EXPERIMENTS WITH BIBLE STUDY

Hans-Ruedi Weber

EXPERIMENTS
with
Bible Study

THE WESTMINSTER PRESS
Philadelphia

Published by The Westminster Press®
Philadelphia, Pennsylvania

PRINTED IN THE UNITED STATES OF AMERICA
9 8 7 6 5 4 3 2 1

Library of Congress Cataloging in Publication Data

Weber, Hans Ruedi.
　Experiments with Bible study.

　Originally published: Geneva : World Council of
Churches, c1981.
　1. Bible—Study.　2. Christian education of adults.
I. Title.
BS600.2.W39 1983　　　　220'.07　　　　82-13398
ISBN 0-664-24461-0 (pbk.)

CONTENTS

REFLECTIONS ON THE WAY

On my desk stands a small wood sculpture, the work of an unknown Tanzanian artist. It portrays an African woman on her knees. What captures one's eyes is her tattooed face, where a big smile is beginning to break through her otherwise severely symmetrical features. It is as if she is going to reveal a great secret which has given her deep joy. The secret obviously relates to the book with the cross which she holds high above her head.

In this sculpture the artist wanted to capture the climax of a story often told in East Africa: A simple woman always walked around with a bulky Bible. Never would she part from it. Soon the villagers began to tease her: "Why always the Bible? There are so many books you could read!" Yet the woman kept on living with her Bible, neither disturbed nor angered by all the teasing. Finally, one day she knelt down in the midst of those who laughed at her. Holding the Bible high above her head, she said with a big smile: "Yes, of course there are many books which I could read. But there is only one book which reads me!"

This, in a nutshell, is the whole secret of Bible study. People start out by listening to an old message, by analyzing ancient texts, by reading — naively or critically — the biblical documents of antiquity. They experience this exercise as dull or instructive, as something Christians ought to do or something they have been led to do by their own historical, literary, or theological interests. Yet a mysterious change of roles can then occur. Listening, analyzing, and reading, students of the Bible meet a living reality which begins to challenge them. Out of the biblical stories, texts, and documents a person comes to life, the God of Abraham, Isaac, and Jacob, and even more intimately Jesus of Nazareth in whom the biblical God chose to be present among us. This divine presence starts to question, judge, and guide us. Perhaps gradually, perhaps quite suddenly, the book which was the object of our reading and study becomes a subject which reads us.

There are no methods to guarantee such a mysterious change of role. It does not come from the power of human scholarship or clever teaching and know-how. It is a change worked by the power of the Holy Spirit.

Therefore the continuous prayer *Veni Creator Spiritus,* "Come Creator Spirit," is essential. Yet not even prayer can force the change to happen.

Bible studies are like experiments in a scientific laboratory. With an open mind, some basic hypotheses, and the best possible tools and methods, we approach a biblical story or text. The experiment may proceed as expected on the basis of our past experiences and present moods. It may simply confirm what we know already, verifying our beliefs or doubts, our assumptions or prejudices. Yet experiments with Bible study, like scientific experiments, can also lead to new discoveries, challenging our preconceptions, our customary styles of life, and in fact our whole outlook on the world and the purpose of life. This is both a frightening and liberating experience.

With this publication I invite readers to join the thousands of groups all over the world with whom I have conducted experiments in this "biblical laboratory". Part One contains some reflections about how the Bible has functioned as an authoritative guide for the Christian way throughout the centuries and in different cultures. Part Two contains 25 fully written-up examples of Bible studies, conducted according to a variety of methods, with suggestions and notes for Bible study enablers. For some of these studies worksheets are appended. The texts and themes were chosen in order to cover the rich plurality of messages and styles within the biblical testimony. Appendix A, "Methods and Tools," offers some advice on how to prepare a Bible study and enable a group to make biblical explorations. The practically minded may actually want to begin by reading Appendix A, especially the section on "leading questions and task assignments."

For thirty years Bible study has been a major part of my work. As secretary of the Swiss Student Christian Movement and then as a theological teacher in Indonesia, later in the work of the Department on the Laity of the World Council of Churches and in teaching at the Ecumenical Institute at Bossey, the ever new questions on the world's agenda forced me to seek guidance in the biblical revelation. In this process other questions and priorities from the Bible, which are not those of the world's agenda, arose. Then, from 1971 onwards, the World Council of Churches gave me the unique opportunity to become involved full-time in this venture. Originally having combined periods of biblical research with the work as a biblical consultant at the World Council's Geneva headquarters, I now spend much of my time in intensive one-week residential training courses for Bible study enablers around the world.

There seems to be a missing link between what happens in biblical scholarship and what happens in the everyday life of Christians. There are excellent biblical scholars, but too often they write only for their colleagues. Their research concentrates on subjects arising from the agenda of biblical scholarship which are often quite distant from the burning issues of faith today. On the other side many believers — both ministers of the church and those fulfilling the ministry of the laity in and for the world — are intimately in touch with the affairs of our time. Yet the biblical knowledge and thinking of ministers often stagnates after they leave seminary and that of lay people often remains on the level of the Sunday school.

In many language areas excellent study Bibles and good tools for exegesis (the understanding and explaining of a biblical text or theme in its own historical and literary context) are now available. The same is true for hermeneutics (the "art of translation," by which the meaning of an ancient message is explored for our present context). Yet, who helps ministers and lay people use these valuable books and tools? In many countries there is no lack of handbooks and training courses in teaching methods and learning techniques, yet unless these are used to discover a message from God, such methods and techniques tend to become "another gospel" in themselves or to serve manipulation rather than participation and learning.

Enablers for Bible study are called for, but present patterns of ministerial training and theological studies seldom produce such enablers. In analogy to the "barefoot doctors" in China, French Catholics speak about *"biblistes à pieds nus"*, barefoot biblical teachers. These mobile ministers must have a good biblical training and discipline for ongoing study combined with the gifts and disposition necessary for participatory teaching. Both knowledge in the field of biblical scholarship and expertise in learning methods are needed to involve believers in relevant Bible study. The good news of the gospel can then be seen in the light of what today's newspapers are reporting, and there is a chance that both our style of life and our decision-making will be brought under the judgment, promise, and guidance of biblical revelation.

The affirmations and scripts in this book arise out of long experience of doing Bible studies, as mentioned earlier. They are reflections and experiments *on the way.* This term "way" refers to three different levels of meanings. First, what is presented here is not the final report of an enquiry, but the provisional thoughts and attempts of someone who is still on the way together with many others who seek in the same direction (see the list of persons and publications mentioned in Appendix B). Second, these reflections and scripts are concerned with the way of doing Bible study, and in this sense they are about methods. The Greek word *methodos* links the noun *hodos* (the "way" or "journey") with the preposition *meta* which means "in the midst of" or "together with." In the most literal sense, reflections about methods are therefore an exploration about the journey which one hopes to take, together with others. Third, according to Luke's testimony the early church called the whole Christian faith and life "the way". It is this third and deepest level of meaning which the following reflections and scripts for experiments ultimately mean to serve.

PART ONE
For All Ages and Cultures

There are plenty of books *about* the Bible. Rather than duplicating or summarizing these, this first part functions as an extended introduction to our scripts for actual biblical explorations. To make such explorations and let the biblical God speak to us is vastly more important than all our historical, dogmatic, or pedagogical reflections about the Bible.

Why not omit this introductory part altogether, then? Because it raises two seldom-discussed questions which need more attention if Bible study is to maintain a central place in the churches of the world.

1. What was the impact of book printing on the function of the Bible in literary cultures? As the readers of this handbook are all marked by a literary culture — or they would not be reading such a thick book! — comments on this question can be relatively short (Chapter 1, "The Bible in Print"). Readers will easily find further illustrations from their own life and environment.

2. How did the Bible function before it became a printed book? This question is examined in three chapters. In essentially oral cultures the biblical message reaches the majority of people not as a written text but through the hearing of an oral tradition (Ch. 2), in the form of visual representations (Ch. 3), and by participation in liturgical enactment (Ch. 4). Examples from biblical times, the ancient church, and Christianity of the Middle Ages, both in the East and the West, are illustrated with extensive quotations from ancient literature, rabbinic writings, and the works of church fathers. For those who have no access to historical and theological libraries nor time to find their way in the labyrinths of this literature, these quotations form a compendium of useful background texts for understanding the Bible.

The answers to these two questions must primarily be sought in the history of the church. Yet such historical considerations also lead back to the Bible itself. What are biblical ways of Bible study? The following chapters thus try to give some biblical justification for the pedagogy proposed in the scripts of Part Two.

Reading the Bible as a book, hearing the Bible as an oral tradition, seeing the Bible as a pictorial presentation, and participating in the Bible as a liturgical drama — all these lead towards a converted life in the here and now. Chapter 5 of this introductory part thus considers the question of the relevance, authority, and interpretation of the Bible for today.

1 THE BIBLE IN PRINT

When Johannes Gutenberg printed the first Latin Bible in the middle of the fifteenth century, something started which was to have a deep impact on Western culture and on the functioning of the Bible itself. Having been for many centuries essentially an oral message, an illuminated manuscript and above all a liturgical drama, the Bible now became a printed book.

For most of us, so deeply marked by a literary culture, it takes a special effort of imagination to conceive of the Bible as anything other than a printed book. Indeed, only those who have lived in essentially oral cultures can fully appreciate the impact and new possibilities, but also the potential dangers, which come with the art of printing. My eyes were opened to this in an unforgettable teaching experience among oral communicators, people whom we often disdainfully call "illiterates" or "uneducated masses."

Oral communicators as teachers

In 1953 the Protestant Church in Central Celebes, Indonesia, gave me a challenging task. On the Luwuk peninsula at the east coast of Celebes, and the extended archipelago of Banggai to the south of it, lived some thirty thousand Christians among a total population of about a hundred thousand. In 1908 the Dutch colonial government had begun to take an interest in this extremely isolated area, and things soon began to fall apart. The traditional tribal communities came into turmoil. Passing Muslim traders won many converts to Islam while other population groups wanted to become Christians. Some had heard the gospel and sincerely desired to worship the biblical God. Others sought to adopt the Christian faith because the colonial officials were Christians. Still others preferred Christianity to Islam because they could thus keep their dogs and pigs, which they needed for sacrifices in their old tribal religion. Yet at the beginning of this century no missionary society working in Indonesia had the means and personnel to begin evangelistic work in this vast and practically pathless mountain and island area.

At the urging of the colonial government the Reformed state church finally sent a minister to Luwuk-Banggai. Within a few years he had baptized many thousands, but without proper baptismal instruction or much aftercare. Later Indonesian evangelists and Dutch missionaries organized these new Christians into congregations and a provincial synod. Yet even in the early 1950s only ten per cent of the baptized members had received Christian instruction and were admitted to Holy Communion. The synod asked me to find ways of teaching these nominal Christians the rudiments of biblical faith. One year was set aside for this task, no funds were available, and only a few Indonesian fellow workers were there to help.

In response to this challenge, five-day Bible courses were planned in a central village of each of the seven church districts. The idea was that a few members from each congregation would follow such a course and then in turn teach their own congregation what they had learned. As long as courses were held on the coast of the peninsula things went reasonably well. Enough literates could be found to participate in this catechetical enterprise. But the farther away we went from these centres the more frequently our invitation was answered: "I would very much like to come to this course, but I am a 'buta huruf' "— "blind with regard to letters." Probably more than two thirds of the thirty thousand Christians could neither read nor write and lived by oral communication.

My typically Western reaction at first was: we must start a literacy campaign. But we lacked the funds and the competence for that, and time was running out. Should we simply write off these masses of people, many of them so eager to learn and obviously intelligent despite their illiteracy? Was there a way of biblical teaching without the printed word? During the last weeks of our stay in Luwuk-Banggai a catechism for illiterates was drawn, hastily multicopied, and introduced to the evangelists. On the one side were simple drawings for the illiterates to fix the teaching in their memory visually. On the other side were written instructions for literate evangelists. Under the title *Kami ini terang dunia* — "You are the light of the world" — this catechism has been reprinted several times by the Christian Publishing House in Jakarta.

The illiterates themselves showed us the way. Their communication through story-telling, proverbs, simple drawings, "painting" with words and dramatic gestures, opened up a whole new world. Not being bound to texts and printed letters, many of them had an astonishing ability to see and hear and remember. A gradual change occurred: the academically trained Western missionary who had come to teach became a pupil. Among the "letter-blind" people, with their many gifts for communication, I discovered myself to be blind and very one-sidedly developed. The most exciting discovery of that time, however, was a new Bible: the Bible as the story and oral tradition of God's great acts, the Bible as God's picture-book, the Bible pointing to the symbols by which God both conceals and reveals himself.

This "new" Bible was in fact the old one, the Bible before Gutenberg.

Printing, the Renaissance and the Reformation

The change from the medieval Bible as an oral tradition, an illuminated manuscript, and a liturgical drama to the printed book of the Bible societies did not happen suddenly. Not everyone felt the impact of printing at first. Only a literate elite could read Latin, and a Bible printed on vellum cost as much as a town house or fourteen fatted oxen. Moreover, editions remained small, even after Gutenberg and his partners had reinvented the art of printing with movable metal letters (Koreans had in fact invented this art more than 200 years earlier). Present estimates about the number of copies printed of Gutenberg's famous 42-line Bible (probably produced from 1450-1455 in Mainz) range from 70 to 270 copies. Nevertheless, the fifteenth century printer Ulrich Han could produce in one day as much as was formerly written in a whole year.

Not until the nineteenth century did Gutenberg's Bible printing have its full impact. In 1803 a machine for making paper was invented, and a year later the process of stereotyping was perfected, enabling printers to mould and cast a whole page of type for use on presses. It is more than a coincidence that the perfecting of this process occurred in the same year as the British and Foreign Bible Society was founded. Soon large numbers of Bibles could be produced at a reasonable price. What had taken a full day's work could now be done in less than an hour. Thus the Bible became first and foremost a printed book, translated and distributed by Bible societies on all the continents. For many language areas and cultures the Bible was the first printed book known and often remains the only one.

Before reflecting further about the Bible and Bible study, we should look at the relationship between book printing and culture, which will also show the influence of printing on the functioning of the Bible. "The medium is the message." Taken literally, this famous slogan by Marshall McLuhan is not true. A variation of it, however, points to an important fact: "The medium is the *massage*." The communications media we use do indeed massage our minds. They are not neutral channels which simply communicate a message; they have an impact of their own. The introduction of a new mode of communication is therefore one of the strongest factors for cultural change. Yet the chain of cause and effect can also be turned around. The medium not only helps to shape the message which is to be communicated, but this message also calls for and creates its own appropriate medium.

Buildings and books were the great passion of the Renaissance in fourteenth- and fifteenth-century Europe. Buildings called for a new way of looking at things, a perspective which delimits space. Books made a way of quick and inexpensive multicopying of manuscripts imperative, especially as the humanists of that time called for a return to the sources. The new medium of multicopying manuscripts in turn increased the hunger for books and facilitated the return to the sources and the study of texts. The early history of Bible printing shows this in a striking way.

By the end of the fifteenth century about a hundred editions of the Latin Bible had been published, many of which contained helps for the reader such as chapter summaries, introductions, glossaries, and lists of scriptural readings for the liturgical year. Moreover, the humanists' call for a return to the sources led to the printing of the Bible in its original languages. Through the efforts of Jews in Southern Germany the whole Hebrew Bible was printed in 1488 at Soncico, a small town near Mantua in Northern Italy. Before the century closed there were no fewer than four Hebrew versions published.

An edition of the Greek New Testament had to wait longer, partly because Greek was regarded as the language of Eastern heretics. Yet the humanists prepared the way with Greek grammars and the search for old Greek manuscripts. The first edition of the whole Greek New Testament, prepared by Erasmus of Rotterdam and printed in 1516 by the Hieronymus Froben Press in Basel, was done in a great hurry. News had come that in Alcala, Spain, Cardinal Ximenes was just finishing the printing of a large Polyglot Bible including the Greek text of the New Testament, and that he was only waiting for the Pope's authorization for publication. Froben therefore pressed Erasmus to complete his work on the text of the Greek Testament, which he had already started in 1507.

Erasmus entitled the first edition of his New Testament *Novum Instrumentum.* Such printed Old and New Testaments in their original languages indeed became instruments for new studies. Special study editions appeared as soon as the original biblical text had been reconstructed on the basis of available old manuscripts. The great Complutensian Polyglot mentioned above, printed in Alcala, was authorized for publication early in the 1520s. Its first four volumes contain the Old Testament with the Latin text (the Vulgate) in the centre of the page. The Greek translation, known as the Septuagint, is printed on the inside column, while the Hebrew text appears on the outside column with an Aramaic paraphrase (called the Targum) and its Latin translation at the bottom of the page. A fifth volume of this Polyglot contains the Latin and the Greek text of the New Testament and the final volume consists of "aids for study" such as dictionaries, a grammar and indexes. Other critical editions listed variant manuscript readings in the margin: for example, the rabbinical Bible (Hebrew Old Testament with Targums and the rabbinical commentaries), published in 1516/17 by the Christian printer Daniel Bomberg of Flanders, and the first attempt at a critical edition of the Greek New Testament, published in 1534 by the Parisian printer Simon Colines.

A direct line leads from the book printing activity of the Renaissance to the rise and expansion of the Reformation. When in 1512 the Augustinian monk Martin Luther was appointed as professor of biblical interpretation at Wittenberg, he could work with the printed Latin Bible and the Hebrew edition of the Old Testament. In wrestling for the right understanding and interpretation of the biblical texts he became a reformer.

During the winter of 1521-22 Luther translated the New Testament from Erasmus' Greek text into Middle German, and this led to the first great success story in the history of book printing. In September 1522 a first edition of 3000 copies was published by the printing workshop of the painter Lucas Cranach and the goldsmith Christian Döring in Wittenberg, illustrated with woodcuts from Cranach's studio. The book was sold for approximately the weekly wage of a carpenter. Within three months a second, revised edition appeared, initiating a long series of subsequent revisions, editions, and reprints. From 1534 onwards Luther's translation of the whole Bible was on the book market, and it is estimated that before Luther's death some 100,000 printed copies of his translation had been sold.

The escalation of Bible printing led to a host of other printing activities: commentaries, hymnals, catechisms, and above all religious pamphlets. During the 1520s more religious pamphlets were published in Germany than in any other decade of German history. A striking example of this intimate link between book printing and the Reformation is the city of Geneva. At the end of the fifteenth century a German had introduced the art of book printing to Geneva. For a few decades the city's one or two printing presses did occasional work for the diocese, but later went out of business. Then the Reformation reached Geneva. From 1533 onwards Protestant printers began to settle in that city, most of them refugees from Italy and France. Among them was Robert Estienne from Paris, probably the most famous printer of the Reformation. His critical editions of the Vulgate and the Greek New Testament served for a long time as the basic texts for biblical scholars. During Calvin's time no fewer than thirty-eight printing workshops were established in Geneva. To a great extent it is due to their work that both Bibles in the language of the people and the teachings of Calvin spread so rapidly into all corners of Europe and beyond, even to Brazil where from 1555 onwards a first Calvinist mission attempt was made.

Reading the Bible in print

The way from the Italian cities of the Renaissance to Luther's Wittenberg and Calvin's Geneva illustrates a deep cultural change which would characterize the history of the Western world. In Italy wealthy princes and prelates gathered ancient manuscripts and artfully illuminated copies of them. The beauty of the library buildings and their embellishment with sculptures and paintings were considered as important as the precious manuscripts they housed. Some collectors despised the new art of book printing: Federigo Urbino, who founded one of the richest libraries of the Renaissance, said he would be ashamed to possess a printed book. Nevertheless, book printing also developed in Italy until it was partly curtailed by the censorship instituted under Pope Alexander VI (1492-1503), which especially affected the publication of biblical texts and commentaries, because Jews and Waldensians had pioneered in this field.

While in Italy the book was essentially treasured as a work of art, in Wittenberg an artist became the servant of the book. Indeed, Luther's friend Lucas Cranach not only directed a large painters' studio, but also had a pharmacy and a bookshop and assets in workshops for paper production and printing. His art became strongly didactic, functioning as an illustration for biblical stories and a visual transposition of Luther's teaching. In this he fulfilled the expectation of Luther who welcomed and encouraged the visual arts, yet saw their importance essentially as Bible illustration and a means for Christian teaching.

The progression from a mainly visual to a literary culture became even more manifest in Geneva. Calvin saw in the visual arts a precious gift of the Holy Spirit which could be used for the glory of God. However, the worship and teaching of the church must be totally centred on God's word and the sacraments, so that the Bible and the arts had little to do with one another. What was needed, according to Calvin, was an easily available biblical text and its study according to the best possible literary methods. The Geneva reformers commissioned no altar paintings like the many produced by Cranach's studio; instead they established a college and theological academy. There Hebrew and Greek were taught, biblical texts were explained by Calvin, and further analyzed by the rector of the academy, Théodore de Bèze, an accomplished biblical scholar.

What happened to the Bible under the impact of book printing in the hundred and fifty years after Gutenberg's invention is typical of what happened over a much longer period to Western culture. Increasingly it became a literary culture.

Obviously not the whole of Europe and the Western world shared equally in this bookish culture. It is difficult to ascertain its actual influence, and exceptions could be found to all the following generalizations. Populations strongly influenced by Protestantism certainly became more deeply involved in the literary culture than people in traditionally Catholic areas. Predominantly Orthodox countries were even less affected. Peasants and many factory workers since the Industrial Revolution remained less affected by it than urban populations, artisans, and intellectuals. Also many women and most children continued to live in a culture which was much less dependent on the printed word. Unfortunately, there are no reliable statistics on the rate of literacy in former centuries. Further studies might show that almost everywhere the literary culture remained the prerogative of a minority.

Nevertheless, during the last three centuries this literary minority has shaped much of the history of the West and especially of Western Christianity. The whole Western school system is moulded by it and therefore centres almost exclusively on printed books. Western theology and theological teaching remain strongly marked by the literary culture. This has had a deep impact on Christian education and Protestant worship. Moreover, both Catholic and Protestant missions have introduced the Western school system into the cultures of all continents. On the one hand this was a great service, for illiteracy breeds exploitation and poverty. Yet behind the marriage between missions and schools is the widespread (though seldom acknowledged) assumption that nobody can become a Christian without being literate — a strange reminder of the demand by Jewish Christians in New Testament times that Gentiles had to be circumcized before being baptized.

What happened to the Bible in the Western literary culture? First of all, it cannot be too strongly emphasized that Gutenberg's invention and its implications have done the Bible a tremendous service. The return to the biblical sources in the Renaissance and the Reformation, the development of modern biblical scholarship from the seventeenth century onwards, the spectacular missionary expansion of the church in the nineteenth century, and the rediscovery of the Bible and Bible studies during the last decades — all this would have been inconceivable without the easily available printed text of the Scriptures. The history of biblical research and of Christian mission and above all of the Bible Societies are full of telling examples of what could well be called Gutenberg's liberation of the Bible: a liberation from ignorance of the biblical message, from the Bible's captivity to dogmatic assumptions, from its imprisonment in the Latin language and concepts.

The medium of the printed book has possibilities and advantages which are not superseded by all the new media for mass communication. Only by working with a synopsis, where we can see and read the texts of the gospels side by side, can we be attentive to both the common tradition and the particular message of each evangelist.[1] Only by comparing with ancient extra-biblical texts from the Near East can we discover their special character and typical accent.[2] Reading texts from ancient historians can also help us understand the milieu in which and for which the biblical texts were written.[3] It is through careful analysis of texts that we can grasp the message which comes through the literary form of a biblical book or passage.[4]

Historical and literary analysis of biblical texts is made possible through the ready availability of printed study Bibles, biblical wordbooks, grammars, synopses, and the like. Such a study of the Bible can simply become an intellectual game and has in fact often undermined faith. Yet, if used in a pastoral way, the historical and literary analysis of texts will be a most

---

[1] For the use of the synopsis, see the studies on a parable (II/9, pp. 130ff), on the institution of the Lord's Supper (II/15, pp. 182ff), or on the resurrection accounts (II/17, pp. 199ff).

[2] Cf. the use of such extra-biblical parallels in the studies on the Exodus (II/2, pp. 73f), on the wisdom literature (II/5, p. 99), or on a healing story (II/11, pp. 142ff).

[3] Cf. the earliest written testimonies of non-Christians about Jesus (II/12, pp. 155ff), the use of ancient historical texts for describing the position of children in the Graeco-Roman world (II/13, pp. 165ff), and for sketching the situation in Thessalonica in A.D. 50 (II/21, pp. 236ff) or in Asia Minor at the end of the first century (II/25, pp. 261ff).

[4] Cf. the comments on Hebrew poetry (II/1, pp. 59ff), the analysis of the end of Matthew's gospel (II/18, pp. 208ff), the use of word statistics in the study on John's gospel (II/19, pp. 219f), or the examination of tenses of verbs in the study on Galatians (II/22, pp. 247ff) and Ephesians (II/23, pp. 353ff).

valuable means for discovering the original meaning of the ancient texts, for taking them seriously as they are written, and for doing Bible study with intellectual honesty.

Liberating the Bible from print

Having acknowledged Gutenberg's liberation of the Bible as well as the advantages of the historical and literary study of biblical texts, one must face also the limiting factors of printing and what could well be called the Gutenberg captivity of the Bible.

If the Bible is known and functions almost exclusively as a printed book, Bible study will remain the privilege of those who can read and who are motivated to read. This excludes too many of our contemporaries. Indeed, illiteracy is constantly growing in today's world, despite all the literacy campaigns. Of all adults over fifteen years of age more than one-third are at present totally illiterate. Most of them live in Latin America, Asia, and Africa where whole societies of non-readers — or, to express it positively, oral communicators — exist. A printed book remains among them a foreign and ineffective medium.

Still more is at stake. Recent surveys in the great book-producing cultures of the West have shown that only three to five per cent of those who can read do in fact read. The whole apparatus of producing and distributing books — including the Bible as a printed book — serves a small minority. With the growth of the audio-visual media of mass communication many potential readers become semi-literate. They may read the headlines or the short and simple sentences of comic strips, but they have lost the motivation and gradually also the capability to read books. Whether these recent surveys indicate only a temporary decrease in incentive and ability to read, or register a progressive tendency towards what some already call a post-literary era, it is too early to tell.

Whatever the cultural impact of the audio-visual mass media may ultimately be, Christians have a twofold — and sometimes contradictory — task in the face of these developments. On the one side they must continue to use and defend the assets of the literary culture. Long before the Reformation the church fathers had already done this. During the first Christian centuries, even without book printing, a literary minority culture had developed in the Jewish and Graeco-Roman world. There is thus a very ancient tradition which links Christian faith with the literary culture, and this tradition must not be easily dismissed. On the other hand there is a difficult second task ahead of us: Western Christian worship and theology — and in fact the Bible itself — must be liberated from its imprisonment in a one-sided literary culture. This is necessary in order to challenge and nurture with the biblical message all those who no longer read. But we must also do this to counteract the one-sided influence of printing on Bible study.

In literary cultures the sounds and gestures, the accents and the music of oral transmission are gradually lost. The copying of biblical manuscripts ceases, and in the course of time the incentive and faculty for memorizing disappears. The Bible becomes a collection of texts: texts to be read silently, analyzed, and interpreted. Uniformly printed pages create the illusion of a uniform and disincarnate message, burying the rich variety of biblical images, styles, and stories into grey blur. Moreover, the Bible as a printed book appeals far more to the human intellect than to human emotion and imagination. The very term "Bible study" is a child of a literary culture in which the capacity for meditation and celebration often remains underdeveloped. Also the tendency to individualism and privacy can be fostered by the printed book: each one has his or her own Bible to read and explain as one wishes. The actual degree of participation in the biblical drama together with God's people of biblical times and of our time remains low.

Bible study in literary cultures tends to concentrate too one-sidedly on the left side of the human brain, where the faculties for rational analysis, thinking, reasoning, and other intellectual activities are located. Because we are called to love God with all our mind, nobody should despise these great gifts of the left hemisphere of our brain. For Bible study this means that text analysis, reflection on meaning, and serious intellectual discernment with a view to the right decision and action are essential.

But our calling to love God embraces much more. "You shall love the Lord your God with all your heart, and with all your soul and with all your mind, and with all your strength" (Mk. 12:30; cf. Deut. 6:5). Faculties other than those of the mind cannot be easily located in our human body. What this text means by "heart" and "soul" goes far beyond the functions of the physiological heart. They have to do with our inner sensibility, the intuitive understanding and grasping of the whole, the spontaneous passions, emotions, and perceptions which lead to specific attitudes, decisions, and actions. Neuro-physiologists locate these faculties in the right hemisphere of the human brain. In Bible study such faculties must be fully used.

The brain with its left and right sides is only a part of the human body. The conversion of our mind without the feet to walk in the new way is of no avail. A feeling of mercy without the loving look in our eyes and the hands for loving gestures and acts will help no one. Bible study addresses itself therefore to our whole body. Moreover, it would be less than biblical to limit ourselves to the faculties of individual human beings. Old and New Testament alike emphasize the individual person's incorporation into the body of the believing community. It is as members of that community and in communion with one another that we are confronted with the biblical message.

2 HEARING GOD'S MESSAGE

Although the Bible takes its name from the Greek word *biblos* ("paper," "book," "scripture"), it originally had nothing to do with paper but was an oral message. Personal witnesses and communities transmitted it with a loud voice. The message was heard in order to be remembered and understood, taught and proclaimed, celebrated and translated into life. This claim made by God's word, addressed to us orally by personal witnesses, remains at the origin of all Christian proclamation, teaching, worship, and ethics.

The primacy of recitation

Even when the oral testimonies were written down, these "scriptures" were not in the first place meant to be read silently and privately, but to be recited aloud. When a book of the law was found in the temple at Jerusalem in 622 B.C., King Josiah gathered all the inhabitants of his kingdom and "read in their hearing all the words of the book of the covenant" (2 Kings 23:2). Some two centuries later we hear again of such a public reading of the law of Moses, this time by the priest/scribe Ezra (Neh. 8:1-8). When Paul sent a letter to a local church he expected it to be read publicly: "I adjure you by the Lord that this letter be read to all the brethren" (1 Thess. 5:27; cf. Col. 4:16). The visionary John pronounced a special blessing on those who read his witness aloud and those who truly heard it (Rev. 1:3). As in many cultures today, even solitary reading in the ancient world was loud recitation. This explains why Philip actually heard the Ethiopian eunuch read Isaiah's prophecies (Acts 8:28, 30).

Such emphasis on oral communication of the biblical message cannot be explained by widespread illiteracy in the ancient world alone. True, many Palestinian Jews of Jesus' time were illiterate. The schools related to the synagogues began to function only in the first century B.C., and historians debate whether there were any such schools outside Jerusalem before the turn of the millennia. Yet the Jews in cities like Alexandria and the growing church in the Graeco-Roman world lived in an environment which was remarkably literate by comparison with other areas of the world and later centuries in Europe. Of course, most women and slaves could not read and remained dependent on oral communication.

Yet even fully literate and highly educated persons in the ancient world maintained a general mistrust of the written word. The educators in the Graeco-Roman world had not yet forgotten the ancient story of the Egyptian god Teuth, the inventor of the letters for writing. As Socrates tells it in Plato's dialogue *Phaedrus*, Teuth brought his invention before the god Thamus, the king of Egypt, saying:

> This invention, O king, will make the Egyptians wiser and will improve their memories; for it is an elixir of memory and wisdom that I have discovered." But Thamus replied, "Most ingenious Teuth, one man has the ability to beget arts, but the ability to judge of their usefulness or harmfulness to their users belongs to another; and now you, who are the father of letters, have been led by your affection to ascribe to them a power the opposite of that which they really possess. For this invention will produce forgetfulness in the minds of those who learn to use it, because they will not practice their memory. Their trust in writing, produced by external characters which are no part of themselves, will discourage the use of their own memories within them. You have invented an elixir not of memory, but of reminding; and you offer your pupils the appearance of wisdom, not true wisdom, for they will read many things without instruction and will therefore seem to know many things, when they are for the most part ignorant and hard to get along with since they are not wise, but only appear wise" (*Phaedrus*, 274f).

This insight of Plato has been forgotten all too often by educators in later literacy cultures.

Not so among the Jews, however. In Jesus' time it was strictly forbidden to transmit and publish the oral law in writing — partly to protect the special place of the written law, which was scrupulously guarded, memorized, and copied, partly from the concern to safeguard the transmission and interpretation of biblical faith as a living process from the mouth of the teacher to the ear and heart and mind of the disciple.

Jesus was an oral communicator. He used the rich register of words, intonations, mnemonic forms (helps for memorization), poetry, parables, and gestures which characterize oral communication. He also maintained the learning community of teacher and disciples, in which the communication of a message is embedded in communication between people. Above all, his whole life and teaching were marked by the most important characteristic and test of oral communication, namely the intimate relationship between the message and the messenger. "You shall *be* my witness" (Acts 1:8). To make of all nations his disciples, to incorporate them through baptism into a living community with him, to teach them what he taught (Matt. 28:18-20) — this was the challenge of the risen Lord to his church.

Memory and manuscript

In their worship, teaching, and proclamation the early Christians followed Jesus' way of oral communication. It is interesting to examine what

Eusebius, the earliest church historian, reports about this. After a lifetime of studying available sources, this learned bishop of Caesarea probably completed his history in A.D. 324.

Except perhaps for the second letter of Peter all documents now contained in the New Testament were written before A.D. 100. Yet three decades later, when Papias, the bishop of Hierapolis, wrote his now lost "Expositions of Oracles of the Lord," he trusted the living testimony of witnesses more than what could be gotten from the books. Eusebius quotes Papias' preface:

> I shall not hesitate also to put down for you along with my interpretations whatsoever things I have at any time learned carefully from the elders and carefully remembered, guaranteeing their truth. For I did not, like the multitude, take pleasure in those that speak much, but in those that teach the truth; not in those that relate strange commandments, but in those that deliver the commandments given by the Lord to faith, and springing from the truth itself. If, then, any one came, who had been a follower of the elders, I questioned him in regard to the words of the elders — what Andrew or what Peter said, or what was said by Philip, or by Thomas, or by James, or by John, or by Matthew, or by any other of the disciples of the Lord, and what things Aristion and the presbyter John, the disciples of the Lord, say. For I did not think that what was to be gotten from the books would profit me as much as what came from the living and abiding voice *(Church History*, III, 39, 3f).

It is uncertain whether the books referred to by Papias include any of the canonical gospels or were already circulating written interpretations of the gospels. In either case, the authority of oral tradition in the early church is clearly documented by this text. The Bible was the Old Testament, and although apostolic letters and written gospels circulated among the churches, the living tradition about Christ was still handed on from mouth to mouth.

Eusebius gives a striking example of this chain of oral tradition alongside the publishing of written testimonies. He quotes a letter which Irenaeus, the bishop of Lyons, wrote shortly before A.D. 200 to his former fellow student Florinus. The two of them had attended lectures or sermons by Polycarp, the bishop of Smyrna, who died as an old man around A.D.155.

> When I was a boy, I saw thee in lower Asia with Polycarp, moving in splendor in the royal court, and endeavoring to gain his approbation. I remember the events of that time more clearly than those of recent years. For what boys learn, growing with their mind, becomes joined with it; so that I am able to describe the very place in which the blessed Polycarp sat as he discoursed, and his goings out and his comings in, and the manner of his life, and his physical appearance, and his discourses to the people, and the accounts which he gave of his intercourse with John and with the others who had seen the Lord. And as he remembered their words, and what he heard from them concerning the Lord, and concerning his miracles and his teaching, having received them from eyewitnesses of the "Word of life,"

Polycarp related all things in harmony with the Scriptures. These things being told me by the mercy of God, I listened to them attentively, noting them down, not on paper, but in my heart (*Church History*, V, 20, 5-7).

"Not on paper, but in my heart!" Yet despite this emphasis on oral communication, the recollections of the eyewitnesses were also put down on paper. The oral tradition was reinforced by notes and, in the second half of the first century, by whole written gospels. The information Eusebius gives about why and how this happened is often contradictory, and certainly not all his facts are correct, but the general development probably followed the way he described it. According to Eusebius, the gospels were written almost as a makeshift substitute for oral teaching.

About Mark's gospel he writes that, after Peter's martyrdom in Rome,

> so greatly did the splendor of piety illumine the minds of Peter's hearers that they were not satisfied with hearing once only, and were not content with the unwritten teaching of the divine gospel, but with all sorts of entreaties they besought Mark, a follower of Peter, and the one whose gospel is extant, that he would leave them a written monument of the doctrine which had been orally communicated to them. Nor did they cease until they had prevailed with the man, and had thus become the occasion of the written gospel which bears the name of Mark (*Church History*, II, 15, 1).

Similar necessities, Eusebius says, lay behind the first and the fourth gospels, which are assumed to have been written by the apostles Matthew and John. The disciples did not

> attempt to proclaim the doctrines of their teacher in studied and artistic language, but employing only the demonstration of the divine Spirit, which worked with them, and the wonder-working power of Christ, which was displayed through them, they published the knowledge of the kingdom of heaven throughout the world, paying little attention to the composition of written works.... Of all the disciples of the Lord, only Matthew and John have left us written memorials, and they, tradition says, were led to write only under the pressure of necessity. For Matthew, who had at first preached to the Hebrews, when he was about to go to other peoples, committed his gospel to writing in his native tongue, and thus compensated those whom he was obliged to leave for the loss of his presence. And when Mark and Luke had already published their gospels, they say that John, who had employed all his time in proclaiming the gospel orally, finally proceeded to write for the following reason. The three gospels already mentioned having come into the hands of all and into his own too, they say that he accepted them and bore witness to their truthfulness; but that there was lacking in them an account of the deeds done by Christ at the beginning of his ministry. And this indeed is true. For it is evident that the three evangelists recorded only the deeds done by the Saviour for one year after the imprisonment of John the Baptist, and indicating this in the beginning of their account (*Church History*, III, 24, 3.5-8).

The literary activity of the church had only begun. Soon other letters, apocalypses, and new gospels began to circulate. Towards the end of the second century such a confusing plurality of written testimonies existed that the church had to sift what should be accepted as a normative witness to Jesus and what not. This establishment of the canon of New Testament Scriptures was a long and painful process.

A list of canonical writings from the church in Rome (the "Canon Muratori") mentions the four gospels, the Acts, and Paul's letters to seven churches in the following order: Corinthians, Ephesians, Philippians, Colossians, Galatians, Thessalonians, and Romans. It adds the letters to Philemon, Titus, and the two to Timothy, and mentions that letters of Paul to the Laodiceans and Alexandrians were also circulating, but that these had been falsified by heretics. It further lists the letter to Judas, two letters with the title John, the intertestamental writing of the Wisdom of Solomon, and two apocalypses — those of John and of Peter. The list adds, however, that some were against the public reading of this apocalypse of Peter in the church. The same caution is made with regard to the public reading of the "Shepherd of Hermas" from the middle of the second century.

This list shows that by A.D. 200 the New Testament canon was fairly complete (only Hebrews, 1 and 2 Peter, and 3 John are not listed). At the same time it is evident that the distinction between intertestamental writings, New Testament apocrypha, and the writings of the church fathers on the one side, and the Scriptures of the New Testament on the other was still blurred. In the Eastern church Athanasius listed in 367 the present 27 books of the New Testament as authoritative. In the Western church the final decisions were taken only at the Councils of Hippo in 393 and Carthage in 397.

Continuing oral communication

Writing down God's message in Christ and fixing the canon did not interrupt the process of oral communication. The manuscripts functioned as bases and helps for memorizing and reciting, proclaiming and teaching, study and celebration. Even when the Bible became a printed book in the fifteenth century this essentially oral communication of God's message continued. The great development of biblical preaching in the time of the Reformation and in Protestant churches since then shows this clearly. The first chapter of the "Second Helvetic Confession" (1566) states that "the preaching of the Word of God *is* the Word of God." But there is much more to oral communication of the Word of God than preaching. In oral cultures like those of the South Pacific, the "speaking papers" — as books and especially the printed Bible were called — functioned among first-generation Christians exactly as the biblical manuscripts did in the early church. The book was used as a help for memorization, dramatic recital, and all the other strongly participatory ways of oral communication.

But in these essentially oral cultures, Christians from the second and third generation on have known the Bible almost exclusively as a printed book, to be read and studied as one reads and studies the text of a schoolbook. Unlike the first converts and their immediate followers they no longer understand and communicate the biblical message with the means of their oral cultures which are so similar to those of biblical times. This process of Westernized Bible reading is accelerated where pastors and priests have followed a Western type of theological education. Future church leaders may learn to distinguish the many ways in which the people of Israel, Jesus, and the early church communicated their faith, but teachers and students alike usually are content with analyzing and defining the diversity of literary genres in biblical texts. They seldom learn how to practise the biblical ways of learning and communicating.

Bible study should not be conducted in such a one-sided literary way. The biblical message must be heard. Radios and cassette recorders give us the means to rediscover the Bible as an oral tradition. While radio may be an efficient means for evangelization, cassette recorders are much better for participatory learning and teaching. They function as a group-medium. Radio programmes prepared by specialists in a studio are sent out to an amorphous mass of people. What they hear can be passively consumed or simply function as background noise. Seldom is the communication of a message embedded in a close communication between the witness and the listeners. But with cassette recorders, participants themselves can for example tape a dramatic biblical reading and then repeatedly listen to their "programme" and discuss it. They can discover aspects of the message which seldom disclose themselves to silent readers of texts. In the following scripts for Bible study cassette recorders play an important role.[1]

In order for the biblical message to be heard it must be told well. Biblical communicators must therefore learn not only how to preach a Sunday sermon, but also how to tell a story.[2] An important part of this learning process is to become sensitive to poetry, for much of biblical theology appears in the form of "theopoetics."[3] Just as form and content are intimately related in poetry, so the biblical message cannot be abstracted from its manifold forms. It must be told and heard as a message through stories and proverbs, through parables and letters, through prayers, confessions, and visions.

God's message must be heard to be remembered. What nourishes us is not how much food we eat, but what we actually digest. Similarly, what matters is not how many biblical stories and teachings we hear and read, but how much of the message we remember and reflect on. Memorization has come to be regarded with disfavour because of abuses of rote learning. Yet a certain degree of learning by rote will always be necessary. It is by no

---

[1] For example, to make recordings (cf. II/20, pp. 228f, II/25, pp. 264f), for listening to already-recorded scripture readings and thus getting an impression of the whole before analyzing the detail (cf. II/2, p. 69, II/18, p. 210, II/19, p. 220), or for enabling a group to do Bible study by a recorded study cassette (cf. II/23, pp. 250ff).

[2] Cf. the exercises in II/21, pp. 233ff, the example of a narrative exegesis in II/13, and the invitations to join in making such a biblical story in II/21, p. 241.

[3] Cf. for example the comments on Hebrew poetry in II/1, pp. 59ff, and on John's language in II/19, pp. 212ff, 219ff, and II/25, pp. 260ff.

means true that we must first understand the message before we can or should memorize it. Often we must live with a saying or a story for a long time before it discloses its meaning to us. In Bible study we must therefore learn again how to memorize.[4]

The true hearing of God's message must lead to understanding. Contrary to ancient and modern mystery religions, biblical faith does not aim at ecstasy, at driving us "out of our mind." Yet our mind *is* being transformed if we truly hear, remember, and ruminate on God's message. We gain a deeper understanding of who we are, of where this earth and the course of history is leading, and of how present earthly and human realities remain open to the transcendent reality of God. This understanding, growing out of the hearing of God's claim, will be deepened if we also attempt to see God's image, to participate in the celebration of God's drama of salvation, and especially if we attempt to walk in God's way.

---

[4] The exercises in reconstructing biblical passages from memory (cf. II/7; II/9; II/15) will probably reveal how much we have forgotten this art. Recent studies in oral communication offer many insights on how to learn it again (cf., e.g., the exercise in II/21, pp. 234f).

3 SEEING GOD'S IMAGE

One can hear God's message and yet remain deaf to it. One can see God's image and nevertheless remain forever blind to it. In the communication of biblical faith seeing is actually much more a problem than hearing.

Idolatry and art

"You shall have no other gods before me. You shall not make for yourself a graven image, or any likeness of anything that is in heaven above, or that is in the earth beneath, or that is in the water under the earth; you shall not bow down to them or serve them" (Exod. 20:3ff). What this commandment prohibits is not pictorial thinking or visual arts in general, but the making of idols, "gods of silver and of gold" (Exod. 20:23), turning to idols and fashioning "molten gods" (Lev. 19:4; Deut. 27:15). The priestly ordinance for making the ark prescribes: "You shall make two cherubim of gold; of hammered work shall you make them, on the two ends of the mercy seat" (Exod. 25:18) — that is, the empty seat where the image of divinity would stand in non-Israelite religions. When Solomon built the temple he called on artists to sculpture the cherubim (1 Kings 6:23ff), to work the pillars of bronze and the molten sea which stood on twelve cast oxen (1 Kings 7:13ff). Only later, when King Rehoboam allowed two calves of gold to be made for his sanctuaries in Bethel and Dan and made sacrifices to these images, was the wrath of God announced to him by an unknown prophet (1 Kings 12:28-13:10).

The attitude of Jews towards images became much stricter in the Hellenistic period when art flourished, the worship of deified political rulers increased, and statues of divinities filled public places. The intertestamental books of Maccabees describe this period. The Seleucid ruler Antiochus IV (175-163 B.C.) sent letters to Jerusalem ordering the people "to build altars and sacred precincts and shrines for idols, and whoever does not obey the command of the king shall die" (1 Macc. 1:47ff). In 167 B.C. he introduced a coin with the head of the ruler as Zeus on one side and on the other Zeus on a throne with Nike, goddess of victory, on his right hand and the inscription: "Of Antiochus King, God Manifest, Bearer of Victory." Such measures triggered the Maccabean revolt, out of which came the movement of the Pharisees. Scrupulous distinctions were made between what should be strictly forbidden as an idol and what could be used as "secular" art. Their discussion is collected in the tractate *Abodah Zarah* ("strange worship") contained in the Mishnah, the first written collection of Jewish oral law).

> "All images are forbidden because they are worshipped once a year." So R. Meir. But the Sages say: "Only that is forbidden which bears in its hand a staff or a bird or a sphere." Rabban Simeon b. Gamaliel says: "That which bears aught in its hand. If a man found fragments of images, these are permitted. If he found (a fragment in) the shape of a hand or the shape of a foot, these are forbidden, since an object the like of these is worshipped" (*Abodah Zarah* 3,1-2).

Even in Palestine many distinguished teachers freely used objects with decorative art. During the First and Second Jewish wars (A.D. 66-70 and A.D. 132-135) the revolutionaries issued coins with such Hebrew inscriptions as "For the liberation of Jerusalem" and with engravings of religious symbols pointing to the temple worship and the great Jewish feasts. In the third century Rabbi Johanan allowed synagogues in Palestine to be decorated by painting. Of Rabbi Nahum in Tiberias it is said, however, that he never looked at an image on a coin during his whole life. At his burial the statues on the road to the cemetery were covered so that even after death he would not do what he had so scrupulously avoided during his life.

At the same time Jews outside of Palestine were applying the second commandment much more freely. From Alexandria comes a Jewish oil lamp which shows in relief David killing Goliath (first to third century). Later in the same city narrative illumination of biblical manuscripts began. But the most amazing early Jewish art was found in the synagogue of Dura Europos on the Euphrates (*ca.* A.D. 250). Its walls are covered with frescoes showing not only Jewish symbolism but also narrative representations of biblical scenes, mainly from the Exodus and the monarchy. Human figures, especially Moses, appear, and even God himself is symbolized by a hand. But where the image of divinity would stand in the paintings of ancient religious cults, the chest with the Torah scrolls or the candelabrum appear as the visible word of God.

Theologians and artists

In the New Testament the second commandment is never quoted. Only unbelievers could possibly exchange "the glory of the immortal God for images resembling mortal man or birds or animals or reptiles" (Rom. 1:23; cf. Acts 17:29). Jesus had no scruples about looking at a Roman denarius on which the head of Caesar Augustus was engraved (Mark 12:15ff). If "the image of the beast" had to be worshipped, however, martyrdom rather than apostasy was to be chosen. This "image of the beast", which plays an important role in the second half of Revelation (13:14f; 14:9, 11; 15:2; 16:2; 19:20; 20:4), almost certainly refers to the image of Domitian, the Roman emperor from A.D. 81-96. There was a provincial sanctuary for the worship of Domitian in Ephesus; in nearby Smyrna coins were struck with Domitian as the father of the gods; and in Laodicea an inscription was made "to Zeus the Supreme, the Saviour, the Emperor Domitian."

While such idolatry is clearly rejected in the New Testament, the general question about visual arts simply did not arise, and no text from the New Testament can be quoted against their use. Most early Christians were too poor to own precious artifacts, and the reservation of Palestinian Jews about translating the biblical message into pictorial forms also prevailed among early Christians. The earliest Christian art — symbolic paintings in the Roman catacombs and sculptured sarcophagi (stone coffins) with biblical scenes — go back only to the beginning of the third century.

A strange discrepancy had developed. During the second and third centuries Christian apologists and church fathers used the oratory and literary means of communication of the Graeco-Roman culture without any hesitation. Until the fourth century, however, the theologians maintained a negative attitude to visual arts and warned against translating the biblical message into pictorial representations, mainly for fear of idolatry. The great North African theologian Augustine wrote (about A.D. 400):

> The eyes love beautiful and diverse shapes, brilliant and pleasant colors. Let these things not occupy my soul; let God occupy it, who indeed made all these things which are very good, still he is my God, not these things.... How many seductions without number have men added to the things which entice the eyes, through the various arts and by the works of craftsmen, in the form of clothes, shoes, vessels, and other artifacts of this kind, even in paintings and all sorts of representations — these things far overstep the bounds of necessary utility, moderation, and faithful representation. In this, men become devotees of their external products, while abandoning internally their own Maker and annihilating the things made by him (*Confessions*, X, 34).

Whatever the theologians said, Christian art began to develop in the East and the West, and it was essentially a pictorial translation of biblical symbols and narratives. The Bible, which had originally been an oral message, memorized, transmitted, and celebrated with the help of biblical manuscripts, now received a new "incarnation": from the fourth century on paintings and mosaics of biblical scenes appeared on the walls of church buildings. The earliest known illuminated biblical manuscript dates from the same century. The "Vienna Genesis" (*ca.* 500) already contains 48 miniatures, telling the story in a narrative style of painting. The written word and painted image were not separated but communicated the message together. From southern Italy in the early twelfth century come rolls with the biblical text on one side and pictorial representations of the same texts on the other. The priest, usually the only literate in the village, would read the biblical stories, while the congregation would see these same stories interpreted by the artist.

Increasingly, artists were commissioned to become the popular communicators and interpreters of the Bible. In both the East and the West the creation of this visible Bible was guided by prescriptions from theologians and bishops. The first clear indication of this is Canon 82 of the Quinisext Council in Trulla (692). At that time many religious paintings ("icons," from the Greek *eikōn*, image) showed Jesus only as the lamb, while John the Baptist was drawn as a person. Acknowledging the meaningful symbolism, the bishops nevertheless felt that this remained too much in the realm of the Old Testament and did not fully take seriously the incarnation. They officially ruled that

> the figure in human form of the Lamb who taketh away the sin of the world, Christ our God, be henceforth exhibited in images, instead of the ancient lamb, so that all may understand by means of it the depths of the humiliation of the Word of God, and that we may recall to our memory his conversation in the flesh, his passion and salutary death, and his redemption which was wrought for the whole world (*Ecumenical Councils*, p. 401).

The widespread use and veneration of biblical and other religious paintings and mosaics soon led to heated discussion, in which iconoclasts (those opposing images), and defenders of icons excommunicated and persecuted one another. These debates were strongly influenced by the political interests of the Byzantine rulers, by growing tension between the Western and Eastern churches, and by the desire to curb the influence of monks and nuns who were strong defenders of the icons and had the overwhelming support of the laity.

In 754 the iconoclasts gathered in the so-called Conciliabulum of Constantinople. By painting Christ, they argued, one either separates the divine-human nature or mingles the two natures — in either case a heresy according to earlier church councils. The iconoclasts therefore decreed:

> The only admissible figure of the humanity of Christ... is bread and wine in the Holy Supper. This and no other form, this and no other type, has he chosen to represent his incarnation.... "There shall be rejected and removed and cursed out of the Christian church every likeness which is made out of any material and colour whatever by the evil art of painters.... If anyone ventures to represent the divine image of the Word after the Incarnation with material colours, let him be anathema! (*Ecumenical Councils*, pp. 544f).

Defenders of icons saw iconoclasm as a denial of incarnation. The great Orthodox theologian John of Damascus (*ca.* 670-750) became their main spokesman. His followers made a clear distinction between the veneration (*proskynēsis*) of icons and the adoration (*latreia*) which is due only to God. Icons were to be considered only as types representing the prototype of Christ. They lead not to a eucharistic communion but to a prayer communion with Christ. The forms of veneration addressed through the icons to Christ, Mary, and the saints were the same as those commonly used in the Byzantine world for greeting personalities like bishops and the empress or emperor — the *proskynēsis*, kissing the feet, and the use of incense. The seventh Ecumenical Council (Nicea, 787) fully accepted the views of the defenders of the icons. As the decisions of this Council were soon misrepresented in the West, it is important to quote the official decrees. The Council reaffirmed the decisions of the first six ecumenical councils, and sought to keep the ecclesiastical traditions unchanged,

> whether in writing or verbally, one of which is the making of pictorial representations, agreeable to the history of the preaching of the gospel, a tradition useful in many respects, but especially in this, that so the incarnation of the Word of God is shown forth as real and not merely fantastic.... We, therefore, define with all certitude and accuracy that just as the figure of the precious and life-giving cross, so also the venerable and holy images, as well in painting and mosaic as of other fit materials, should be set forth in the holy churches of God, and on the sacred vessels and on the vestments and on hangings and in pictures both in houses and by the wayside.... For by so much more frequently as they are seen in artistic representation, by so much more readily are men lifted up to the memory of their prototypes, and to a longing after them; and to these should be given due salutation and honourable reverence (*proskynesis*), not indeed that true worship of faith (*latreia*) which pertains alone to the divine nature; but to these, as to the figure of the precious and life-giving cross and to the book of the gospels and to the other holy objects, incense and lights may be offered according to ancient pious custom. For the honour which is paid to the image passes on to that which the image represents, and he who reveres the image reveres in it the subject represented (*Ecumenical Councils*, p. 550).

These decisions were received and acknowledged also by the bishop of Rome, Pope Hadrian, although some parts of the Western church questioned them. In the Eastern church the debate started once again when iconoclastic emperors came on the throne. Yet the synod of Constantinople (842) reaffirmed the role of icons in the worship of the church and sealed this decision by instituting the Feast of Orthodoxy.

"What the gospel tells us by words, the icon proclaims by colours and makes it present for us." This statement from a council in 860 sums up the role icons have played in the Eastern church. Icons were painted mostly by monks according to painters' manuals, one of which (possibly from the eleventh century) was found on Mount Athos. They show the life of Christ and of the church from the perspective of transfiguration.[1] In Orthodox life and worship, both in church buildings and in homes, hearing God's message from the written gospel and the meditation on God's image in the "painted gospel" of the icons remain intimately united.

The pedagogic use of images

While theologians in the East discussed the legitimacy of images in Christian worship, the manuscripts of the Bible in both the East and West were being illuminated with more and more illustrative drawings and miniatures (paintings with *minium*, red lead). The walls of church buildings

---

[1] For a meditation based on icons, see the script on John's gospel, II/19, pp. 221ff.

were covered with paintings and mosaics, mainly of biblical scenes and persons. The most glorious of these are the sixth-century mosaics in Ravenna. Reliefs with incidents from Christ's life were made still earlier. Eusebius even tells of a full sculpture he had seen in Caesarea Philippi, supposed to be the home town of the woman healed of a hemorrhage (Matt. 9:20ff).

> There stands upon an elevated stone, by the gates of her house, a brazen image of a woman kneeling, with her hands stretched out, as if she were praying. Opposite this is another upright image of a man, made of the same material, clothed decently in a double cloak, and extending his hand towards the woman.... They say that this statue is an image of Jesus. It has remained to our day, so that we ourselves also saw it when we were staying in the city. Nor is it strange that those of the Gentiles who of old were benefited by our Saviour should have done such things, since we have learned also that the likenesses of his apostles Paul and Peter, and of Christ himself, are preserved in paintings (*Church History*, VII, 18, 2-4).

Eusebius himself did not approve of such images. Yet about a hundred years later Nilus of Sinai advised that churches not be decorated with hunting scenes, but with scenes from the Old and New Testaments. Those unable to read might contemplate the paintings, note the example of the saints, and endeavour to copy in their own lives the virtues suggested. He quoted the Roman poet Horace, who believed that our spirits are less keenly stirred by what passes through our ears than by what is set before our eyes.

> To adore a picture is one thing, but to learn through the story of a picture what is to be adored is another. For what writing presents to readers, this a picture presents to the unlearned who behold, since in it even the ignorant see what they ought to follow; in it the illiterate read. Hence, and chiefly to the nations, a picture is instead of reading (*Selected Epistles*, XI, 13).

The decline of literacy resulting from the invasion of "barbarians" from the East and the North made new ways of biblical communication necessary. In 800, when the Frankish conqueror Charlemagne became emperor and patron of the Western church, he faced a tremendous educational task. He ordered his illiterate subjects to memorize the "Our Father" and to participate regularly in worship where the Bible was read and explained. He founded schools and a court academy. What was his attitude towards images? Pope Hadrian had sent him a rudimentary Latin translation of the acts of the seventh Ecumenical Council in Nicea. This mutilated text quoted a council father as saying that images were to be adored with the same supreme worship due the Holy Trinity. On the basis of such inaccurate information Charlemagne's theologians wrote the Caroline Books, in which the decrees of the council of 787 were refuted. Charlemagne himself, however, called Syrian, Greek, and Roman artists to his court to help illumine the famous Carolingian Bibles. No matter how much the theologians insisted on the Word and the Bible as a text, Christian art had become a pedagogical necessity. The time for the Bible as a visual message had definitely arrived.

In the West Christian art was not regulated by ecclesiastical synods as it was in the East. Nevertheless, the artists' commissions indicated clearly what they were to paint, sculpture, or represent in stained glass windows. Special emphasis was made on showing the correspondence between the Old and New Testaments. As early as 520 Elpidius Rusticus, a deacon of Lyons, had written a poem relating events from the two Testaments to each other. Medieval biblical theologians fervently pursued such typological interpretations. About 1200 an English monk composed — especially for painters — a long poem coordinating no fewer than 508 types from the Old Testament and the liturgy with 138 scenes in the New Testament.

Medieval cathedrals are visible translations of the typological understanding of the Bible. They were in fact "Bibles in stone and stained glass." Their beautiful altarpieces — painted, sculptured, or enameled — "preached" powerful sermons. The enameled altarpiece Nicolas of Verdun made in 1181 for Klosterneuburg in southern Germany consists of thirteen groups of three images. In each group a scene from Jesus' life is superimposed on one scene from the time before Moses and another from the period under the law, both prefiguring the New Testament episode.

The most famous example of late medieval pictorial Bible teaching is the *Biblia pauperum*. These picture books began to circulate around 1300, and in the next two centuries their influence reached far beyond their region of origin. The original model was probably conceived and drawn in a Benedictine monastery in southeastern Germany. In the process of copying three different styles developed in Bavaria, Austria, and around Weimar. Contrary to what one might assume from their name, these books were not primarily designed for poor or illiterate laity, but as helps for the teaching and preaching of mendicant friars and village priests. They are in fact an ingenious biblical and dogmatic compendium.

The oldest copies of the *Biblia pauperum* contain thirty-four scenes from the New Testament, two on each page, beginning with the annunciation and ending with the descent of the Spirit and the extra-biblical scene of the coronation of the Virgin. Each New Testament episode is drawn within a circle or rectangle framed by banners held by four prophets, on which their prophecies of the episode are written. Two Old Testament scenes, as types of the New Testament event, appear at the left and right sides, and the whole is completed with corresponding titles and interpretative texts. Those who used these small books began to see the Bible as a whole, thus receiving the framework for a biblical theology.

From the early fifteenth century on the images of the *Biblia pauperum* were printed with wood blocks, and the text was added later by hand, in Latin in the older copies, but subsequently also in German. The earliest printed Bible is therefore not a printed text with a few illustrations, but a pictorial Bible, in which a short, handwritten text serves the printed drawings.

Gutenberg's invention did not immediately displace this pictorial Bible. Yet, as we have seen, the printing of the biblical text did gradually change the function of the Bible. The Reformers considered the translation of this biblical text into the common language of the people most important, so that the biblical message could be preached, studied, and sung. In some places this new concentration on the biblical text went hand in hand with radical iconoclastic movements, and the "Bible in stone," the medieval sculptures in the cathedrals, were smashed.

Martin Luther did not approve of such measures. In his catechism he omitted the second commandment, which he considered valid only for the Jews (which is why the Lutheran numbering of the Ten Commandments differs from that of other Christian confessions). In his preface to a prayer book, published in 1545, Luther wrote:

> It seems good to me to include the old (illustrated) passion booklet in this prayer book, especially for the sake of children and simple folk. Through images and parables they are more deeply motivated to remember the divine stories than simply by words and teaching. Saint Mark, after all, testified that also Christ preached to simple people for their sake only in parables.... I also do not think it to be wrong to paint Scripture texts in parlours and rooms so that one has God's work and word constantly before one's eyes and can thus train oneself in the fear and faith of God. And what is wrong if someone would paint all the major stories of the whole Bible into a book and if such a book would truly be a Bible for the laity? Indeed, the words and works of God can never be held enough before the common people.

Quite a different view was taken by John Calvin. Never would he have omitted the second commandment! In his *Institutes* of 1560 he wrote:

> As sculpture and painting are gifts of God, what I insist for is that both shall be used purely and lawfully — that gifts which the Lord has bestowed upon us for his glory and our good shall not be preposterously abused, nay, shall not be perverted to our destruction. We think it unlawful to give a visible shape to God, because God himself has forbidden it, and because it cannot be done without in some degree tarnishing his glory. And lest any should think that we are singular in this opinion, those acquainted with the productions of sound divines will find that they have always disapproved of it. If it be unlawful to make any corporeal representation of God, still more unlawful must it be to worship God in it. The only things, therefore, which ought to be painted or sculptured are things which can be presented to the eye; the majesty of God, which is far beyond the reach of any eye, must not be dishonoured by unbecoming representations. Visible representations are of two classes — viz. historical, which give a representation of events, and pictorial, which merely exhibit bodily shapes and figures. The former are of some use for instruction or admonition. The latter, so far as I can see, are only fitted for amusement (*Institutes*, I, 11, 12).

Three years later the Heidelberg Catechism spoke categorically to the question of using images for biblical teaching: Question 98: "May not pictures be tolerated in churches in place of books for unlearned people?" Answer: "No, for we must not try to be wiser than God who does not want his people to be taught by means of lifeless idols, but through the living preaching of his Word."

This raises again the question of whether it is legitimate to translate the oral and written biblical message into pictorial form. Can we see God's image? Are we allowed to see it? Or was the development of biblical art from the third century onwards a tragic mistake?

The incarnate image of God

Human hands cannot create the image of the true God. Those who try to do so or who worship such "molten gods" are idolaters. The danger of idolatry is great everywhere. Not all Orthodox believers praying before the icons make the subtle distinction between veneration and adoration. In popular Roman Catholicism there is still much image worship which makes the protest of the Reformers valid even today. But idols are worshipped among Protestants, too — not images or sculptures, perhaps, but work or money or success. The second commandment remains an ever timely warning.

Nevertheless, it was God who created this universe. Biblical faith affirms that God is involved in the history of this world, that through pain and struggles he leads human history and the unfinished creation to their goal. The eyes of Christian hope see that God's glory breaks through here and there and can be perceived already now. The biblical witnesses speak about this hidden presence of God in such highly evocative language that it calls for visualization. Not surprisingly, the earliest Christian art — that of the catacombs — was deeply symbolic: the fish, the anchor, the Good Shepherd. Like the biblical words these images point to a reality beyond what meets the eye. Rather than reproduce the visible, they make visible a hidden presence. This God from afar is involved in the concrete history of a particular people. Both Jewish and early Christian art were therefore not only symbolic, but also narrative. Scenes in which God intervened in the lives of the patriarchs, shaped the events of the Exodus, and spoke and acted through prophets are portrayed, with the acting God himself appearing through the symbol of his hand.

The biblical message is still more explicit with regard to God's image. This image is not created *by* human beings. It is shaped by God's hand *in* human beings. "God created the human in his own image, ... male and female he created them" (Gen. 1:26f). Jewish rabbis in Palestine related this affirmation to the second commandment and strictly forbade the visual representation of a human being. To do so would mean to make an image of God. Jews of the diaspora and Christians did not argue in this way. On the contrary: God's image, which God himself had shaped in human beings, reflects God's action. Not only must it be told about; it can also be seen and represented pictorially.

The New Testament affirms much more: God's image has been personally present in Jesus Christ. "The Word became flesh and dwelt among us, full of grace and truth; we have beheld his glory, glory as of the only Son from the Father" (John 1:14). "He is the image of the invisible God, the first-born of all creation" (Col. 1:15; cf. 2 Cor. 4:4). The word of the biblical God tends to incarnation. It becomes visible. Paradoxically, the invisible God appears before our eyes in Jesus Christ.

Wherever artists have attempted to grasp this biblical message, and represent it visually, it is not only subject-matters but also the criteria of art which gradually change. The portrayal of gods and heroes and the glorification of the beauty of the human body are replaced by symbols and scenes of God's action in history. The beauty of the expected transfiguration of all things in Christ is prefigured (as in the Orthodox icons and early medieval Western art). Yet the ugliness of pain and God's image in suffering and struggling humanity are also made visible (as in the late medieval art and the work of Rembrandt). Such art becomes a genuine communication and interpretation of the biblical message.

Not all pictorial translations of biblical themes and scenes nor all the works of Christian artists have been biblical. Just as a sermon or a book of theology may dilute the biblical message rather than communicate it, much "Christian" art betrays God's true image rather than making it visible. Yet as the medieval church called on artists to become biblical communicators and interpreters, so we today must call on them. Their work can open our minds and hearts and eyes to discover dimensions in God's message which a purely literary study of texts will never disclose.

That is why the visual element plays an important role in the following scripts for Bible study. Modern inventions like the camera, the slide projector, and duplicating equipment can help us discover the pictorial Bible. Such expensive media as motion pictures, television, and video tape have so far proved to be of limited use for participatory Bible studies. The very traditional medium of drawing on paper or blackboard, however, remains as good as ever.

In the scripts of Part Two, visual elements are first of all used for purely informative purposes.[2] "Chalk and talk" and making simple line-drawings are mainly used for pedagogical reasons.[3] Diagrams can be helpful to show the complicated process of interpretation.[4] More demanding are the exercises of visualization proposed in the study on the coming of the Messiah and the meditation on Levi's calling.[5] Artists can deepen a group's study of a biblical passage or theme; and works of art are especially helpful for meditating the biblical message and summing up and fixing the insights of a Bible study in our mind and heart.[6]

---

[2] Cf. the showing of slides of archaeological discoveries and geographical sites in II/2, p. 70.
[3] For example, in II/1, pp. 63, 65 and II/20, pp. 226 and 230.
[4] Cf. worksheet on p. 304.
[5] Cf. II/7, pp. 115ff and II/10, pp. 136ff.
[6] Cf. II/3, pp. 82ff, II/6, pp. 103f, 111, II/7, p. 116, II/17, pp. 198f and II/19, pp. 221ff.

4 CELEBRATING THE DRAMA OF SALVATION

The Bible as a written manuscript developed alongside the Bible as a liturgical enactment. The recollection and oral traditions of the Exodus event led both to its liturgical re-enactment in the Jewish Passover feast and to the writing down of the Exodus traditions. The enactment shaped the manuscripts and vice-versa. This Bible as a manuscript and as a liturgical drama (including the cycle of feasts in the ecclesiastical year) forms a whole. Throughout the centuries, and probably even today, the majority of Christians — Orthodox, Roman Catholic, and Protestant — know the biblical message not from their own reading of the Bible-book, but from participating in the biblically shaped liturgical drama.

Lessons, interpretation and prayers
How does the Bible function in worship? The public reading of the law in the time of Ezra gives us a vivid picture of the later synagogue assemblies, which had a strong influence on early Christian worship:

> Ezra the priest brought the law before the assembly, both men and women and all who could hear with understanding.... (He) stood on a wooden pulpit which they had made for the purpose.... And Ezra opened the book in the sight of all the people ... and when he opened it all the people stood. And Ezra blessed the Lord, the great God; and all the people answered, "Amen, Amen", lifting up their hands; and they bowed their heads and worshipped the Lord with their faces down to the ground.... And (Ezra and the Levites) read from the book, from the law of God, clearly; and they gave the sense, so that the people understood the reading (Neh. 8:2-8).

In this account we notice the people's worshipful attitudes and liturgical gestures before the Lord, the prayers, but above all the reading and exposition of the scriptures. The message of God was both read aloud and interpreted. In the time of Jesus this interpretation began with the Aramaic translation and paraphrase (Targum) made immediately after the reading of the scripture in Hebrew. Often it was followed by a Midrash (from the Hebrew *darash*, "to seek," "to search out," "to interpret scripture"), which made the biblical text understandable and applied it to the situation of the hearers. The texts were thus not considered as documents fixed once for all, but were reread and continuously reinterpreted within the living tradition and experience of faith. Jews in Jesus' time assumed that this synagogue worship had been instituted by Moses himself. Josephus, the Jewish historian of the late first century wrote:

> (Moses) has proclaimed the Law to be the best and most necessary instruction of all; not once or twice or many times, must one listen to it; for he has ordained that every week, other works being set aside, the people should come together to hear the Law and learn it exactly (*Against Apion*, II. 17, 175; cf. also Acts 15:21).

It was in the context of such a synagogue worship that Jesus made his first programmatic scripture lesson and one-sentence sermon in Nazareth (Luke 4:16-21).

The Jewish worship assembly, with its regular scripture lessons and exposition, was the pattern for early Christian worship (cf. 1 Tim. 4:13). Scholars disagree over which parts of the New Testament are in fact early Christian interpretations of Old Testament lessons and over the extent to which whole books of the New Testament were written to serve in Christian worship as new scripture lessons alongside those from the Old Testament. It is certain, however, that many of the writings of the New Testament contain parts of early Christian worship and are to a certain extent patterned according to the sequence of feasts or the sequence of the liturgy.[1]

Since the only description in the New Testament of early Christian worship is found in a few summary comments in Acts (2:42, 46; 5:42) and in Paul's prescriptions for the Corinthians (1 Cor. 11:20ff and 14:1ff; cf. below pp. 271ff on 1 Cor 14:26), it is instructive to examine one of the earliest Christian testimonies about what happened when the church met for worship. Around A.D. 150, the converted philosopher Justin Martyr wrote:

> On the day which is called Sunday we have a common assembly of all who live in the cities or in the outlying districts, and the memoirs of the Apostles or the writings of the Prophets are read, as long as there is time. Then, when the reader has finished, the president of the assembly verbally admonishes and invites all to imitate such examples of virtue. Then we all stand up together and offer up our prayers (*First Apology*, 67).

Justin's description goes on to speak about the celebration of the eucharist which followed immediately. Notice how the reading and interpretation of the scriptures were held intimately together. Just as the rabbis reinterpreted an Old Testament lesson in their Midrash with a view to the situation of the hearers, so the early Christian teachers and "presidents" (probably the bishops) reinterpreted both the Old Testament lessons and the "memoirs of the apostles" with a view to current questions in the life of the assembled church.

---

[1] On this, see below scripts II/19, p. 218, II/23, pp. 253ff, II/25, pp. 263ff.

Much of the present New Testament arose from this process of handing down the tradition of oral and written testimonies and interpreting them for the hearers' needs. Papias clearly stated this with regard to the origin of Mark's gospel. Whether or not his information was accurate, the general process of the growth of the New Testament almost certainly followed the way indicated.

> Mark, having become the interpreter of Peter, wrote down accurately, though not indeed in order, whatsoever he remembered of the things said or done by Christ. For he neither heard the Lord nor followed him, but afterwards, as I said, he followed Peter, who adapted his teaching to the needs of his hearers, but with no intention of giving a connected account of the Lord's discourses, so that Mark committed no error while he thus wrote some things as he remembered them (*Church History*, III, 39.15).

Exactly when the scripture lessons in the eucharistic services and daily offices of the church were fixed through lectionaries is not known. The earliest known lectionaries date from the fifth century, but we know from the writings of the church fathers that from the third century on there were regular lessons from the Old Testament, the New Testament epistles, and the gospels. There was a continuous reading of and commenting on whole books, as well as a special choice of scripture lessons for particular times and celebrations in the ecclesiastical year. This practice has been continued in church services throughout the centuries.

Such scripture lessons combined with biblical interpretation are at the heart of Bible study. Listening to previously recorded readings is thus emphasized in some of the following scripts.[2] Most of the scripts also involve exploring the meaning of biblical stories and passages in the light of present questions and situations both in church and society.[3]

God's message addressed to us evokes a response. The passages we have cited from Nehemiah and from Justin's *Apology* show that among Jews and early Christians scripture lessons and interpretations were embedded in prayer. No wonder so many parts of the Old and the New Testaments are in fact prayers.

We hear desperate cries for help in the psalms of complaint and painfully honest confessions by Jeremiah and Job. We see Hannah weeping as she utters her humble petition and exulting in the Lord when her son is born (1 Sam. 1-2). The Israelites' confessions of faith (e.g., Deut. 26:5-9), the solemn prayer of Solomon (1 Kings 8:22-53), and Daniel's invocation, confession, and petition (Dan. 9:3-19) take us into the pilgrimage of God's people of the old covenant. In the gospels we meet Jesus, who teaches us how to pray (Matt. 6:5-13). Again and again he himself went out to a lonely place to pray (Mark 1:35). We are included in his high priestly prayer (John 17), and his struggle in Gethsemane sets the pattern for all truly Christian prayer: "Not as I will, but as thou wilt" (Matt. 26:39).

---

[2] E.g. II/2, p. 69, II/19, p. 220, II/25, p. 264.
[3] See, for example, II/4, pp. 90f, II/6, pp. 104f, II/12, pp. 162f, II/14, pp. 169ff.

The early church's steadfastness in prayer is abundantly evident from Acts and the epistles. With one exception — the angry letter to the Galatians — Paul began his epistles with prayers of thanksgiving or blessing (which, as in the Old Testament, are not only a blessing given and received, but a thankful response of praise which tells the glory of God), and ended them with a blessing or a grace.

Many New Testament prayers are taken over from early Christian worship. In these cases, the Bible as prayer preceded the Bible as manuscript. This is also true for the many confessional formulas (such as 1 Cor. 15:3-5), prayerful affirmations of faith which also served for teaching. Similarly, the many biblical hymns were sung in worship before they were written down and included in the biblical manuscripts. Those in Revelation may have been taken over directly from the service of "the Lord's day" when the seer received his visions (Rev. 1:10). Perhaps the earliest typically Christian prayer of the church was the Aramaic "Maranatha!", which can express both the petition "Our Lord, come!" (*marana-tha*) and the affirmation "Our Lord has come!" (*maran-atha*). First used in the Aramaic-speaking church in Palestine, it had by A.D.55 become an integral part of Christian worship elsewhere and Paul could use it without translation when writing to the Corinthians (1 Cor. 16:22).

Not only were the prayers of the church integrated into the biblical manuscript, but the movement was also reversed, beginning with the liturgical use of the Our Father. This prayer appears already in the *Didache*, the oldest Christian catechism, worship book, and church order, probably written in Syria only a few decades after the gospels. There for the first time it appears with a concluding doxology ("for thine is the power and the glory"), which is not in the oldest manuscripts of Matthew's gospel nor in Luke's version of the prayer.

Throughout the centuries the church has continued this biblical way of praying and confessing. Besides the Our Father, many psalms and the great prayers in Luke 1 and 2 have become integral parts of the liturgy. Other liturgical prayers take up biblical themes and sayings. The oldest known extra-biblical Christian document, a letter written about 96 from the church in Rome to the church in Corinth, includes a long prayer probably taken from the Roman liturgy. Its many allusions to Old and New Testament texts show how the early church used the Bible in prayer:

> (Grant us, Lord) to hope in his (Christ's) name, the beginning of all creation; open the eyes of our heart to know thee, that thou alone art the "Highest in the highest" and remainest Holy among the holy. Thou dost humble the pride of the haughty; thou dost destroy the conceits of nations, lifting up the humble and humbling the exalted. Thou art he who makes both rich and poor, who kills and who vivifies, the sole benefactor of spirits and God of all flesh. Thou "lookest on the abysses," thou seest into the works of man. Thou art the helper of those in danger, the "saviour of those in despair"....

We beseech thee, Lord, to be our helper and protector. Save those of us who are in affliction, have mercy on the humble, raise the fallen, show thyself to those who are in need, heal the sick, turn back the wanderers of thy people, feed the hungry, ransom our prisoners, raise up the weak, comfort the faint-hearted. Let all the nations know thee, that thou alone art God, and that Jesus Christ is thy Servant, and that "we are thy people and the sheep of thy pasture."

Yes, Lord, let thy countenance shine on us for good in peace, that we may be protected by thy strong hand and delivered from all sin by thy uplifted arm, and deliver us from those who hate us unjustly. Give concord and peace to us and to all inhabitants of the earth, as thou didst give it to our fathers when they invoked thee reverently in faith and truth, so that we may be saved, and grant that we may be obedient to thy almighty and excellent name, and to our rulers and governors on earth.... Direct their counsels, Lord, according to what is good and well-pleasing before thee, that by piously administering in peace and gentleness the authority granted them by thee they may obtain thy mercy. Thou who alone art able to do these good things for us and other things more abundantly, we praise thee through the high priest and protector of our souls, Jesus Christ, through whom be glory and majesty to thee both now and for all generations and for all ages. Amen (*1 Clement*, 59-61).

The Bible as prayer thus entered the corporate Christian memory. Local congregations recite it Sunday after Sunday. Day after day it is chanted in religious communities. This corporate memory is meditated on by many of the faithful when they are ill or in prison. Consciously or unconsciously it guides the decisions of those who find themselves at a crossroad in their life. Bible study must therefore lead to the praying of the Bible.[4]

It is not only the formal prayers of the Bible, but also the prayerful and meditative way of looking at creation and history which has had an impact on the spirituality of the church. This is an attitude which takes a long-term view, confronting the present state of earthly realities with the reality of God. One finds it emphasized very differently in the prophetic interventions, the wisdom-sayings, and the apocalyptic visions of the Old Testament. In the New Testament it appears fully in the way Jesus looks at people and events (especially in his parables of the kingdom), in the deeply meditative epistles of Romans, Colossians, and Ephesians, and above all in the Johannine writings. Throughout the centuries this biblical way of looking at things has been an inexhaustible source for Christian meditation and action. Bible study must foster it.

Music, dance and processions

Long before the psalms were written down and collected to become "the hymn book of the Second Temple," they were sung to the accompaniment of *musical instruments*. One of the earliest Old Testament songs is the one Miriam sang after the Israelites' passage through the sea. She beat the

---

[4] Such transformations into prayer are suggested in II/1, p. 66, II/7, p. 118, II/10, p. 140.

rhythm with her timbrel and all women followed her with timbrels and dancing: "Sing to the Lord, for he has triumphed gloriously; the horse and his rider he has thrown into the sea" (Exod. 15:21).

David, the poet and harpist who danced before the ark (2 Sam. 6:5, 14f), has become the symbol of this Bible which is sung and danced. A scroll of Hebrew psalms from the time of Jesus makes the exaggerated statement that David wrote 3600 psalms as well as a hymn for each day of the year to be sung during the daily sacrifice. Together with his other songs for each month and the feasts, he is said to have been composed four thousand musical pieces. In the temple built after the exile some "two hundred and forty-five singers, male and female," participated (Neh. 7:67) with more than a hundred trumpeters. Psalm 150 enumerates the musical instruments used for praise.

The splendour of such worship ceased when the temple of Jerusalem was destroyed in A.D. 70. Meanwhile a much simpler form of worship had developed in the synagogues where musical instruments were forbidden. The early church followed this simpler pattern, but in the New Testament and early Christian worship the singing of the biblical message continued. Filled with the Spirit, the believers were called upon to address "one another in psalms and hymns and spiritual songs, singing and making melody to the Lord" (Eph. 5:19). Immediately preceding this exhortation the words of an early Christian baptismal song are quoted (Eph. 5:14) — only one example of the many hymns found in the New Testament and the ancient Christian liturgies.

How the psalms and these hymns were sung remains uncertain. A Roman procurator wrote to the emperor Trajan at the beginning of the second century that Christians "were in the habit of meeting on a certain fixed day before it was light, when they sang in alternate verses a hymn to Christ, as to a god" (Pliny, *Letters*, X, 96.7). For a long time the melodies were not fixed in writing, but sung from memory or freely improvised. Until the ninth century they were sung in unison. The early church already had cantors, however, who sang antiphonally with the congregation or chanted parts of the liturgy while the whole assembly participated with sung responses.

As in the case of images, the church fathers at first had some misgivings about music. Augustine sometimes wondered whether all the melodies of the Psalter should not be banished from the church. But he continues:

> When I recall the tears which I shed over the hymns in thy church at the early period of the recovery of my faith, and now today when I am affected not by singing, but by the words which are sung, provided they are sung in a clear voice and with the most appropriate modulation, I again recognize the great usefulness of this practice. So, I waver between the danger of sensual enjoyment and the experience of healthful employment, and — though not, indeed, to offer an irrevocable decision — I am more inclined to approve the custom of singing in the church, in order that the weaker mind may rise to a disposition of piety through these delights of hearing. Nevertheless, when it

happens that I am more moved by the song than the thing which is sung, I confess that I sin in a manner deserving of punishment, and then I should rather not hear the singing (*Confessions*, X. 33).

As liturgical music developed, the piety of the age submerged the biblical content. Although the message was often lost in the music, the Bible continued to be sung. The Huguenot psalms gave consolation and the courage of faith in many persecutions. The passions of J.S. Bach communicate central parts of Matthew's and John's gospels to people who never read the Bible. Bible study also should never be deprived of music and songs.[5]

The biblical message in the form of a *dance* remains more problematic. Old Testament Hebrew uses eleven different verbs for dancing and acknowledges that there is "a time to dance" (Eccl. 3:4). Even the prophet Jeremiah, better known for weeping than rejoicing, described the time of salvation as an occasion for Israel to "go forth in the dance of the merrymakers" (Jer. 31:4, 13). Yet the memory of the Israelites' dance before the golden calf (Exod. 32:6, 19) was never lost. As in many cultures, dancing in the Canaanite environment was intimately linked with idolatry and lascivious living. Thus the rabbinic writings warn against the dangers of dance, though the Mishnah also includes a vivid description of liturgical dancing during the feast of tabernacles:

> Men of piety and good works used to dance before them with burning torches in their hands, singing songs and praises. And countless Levites (played) on harps, lyres, cymbals and trumpets and instruments of music, on the fifteen steps leading down from the Court of the Israelites to the Court of the Women, corresponding to the Fifteen Songs of Ascents in the Psalms; upon them the Levites used to stand with instruments of music and make melody. Two priests stood at the upper gate which leads down from the Court of the Israelites to the Court of the Women, with two trumpets in their hands. At cock-crow they blew a sustained, a quavering, and another sustained blast (*Sukkah* 5.4).

Dancing appears only three times in the New Testament, in Jesus' parable about children unwilling to dance (Matt 11:17; Luke 7:32), in connection with the daughter of Herodias dancing before Herod (Matt. 14:6; Mark 6:22), and in an Old Testament quotation referring to the dancing before the golden calf (1 Cor. 10:7; cf. Exod. 32:6). Paul exhorted the Corinthians: "Glorify God in your body!" (1 Cor. 6:20), but he did not link this with the dance. Nevertheless, the early church did not at first exclude dancing as a liturgical act. It played an important role in the feasts of the martyrs. John Chrysostom himself, later Patriarch of Constantinople, acted as a dance leader in such martyrs' feasts. In a sermon in Antioch during Lent 387 he said, "Ye have danced a goodly dance throughout the whole

---

[5] The following scripts use both rediscovered ancient melodies of the Psalms (II/1, p. 59) and popular spirituals (II/2, p. 67, II/8, pp. 119ff), Orthodox hymns (II/19, pp. 212f), as well as melodies without words (II/10, p. 138). Bible studies should also lead to new songs (cf. the tasks in II/9, p. 135 and II/23, pp. 255f).

city; this, your noble captain (Bishop Flavian) leading you on; but sickness compelled me to remain at home, although against my will..." (*Concerning Statues*, Hom. XIX).

In the apocryphal Acts of John (second half of the second century) Jesus himself is shown as a divine dancer on the eve of his crucifixion:

> Before he was arrested Jesus told us to form a circle, holding one another's hands, and himself stood in the middle and said, "Answer Amen to me." So he began to sing the hymn and to say: "Glory be to thee, Father." And we circled round him and answered him, "Amen." ... "Now if you follow my dance, see yourself in me who am speaking, and when you have seen what I do, keep silence about my mysteries. You who dance consider what I do, for yours is this passion of man which I am to suffer." ... After the Lord had so danced with us, my beloved, he went out (*Acts of John*, 94-97).

Such teachings, together with the practice of ecstatic dancing by Christian heretics and an ever-present suspicion of the life-style to which dancing was related, brought the liturgical dance into disrepute. Augustine called dance "a circle with the devil at its centre," and several church councils later condemned its liturgical use. Only in the Church of Ethiopia has it continued through the centuries.

There are no indications of liturgical dance being used for understanding, expressing, and interpreting the biblical message through body movement. Thus one of the most basic and childlike human potentialities for expressing a range of emotion and insight has never been called upon in the practice of Bible study. There are now signs of a change, especially with Christians in Asia, Africa, and the Pacific becoming more conscious of their cultural heritage.[6]

If most Christians have yet to discover the biblical message in the form of a dance, another type of movement has long been related with the biblical message — *processions and pilgrimages*. The Exodus of the Israelite tribes from Egypt and their journey through the desert to the promised land foreshadowed subsequent pilgrimages. Year after year Israelites came to Jerusalem, and the processions in the temple were a Bible in movement, for which many psalms were composed (cf. Isa. 30:29): the songs of Zion (Ps. 48; 76; 87), the psalms of procession, where the movement can still be followed in the text (Ps. 24; 95:1-7), but also complaints such as Psalm 42. This cultic movement inspired the prophetic visions of the coming of the nations to Zion (cf. Isa. 2:2ff; 60:1ff; Zech. 8:20ff; 14:16ff).

The gospels portray Jesus taking part in pilgrimages to Jerusalem as a child, as a boy, perhaps several times during his public ministry, and for his passion. His travels through Palestine have made that country a very special land for Christians everywhere throughout the centuries. When the end of persecutions permitted it, Christian pilgrims went to Galilee and Jeru-

---

[6] In the following scripts the use of simple body movement is suggested for meditating on a Psalm (II/1, p. 66) and for memorizing a biblical hymn (II/23, p. 255), but much more can be done in this field.

salem. Visiting the places Jesus had stayed and reading and meditating on the appropriate gospel passages, these pilgrims were in fact doing Bible study. Jesus' movements in Jerusalem — his entry into the city, his prayer in Gethsemane, the way to Golgotha, his visit with the disciples to the Mount of Olives after his resurrection — strongly mark the feasts of the ecclesiastical year and are represented in many liturgical processions.

The diary of Egeria, a late fourth-century Christian pilgrim, probably from Northern Spain, gives us a glimpse of how the biblical drama of salvation can be re-enacted in processions. About the celebration of Palm Sunday she writes:

> At the seventh hour all the people go up to the church on the Mount of Olives, that is, to the Eleona. The bishop sits down, hymns and antiphons appropriate to the day and place are sung, and there are likewise readings from the Scriptures. As the ninth hour approaches, they move up, chanting hymns, to the Imbomon, that is, to the place from which the Lord ascended into heaven; and everyone sits down there. When the bishop is present, the people are always commanded to be seated, so that only the deacons remain standing.... As the eleventh hour draws near that particular passage from Scripture is read in which the children bearing palms and branches came forth to meet the Lord, saying: "Blessed is he who comes in the name of the Lord." The bishop and all the people rise immediately, and then everyone walks down from the top of the Mount of Olives, with the people preceding the bishop and responding continually with "Blessed is he who comes in the name of the Lord" to the hymns and antiphons. All the children who are present here, including those who are not yet able to walk because they are too young and therefore are carried on their parents' shoulders, all of them bear branches, some carrying palms, others olive branches. And the bishop is led in the same manner as the Lord once was led. From the top of the mountain as far as the city, and there through the entire city as far as the Anastasis (the sanctuary of the resurrection in Constantine's basilica of the Holy Sepulchre), everyone accompanies the bishop the whole way on foot, and this includes distinguished ladies and men of consequence, reciting the responses all the while; and they move very slowly so that the people will not tire. By the time they arrive at the Anastasis, it is already evening. Once they have arrived there, even though it is evening, vespers is celebrated; then a prayer is said at the (atrium of the) Cross and the people are dismissed (*Diary of a Pilgrimage*, 31).

In many pilgrimages and processions legends and even superstitions prevail over the biblical content. But well-conducted biblical pilgrimages and processions can become a deeply impressive form of Bible study, relating the places and events of Scripture with the present reality of a Christian fellowship and one's own interior journey.

Symbolic acts, sacraments and drama

In celebrating the drama of salvation the church remembers the great acts of God, past and future. This remembrance (Greek, *anamnesis*) happens in the strong sense of that term: past or future events are *made present*, so that the church today can liturgically participate in them.

The covenant renewals under Joshua (Josh. 24) and Josiah (2 Kings 22-23) functioned in this way. In the latter a book of the law was read, the Deuteronomy, where Moses says at the end of his life: "Hear, O Israel, the statutes and ordinances which I speak in your hearing this day, and you shall learn them and be careful to do them. The Lord our God made a covenant with us in Horeb. Not with our fathers did the Lord make this covenant, but with us, who are all of us here alive this day" (Deut. 5:1-3). The Israelites of a later generation thus became participants in the establishment of the covenant at Sinai. Similarly, in the temple feasts, the past great events of salvation were made present and the future messianic time was anticipated.

The spoken words retelling the story are important in this remembering, but *material tokens and gestures* are equally significant. Joshua not only wrote the words of the covenant in the book, but he also erected a great stone as a token and witness (Josh. 24:26f; cf. 4:21f). A good example of such a remembrance is the Jewish Passover meal. Jesus often participated in it, and this family meal with its many symbolic acts had as strong an influence on early Christian worship as the more formal Jewish services in the synagogue. Thus for studying the New Testament it is important to know how this remembrance is celebrated. The *Passover Haggadah*, from which the following quotations are taken, did not receive its present form until the Middle Ages, but much of it goes back to biblical and rabbinic times (cf. Exod. 13:8 and the Mishnah tractacte *Pesahim* 10, 4).

Haggadah means narration — in this case the telling of the Exodus story in the context of a family meal. The night before, a symbolic "search for the leaven" is made. Then the table is set with glasses for each and material tokens in the centre: three pieces of unleavened bread (*Matzah*), herbs to be dipped into salt water, a mixture of apple and nuts, the cup of Elijah, and two symbolic dishes, a roasted shankbone representing the paschal lamb and a boiled egg commemorating the festival offering made by pilgrims in Jerusalem.

After sunset the family and guests assemble, the mother lights the candle, the first cup of wine is blessed, and all drink it. The participants wash their hands and green herbs are eaten. Then the middle *Matzah* is broken, one part put back on the table, the other hidden to be eaten at the end of the meal. The remaining *Matzah* is lifted up and the master of the meal says:

> This is the bread of poverty which our forefathers ate in the land of Egypt. Let all who are hungry enter and eat; let all who are needy come to our Passover feast. This year we are here; next year may we be in the land of Israel. This year we are slaves; next year may we be free men.

The second glass of wine is poured and usually the youngest child asks a series of questions, beginning with: "Why is this night different from all other nights?" In response the father tells the Exodus story with many biblical quotations, later rabbinic interpretations, and symbolic acts. A hymn of thanksgiving is sung, the Passover symbols are pointed out and explained with quotations from the Exodus story. Here the present participation in the past event is clearly stated:

> In every generation let each man look on himself as if he came forth out of Egypt. As it is said: "And thou shalt tell thy son in that day, saying: It is because of that which the Lord did for me when I came forth out of Egypt" (Exod 13:8). It was not only our fathers that the Holy One, blessed be he, redeemed, but us as well did he redeem along with them. As it is said: "And he brought us out from thence, that he might bring us in, to give us the land which he swore unto our fathers" (Deut 6:23).

This is immediately followed up by the reciting of the first part of the psalms of praise (Ps. 113 and 114) and the blessing and drinking of the second cup.

Now the participants wash their hands for the meal. The upper and middle *Matzah* are blessed, broken, and distributed, the bitter herbs are dipped into salt water, blessed, and eaten. In remembrance of the temple the third *Matzah* is eaten with herbs. Then the actual meal is served. After the meal the hidden part of the unleavened bread is searched for and distributed to be eaten as a remembrance of the paschal lamb. The meal ends with a series of thanksgiving prayers, beginning with Psalm 124. The participants drink the third glass of wine, the cup of Elijah is filled and a door is opened (this symbolic act may be related to the ancient expectation that Elijah will come to herald the Messiah on Passover night). Then the remainder of the psalms of praise (Pss. 115-118 and 136) are recited, the fourth glass of wine drunk, and the closing prayer spoken, always ending with the expectant petition: "Next year in Jerusalem!"

When Jesus participated in such Passover meals the rituals were certainly not so elaborate; nevertheless, he learned even as a boy that Bible study can be done through participation in symbolic acts and prayers around the family table. When he began his public ministry he knew that teaching, ministering, and worship happens as much through material tokens of remembrance and symbolic gestures as through words. Therefore he allowed himself to be baptized by John the Baptist. He healed the sick and did other signs. He embraced children, ate with tax collectors and sinners, rode on an ass into Jerusalem, upset the tables of money changers in the temple court. Finally he washed the feet of his disciples and broke the bread.

Under the influence of a literary culture biblical scholars have published a great number of books about the sayings of Jesus, but his gestures and actions have received relatively little attention. Similarly, the endless theological debates about the Lord's Supper centre on the nature of the elements and the meaning of the words of institution. But "This is my body" referred probably as much to the whole series of *sacramental gestures* as it did to the elements (cf. the interpretation suggested below on pp. 188ff).

Early Christian worship was much more than words. Through baptism entry into the church became an unforgettable death and life experience. A third-century baptismal liturgy of the church in Rome details the following symbolism. After the catechumens had received baptismal instruction and had prepared themselves through prayer, fasting, and a night's vigil, they gathered early in the morning at the baptismal place. There they were asked to undress and say: "I renounce you, Satan, and all your service and all your works." As they were anointed with the oil of exorcism, the priest said: "Let every spirit depart far from you!" Baptism followed, with the catechumen standing in flowing water and confessing the Christian faith in God the Father, Son, and Holy Spirit. Coming out of the water each person baptized was anointed by the priest with the oil of thanksgiving. Then they dressed and entered the church, where the bishop laid his hands on each, saying:

> Lord God, you have made them worthy to receive remission of sins through the laver of regeneration of the Holy Spirit: send upon them your grace, that they may serve you according to your will; for to you is glory, to Father and Son with the holy Spirit in the holy Church, both now and to the ages of ages. Amen.

The bishop then anointed them with the oil of thanksgiving, made a sign on their foreheads, gave the kiss of peace, and said: "The Lord be with you." The newly baptized were thus integrated into the community of believers and ordained for their ministry as Christians in the world. This was sealed with the kiss of peace exchanged among all members and celebration of the eucharist, which followed immediately (Hippolytus, *Apostolic Tradition*, 21).

New Testament baptismal liturgies were not so elaborate, but even then gestures played an important role in worship. The position of the body — standing with lifted arms, kneeling, lying prostrate — was an integral part of prayer. The "holy kiss" (Rom. 16:16) expressed fellowship. The laying on of hands conferred authority for ministry (1 Tim. 4:14). To anoint the sick and pray with them brought healing (James 5:14). Above all the celebration of the Lord's Supper became from the beginning an integral part of early Christian worship.

Scholars are not agreed about the exact relationship between Jesus' last meal with his disciples and the early eucharistic celebrations of the church. It is possible that a joyful communal celebration (Acts 2:46) was related in the first place to the announced messianic feast (Mark 14:25) and the meals of the risen Lord with his disciples (Luke 24:30, 36ff; John 21:12ff; Acts 1:4; 10:40f), while a more solemn type of celebration stressed the remembrance of Christ's death (1 Cor. 11:26). But these are only different emphases. The first type is found mainly in the *Didache*, and strongly accents the sense of community and expectation as is shown in this well-known eucharistic prayer and closing grace, probably said antiphonally:

> As this broken bread was scattered upon the mountain tops and after being harvested was made one, so let thy church be gathered together from

the ends of the earth into thy kingdom, for thine is the glory and the power through Jesus Christ forever.
(Leader:) Let grace come, and let this world pass away.
(Congregation:) Hosanna to the God of David.
(Leader:) If anyone is holy, let him come; if anyone is not, let him repent. Maranatha.
(Congregation:) Amen (*Didache* 9.4; 10.6).

Such worship assemblies included not only Scripture lessons and interpretations, but also hymns, spontaneous prophecies, and revelations (1 Cor. 14:26). The writer of Revelation probably received his visions during a eucharistic service (Rev. 1:10). Later what is now commonly called the "service of the word" and the "service of the sacrament" were more formalized.

> After we finish our prayers, bread and wine and water are presented. He who presides likewise offers up prayers and thanksgivings, to the best of his ability, and the people express their approval by saying "Amen." The eucharistic elements are distributed and consumed by those present, and to those who are absent they are sent through the deacons. The wealthy, if they wish, contribute whatever they desire, and the collection is placed in the custody of the president. (With it) he helps the orphans and widows, those who are needy because of sickness or any other reason, and the captives and strangers in our midst; in short, he takes care of all those in need (Justin Martyr, *First Apology* 67).

The biblical message as lesson and interpretation and the biblical drama as liturgical enactment (including the collection of money!) belong together. Even the churches of the Reformation, with their insistence on the scriptures alone - *sola Scriptura!* — have accepted as true faith that God's message of salvation is communicated to us both through the preaching of the word and the celebration of the sacrament.

It was not only in the sacraments that the biblical message broke the confinement of a book and led to *dramatic representations*. The cycle of feasts in the ecclesiastical calendar made the church participate each year in the drama of salvation. In the Middle Ages Christ's resurrection was portrayed in monasteries and cathedrals by the solemn liturgical Easter plays in Latin. From the fourteenth century on the Bible appeared in vernacular as a full-day passion play in the market place. These later developed into mystery plays. For four days a cast of as many as three hundred enacted the whole history of salvation from creation to judgment.

Symbolism and drama can be overemphasized. The Eastern Orthodox churches developed a rich liturgical symbolism, in which the Bible-book itself is placed on the lectionary in a solemn procession. Yet is the message of this book still taken so seriously that it not only authorizes the ecumenical councils and the church's liturgy, but maintains a critical authority over both of them? The medieval Roman Catholic mass re-enacted Christ's sacrifice so massively that the uniqueness of his death on the cross was lost. Against such one-sidedness, the Reformation confessions rightly protested in the name of the biblical God. However, many Protestant churches then fell into the opposite one-sidedness. Partly under the impact of the literary culture they lost a sense for symbolic acts and the biblical drama. Studied in an ecumenical context, the Bible itself corrects such one-sidedness.[7]

We have seen how the Bible may appear in the church's worship in numerous ways: as scripture lesson, exposition, prayer, hymn, dance, movements in procession, sacraments, and drama. Printing the biblical text has enhanced some of these ways of entering into God's drama of salvation but stifled others. Therefore worship and Bible study must be kept together. Yet our whole Christian life must become worship — a living Bible. We are called to walk God's way.

---

[7] Scripts emphasizing symbolic acts, sacraments, and biblical drama include II/2, pp. 67ff; II/3, p. 84; II/14, p. 174; II/15, pp. 183f, 188ff; II/16, pp. 191ff; II/20, p. 228.

5 WALKING ON GOD'S WAY TODAY

Bible study is not an end in itself. The printed Bible which we study, God's message which we hear, God's image which we see, the drama of salvation in which we participate, all direct us on a way that we do not usually want to follow. Bible study *converts*. In the biblical languages this word means to return, to change one's mind, to set one's feet walking in a new direction. Yet is God's way relevant to the modern world?

Relevance or conversion?
Throughout the ages, in many cultures, the Bible has worked in a converting way. It has deeply marked the culture and conduct of strongly Orthodox islands and countries in southern and eastern Europe. Under the influence of Roman Catholicism and Protestantism the Bible was a formative element in the rest of Europe and the Americas. The missionary movement and the work of Bible Societies made the biblical message operative in Asia, Africa, and the Pacific. The love of God, together with human potentialities, has led to the love of the neighbour, as indeed should happen according to Jesus' summary of the law and the prophets (Mark 12:30f).

People tend to forget how deeply their cultures and conduct have been influenced by the biblical message. This is especially so in areas where this impact has extended over several centuries and where the Bible's influence is now fading. A study of the history of the South Pacific islands, for example, where the Bible and its message reached isolated peoples less than a century or two ago, helps one see anew the changes in culture and conduct which a personal love relation with the biblical God can effect.

Yet there is nothing automatic about this converting power. As Jesus himself told some Jews: "You search the scriptures, because you think that in them you have eternal life; and it is they that bear witness to me; yet you refuse to come to me that you may have life" (John 5:39f). For many centuries the Jews have indeed studied the scriptures and yet not recognized and accepted Jesus as the Messiah. People can read and appreciate the Bible as ancient Near Eastern literature; they can study biblical texts in comparative religion courses; and yet not be challenged to change the direction of their life. Often Christians, too, study the scriptures without being involved. Consciously or unconsciously, they misuse the Bible. They may treat it as a quarry for prooftexts to defend their own theology and spirituality or to justify their own unconverted thinking and selfish way of life. An important function of Bible study is to check such misuses of the Bible.

We must also face the disturbing fact that, despite statistics showing that the Bible remains a best-seller, most of our contemporaries know nothing about its message and its converting power. Either they have never been told of its message and power or they have decided in advance that such an old book could have no relevance for today.

In what follows there are few recipes for making the message relevant, for bridging the gaps between ancient traditions, texts, and concepts and contemporary questions and problems. There are of course pedagogical devices for making Bible study easier and more attractive,[1] and these should be used wherever they can serve to let God's message address us, his image transform us, and the chief actor in the drama of salvation engage us. Yet even so Bible study will soon become difficult and sometimes threatening. For long stretches of the way it will seem to fall short of our demands for immediate relevance, because the God who meets us in the Old Testament is not one of our beloved idols but a God from afar, and in the New Testament we come face to face with Jesus on the way to the cross. Sooner or later he will say to us also: "Follow me!"

There are no short-cuts from studying the Bible to solving our own problems or the world's. To learn to love our neighbours and ourselves we must learn to love God. Biblical ethics takes the long way around, through the worship, fellowship and mission of a people — Israel in the Old Testament and the church in the New Testament. It is rooted in a spirituality from which a harvest of the Spirit is promised (Gal. 5:22). The special community of persons which Bible study shapes can be described in the terms of Romans 12:2. They are people who do not conform to this age. They dare to be "irrelevant," as measured by present-day fashions. For they are in the process of being transformed by the renewal of their mind; that is, by constantly conforming their own mind to the qualitatively new mind of Christ. In this way they are enabled to discern, step by step, what is God's will and way. They experimentally discover what is truly good, what is acceptable and relevant to God's plan, and what therefore leads towards the final goal of human life and world history.

Can we explain — if only partially — the mystery of the change of roles we referred to in the Preface, by which the book we are reading begins to read us? Here we must take up the age-old discussion of the authority of the Bible. All Christian confessions acknowledge that God has spoken authoritatively to his church throughout the centuries in and through the

---

[1] Cf. Appendix A on "Methods and Tools," especially the suggested "leading questions and task assignments."

Bible. What is the nature of this authority? How does it relate to human experience? And how must we interpret the Bible for today?

The ecumenical discussion on the Bible
Rather than providing an historical survey of how the Bible has in fact functioned authoritatively throughout the years in various cultures and confessions, I would invite readers to participate in an ongoing ecumenical discussion. The present basis of the World Council of Churches describes the WCC as "a fellowship of churches which confess the Lord Jesus Christ as God and Saviour according to the scriptures, and therefore seek to fulfil together their common calling to the glory of the one God, Father, Son and Holy Spirit." What does "according to the scriptures" mean? How can it become operative in the life of the WCC, its member churches, and individual Christian believers?

During World War II many Christians rediscovered the power of the biblical message. Confronted with demonic powers and perplexing social and political issues, they found little guidance in the traditional dogmatic teaching of their churches. Many of them had faithfully read the Bible for their own personal piety, but now they reread it in the context of the world situation which faced them with grave decisions. Often this happened in prisons and concentration camps, sometimes individually, sometimes in small groups of Catholics, Orthodox, and Protestants, sometimes together with Jews, Marxists, and secular humanists. Dietrich Bonhoeffer's *Letters and Papers from Prison* is no doubt the best-known account of this rereading of the Bible.

On the basis of this experience the study department of the WCC (then in process of formation) organized, from 1946 onward, ecumenical consultations on the authority and interpretation of the Bible. The WCC Commission on Faith and Order later continued this process, and a series of ecumenical statements has resulted. The reports of these studies have been published with an interpretative introduction,[2] and in the following paragraphs and quotations I have selected some of those insights which have been particularly helpful to me (with occasional references to how these insights operate in Bible study).

a) 1946-1951: The Wadham statement
The main document of the first round of discussion was the statement "Guiding Principles for the Interpretation of the Bible," accepted by the ecumenical study conference at Wadham College, Oxford, in 1949.[3] Those

---

[2] Ellen Flesseman-van Leer (ed.), *The Bible: its Authority and Interpretation in the Ecumenical Movement* (Geneva: WCC, 1980, Faith and Order Paper No. 99). Page numbers cited in this chapter refer to this book.

[3] The major contributions to this round of discussion were published in two volumes, whose titles and subtitles clearly indicate the starting point of the discussion: *From the Bible to the Modern World* (1947), and *A World Council of Churches Symposium on "The Biblical Authority for the Churches' Social and Political Message Today"* (1951).

who have followed biblical scholarship over the last three decades may find these "guiding principles" outdated. They clearly reflect the "biblical theology" movement which characterized ecumenical discussions in the 1940s and 1950s. I doubt that it does justice to the particular messages of the Old Testament and the whole of the New Testament to state categorically:

> It is agreed that the primary message of the Bible concerns God's gracious and redemptive activity for the saving of sinful man that he might create in Jesus Christ a people for himself... It is agreed that the centre and goal of the whole Bible is Jesus Christ. This gives the two Testaments a perspective in which Jesus Christ is seen both as the fulfilment and the end of the law (p. 14).

But it seems to me that two basic trends of the Wadham statement remain fully valid.

The first has to do with hermeneutics, the art of interpretation. Hermeneutics has become a science of its own, developing a highly philosophical language. Theologians of the literary cultures continue passionately to discuss "the hermeneutical problem." Whatever its value in other fields, this modern hermeneutics does not prove to be very fruitful for the practice of Bible study. The Wadham statement, however, examines the interpretation (hermeneutics) of the Bible not only with a view to understanding biblical texts, but very specifically with a view to the practice of walking on God's way, the *praxis pietatis*. It rightly states that through the Bible "an authoritative claim is placed upon man and he is called upon to respond in faith and obedience throughout the whole of his life and work" (p. 14). Thus Christian interpretation has to happen within the context of the pilgrim people (p. 14) and with a view to its journey in the midst of "the tension between life in the kingdoms of this world and participation in the Kingdom of God" (p. 15). The search for biblical guidance on this way of obedience must not start with a particular theory of understanding or a general biblical theology.

> It is agreed that one must begin with a direct study of the biblical text in relation to a given problem; otherwise the general principles which we establish will reflect more the presuppositions of our own time than the message of the Bible (p. 15).

In the following scripts I have attempted to apply this hermeneutics from within the church and with a view to the church's worship (a purpose not dealt with in the Wadham statement), work, and mission in the world. I have tried to let the biblical story and text have first authority, even if it contradicts my own preconceptions and theology or cherished affirmations in the current ecumenical debates. Of course, no one can totally escape his or her own bias and we all need mutual correction.

The second abiding value of the Wadham statement is its insistence on seeing the Bible as a whole:

> It is agreed that in the case of an Old Testament passage, one must examine and expound it in relation to the revelation of God to Israel both

before and after its own period. Then the interpreter should turn to the New Testament in order to view the passage in that perspective. In this procedure the Old Testament passage may receive limitation and correction, and it may also disclose in the light of the New Testament a new and more profound significance, unknown to the original writer. It is agreed that in the case of a New Testament passage one should examine it in the light of its setting and context; then turn to the Old Testament to discover its background in God's former revelation. Returning again to the New Testament one is able to see and expound the passage in the light of the whole scope of *Heilsgeschichte* (history of salvation). Here our understanding of a New Testament passage may be deepened through our apprehension of the Old (p. 15).

I doubt that there is just one *Heilsgeschichte* in the Bible or that the whole of it can be subsumed under the title "salvation history," but this procedure of interpretation is a sound one.[4]

b) 1952-1963: The Montreal report on Scripture and Tradition

Meetings across confessional and cultural boundaries made it increasingly clear that no church or group of Christians understands and lives the Bible in a vacuum. All of us are conditioned by our particular Christian confession and the cultural milieu in which we live, even if we react against both. History — including the history of how the Bible has functioned and how it has been understood in the past — cannot be short-circuited. And so the Fourth World Conference on Faith and Order (Montreal, 1963) faced the question of the relationship between scripture and the various traditions. I would highlight two basic insights from its report, "Scripture, Tradition and Traditions."

The report makes a helpful distinction between Tradition (capital T) and tradition(s) (lower case t). The former designates "the Gospel itself, transmitted from generation to generation in and by the Church, Christ himself present in the life of the Church" (p. 19); whereas "traditions" — and the "process of tradition" — indicate how in different Christian confessions and different cultural situations this one Tradition has been diversely understood and transmitted. Recognizing that "Tradition precedes the Scriptures," the report states:

> We exist as Christians by the Tradition of the Gospel (the *paradosis* of the *kerygma*) testified in Scripture, transmitted in and by the Church through the power of the Holy Spirit. Tradition taken in this sense is actualized in the preaching of the Word, in the administration of the sacraments and worship, in Christian teaching and theology, and in mission and witness to Christ by the lives of the members of the Church (p. 20).

How, then, do we determine what in our various traditions is a faithful transmission of the Tradition "testified in Scripture?" Beyond enumerating criteria which are in fact applied in different Christian confessions, the report does not give much guidance. But by asking the right questions, at

---

[4] For applications, see scripts II/1, II/3-8, II/11, II/15, and II/18.

least, it leads the ecumenical search for truth beyond the classic debate on whether Scripture or Tradition is the source of revelation. Scripture itself is after all embedded in Tradition and has been a result of the process of tradition.[5]

A second important emphasis was the insistence on the role culture plays in the transmission of faith. The Tradition must never be confused with *traditionalism*, for it is not only backward-looking.

> Tradition looks also to the present and to the future. The Church is sent by Christ to proclaim the Gospel to all men; the Tradition must be handed on in time and also in space. In other words, Tradition has a vital missionary dimension in every land, for the command of the Lord is to go to all nations. Whatever differences of interpretation there may be, all are agreed that there is this dynamic element in the Tradition (p. 26).
>
> When the Word became flesh, the Gospel came to man through a particular cultural medium, that of the Palestinian world of the time. So when the Church takes the Tradition to new peoples, it is necessary that again the essential content should find expression in terms of new cultures (p. 26).
>
> The traditionary process involves the dialectic, both of relating the Tradition as completely as possible to every separate cultural situation in which men live, and at the same time of demonstrating its transcendence of all that divides men from one another. From this comes the truth that the more the Tradition is expressed in the varying terms of particular cultures, the more will its universal character be fully revealed. It is only "with all the saints" that we come to know the fullness of Christ's love and glory (p. 28).

In the following scripts the diversity of cultures and the importance of this for Bible study appear in the different methods used to complement those of Western literary culture.

c) 1964-1967: The Bristol report on hermeneutics

The Montreal report had stated that throughout church history the criterion for the genuine Tradition was sought "in the Holy Scriptures rightly interpreted" (p. 22). Yet what is right interpretation? The "Guiding principles" of 1949 had not taken sufficient account of the great diversity of testimonies within the Bible itself. This was brought home in Montreal when both a Protestant and a Roman Catholic New Testament scholar (E. Käsemann and R. E. Brown) showed that, from a purely exegetical point of view, it is impossible to speak about a single New Testament conception of the church (ecclesiology). The New Testament contains a diversity of ecclesiologies. Can any unity be found in this diversity? What process of interpretation can do justice to this biblical diversity?

---

[5] For examples in the Bible study scripts, see the several oral and written traditions which together formed the present Exodus story (II/2, pp. 70f), the updating of the old Mosaic tradition in the Deuteronomy (II/3, p. 79), the way in which the early church worked with the gospel tradition (II/9, p. 134; II/12, pp. 159ff and II/15, pp. 183ff), and superimposed layers of traditions in John's gospel (II/19, pp. 215ff).

A report on "The Significance of the Hermeneutical Problem for the Ecumenical Movement" was presented to the Faith and Order Commission meeting at Bristol in 1967. It points out that "awareness of the differences within the Bible will lead us towards a deeper understanding of our divisions and will help us to interpret them more readily as possible and legitimate interpretations of one and the same Gospel" (p. 40). Strong emphasis was placed on the necessity and value of literary and historical analysis of the Bible, which "contains a collections of very diverse literary traditions, the contents of which often stand in tension with one another" (p. 31).

Honest coping with literary and theological diversity is the most helpful contribution of the Bristol report:

> The diversity of thought within the Bible reflects the diversity of God's actions in different historical situations and the diversity of human response to God's actions (p. 32).
>
> When scholarship discerns several layers in a document or passage — some of which may be from a primitive or preliterary stage while others are carefully and reflectively developed, and yet others are late glosses or additions — it must work on all of these layers, since any or all of them may be theologically relevant. Each layer may indicate how an earlier one was later understood, and thus a passage may have not only one meaning but several meanings (p. 34).

The following scripts try to show something of the biblical diversity both in forms and theological accents — comparing, for example, the poetic style of Psalm 8, with its insistence on the Creator's glory and human stewardship, with the narrative style of the Exodus, with its emphasis on God acting as Saviour in history; comparing the lonely Jesus on the cross according to Mark's testimony with the majestic Jesus according to John's witness, in which even Golgotha becomes part of the story of transfiguration; comparing the reasoning theology of Paul in Galatians with the visual theology of the seer on Patmos in Revelation. Several scripts analyze the presence of subsequent layers of meaning in biblical texts.[6]

d) 1967-1971: The Louvain report on biblical authority

The Bristol report had envisaged the Bible in the first place as a collection of human writings, without denying that it witnesses to God's actions. Does this not undermine its authority? After all, it is not enough to ascertain the meaning of a biblical story or text for its first hearers; we must also ask how this story or text can become authoritative for Christian thought and action today. A report on "The Authority of the Bible" was accepted by the Faith and Order Commission at Louvain in 1971. Realistically

---

[6] Cf. for example the rereading of Psalm 8 in the light of Christ (II/1, p. 65), the changing image of the Messiah (II/7, pp. 114ff), the changing understanding of "Peter's confession" in the Caesarea Philippi episode (II/12, pp. 159ff), or the growing perception of what happened during the Lord's Supper on the basis of clue-texts from the Old Testament (II/15, pp. 184ff).

facing the difficulties with the Bible in present church life and the ecumenical movement, this report clarifies the concept of authority and then goes on to discuss the relationship between God's revelation and the diversity of interpretations and the significance of the Holy Spirit, the church, and inspiration with regard to the authority of the Bible. The report ends with some general comments on the use of the Bible. For three questions which often arise in the practice of Bible study the Louvain report offers new insights.

(i) How does biblical authority relate to present human experience? We may turn to the Bible simply because it has authority as an important literary document which deserves to be read. As Christians we also turn to it because it contains those testimonies to the biblical God which the church has recognized as canonical, as the indispensable source of Christian knowledge and conduct. Yet can this authority be stated more theologically? The Louvain report considers some attempts to do so, among them the classic dogma which regards the Bible as a book inspired by the Holy Spirit and sees its authority as resting on this inspiration. Such a dogmatic assumption is rejected. The Spirit's impact on the authors of the biblical scriptures and on those who hear or read them today is by no means denied; however, "to assume inspiration in advance would lead to a legalistic view of Scripture" (p. 54).

> The authority of the Bible only becomes evident as it "proves itself to be authoritative." It "cannot be derived from external criteria" (p. 53).
> Ultimately, of course, this authority is the authority of God himself and not that of the Bible as a book. Authority in this sense can only be claimed for the Bible because by its witness it makes possible the knowledge of God and of his authority. Therefore it only has derived authority. Nevertheless, anyone who has once encountered the living God in Christ in the Bible will again and again return to this source (p. 47).
> Authority is therefore a present reality only when men experience it as authority; at the same time, it transcends human experience. Special and explicit emphasis must be placed on this supra-individual character of authority (p. 48).

This dynamic understanding of the biblical authority explains why not every biblical story or text speaks to every believer or church in the same way. Many biblical passages remain "silent" for us today, though they spoke strongly to our fellow believers in other times and circumstances. Other passages suddenly come alive because it is through them that God puts his claim on us today. Inspiration here is not limited to the letter of the Bible. "Just as the Spirit once called his witnesses, so today will He also awaken faith, obedience and witness as He opens up to us these indispensable witnesses. The Spirit works in the Church" (p. 55). That is why this handbook is entitled *Experiments with Bible Study*. By such experiments we test how and through which biblical passages the God of Abraham, Isaac, and Jacob, the God who came in our midst through Jesus Christ, proves himself to be the way, the truth, and the life for us and this world.

(ii) How are event, interpretation, and today's situation related to each other? What was canonized by the church — in other words, accepted as a measure, the compass for God's way — was a certain number of interpreted events and revelations. God acted in human history: in the Exodus, in the Davidic monarchy, in the exile, by giving wisdom to the sages, discernment to the prophets, visions to the seers. He especially acted in the incarnation, in Jesus' teaching and healing, in the death and resurrection of the Messiah.

> (All these) events which the Bible claims to be decisively important have already in every case been subject to interpretation. (They) are therefore never the "bare facts", but are always accessible to us only in the clothing of their interpretation by the biblical authors.... "The events as such have no revelatory significance at all but are, so to speak, dumb and in need of interpretation if God's voice is to be heard in them. In a sense, therefore, the interpretation *is* the event. On the other hand, the historical character of the revelation is of central importance" (p. 48).

I am not quite happy with this last statement. It is undoubtedly true that there are no uninterpreted events. But the biblical events and revelations, the way God acts in history, have in themselves something astonishing, something odd. Why should he have especially chosen the insignificant nomadic tribes of Israel rather than people of such highly developed cultures as the Egyptians, the Babylonians, the Indians, or Chinese? Why was it that Jesus said about ordinary children "to such belongs the Kingdom of God?" Why did the Messiah have to die on the cross? These events are deeply significant in themselves and call for the unfolding of their significance in the process of interpretation. Like all events in history, the events recorded in the Bible are open-ended, pointing towards the kingdom. We still continue to remember and interpret them, to respond to them and unfold their meaning.

The biblical authors responded not only to events and revelations, but also to the situation in which and for which they memorized and interpreted the biblical traditions.[7] This is true also for us today. One might say — though the Louvain report does not state it in this way — that it is not only the content of the Scriptures which is canonical for us, but also the interpretative process observed in the Bible.

> If the process of contemporary interpretation is seen as the prolongation of the interpretative process which is recognizable in the Bible, then considerable importance must be attached to the situation at any given time in our interpretation of the Scriptures (p. 51).

> The biblical writers sought to speak and act in response to the challenge of their own times. The supreme challenge was the message itself but besides this there was also the confrontation with contemporary movements, such as syncretism, the emperor cult, gnosticism and so on. The message had to prove itself in the midst of constant controversy. The Bible begins to speak most

---

[7] Examples are found in II/9, pp. 131ff, II/12, pp. 157f, II/15, pp. 187ff, II/19, pp. 215ff.

effectively when it is read in the context of the corresponding controversies of our own times. It has, therefore, to be exposed to the challenge of the situation existing at any given time. This also means that the Bible is not a religious book in the usual sense, meant only for use in the liturgy. It has, on the contrary, to be brought into a two-way relationship with the questions of the time (pp. 56f).

Interpretation here takes the present historical situation and the insights and questions of our own culture as seriously as the situation and culture of first-century Palestine. This frees Bible study from being dominated and stifled by former times, or by authorities such as the church fathers, the reformers, or the biblical scholars of literary cultures. Such earlier insights can help greatly, but there are still new discoveries to be made in the treasure of the Bible, new aspects of significance to be unfolded in the biblical events.

Does such a practice of Bible study not blur the line between what is canonical and what is not? Does it not relativize the biblical revelation? We must therefore ask a third question.

(iii) What is biblical? What is "canonical" in the canon? One answer has already been given: the interpretative process observed in the Bible. The primary concern of this process is to transmit the Tradition, but the motivation for doing so is not that of an archivist. The transmission happens with strong missionary and pastoral concerns. The Tradition is received, understood, accented and interpreted within the context in which the church lives and for the milieu in which it witnesses. Both those who think and act exclusively in a traditional way or exclusively in a contextual way are less than biblical. To think and act biblically means to be so deeply rooted in the Tradition and the various biblical ways of transmitting and understanding it that one can interpret it appropriately for each new historical situation and cultural context.

Yet the canon does not only provide this biblical process of tradition and interpretation. It also canonizes content. As the Bristol report rightly emphasized, this content contains a limited but nevertheless astonishing theological variety. How can such a diverse content act as the compass for God's way? Is it possible to establish a "canon within the canon," a "material centre" to guide our judgment about what is truly biblical and what not? Consciously or unconsciously, most churches and individual Christians do just that. It may be the lordship of Christ, or justification by faith, or God's liberating act in the Exodus, or the regenerating work of the Holy Spirit. Some of the groups working towards the Louvain report rejected the establishment of such a static centre. In place of it they suggested a whole network of "relational centres" (German *Beziehungsmitten*) to be found in the Bible.

> We cannot, therefore, attribute permanent authority to an inner circle of biblical writings or biblical statements and interpret the rest in terms of this inner circle. But the biblical statements do have certain internal connections and many of these connections are directly related to central saving facts

whereas others are derived from these primary statements, as conclusions from them or as fuller explanations of them. Different sets of statements, different writings and groups of writings each have different centres" (p. 51; later in the report the messiahship of Jesus, the kingdom of God, the death and resurrection of Jesus Christ are given as examples of such relational centres for the entire New Testament).

This notion can be very fruitful for Bible study in an ecumenical context. Christians from different church traditions and cultural contexts will have different "relational centres" from which they think and act. This is perfectly legitimate, as long as two cautions are borne in mind: First, the relational centre for biblical thinking and action cannot be chosen arbitrarily nor selected simply because it seems best adapted to the inherited tradition or the present context. It must be discerned under the guidance of the Spirit. It can then lead either to the affirmation of the inherited tradition and present context or to a prophetic confrontation with them, to a process of acculturation or culture criticism. Secondly, if it is not to become sectarian, all such avowedly one-sided biblical thinking and action must continuously submit itself — and contribute — to the mutual correction within the ecumenical movement.

e) 1972-1977: The Loccum statement on the Old Testament

A question about which the Louvain report registered considerable disagreement was the authority of the Old Testament. As a consequence, a small intercontinental and interconfessional consultation was convened in 1977 at Loccum. Its report on "The Significance of the Old Testament in its relation to the New" is in many ways the most stimulating of all the documents mentioned so far, especially because of its unfinished and tentative character which invites criticism and further thought.

The Loccum report continues and applies insights gained earlier, showing how the interpretative process works in the relationship between the New and the Old Testament and commenting on three relational centres for the whole Bible: covenant, hope, and wisdom. Some of the earlier insights are critically reviewed from a broader ecumenical perspective. Moreover, new questions — some of them controversial — are put on the agenda: How is the historical continuity between the Old and the New Testament to be theologically evaluated? Some churches accept the Hebrew Old Testament as canonical; others its expanded Greek translation (the Septuagint). How does our not having the same Bible affect our understanding of Jesus and of Christian faith and life? What is the theological significance of the different rereading of the Old Testament in rabbinic Judaism, the Christian church, and Islam? What role does the Old Testament play in the dialogue with people of other faiths and ideologies?

The great significance of the Loccum report is its strong emphasis on the unity of the whole Bible.

> The Bible is a collection of many varied books which in their two collections are held together by one subject. We meet in them one and the same

God in his dealings with his whole creation, with the nations and with individual people. It is he who creates the unity in the diverse testimonies of Old and New Testaments (p. 66).

Just as the Old Testament forms the background for the New Testament, Jesus Christ is the horizon for the Old Testament (p. 74).

This emphasis on the unity of the Bible does not overlook the diversity of testimonies. Two interesting paragraphs spell out the specificity of the New and the Old Testament. Having examined what it means to affirm that in Jesus Christ the scriptures, the time, the law, and the promises of the Old Testament have been fulfilled, the report continues:

Perhaps even more attention should be given to those things in which the Old Testament surpasses the New Testament, because they are often neglected. There are many elements which are more clearly expressed in the Old than in the New Testament. It is mainly from the Old Testament that we come to know God as the Creator of all that is, as the Lord of history, as the Judge who upholds the rights of the poor and downtrodden. There too his holiness, majesty and hiddenness are emphasized, his concern with world politics, his exclusive claim upon his creatures and what the Old Testament calls his jealousy. Other specifically Old Testament notions are the creation of man and woman in the image of God, their place in the cosmos as God's caretakers, and the much greater attention given to nature; the warning against the constant temptation to idolatry, the fight against the deification of any part of creation and the danger of a dead, formal religion; moreover the interest in social structures, the insistence on righteousness, the fight against poverty and oppression, the concern with sorrow and the complaint of having been forsaken by God, and the importance of faith in providing wisdom for everyday life.

All these elements are assumed in the New Testament and most of them are mentioned too. However, they receive there less explicit attention because the New Testament is focused on the appearance of Christ and the radicalization of faith and on the individual conduct of life which comes with it. These specifically Old Testament elements should not be neglected. Otherwise we might come to misconstrue the context within which the appearance of Christ happens, thus running the risk of placing him in a wrong framework - possibly an individualistic, introverted or idealistic one. As a consequence the New Testament would be robbed of its purport. Especially in our time, with its worldwide ethical and structural problems, we need the width and depth of the Old Testament more than ever (pp. 71f).

The mystery remains

Despite this long search for understanding the authority of the Bible and how it functions as the compass for God's way, the mystery remains. None of those involved in the ecumenical discussion we have reviewed would claim to have found the final answer. The search must continue. Yet even this ongoing search will probably lead again to the question asked in the Louvain report: "If God's claim is experienced in the compelling way it undoubtedly is in the Bible, does this not mean that behind the Bible is the activity of God himself, i.e. of his Spirit?" (p. 54). And the wind of the Spirit blows where it wants.

It is because God has already found us that we search for him. And only those who are already on God's way can begin to understand the truth of that way and life. "The Bible is food for wrestlers," D.T. Niles used to say. It is not those who simply gather in pious circles to edify themselves for whom the biblical message will become a converting and strengthening power, but those engaged in the struggle of prayer and the struggles of faith in the world.

If God were not already at work in us and in history, who would dare submit to the converting exercise of Bible study and hold fast to the biblical promise and hope? The paradox about which Paul once wrote — in an almost untranslatable sentence — applies to Bible study and its harvest of a Christian life: "With fear and trembling do your best to bring about your own salvation; for it is God who is at work as he pleases, activating in you both the willing and working" (Phil. 2:12f).

PART TWO
Scripts for Experiments

There are limits to how successfully one can fix a Bible study in writing. True, the original context of a biblical passage remains the same and may be relatively easy to describe. But the context of the people involved in the study process constantly changes, altering the perspective, the questions, the preconceptions with which the passage is approached. There is no such thing as totally objective learning, seeing, or reading. Bible studies are therefore "happenings." There is always an element of surprise. Experiments with Bible study can be prepared for and planned, but they can never be fully predicted.

This element of surprise — the unexpected response which changes the anticipated course of things — is obviously missing from the following scripts. It can be present again if enablers use these studies with groups, provided the scripts are not slavishly followed. These biblical explorations are meant to help enablers prepare and plan, not to serve as the texts for lectures. They will have to be adapted according to the time and facilities available, the composition of the group, and the special gifts of the enabler.

Some scripts will prove too long for the time available. Such long studies as the one on the time of Jeremiah (II/3) and on the coming of the Messiah (II/7) were prepared for residential seminars or weekend retreats; yet they can easily be subdivided for a series of shorter study sessions. The shorter the time available, the more difficult it is for group members to participate actively in the biblical exploration. Occasionally this may require use of the lecture style of teaching (as with radio Lenten talks, II/8), but even so one need not speak in abstractions. Once I was asked to conduct a participatory Bible study for a fairly large group with a time limit of five minutes. Such a restriction is certainly not ideal, but one can still try to make the best of it (cf. II/24).

The following studies have been tried in this form or a similar one, with groups in various cultural settings, though most of them are being published here for the first time. Since almost none of the art, music, or recorded readings suggested for use with several of the following Bible studies are reproduced here, I hope Bible study enablers will be stimulated to discover and collect audio-visual material particularly appropriate for their own cultural setting.

The material in small print contains information about the groups and occasions for which some of these studies were originally prepared and suggests how study enablers may want to proceed and what alternative methods could be used. However, the reasons for using various media, given in Part One, and the remarks on approaches in Bible study, methods, and tools, given in Appendix A, are not repeated here.

Since each study is self-contained, there are some overlaps. But this also means that any of the twenty-five scripts can be picked out and adapted for use regardless of its position in the book. The sequence chosen here — starting with a creation psalm and the Exodus story, concentrating on the Jesus of the gospels, and ending with a passage from Revelation — gives individual readers a broad perspective on the whole biblical testimony.

1 WORSHIP AND WORK

Psalm 8

To make the following study and do the group work on all the suggested tasks will take two to four hours, especially if the group has never used mime and must therefore be acquainted with that method. By omitting the introduction to Hebrew poetry and the transposition into mime the study can be done in an hour and a half. If the Vantoura record is unavailable, music should nevertheless be part of the study of the psalm. One of the several hymns based on Psalm 8 could for instance be sung at the beginning or end of the session.

Hebrew poetry

Psalms are first of all poetry, hymns to be sung, prayers, complaints, or shouts of joy. They are personal or corporate affirmations of faith. Often they were part of liturgical celebrations in the temple courts of Jerusalem. Hundreds of well-trained singers sang them to the accompaniment of trumpets, strings, and percussion instruments.

Though we have no recordings of such ancient celebrations in Solomon's temple, the key to biblical music may have been found. For centuries scholars were intrigued by some enigmatic signs in the text of the Hebrew Bible. Are these musical annotations? An Israeli musician, Suzanne Haik Vantoura, claims that they are, and that she has been able to decipher them. Here is her musical reconstruction of Psalm 150, perhaps as it sounded almost three thousand years ago in Jerusalem.

Psalm 150 is played from the record "La musique de la Bible révélée", Harmonia mundi, HMU 989, Paris, 1975.

To appreciate the psalms — and in fact many other parts of the Old Testament — it is important to know something about Hebrew poetry. In traditional Western poems, rhythm usually depends on the number of syllables and on rhymes created by the similar-sounding words at the end of the line. In Hebrew poetry, both rhythm and rhyme are much more intimately connected with content.

The *rhythm* is created by a fixed number of accents or stresses, ideally corresponding to the number of substantial ideas in the line. The most common meter is that with three accents per line, repeated in the corresponding second line. Other rhythms have a two-accent meter in two or three corresponding lines, or lines with four accents, or an unequal meter such as three accents in the first line and two in the second.

To this rhythm of content corresponds a *rhyme* of content, with three types of parallelism:

(a) The second line paraphrases the first, adding fresh nuances by using other words and imagery:

> O Lord, who shall sojourn in thy tent?
> Who shall dwell on thy holy hill? (Ps. 15:1).

(b) The second line forms the antithesis to the first, often contrasting a positive statement with a corresponding negative one:

> A wise son makes a glad father,
> but a foolish son is a sorrow to his mother (Prov. 10:1).

(c) The second line takes up and develops the thought begun in the first, sometimes drawing out the meaning of the preceding image:

> As a hart longs for flowing streams,
> so longs my soul for thee, O God (Ps. 42:1).

What characterizes all these types of Hebrew poetry (and others not mentioned here) are short lines where nouns and verbs are prominent. Action and imagery are emphasized, and there are seldom abstractions.

Task 1: Compose several two-line poems on subjects from your everyday life, using the most common three accent-meter of Hebrew poetry and the three different types of parallelism or content-rhymes mentioned above.

> This task should be divided among the members of the group, some making "Hebrew" poems according to type *a*, others type *b*, still others type *c.* The best examples of these two-line poems are recited aloud and discussed briefly in order to make sure that all members of the group have grasped the major characteristics of Hebrew poetry.

Task 2: Read Psalm 8 in the light of these rules of Hebrew poetry. What examples of rhythms and types of parallelism can you discover, even in the English translation of the psalm? Which type of parallelism is missing? How does the knowledge of Hebrew poetry help you understand the psalm and safeguard you from misunderstandings?

> This task can best be done individually at first, followed by exchange of discoveries among group members sitting next to one another, and then in general discussion. The group will have noticed the uneven meters at the beginning and the end of the psalm, the prevalence of the three-accent meter with an occasional two-accent in v. 7, the frequency of the type *a* parallelism (e.g., in vv. 3, 4, 6), with type *b* parallelism in v. 5, while the parallelism of type *c* is missing. Knowledge of the basic laws of Hebrew poetry prevents us,

for example, from wrongly interpreting the "son of man" in v. 4 in terms of the "Son of Man" passages in Daniel and the New Testament.

The setting of Psalm 8

Long before the Babylonian exile (598-538 B.C.) several collections of psalms had already been made. One of these was the seventy-three psalms entitled *le-David*. This Hebrew expression can be translated "of David," but a more correct translation would be "to David," "according to the manner of David," or "in honour of David." Some of these psalms may actually have been composed by David, but most are later. Thus in one of the psalms *le-David* — Psalm 122 — the singer rejoices that he is going up to the temple, which did not yet exist in the time of David.

Thus we cannot ascertain who first sang Psalm 8 or when it was composed. The instruction to the choirmaster —"according to the Gittith" — does not help, because the meaning of "The Gittith" is uncertain. It may refer to a musical instrument or a melody common in the city of Gath; or it may derive from the Hebrew word for wine-press and thus have something to do with the vintage festival.

For over six hundred years kings, priests, prophets, and above all many unknown poets and temple singers added their contributions to the treasury of Hebrew songs and poems. Only after the Babylonian exile were the ancient collections of psalms brought together with some recent hymns and prayers to form the hymnal and prayer book of the Jewish congregation in Jerusalem.

The content varies greatly. There are hymns and prayers to be said and sung by individuals, and there are some to be used by the whole worshipping community. Some are acts of adoration and praise, others are cries of complaint and lamentation. Some psalms proclaim the great deeds of God in creation and history. Others were composed for special occasions, be it times of illness or great joy, for the coronation festival of a king, for harvest festivals, processions, and various religious ceremonies in the households or in the temple. When the ark was brought into Jerusalem around 1000 B.C. "David and all the house of Israel were making merry before the Lord with all their might, with songs and lyres and harps and tambourines and castanets and cymbals" (2 Sam. 6:5). Some 300 years later King Hezekiah composed a psalm of complaint and praise after he had recovered from a serious illness (Isa. 38). Another occasion for psalm-making was the dedication of the rebuilt wall of Jerusalem under Nehemiah shortly after 450 B.C. (Neh. 12:27-43).

No such clear indication is available for the origin of Psalm 8. Nevertheless, the text of the psalm itself gives some clues about where and when it was sung and what function it fulfilled in the worship.

Task 3: Reread Psalm 8, looking for clues about where and what time of day it was sung. Was it sung by an individual or an assembly or worshippers? To what part of worship is this psalm most intimately related (e.g., procession, praise, confession, teaching, sacrifice)?

Again, individuals should do this first, then exchanging their discoveries in small groups and finally in plenary discussion. The group will easily discover that the psalm was sung in the evening or at night in an open space. It is a mixture of corporate praise (cf. "our Lord," in vv. 1 and 9) and individual confession and teaching (vv. 3-8). Some group members may suggest that the "sheep and oxen" point to the shepherd David as the author, yet the psalm has obvious relations with the creation stories in Genesis, which were written after the time of David.

The most likely setting of Psalm 8 is one of the solemn noctural celebrations in the temple courts of Jerusalem. The occasion was probably the new year festival, when God's enthronement as king was celebrated and when the act of praise often centred on the greatness of the Creator in his creation. Let us imagine that we are part of this assembly, gathered late in the evening on the temple court illuminated by burning torches. A hymn of praise is intoned and we all join in. Then a priest appears in the portal leading to the inner court where the altar stands, and he teaches us about the human vocation in God's creation. Finally the chorus of praise is taken up again by the whole assembly. To enter into the responsive litany of this psalm it is good to recite it aloud with gestures expressing its mood and content.

At this moment the psalm is enacted by dramatic reading and simple gestures, vv. 1-2 and 9 being recited by all in an attitude of praise, while vv. 3-8 are confessed and taught by an individual representing the priest, standing in an improvised portal.

Form and content

By examining the poetic form and by the dramatic reading we have already entered into the message of the psalm. Form and content can never be neatly separated, particularly in Hebrew poetry, but we must now examine the meaning of these verses more directly.

The most difficult part is verses 1b-2. The original Hebrew text of this passage is unclear, and the mention of God's enemies and avengers contrasts strangely with God's royal authority in verses 3-8. No wonder that translations and interpretations of this passage differ considerably. Most commentaries offer one of two explanations: (1) These verses refer mythologically to supernatural powers of chaos which God had to overcome in his act of creation. The "babes and infants" are sometimes interpreted as angels of the heavenly host which accompanies the Creator. Parallels from Canaanite Syrian (Ugaritic) psalms are quoted in support of this interpretation. (2) More probable is the explanation that there as elsewhere in the Old Testament the enemies of God are human kings and powers who fight against his purpose within history and on the earthly scene. It is through frail and apparently insignificant human beings such as babes and children that the biblical God lays the foundation of his strength and thereby confounds his enemies. (Many modern translations follow the ancient Greek translation by relating the children to the singing; in the original Hebrew the children are related to the founding of a bulwark rather than the chanting of God's glory.)

Another difficulty in translation and interpretation is verse 5a. Did God make human beings "a little less than God" or "a little less than the angels?" The original Hebrew text clearly states the former, using the same word for God as in Genesis 1 — *Elohim* which refers to God, sometimes including the whole heavenly host. Those who made the Greek Septuagint translation were apparently shocked by this statement and changed "God" to "angels," and this is the wording quoted in the New Testament (Heb. 2:6-8).

Looking now at the psalm as a whole it is clear that there emerge three or four interrelated themes: the creator God, his creation, and the human vocation. A fourth theme is added if one includes the perspective of the New Testament, where this short psalm is applied to Christ three times.

> In certain groups it may be helpful for the Bible study enabler to enumerate these themes using a "chalk-talk." A simple drawing like this one gradually appears:

What is important is that these three or four themes are all held together. According to biblical thinking it is impossible to speak about God, to do theology, without at the same time speaking about his creation, about the human vocation, and about the revelation of Christ. Conversely it is impossible to speak about men and women and children, to do anthropology, without seeing them in relationship with God, his creation and his revelation in Christ. The same intimate interrelationship must be noticed if one speaks about creation (the cosmological theme) and about Christ (the christological theme).

Task 4: What does Psalm 8 reveal about these four interrelated themes? State briefly what kind of God we meet in this psalm, what is said about the creation and about the vocation of human beings, and how the writers of the New Testament epistles reread this psalm in the light of what they believed about Jesus (cf. 1 Cor. 15:27; Eph. 1:22; Heb. 2:6-8).

This task can best be done in small discussion groups. The participants are divided into "theological," "cosmological," "anthropological," and "christological" subgroups. After a sufficient period for group work the sub-groups report to one another in a plenary discussion.

Human trustees in God's creation

The *God* whom we meet in this psalm is first of all the majestic creator. Notice that in verses 4-8, which speak about the human vocation, God remains the grammatical subject: "*thou* art mindful of him ...," "*thou* hast made him little less ...", "*thou* hast given him dominion ...." The biblical God is not only a first cause who set things in motion and then retired. He continues to be involved in his creation. Furthermore, God is not simply interested in religious matters, but in the things, the animals, and the people of this earth. That involvement comes out with special poignancy in the enigmatic verse 2. He is being contested by enemies and engaged in a battle. If the second explanation of this verse mentioned above is correct, we have here a hint about the peculiar characteristic of the biblical God. He is not neutral but chooses the weak and the poor to fulfil his purpose (cf. Deut. 7:7-8). The most amazing characteristic of this God, however, is his trust in human beings. Taking a great risk, he entrusted his creation to the stewardship of one kind among his creatures.

This psalm sees the *cosmos* not as something which grows, develops, and decays by itself. This cosmos is first of all God's creation. Many people in the world around the biblical writers worshipped the moon and the stars as divine beings. But this psalm testifies that the moon and the stars are part of God's creation. This origin in God gives all creation worth and dignity. What was created is not simply a "thing," not just raw material to be used, but it remains "the works of thy hands" (v. 6). This creation is entrusted to the human beings. They are given dominion over the works of God's hands. (Notice that according to this psalm that empowerment does not include dominion over fellow human beings.) The destiny of the cosmos thus depends on how human beings fulfil their stewardship.

Human beings have a double status. On the one hand they are mortal creatures like the animals. Together with animals they were created on one and the same "day" (Gen. 1:24-31), and according to Old Testament thought not only humans but also animals have a *nephesh*, a "soul." On the other hand human beings are elevated to become God's viceroys and trustees in creation. This happened not as an act of proud self-assertion, but through a gift and commissioning. God remains the authoritative subject. The humanity of the human kind remains deeply rooted in God's divinity. Nevertheless, this second status makes out of a vulnerable creature somebody "a little less than God."

A twofold human task corresponds to this double status: praise of God (vv. 1 and 9) and stewardship over the earth. The two belong together. In the psalm the work of stewardship flows out of praise and leads up to praise. Without this intimate interrelation between worship and work both degenerate. Worship becomes meaningless and work a tragic way of oppression. If human viceroys cease to praise God they soon become the destructive usurpers who exploit the creation.

If the study enabler used a drawing earlier, that graphic is further developed during the preceding paragraph on human beings. Lines are drawn to indicate the double status, and the different positions of the humans illustrate the double vocation:

The person described here hardly resembles the men, women, and children whom the writer of this psalm knew or whom we meet today. Psalm 8 stands in the middle of history like a misplaced fragment from the time before the fall (Gen. 3). Except for the enigmatic enemies and avengers in v. 2 nothing is said about human self-assertion and revolt. Today's worldwide ecological problems and the increasing scarcity of non-renewable resources show clearly that humans have not fulfilled their vocation as trustees of this earth. Both the irrelevance of much worship today and the dehumanizing effects of work reveal that the intimate relationship between worship and work has been lost. No wonder that later this psalm was reread in the light of Christ.

Paul and other New Testament writers indeed saw *Christ* foreshadowed in the "man" and "son of man" of Psalm 8. The poem was certainly not understood this way in Old Testament times. This psalm never occurs in the lists of messianic texts. Already within the Bible, however, biblical events and testimonies were constantly being reread in the light of the new acts of God. The early Christians thus identified Jesus, the Son of Man, with the son of man in Psalm 8. Even if we question this early Christian interpretation we can nevertheless in our turn reread the ancient poem in the light of Christ. He is the true human being, the new Adam. He was the one who totally lived in the rhythm of worship and work. It is difficult for us, who have failed so often in our double human task, to recognize ourselves in the man of Psalm 8. Yet Christ we recognize in this song of praise and commissioning. He recovered the true image of God (Gen. 1:26-31). By the new humanity which we receive in him, we can be reinstated into the double human status. In communion with him we can be enabled to fulfil our twofold human task: worship and work.

Translation into prayer and mime

We live in another time and environment than the writer of Psalm 8. For those of us in large cities, the glare of streetlights and neon signs and industrial haze often hide the moon and the stars. Daily work for many of us more often has to do with producing and selling goods, with administering organizations, with shuffling people and paper, than with sheep and oxen. Nevertheless the basic affirmations of Psalm 8 are today even more pertinent than they were in biblical times.

Task 5: Paraphrase the basic affirmations of Psalm 8 as a prayer of praise and commitment for your own life and environment. Following the pattern of Hebrew poetry, try to avoid abstractions but use images from your everyday world and short rhythmic sentences.

> If only little time is available this task can be given as homework. The next session could then begin with the hearing and praying of some of these modern paraphrases.

Psalm 8 reveals basic attitudes and transformations in the process of becoming truly human. It is therefore helpful to get this psalm into one's own body and meditate on it by means of a mime.

Task 6: Either individually or as a small group make a mime of Psalm 8. What attitudes of the body best express the praise in vv. 1 and 9? (Since the meaning of vv. 1b-2 is not very clear, and since mime involves concentrating on just one essential message, it is better to disregard these verses for the translation into mime.) How can the transformation from "What is man?" to "Thou hast given him dominion" (vv. 3-8) be expressed in a bodily movement so that it does not appear as natural growth or as arrogant self-assertion? How can responsible dominion over the works of God's hand be expressed bodily?

> One group which worked on this task rediscovered for vv. 1 and 9 the attitude of the *orantes* (the early Christians in prayer as depicted on the walls of the catacombs) with their hand open and raised. Out of the group standing in a semi-circle, one member moved into the middle and depicted the small form of a fetus in the womb (vv. 3-4). During the subsequent transformation (v. 5) the group remained in a semi-circle, pointing to the person in the middle who represented the "man" of Psalm 8. Rising to his feet as if someone invisible and strong had lifted him up by placing hands from behind under his shoulders, the central actor then showed by facial expressions and simple bodily movements the joy of discovering the power and authority entrusted to him (vv. 6-8). He began to walk and with gentle hand and arm movements to represent ordering and dominating the surrounding world. (One must take care to maintain the spirit of miming and not make things ridiculous by trying to figure sheep and oxen, birds and fish.) Finally, the main actor rejoined the semi-circle and together with the others resumed the initial attitude of praise.
>
> This is only one of several possibilities for translating psalm 8 into mime. Together with modern paraphrases (Task 5) such a mime can become part of a closing act of worship.

2 A STORY OF LIBERATION

Exodus 1-2

> This script was prepared for a biblical presentation during a plenary session (more than 300 people) of the World Mission Conference in Bangkok, December 1972, under the theme "Salvation Today" (cf. II/25). I have reconstructed from memory the quite spontaneous dialogue at the beginning. The presentation was scheduled to last one hour and forty-five minutes. Omitted here is a short concluding part dealing with salvation as healing and forgiveness, the spiritual "There is a Balm in Gilead" and Luke 4:16-21. The participants had worksheets with an outline of the presentation, the words of the songs used, the biblical passages, and the text of the two myths about Sargon I and Horus.
>
> This study can also be conducted without the dramatized beginning, the slides, or the recorded reading. A record of the spiritual "Go Down, Moses" might be played, the words of this song reread, and the participants asked how the Exodus story is told and interpreted in this spiritual. Who are "old Pharaoh" and "my people" according to this song? After a discussion of the possibilities and dangers of such direct application of an Old Testament story to present-day suffering and hope for liberation, the study can proceed to the introduction to Task 1.

A story which shaped history

The presentation begins with an empty stage. The spiritual "Go Down, Moses" is played, and the assembly joins in singing the chorus:

> Go down, Moses,
> Way down in Egyptland;
> Tell old Pharaoh
> To let my people go.

During the first verse a black American comes on stage, singing the spiritual and encouraging the assembly to shout the chorus. As the song comes to an end a friend of the Jews enters and addresses the American black.

Friend of the Jews: "Do you know what story you're singing?"

American black: "Sure. It comes from the Bible. My fathers who were brought by slave traders from Africa to the Americas heard this story, and soon they began to understand it with their hurting backs as well as their minds. So they sang this story which tells about our own slavery and liberation."

Friend of the Jews: "Yes, but don't forget that this was first of all the story of the Israelite tribes and their slavery in Egypt some three thousand years ago."

American black: "You mean to say that this story has nothing to do with me and my people? When my forefathers sang this song they thought about their own slave-masters. When we sing it now we think of today's economics and the big corporations. Yet we know that wherever there is a Pharaoh, there also will come a Moses, *our* Moses. Do you mean to say that this is wrong?"

Friend of the Jews: "Not exactly. For Israel too this story hasn't just remained a memory from the ancient past. It's through this story that they have seen and evaluated what has happened to them throughout the centuries. Even today the Jewish people celebrate their Passover feast every year and recall their liberation from slavery under Egypt's Pharaoh. This isn't simply remembering an old story; in the Passover celebration the story is re-enacted for today."

American black: "So you see, we are right in applying this story to our own history of suffering and liberation. For us, American blacks, Pharaoh is not an Egyptian. He is the symbol of oppression, of the oppressor. We read this story as a political act in which God was working in a concrete situation, struggling for the liberation from a concrete bondage."

Friend of the Jews: "You have a point there. In the biblical story Pharaoh has no name. So you can fill in the name of any contemporary tyrant. In fact the Jews filled in the names of their persecutors when they suffered from the crusaders in the Middle Ages, from the Inquisition in Spain and in our century from the Russian czars and Hitler. That is why the Passover feast has remained so meaningful for them throughout the centuries."

American black: "Tell me more about this feast of liberation."

Friend of the Jews: "The Passover is a meal. There are bitter herbs to symbolize how the slave-drivers embittered the lives of the Israelites. A dish of stewed apples and almonds represents the bricks and mortar used in forced labour. It's a family feast, and at its centre is the telling of the Exodus story. The youngest child asks: 'Why is this night different from all other nights?' and the father replies: 'We were slaves of Pharaoh in Egypt, and the Eternal our God brought us forth from there with a mighty hand and an outstretched arm.' Then he continues the story of liberation with words and symbolic gestures leading up to an act of thanksgiving."

American black: "But how can we give thanks when there are still so many people suffering and oppressed?"

Friend of the Jews: "In the middle of the Passover celebration this very paradox is recalled. When the ten plagues are mentioned, some drops of wine must be spilled from the cup of thanksgiving, because the cup of joy cannot be full as long as so many human beings — and in this case the

Egyptians — are suffering. There's also a saying of the rabbis that God, the Almighty, rebuked the angels when they sang songs of rejoicing as the Egyptians were drowning: 'My children are perishing in the sea,' God said, 'and you want to *sing*?' And we have to face an even more tragic paradox of liberation stories: the oppressed of yesterday may become the oppressors of today."

> At this point the Bible study enabler enters the scene and begins to direct the study. Together with the two dialogue partners the enabler forms a panel on the stage. After each of the subsequent tasks, discussed in the whole assembly by each participant with his or her neighbour, this panel spontaneously comments on the questions asked, thus substituting for the plenary discussion that would be impossible in a large assembly.

The story of Moses and Pharaoh has made history. For three thousand years the Jews have remembered and re-enacted it. It also played a crucial role in the struggle for the liberation of slaves and in North American civil rights movements. Examples from other areas of people for whom this story suddenly came alive, evoked new hopes, and inspired new movements of liberation could be given.

No wonder some claim today that "the Exodus is the primary fact," as an outstanding Latin American theologian has written. According to him the rest of the Bible, including its testimonies about Jesus, must be interpreted in the light of this story: salvation means in the first place liberation of the oppressed. Others, however, refuse to give the Exodus such a central place and protest against a one-sided political interpretation of this story and its direct application to the liberation struggles of today.

The story and historical events

Were we immediately to plunge into such a debate, we would probably soon be deeply divided. For Christians of course there is no legitimate escape from that debate, but it is a good idea beforehand to listen together to the story itself. Stories, after all, are in the first place told to be listened to, not to be linguistically and theologically analyzed and explained. So sit back and listen to this story as if you had never heard it before.

> At this point a previously recorded dramatic reading of the following passages is played back: Exod. 1:6-2:15a; 2:23-25; 2:23-3:7; 3:10-15; 4:18; 4:27-5:9; 5:22-6:1a; 6:6-9; a short summary of the intervening events by a commentator; 19:1-6. This reading takes 16 minutes.

A fascinating story. Yet our modern critical mind immediately asks: Did it actually happen? Is this story rooted in history? The setting, in any case, sounds familiar to people who read newspapers in the twentieth century. As in our time, the world of the Exodus was one of power politics, a society in which a migrant labour force was exploited, a time in which oppression and fear dictated action. Yet was Moses a historical person?

No written sources outside of the Bible directly confirm or deny what is told in the book of Exodus. Nevertheless, the description of the social and political situation fits very well with what we know of Egypt in the thirteenth century B.C. Sculptures and wall-paintings from that period as well as photographs from the Sinai can help our imagination visualize what happened.

A series of slides is now shown with a brief commentary: *Sculpture of Rameses II with close-up of his face*: The "new Pharaoh" mentioned in Exodus 1 was probably Rameses II, whose larger-than-life-size statue in granite we see here. He ruled Egypt, probably from 1301-1234 B.C., and the Exodus might in this case be dated around 1250. Rameses does not look cruel, yet portrayals of great rulers are usually more flattering than reality. *Egyptian wall painting from fifteenth century B.C., showing brickmaking and the building of walls by slaves from various ethnic groups (with several close-ups)*: Rameses II built a chain of border fortresses and supply stores for his large army. Both store-cities mentioned in Exodus 1:11, Pithom and Raamses, are known from Egyptian sources, which indicate that they were built by Rameses II. Foreign slaves and forced labour were used for this vast building activity. On the ancient Egyptian wall painting we can discern the darkskinned Nubian slaves. Those with a lighter skin and a beard are probably Semites. The slave-driver with the whip portrays the hardship of forced labour. No escape seemed possible from this "house of slavery." *Egyptian wall-painting with marching army; close-up of horses with chariot and rider*: Indeed, Rameses II was not only a great builder, but also the leader of successful military expeditions with a well-equipped army, as this ancient wall-painting shows. A few tribes of Hebrews were no match for him.

Map indicating the three major hypotheses about the route of the Exodus: It will probably never be possible to ascertain the exact itinerary of the Israelite tribes. This map shows three possible locations for Mount Sinai. On any of the three routes travelers would have met similar types of deserts, mountains, and oases. *Photographs from the Sinai peninsula*: This landscape has not changed much during the last three thousand years. It is not difficult to imagine why the Israelites complained bitterly in such a hot and inhospitable wilderness. *Photograph of Jebel Musa, traditionally identified with Mount Sinai*: Although it is not certain whether this is indeed the biblical Mount Sinai, near such a mountain the decisive event of the Exodus story happened: the revelation of the Torah, of God's will, and the conclusion of the covenant.

The Exodus story is definitely rooted in history. However, it is not *simply* a chronicle of what really happened. Nor was the story recorded by one man or even by one generation. Each new generation discovered and added new layers of meaning as the story was transmitted orally throughout centuries. From the beginning the aim of this transmission was not to describe "how it really was," but to teach and celebrate the Torah, God's mighty saving words and acts. Then, from the tenth century B.C. onwards, the story was written down. A first tradition is commonly called the "Jahvist source" (J) because it uses the name *Jahve* (or Yahweh) for the biblical God. This tradition was probably preserved in the royal circles of Jerusalem and written down in the time of Solomon. Other traditions about the Exodus were preserved in a milieu strongly under the influence of prophetic teachings in the northern kingdom. Perhaps around 750 B.C. these traditions were gathered and written down in the "Elohist source" (E), so called because the term *Elohim* is used for God up to Exodus 3:14. Much later, during the Babylonian exile in the sixth century B.C., priestly circles wrote down their own account and interpretation of the Exodus story in the "sacerdotal source" (P).

The meaning of the Exodus

The best guide for our reflection on the meaning of the Exodus event is a passage from this latest and most "theological" source. According to the priestly tradition God himself explained to Moses what he was going to accomplish: "Say therefore to the people of Israel, 'I am the Lord, and I will bring you out from under the burdens of the Egyptians, and I will deliver you from their bondage, and I will redeem you with an outstretched arm and with great acts of judgment, and I will take you for my people, and I will be your God; and you shall know that I am the Lord your God, who has brought you out from under the burdens of the Egyptians. And I will bring you into the land which I swore to give to Abraham, to Isaac, and to Jacob; I will give it to you for a possession. I am the Lord'" (Exod. 6:6-8).

Task 1: What are God's saving acts in the Exodus according to this passage? Examine especially the verbs and their relationship with one another.

> After a short period of silent individual study all participants exchange their findings with those sitting next to them. Then the panel shares with the plenary its own insights, which the Bible study enabler complements — if necessary — and then sums up as follows.

According to this text salvation appears in the first place as a social and political liberation. God saves by releasing the oppressed from their labours, by rescuing them from slavery. This implies judgment of the oppressor. It also means that God makes available a land for the oppressed to live in. In fact, this corresponds to the original meaning of the verb "to save" in the Hebrew language: *jasha* (from which the names "Joshua" and "Jesus" are derived) means "to give space," to free from their confinement those who have no air to breathe and no space to live. The notion of salvation according to the book of Exodus and according to the Old Testament in general is therefore indeed a social, political, this-worldly concept and can often best be translated with "liberation."

However, Exodus 6:6-8 emphasizes also another equally important aspect of the reality of salvation. The people of Israel are being adopted by the God of Abraham, Isaac, and Jacob. "I will be your God." This is the first half of the famous covenant formula which calls for a response: "You shall know that I am the Lord your God." We totally misunderstand the biblical Exodus story if we emphasize only the element of liberation and do not put equal stress on the fact that the Exodus leads to the covenant between the liberating God and the liberated people. Freedom from slavery aims at a life in obedience to God's will (cf. Exod. 19 and 20).

Notice finally that throughout the passage of Exodus 6:6-8 God remains the subject. The event of salvation as liberation begins and ends with the affirmation: "I am the Lord." To be liberated in the sense of the biblical Exodus story means therefore to acknowledge that reality which transcends this earth and human history. Without such self-transcendence, the liberty gained would soon become slavery again.

The agents of salvation

We now turn to the Exodus story itself and examine its beginning, as it is recorded in an integrated text which originated mainly from the Jahvist and Elohist sources.

Task 2: Read Exodus 1:6-2:10. Who are the agents of salvation in this beginning of the Exodus story? Who are notably present — and strangely absent — in this passage?

> After a period of individual study participants exchange their discoveries. The panel then comments on the questions and the Bible study enabler sums up.

This passage could very well become a key text for the women's liberation movement. Only one man plays an important role — Pharaoh — but he is the agent of oppression. Moses' father appears briefly, only to fade back again, and the scene is literally dominated by one woman after the other. First there are the midwives who dare to disobey the almighty Pharaoh and get away with it. Then there is the mother of Moses who struggles for the survival of her baby with all the inventiveness and confidence of somebody who loves. She is helped by the sister of baby Moses, a very clever girl. At the critical point at which the Egyptian princess discovers the basket and recognizes the baby as an Israelite boy, Moses' sister makes the brilliant suggestion which brings the baby back to its mother's breast. Finally, there is Pharaoh's daughter with her ladies-in-waiting and her slave girl. What happened in the heart of the princess undid all of her father's repressive measures. Ironically she not only spared the life of the one who would later challenge and defeat her father's authority and military power, but she even educated him for this liberating task.

True, God often fulfils his plans of salvation by great men of faith whose names we all know — Abraham, Moses, David. But here at the beginning of the Exodus story Moses is only a crying baby. Later in the story, too, he appears as something less than a glorious hero. He is the frightened murderer who escapes, then the unwilling and stammering spokesman for his people. Where would Moses be without the midwives, without his loving mother, without the shrewd sister, without the very womanly princess? These nameless and ordinary people have become agents of salvation. (The names of the midwives are probably not their proper names, but attributes given to them because of their courageous acts of civil disobedience. The translation of "Shiphrah" and "Puah" is not certain, but probably they mean "beauty" and "splendour".)

The hidden presence of God

Biblical stories did not fall from heaven. Just as God became incarnate in Jesus Christ, living as a Jew in a definite historical and cultural situation, so the stories of the Old and New Testaments are not unrelated to the literature of the ancient Middle East. Old Testament authors, Jesus himself, and later the New Testament writers often borrowed stories, images and parables which were well known in Egypt, Palestine, or Mesopotamia. They used them to make a point, to communicate the message concerning the mighty acts of God in the history of the people of Israel, in the life, death, and resurrection of Jesus, and in the early church.

The passage on the birth of Moses and his almost miraculous survival resembles several birth stories of heroes commonly known in the ancient Middle East. *Sargon I* of Akkad, a Mesopotamian monarch who ruled about 2500 B.C. is one of these heroes. After his secret birth his mother (some suggest that she was a virgin priestess of the sun god) put him in a little basket made of reeds and sealed with pitch, and cast the basket upon the river Euphrates. The child was found and adopted by Akki, a peasant who drew water from the river. Later the goddess Ishtar grew fond of the child and made Sargon a great and powerful king.

A similar story was common knowledge in Egypt. It concerns the birth and survival of the god *Horus*. After the death of the Egyptian god Osiris, his pregnant wife, the mother goddess Isis, fled the wrath of her brother-in-law Seth, the Egyptian god of darkness and drought. Seth had killed and mutilated Osiris and he was determined to exterminate Osiris' son. Isis fled into the impenetrable marshes of the Nile delta, where she gave birth to Horus, the falcon. He was hidden among the papyri, the water reeds. A later version of the myth, written in Greco-Roman times, speaks of a boat of papyrus in which Horus was covered by the mat of his nurse, the goddess Nephthys. When Horus had grown up he avenged his father's death by driving his uncle Seth out of Egypt.

Task 3: Compare these ancient myths with Exodus 1:6-2:10. What are the basic similarities and differences? What does this comparison teach us about God's saving acts?

> Individual silent study, exchange with neighbours, comments by the panel members, and summing up by the enabler.

When the story of the birth of Moses was first told it was probably patterned after these well-known ancient myths. This of course does not mean that the account of Moses' birth and childhood was simply invented. Moses was an historical personality. His Egyptian name makes it probable that he was adopted into an Egyptian family in his childhood. Only an aristocratic family, perhaps a branch of the royal house, was rich enough to do so. Nevertheless, the telling of the story and perhaps also some details of the narrative itself have been influenced by ancient legends and myths.

The obvious parallels and the probable influence of the very old myths on the birth story of Moses must not overshadow the great differences and the particular features of the biblical story. The Mesopotamian and Egyptian myths tell about gods and super human heroes. Their setting is somewhat removed from the scene of human history to a world in which gods, nature, and human beings interact. Those who told, transmitted, and wrote down the Exodus story not only used these myths but at the same time demythologized them. The main actors became ordinary human beings. Even Pharaoh's daughter, the princess, appears not as a fairy tale queen, but as someone with deep motherly instincts and feelings. Salvation history does not happen somewhere outside human history. Its setting is the hard facts of human fear and cruelty. It also concerns how history is being changed by human inventiveness and human love. In and through such everyday human feelings and acts salvation is being accomplished. Does this mean that God is absent at the beginning of the Exodus story?

Task 4: Where are the signs of God's presence in Exodus 1:6-2:10?

> This question may have been dealt with satisfactorily in connection with Tasks 2 and 3. If so, the enabler should recall and sum up the main affirmations then made. Otherwise the above question is again studied privately, discussed in groups, and by the panel.

The hidden presence of God first appears in the decisions of the Hebrew midwives. They "feared God, and did not do as the king of Egypt commanded them" (Exod. 1:17). The source of the midwives' civil disobedience was their "fear of God," an expression which in the Old Testament means the awe of humans before God, reverence of God, and obedience to his will. This hidden presence of God overruled the will of Pharaoh.

Another sign of God's presence, even more powerful for Old Testament and Jewish thinking, is the refrain that "the descendants of Israel were fruitful and increased greatly; they multiplied and grew exceedingly strong" (Exod. 1:7). This affirmation is the basic melody of the first chapter of Exodus (cf. vv. 7, 9, 10, 12, 17, 19). The account of Moses' almost miraculous survival in the second chapter is a variation on this theme. To persons in the last part of the twentieth century a phenomenal population explosion is rather frightening. For believers of Old Testament times and for many Jews through the centuries, however, this fertility is a great sign of God's blessing. By insisting on this fact of the growth of the people of Israel despite all measures of birth control, the narrators of the Exodus story wanted to remind their hearers of texts like Genesis 1:28 and the great promise of Genesis 12:2. Now the promised blessing was becoming a reality. Now God was indeed present with his people. Now salvation — and therefore liberation from slavery — was at hand.

3 THE TIME OF JEREMIAH

God's ministers in the Old Testament

The main part of the following study was prepared for the world consultation which the Vatican "Council of the Laity" organized in Rome as part of the Holy Year celebrations in October 1975. Under the title "Christ and the Ministries of the Old Covenant" this study was held during the first main session. Its purpose was to draw participants from all continents and diverse church-world situations into the common tradition of faith. The study started with six slides of modern "secular" art which communicated something of "the joys and the hopes, the griefs and the anxieties" in the present world (cf. the Pastoral Constitution on "The Church in the Modern World" of the Second Vatican Council). On that basis participants discussed with one another the particular human condition from which they came.

Having started with the here and now, we then went back to the time of Jeremiah and from there to Christ. The study led towards the consultation's first celebration of the eucharist, which included prayers written during this Bible study. The version of the study reproduced here was planned for a whole day's session with a group of at least 18 participants (so that six subgroups of three or more can be formed). If the group is smaller or if a series of short sessions is preferable to a one-day session, this study can be subdivided. The first session starts as the original version, with an art meditation on the human condition today and information about the religious and political situation in the time of Jeremiah. Sessions two to seven examine each one of the six ministries mentioned and connect them to the ministry of Jesus. On the basis of this process a worship service is prepared and conducted on the eighth session (cf. the appended worksheet on "The time of Jeremiah").

The hopes and fears of people today must not be forgotten as we cross many centuries to go back to Old Testament times. The biblical God acts in history; not only in past history, but also on the large scene of present world history and the smaller scenes of our national and personal lives today. Yet in order to discern who this God is and how he acts, it is good to sharpen our eyes by examining how God was present in a crucial period of past history, the time of Jeremiah.

World politics in Jeremiah's time

(Cf. the historical synopsis and map on the worksheet.)

What did Jeremiah see on the stage of world history during his lifetime? Born about 650 B.C. in the village of Anathoth, he spent most of his life as a prominent and much-hated prophet in the nearby city of Jerusalem and died about 586 B.C. as a political refugee in Egypt. Even this brief outline of his personal destiny shows that he lived in troubled times.

Jeremiah certainly knew nothing about the great pre-Columbian cultures in the Americas — the Zapotecs in Mexico, the beginning Maya culture in Central America, or that of the Chavins in Peru. It is unlikely that he had ever heard of the Chinese kingdom and culture on the other side of the globe, where Confucius (551-479 B.C.) was soon to bring together and transmit the great tresure of ancient Chinese wisdom. Nor was Jeremiah familiar with the Vedanta period in India and its religious philosophy, which would soon receive a new impulse through the life and teaching of Buddha (563-483 B.C.).

Jeremiah's world was the Middle East, the cultures of Egypt and Mesopotamia, confronting one another again and again on the bridge of land between the Mediterranean Sea and the Arab desert. On this bridge of the Fertile Crescent, with Jerusalem and the small kingdom of Judah situated in the middle, world history was being made. There the big powers met, Egypt and Assyria and the upcoming Babylonian Empire in Jeremiah's time, just as the great powers meet there today.

Egypt had become a vassal of Assyria, but Jeremiah was witnessing the growing strength of a new Egyptian dynasty. He may well have met Pharaoh Necho II when this Egyptian ruler made his great military campaign towards the east and recaptured Palestine in 609. In the east the big power was still Assyria, whose emperors had destroyed Samaria and deported the greatest part of the people of Israel into exile. When Jeremiah was a boy the mighty king Ashurbanipal still seemed invincible. But around 630 B.C. hordes of Scythian warriors from central Asia swept over the Assyrian empire. Later other warriors from the north east, the Medes, captured Asshur in 614 B.C. Yet an even more dangerous enemy was arising in the south, Babylonia, a province of the Assyrian empire. It revolted and began to expand its territory until in 612 B.C. it destroyed the great city of Nineveh. It was the second great emperor of the neo-Babylonian dynasty, Nebuchadnezzar, who captured Jerusalem in 597 B.C. and later destroyed that city and its temple.

All these catastrophic events of world history did not escape Jeremiah's perceptive eyes, for the Judean kingdom was caught up in this political power struggle. What did Jeremiah see in and around Jerusalem?

The dark age of the kingdom of Judah

The history of the Judean kingdom in the seventh century is known as "the dark age of Judah." The glorious days of David and Solomon had long since passed and were but a fading memory. The inhabitants of Jerusalem had not only lost their political freedom, but they were also losing their cultural and religious identity. In the temple of Jerusalem sacrifices were offered to the gods of Canaan and Assyria, and the land was full of witchcraft. King Manasseh even burned his own son as a sacrifice (2 Kings 21; 2 Chron. 33).

Then in 640 B.C. Josiah became king of Judah. He was a boy of only eight years and his tutors and ministers profited all the more from the general corruption. What was even worse, however, was the feeling that God seemed to have abandoned his people. Ever since Isaiah had died (ca. 700 B.C.) no prophet from God had appeared among his people, and this silence had lasted more than seventy years. The heavens were closed.

Jeremiah saw not only what human actors were doing on the scene of world history but how God was acting through his servants. These servants we will now come to know more intimately: prophets, sages, priests, kings, the poor, and heralds of hope. After sketching these agents of God we will discover how Jesus has, according to the witness of the New Testament, taken up each of these ministries of the old covenant. Finally we will explore how we ourselves can participate in this sixfold ministry here and now.

> Divide the participants into six subgroups, one for the prophets, one for the sages, one for the priests, one for the kings, one for the poor, and one for the heralds of hope. During the rest of the study they will identify themselves with their particular ministry.

Task 1: Each subgroup reads the passages assigned to it on the worksheet. Who are the actors we meet in these passages? In what literary style were these texts edited? With what voice and gestures could these passages best be recited and enacted? After discussing these questions, each subgroup practises reciting and enacting the scripture reading assigned to it.

> Subgroups work for 20-30 minutes on this task. Back in the plenary they must sit together so that they can recite and enact their passages at the appropriate time. During the subgroup sessions the enabler should find out how each of the six ministries will be presented, so that these dramatic recitations can be properly integrated into the teaching. For example, will the two passages assigned to the priests be recited separately from one another, or will Deuteronomy 6:4-7 be integrated into the recital of 2 Kings 22, between vv. 10 and 11?

Prophetic watchmen

Jeremiah was still young when the frightening silence of God was broken. A prophetic voice was heard, the oracles of the little-known prophet Zephaniah, probably about 630 B.C. Like the judgment Amos had announced more than a hundred years earlier, the words of Zephaniah sound like a trumpet of the last days. (*Zephaniah 1:14-18 is recited by the "prophets."*)

Prophets interpret the signs of time as the signs of the end. Seeing through the surface of what is happening, they detect and announce the deep meaning of world history, past, present, and future. Possibly Zephaniah was alluding to the sudden invasion of the warriors from the north. He may also have detected signs of weakness in the Assyrian empire. But he interpreted these events of history as signs of even greater apocalyptic catastrophes, and so he warned the mighty ones in Jerusalem.

Two or three years later the young Jeremiah also received his prophetic calling. No longer could he remain a mere spectator. He had to become a voice from God, even if an unwilling voice. In his earliest prophecies he immediately saw the heart of the matter: the people of Israel had broken the love relationship with their God and become unfaithful. Therefore the prophet calls on the heavens to be witnesses and judges in the lawsuit between God and his people. (*Jeremiah 2:11-13 is recited by the "prophets."*)

The prophets often telescope events in world history. In the midst of penultimate realities they point towards the ultimate outcome and goal. Apparently neither Zephaniah nor Jeremiah was at first aware of the great reform-movement which gained momentum in the dark age of Judah. Indeed, the biblical God has other agents than the prophets, and through the ministry of these other agents a promising renewal movement was at hand.

The sages: counselors of the powerful

David and Solomon had gathered wise men to become their counselors. Most of these sages remained anonymous, doing their work behind the scenes as advisors to the powerful. Yet already in Jeremiah's time some of the counsels of the wise men and women had been collected and written down in the most ancient parts of the book of Proverbs (parts of chapters 10-31).

Unlike the prophets, the sages dealt much more with the penultimate realities of everyday life: the difficult process of decision-making, the discernment of good and evil in a world full of compromises and ambiguities. What is a wise or a foolish style of life? What leads to life and what to death? In answering such questions the sages had an ultimate frame of reference which became the source of their wisdom. They called it "the fear of the Lord," an expression which can better be translated as "confidence in the Lord" and "submission to God's will." (*The "sages" recite Proverbs 15:17; 12:28; 15:33.*)

The sages proclaimed their wisdom not as absolute truth but as a suggestion for action. They wanted to train people not simply to conform to an outward law but to make responsible and wise decisions based on inward convictions. Echoes of this pleading are heard in Deuteronomy, and many scholars think that during the dark age of Judah the sages played an important role in editing that book. (*Deuteronomy 30:19b-20 is recited by the "sages."*)

Priests: guardians of the law

The book of Deuteronomy consists of a series of long discourses of Moses addressed to the people of Israel. It is in fact a restatement of the Mosaic faith and law for a new time. Priestly circles in the Northern Kingdom had handed this tradition on from generation to generation, and later it was transmitted to priestly circles in the Southern Kingdom of Judah. During the dark age of the seventh century sages and priests worked further on the tradition, updating and reinterpreting it for the new time and situation of Jerusalem.

Usually when we think of priests, it is altars, sacrifices, and prayers that come to mind. This was not so in the time of Jeremiah. Before the Babylonian exile, priests were in the first place guardians and interpreters of the Torah, the law and will of the living God. Thus it is no surprise that it was a priest who found the book of the law in the temple of Jerusalem in the eighteenth year of Josiah's reign (2 Kings 23; 2 Chron. 34-35). The scroll which the high priest Hilkiah found was the old law which is contained in the book of Deuteronomy and which played such an important role in the subsequent reformation. Reading between the lines, we can guess that the book was not actually found. Priests and sages knew it and had worked on it. Now they felt that the time was ripe to play it into the hands of the king.

The "discovery" of the law happened in 622 B.C. Josiah had grown into manhood and taken over the power from his irresponsible ministers. He already had begun a political and religious reform, among other things restoring the temple in Jerusalem. In this connection he sent his secretary Shaphan to the temple to collect money to pay the workers. (*The "priests" recite 2 Kings 22:8-10; Deuteronomy 6:4-7; 2 Kings 22:11*).

No wonder King Josiah tore his clothes as a sign of deep concern and contrition. Deuteronomy specifies mighty curses against those who do not follow its commandments. But its main emphasis is the insistence that God demands not simply outward conformity to his will but expects a response of love, inward trust, and commitment from his chosen people. This is most clearly expressed in the commandment of Deuteronomy 6:4-7, a passage which has become the key sentence in the daily prayer of all Jews throughout the centuries.

The king: mediator between God and his people

Prophets, wise men, and priests had prepared the great updating of the Mosaic faith and law, but the main actor now became the king. And unlike his predecessors Josiah was a ruler according to God's will. Like his forefather David he was a true "son of God," as the kings are sometimes called in the Old Testament, a mediator between God and his people, a trustee of the covenant. The discovery of the book of the law gave Josiah the impetus to transform the acts of reform he had already begun into a far-reaching reformation. (*2 Kings 23:1-2; Deuteronomy 5:2-3; 2 Kings 23:3 are recited by the "kings."*)

Not only was there a public reading of the newly discovered law of Moses, but Josiah went one step further: as the royal guarantor of God's covenant with his people he renewed this covenant. From Deuteronomy he had learned that the covenant must not remain a past event, but must be continuously renewed and updated to become a present reality.

We have no time to examine the further development of Josiah's reformation. This serious attempt to live according to the prophetic teachings and to return to the covenant faith of Moses must have made a deep impression on the inhabitants of Jerusalem and the villages of Judah. Jeremiah himself probably supported the reformation for a while. We know that he went through the cities of Judah and the streets of Jerusalem appealing for the people to accept "this covenant" (Jer. 11:1-8). However, the prophet must soon have seen that this reformation did not result in a change of heart. There was still no intimate response of love and trust towards the God who had liberated the people of Israel from slavery and called them into his service. Josiah's reformation became too tied up with his own power politics, his strategy of territorial expansion in Samaria, and his policy of concentration of power in Jerusalem. The reformation which had begun with so much spiritual fervour ended miserably, when Josiah was fatally wounded in his futile battle against the army of Pharaoh Necho at Megiddo in 609 B.C.

The poor of the Lord

The period of great excitement and expectation was followed by a period of deep disillusionment. Yet the biblical God could work through still another agent when the classic ministries of prophets, sages, priests, and kings had failed. This last resort in God's purpose of salvation are the poor (Hebrew, *anawim*).

Zephaniah had already announced that in the catastrophic days of judgment the humble ones, the *anawim*, could survive: "Seek the Lord, all you *anawim* of the land, who do his commands; seek righteousness, seek humility (="poverty"); perhaps you may be hidden on the day of the wrath of the Lord" (Zeph. 2:3). These "poor of the Lord" are not *simply* the economically poor or *simply* the spiritually poor. They were neither revolting against God in their poverty nor had they become passive and apathetic in their deprivation. In the midst of their material and spiritual misery they struggled with God in prayer, for they had learned to put their whole trust in God. Even in their God-forsakenness they cried out to him. The poor struggle with God as Job did in his illness and poverty, as Jesus did on the cross when he prayed in the words of the psalmist: "My God, my God, why hast thou forsaken me?" (Ps. 22).

The first to incorporate this spirituality of the poor was in fact Jeremiah. In his famous "confessions" (Jer. 11:18-12:6; 15:10-21; 17:14-18; 18:18-23; 20:7-18) we see him struggling with doubts and fear. He is publicly denounced and deserted by all his friends, and even God seems to have let him down and become his enemy. Nevertheless Jeremiah calls on the biblical God and trusts in his purpose of salvation. (*Jeremiah 20:7-13 is recited by "the poor."*)

Heralds of hope

After Josiah's death the situation in Judah deteriorated rapidly. The vacuum created by the decline of Assyria was soon filled by Egypt, which gained in strength, and especially by the upcoming Neo-Babylonian empire. Jerusalem was conquered in 597 B.C. and totally destroyed ten years later. The remnant of Israel were led as slaves and prisoners to Babylonia for their long exile. Yet in the midst of famine, murder, and deportations, at a time when, humanly speaking, the people of Israel was finished and its hopes frustrated, Jeremiah the prophet of doom became a prophet of hope. When his people were losing their land, Jeremiah went out and bought a field, as a prophetic sign of the coming peace and joy (Jer. 32). Indeed, in the midst of destruction the seer saw the coming new initiative of God, the truly new covenant. (*The "heralds of hope" recite Jeremiah 31:31-34.*)

Josiah's deuteronomic reformation had been an attempt to recapture the past. People looked back to Moses and David, and the reformation was no more than a restoration of the old traditions and hopes. When all this had failed, Jeremiah resolutely turned his eyes into the future, expecting and announcing a new intervention of God. He no longer called for a restoration of the past but expected and worked for an anticipation of the future.

The ministries of Jesus

This in short is what God was doing through his servants at the end of the seventh century B.C. on the great theatre of world history. If we were Jews, we could jump immediately from that faraway historical period to the joys and hopes, griefs and anxieties of men and women today, for Jews see an unbroken continuity from the time of Jeremiah to the present. As Christians we must not ignore what God did in the time and world of Jeremiah, but this ancient history is of special significance for us only through a new intervention of God, which has extended salvation history to all the nations. We confess that this decisive divine intervention in world history has happened in the life, death, and resurrection of Jesus Christ.

There is both continuity and discontinuity between God's action in the time of Jeremiah and his action in the life, death, and resurrection of Jesus Christ. We must now examine how Jesus has taken up and continued but also transformed the ministries of prophets, sages, priests, kings, the poor, and the heralds of hope.

Task 2: According to the testimonies of the New Testament, how did Jesus take up, continue, and transform the six ways God acted during the time of Jeremiah? Answer on the basis of what you remember about Jesus as he is presented in the four gospels and the letters of the New Testament. Each subgroup concentrates only on its own ministry and appoints one person to report to the plenary.

After an appropriate time the six speakers report briefly the main findings of their subgroups to the plenary session. This stage of the Bible study can well be concluded with an art meditation. I have used the following eleven slides, but others can serve as well. Each slide should be projected on the screen for about one minute, during which short texts of meditation are embedded in silent contemplation.

1. *Prophet.* Au Ho Nien: coloured Chinese print, showing a prophetic figure hurrying against the wind with fluttering hair and clothes and a stern, determined expression on his face. Reproduction in the art folder "The Bible in Art Around the World," United Presbyterian Church in the USA, New York (no publication information provided).

Jesus, the prophetic watchman: He is alone, going his way of obedience against the gathering storm of world history, like this prophet in a modern Chinese print.

2. *Sage.* Hezekiel Ntuli: South African clay sculpture, showing the head of an African man with deep and perceptive eyes, looking beyond immediate appearances to the heart of the matter. Photograph from a private collection.

Jesus, the incarnate wisdom: He is the one who sees through the surface of what happens, who knows how to learn from life and is thus able to teach the ways which lead to life, like this African sage sculptured by the South African artist Ntuli.

3. *Priest.* Marc Chagall: drawing of a Jew, carrying in his arms a Torah scroll away from a burning village, bent over backwards by the heaviness of his precious burden. Lunacharsky Art Museum.

Jesus, the priestly guardian of the law: He is the one who not only teaches the Torah, the will of the living God but first of all submits himself to this will and keeps it as the most precious treasure in his life, like the man carrying the heavy and precious Torah in this drawing by Marc Chagall.

4. *King.* Marc Chagall: pen-sketch of the torso and head of King David with a crown, bent forward slightly in humility but at the same time manifesting royal authority. Reproduction in H. M. Rotermund, *Marc Chagall und die Bibel* (Lahr, 1970), p. 98.

Jesus, the royal mediator: He is a humble king who submits himself to the one true king, God, creator and saviour of the world. Through his submission he receives the authority to rule, as Chagall shows us David in this sketch.

5. *The poor.* Erdmann-Michael Hinz: clay sculpture of a young man standing in prayer, looking upward and holding his very large and empty hands up to receive or to dedicate himself. Reproduction in P. Hinz, *Bettler und Lobsänger* (Berlin, 1965), p. 90.

Jesus, the true poor of the Lord: He is the one with the empty hands, with nothing left to give but his own life, as the young East German artist Erdmann-Michael Hinz has shown him in this clay sculpture of the praying beggar.

6. *Herald.* Marc Chagall: Jeremiah — detail from a stained glass window in the Fraumünster church, Zurich. The blue figure of the prophet sitting against a blood-red background, closed eyes looking inward, waits for new prophe-

cies and receives a vision of the new covenant. Reproduction and colour slide in I. Vogelsager-de Roche, *Marc Chagalls Fraumünsterfenster* (Zurich, 1970). *Jesus, the herald of hope: He is the one who in the chaos of first-century Palestine announced the coming of the kingdom, like Chagall's Jeremiah who, crushed by the misery around him nevertheless sees and announces the new covenant.*

As we reflect on the particular way in which Jesus has continued and transformed these six ministries of the old covenant, our thoughts converge at Golgotha, the cross, where we meet the ultimate suffering, the decisive turning point of history, the deepest love, and the final victory.

7. *Righteous sufferer.* Edilberto Merida: clay sculpture of the crucified Jesus on a wooden cross. The artist emphasizes the suffering and torture of the cross by representing the hands, feet, and mouth of the crucified one much larger than their natural proportions. Reproduction in Hans-Ruedi Weber, *On a Friday Noon* (Geneva, 1979), Plate XVIII.

The righteous sufferer: He obeyed the will of God; he was the prophet and the poor; he struggled for justice and freedom. Therefore he had to suffer, as the Peruvian Indian artist Edilberto Merida shows the crucified Jesus as an executed freedom fighter.

8. *The apocalypse of the cross.* Marc Chagall: painting, "white crucifixion." The cross, with the crucified one, stands in the middle of scenes of war — with refugees escaping a burning synagogue, houses collapsing in the village, everything turned upside down. The painting is in the Art Institute of Chicago; reproduction in Rotermund, *op. cit.*, p. 123.

The apocalypse of the cross: Jesus not only announced the kingdom in his life, death, and resurrection, but also anticipated the judgment of this world and initiated the new creation. Thus his death had cosmic significance, overturning the structures of this world, as Chagall shows us in his white crucifixion.

9. *Sacrifice of the cross.* Gebre Kristos Desta: painting of the crucifixion. Christ appears as a stain of blood in the form of a cross, with drops of blood around, in this almost abstract painting. Reproduction in Weber, *op. cit.*, Plate XXX.

The sacrifice of the cross: The ultimate wisdom is giving oneself for the sake of others; the ultimate priestly act is self-sacrifice. Therefore Jesus had to go the way to the cross to be spent for us, as the Ethiopian artist Gebre Kristos Desta shows us in this painting.

10. *The king who reigns from the cross.* Engelbert Mveng: wall-painting in the altar recess of the chapel at the College Libermann, Douala, Cameroon. The crucifixion is represented in the highly stylized way of traditional African art, using colour symbolism of black (= suffering), white (= death), and red (= life). Reproduction in Weber, *op. cit.*, Plate XXXI.

The king reigning from the cross: Yet suffering and self-sacrifice are not the last words in connection with the cross. It is at Golgotha that Jesus was enthroned as King. It is here that he established the new covenant, gathering all the nations. It is from the cross that he reigns and gives his benediction, as the artist Engelbert Mveng, of Cameroon, has interpreted the victory of the cross.

11. *Early Christian baptistery.* Fifth- or sixth-century cross-shaped baptistery at Jalyssos, Isle of Rhodes. Reproduction in Weber, *op. cit.,* Plate XXXIII.

An early Christian baptistery: The last image for our meditation is not a painting or sculpture but an early Christian baptismal place on the Isle of Rhodes, cut into the rock in the shape of a large and deep cross lying on the ground. Here, early on Easter mornings, converts were literally buried in the water of the cross, so that in the future life they would participate in Christ's resurrection and in this life participate in Christ's ministry for the world.

Joining Jesus' ministries today

What happened to those early Christian converts on Rhodes happened to all of us in our baptism. We were taken into the death and life of Jesus. We have been commissioned to participate in his sixfold ministry. This is no more simply a matter of study, but a matter of life and witness in our own particular time and situation.

A good way to enter into this participation in Jesus' sixfold ministry is to prepare and celebrate together a worship service.

Task 3: Each subgroup translates what it has learned from this Bible study into a contribution to a common act of worship. These six short contributions (no longer than five minutes each) will follow the sequence of the six ministries in Jeremiah's time. The *prophets* start with a prophetic word and act for today (perhaps a traditional "call to worship" and song of praise, which is then interrupted by the new prophetic word or act). The *sages* continue the worship with some proverbs of wisdom for today. In cultures where popular wisdom is mainly communicated through songs, such modern proverbs could take the form of a new *chanson* with a refrain sung by all. The *priests* then propose, within the context of worship, some necessary new legislation for today which takes account of God's will. This might be in the form of affirmations followed by confessions of sin. This leads to a covenant renewal led by the *kings,* who have been asked to find a new liturgical act symbolizing what covenant renewal means to people living in today's world. The worship is continued by a prayer of the *poor* today, possibly in the form of a mime. In conclusion the *heralds of hope* proclaim a message of hope for the world of today. This can lead to an act of commitment by the whole group.

Such a translation of the Bible study into worship demands much time, whether or not there are many creative people present. Up to an hour should be allowed for the subgroups to prepare their contribution. The enabler must encourage the subgroups to find new words for prayer, new liturgical responses and gestures, if possible a new song for the Lord. The enabler must also coordinate the preparatory work so that there is neither too much overlap nor too abrupt a transition from one group's contribution to the next. Physical arrangements for the worship service must be prepared according to the shape which the several acts of worship will take.

When the subgroups regather for worship, any new liturgical responses and gestures and new songs must be taught to the whole group. After the hurry and pressure of these preparations, a moment of silence will be necessary before the worship service starts.

4 LAND AND LIBERTY

Leviticus 25

For its 1975 world consultation in Rome (cf. introduction to study II/3), the Vatican "Council of the Laity" asked me to lead a Bible study on the Holy Year. What follows is the slightly edited script of that study. It will be helpful to provide participants with a sheet on which Luke 4:16-21; Isaiah 61:1-3; Leviticus 25: 3-5, and 25:8-17, 23, 54f are printed.

The celebration of the Holy Year has its origins in the church history of the Middle Ages. However, if this celebration is to receive full ecumenical significance, we must go back many more centuries to the Old and the New Testaments. By "ecumenical" I mean not only that members of the Orthodox and Protestant Churches would be able to celebrate this year wholeheartedly together with their Roman Catholic sisters and brothers. The term "ecumenical" refers after all in the first place not to the churches, but to the *oikoumene*, the whole inhabited world. To become fully ecumenical the Holy Year would have to be celebrated to God's glory by all Christians together, for the sake of all human beings on earth and for the sake of the whole creation. It would have to be as much an ecological as an ecclesiastical event.

The few texts in the Bible which refer to such a Holy Year point exactly in this direction. Let us start with an incident in Jesus' life, his first public appearance according to the testimony of the evangelist Luke.

The shortest sermon ever preached (Luke 4:16-21)

The scene is the synagogue in Nazareth, where Jesus grew up. The time is a Sabbath morning. All the pious Jews of the town have gathered for a worship service, which is now coming to an end. As usual the congregation has recited the *shema*, "O Hear Israel ...," the famous commandment from Deuteronomy 6:4ff. Then the prescribed prayers and benedictions were said, followed by scripture lessons from the Torah, the first five books of the Bible. It was a custom of the synagogue to invite visiting teachers to read the last scripture lesson, the one from the books of the prophets, and to give a sermon. Usually the local synagogue leader would issue such an invitation, but Luke's record suggests that Jesus himself took the initiative on this occasion: "He stood up to read." He goes forward on the podium and waits until the servant of the synagogue has given him the scroll.

Now all eyes are fixed on him, those of the older men and women who remember him as a boy and those of his own age who have played together with him in the streets of Nazareth. Which passage would he choose? In the time of the New Testament the scripture readings from the prophets were probably not yet fixed. There was a prescription, however, that the reading should be no longer than 21 verses and no shorter than 3 verses.

The scroll of Isaiah is given to Jesus. He opens it, rolls it down almost to the end, then fixes his eyes on the passage he is going to read from chapter 61. Having finished the reading with the customary blessing, he sits down on the chair — the indication that a sermon will follow. Let us listen. Jesus says: "Today this scripture has been fulfilled in your hearing."

That was it. A shorter and more powerful sermon has never been preached. The actual sermon was shorter than its text. No more words were needed, for the sermon really consisted of the presence of the person of Jesus himself. In this presence the scripture reading is being fulfilled.

What does the passage chosen by Jesus actually promise? The first three verses of Isaiah 61 are a prophecy in which the "anointed" one speaks in the first person singular, something which occurs only twice in the whole Old Testament: here and in King David's last words (2 Sam. 23:1ff).

> The Spirit of the Lord God is upon me,
> because the Lord has anointed me
> to bring good tidings to the afflicted;
> he has sent me to bind up the broken-hearted,
> to proclaim liberty to the captives,
> and the opening of the prison to those who are bound;
> to proclaim the year of the Lord's favour,
> and the day of vengeance of our God;
> to comfort all who mourn;
> to grant to those who mourn in Zion —
> to give them a garland instead of ashes,
> the oil of gladness instead of mourning,
> the mantle of praise instead of a faint spirit;
> that they may be called oaks of righteousness,
> the planting of the Lord, that he may be glorified.
>
> Isaiah 61:1-3

If we compare this text with the words which — according to Luke's testimony — Jesus actually read at Nazareth, we immediately discover several differences. Perhaps the version of Isaiah 61 Jesus read was different from the one we use today for the Old Testament. Perhaps what is quoted is not the actual scripture reading, but the Aramaic paraphrase (or Targum), which always immediately followed the reading of the Hebrew scripture. It is more likely that Luke quoted from memory and in the process left out some expressions and added similar ones from other parts of the book of Isaiah (42:7 and 58:6). These differences need not further attract our attention here. But there is one very striking thing about Jesus' scripture lesson at Nazareth, if it is read in the light of what we said earlier about the procedures of Jewish synagogue worship and Jesus' short sermon.

Task 1: What is the most striking thing in Jesus' scripture lesson at Nazareth? Discuss its significance for the first public appearance of Jesus.

After a moment of individual reflection on Luke 4:16-21, participants discuss their discoveries with their neighbours. The enabler then solicits contributions from participants and sums up and complements the findings.

It is the presence of Jesus which fulfils the prophecy of Isaiah 61. The "today" in Jesus' short sermon is emphasized. Yet what does this fulfilment *today* refer to?

Many expositors have said that in this first public appearance Jesus reveals himself as the Spirit-filled Messiah, the Lord's anointed, by applying the prophecy of Isaiah 61 to his own person. True enough, but both the scripture reading and the sermon point in a different direction. It is not simply in the person of Christ, who appears as the Messiah before the eyes of people, but also in what he declares that the main point lies. "Today, this scripture has been fulfilled in our hearing." What was extraordinary in Jesus' scripture reading?

Earlier we mentioned that the minimum reading from the prophets should be three verses. We do not know exactly how the Jews divided the verses in the time of Jesus. The present division of chapters and verses was much later. Nevertheless, according to Luke's testimony, Jesus certainly did not read three full verses. He stopped short in the middle of a sentence, omitting a reference to the "day of vengeance." He ended his lesson with the announced proclamation of "the acceptable year of the Lord." The accent lies on the proclamation of this year of the Lord — almost certainly a reference to the Year of Jubilee. The terminology used at the beginning of Isaiah 61, especially the Hebrew verb *deror* ("to liberate"), occurs in the Old Testament essentially in connection with the Sabbath Year and the Year of Jubilee. What Jesus did according to the witness of the evangelist Luke during his first public appearance was nothing else than to proclaim the beginning of the true Year of Jubilee.

The Sabbath and the Sabbath Year

To understand what the Jubilee originally meant we must start with one of the ten commandments, that concerning the Sabbath. The Old Testament gives two reasons for this weekly day of rest: (1) it is to be a day of remembrance of God's act of creation (Exod. 20:11) and salvation (Exod. 16:22f; Deut. 5:15); (2) it is to be a day of rest and recovery from labour for all people and animals in the household (Exod. 20:9f; 23:12; Deut. 5:13f). The Sabbath has both a liturgical-religious and a social-ethical purpose. In the Babylonian culture some days of rest were already observed. But it is only through the purpose and centrality given to the Sabbath by Jews — and later to Sunday by Christians — that a weekly day of rest has found acceptance in almost the whole world. This is indeed one of the greatest gifts which the Jewish-Christian faith has given to humanity. But as with so many other gifts we have to a great extent misused it and lost its blessing.

Among the Israelites the Sabbath was soon extended to include not only people and animals but also the land. This led to the institution of a Sabbath Year at the end of every six-year period. Already in the very old "Covenant Law" (Exod. 20:22-23, 33) the institution of the Sabbath Year is known:

> For six years you shall sow your land and gather in its yield; but the seventh year you shall let it rest and lie fallow, that the poor of your people may eat; and what they leave the wild beasts may eat. You shall do likewise with your vineyard, and with your olive orchard (Exod. 23:10-11).

The Sabbath Year is mentioned more explicitly in the "Holiness Laws" (Lev. 17-26). The oldest parts of these laws (especially those phrased in the form of a singular "you") date back to the time just after the people of Israel had entered Canaan. The present form of these laws was not written down until the Babylonian exile, and the old law and later editorial and theological additions by the priestly redactors can be distinguished. The oldest part of the provisions concerning the Sabbath Year in Leviticus 25:1-7 is found in verses 3-5, and the recollection of the institution of the Sabbath Law functions here only as an introduction to the main subject of Leviticus 25, namely the Jubilee.

The Year of Jubilee

In verses 8-11a there are complicated instructions on how the Year of Jubilee is to be counted and initiated. The priestly redactors probably tried to combine two old traditions, according to which the Jubilee was to be proclaimed either every 49th or 50th year, leading up to the sentence: "On the day of atonement you shall send abroad the trumpet throughout all your land. And you shall hallow the fiftieth year, and proclaim liberty (*derōr*) throughout the land to all its inhabitants." Then follows the old Law (vv. 11b-17).

In the midst of the many detailed prescriptions, the redactors of the Holiness Law indicated the theological reasons for the institution of the Jubilee: "The land shall not be sold in perpetuity, for the land is mine; for you are strangers and sojourners with me" (Lev. 25:23). "And if he (that is, an Israelite slave) is not redeemed by these means, then he shall be released in the Year of Jubilee, he and his children with him. For to me the people of Israel are servants, they are my servants whom I brought forth out of the land of Egypt; I am the Lord your God" (Lev. 25:54f).

Task 2: What must happen after a Jubilee has been declared? Reread Lev. 25:11-17, 23, 54-55, and state in your own words the main prescriptions of this special year.

Participants work on this assignment either individually followed by exchange among neighbours or by dividing into study groups. Their reports back to the plenary may make the following summary comments unnecessary.

Four main acts of obedience were asked from the Israelites in the Year of Jubilee:

First of all the Jubilee had to begin with the day of atonement, when the scapegoat carried the sins of the people and their leaders off into the desert (Lev. 16).

Second, the Jubilee was a Sabbath Year. Not only the people and domestic animals but also the land itself had to be given a time of rest and restoration. How could people survive in such a Sabbath Year? The priests answer that question with God's promise:

> I will command my blessing upon you in the sixth year, so that it will bring forth fruit for three years. When you sow in the eighth year, you will be eating old produce; until the ninth year, when its produce comes in you shall eat the old (Lev. 25:21-22).

The Jubilee was to be an interruption in the business of life. To a certain extent it was a return to Paradise, a state of life where it is said that Adam and Eve and all the animals ate what grew naturally. They did not need to labour with sweat nor struggle for survival. They had time to sing and to dance, to enjoy one another's company and to be in communion with their Creator.

Third, the Jubilee implied something like land reform and just economic legislation. Land purchased from impoverished Israelites had to be restored to its original owners. "Each of you shall return to his property" (v. 10) for "land shall not be sold in perpetuity" (v. 23). What could be sold was not the land, but "the number of crops" (v. 16), the fruit of one's own labours. The whole economic system was to be arranged according to this principle. Within the period between two Jubilees land prices were not allowed to rise but had to go down, because the number of harvests — and thus the possibility of gain from one's labour on the land — decreased (vv. 14-16). With this in mind the Holiness Law contains severe regulations against permanent land ownership and against any economic fraud. Theological reasons command this. Land must not be sold in perpetuity because "the land is mine; for you are strangers and sojourners with me" (v. 23). There is only one true landowner, namely the Creator God. We are but stewards of God's land, trustees of his creation who may neither neglect nor exploit and pollute it.

Fourth, the Jubilee is a year of liberation for all Israelites who have become slaves. The old custom that Israelite slaves had to be released after six years of slavery (Deut. 15:1-11; Jer. 34:13-14) must have influenced the prescriptions for the Jubilee. The key Hebrew term here is *derōr*, which means both remittance of debts and liberation of slaves. Again, a theological reason is cited. Slaves must be liberated because "to me the people of

Israel are servants, they are my servants whom I brought forth out of the land of Egypt" (v. 55). Human liberation is firmly based on God's acts of salvation recorded in the book of Exodus, when God liberated the tribes of Israel from their slavery in Egypt. As Christians we look back not only to this Exodus event but also to the great act of salvation accomplished in Christ. For us it concerns all nations, not only the Israelites. A Christian celebration of the Jubilee must therefore consider all forms of slavery and respond to the cry of all oppressed people who long for liberty.

A utopian model

Can such a far-reaching economic and social institution ever become a reality in the hard power struggles of our world? The Sabbath Year and the Jubilee were never fully implemented among the Israelites, but there have always been attempts to put this theologically based economic and social legislation into practice. Indications of this can be found both in the Old Testament (Num. 36:4; Ezek. 46:16ff; Neh. 5:1-13) and during the centuries immediately before and after Christ. We know for instance that conquerors of Palestine took account of the Sabbath Year: Alexander the Great ordered that the Jews need not pay taxes during the seventh year, and the same fiscal concession was later made by Julius Caesar.

One revealing attempt to celebrate a year of liberation was made by King Zedekiah at the beginning of the sixth century B.C. On the basis of a covenanted promise, the rich in Jerusalem had committed themselves to free their slaves. Later they changed their mind. At that moment the prophet Jeremiah intervened and said to the king and the people in Jerusalem:

> You turned around and profaned my name when each of you took back his male and female slaves, whom you had set free according to their desire, and you brought them into subjection to be your slaves. Therefore, thus says the Lord: You have not obeyed me by proclaiming liberty, every one to his brother and to his neighbour (Jer. 34:16-17).

Then Jeremiah makes a wordplay on the Hebrew verb *derōr*: against those who do not free (*derōr*) their slaves God will loose (*derōr*) the sword, famine, and plague. This is the grim prospect for people who only pay lip-service to the commitment of liberation and who observe a hypocritical Jubilee.

Yet the question remains: Is the Jubilee not a totally unrealistic utopia? In the last few decades there has been an interesting change in the connotation of the term "utopia." Once this term had mostly a pejorative meaning. It was associated with impractical dreamers and dangerous idealists. Today many discerning observers of the human prospect speak much more positively about the function of utopias. It is more clearly recognized that we are prisoners not only of the past and the present, but increasingly also of the forecasted future. For instance, we are prisoners of modern city planning which squeezes us into the mould of a forecasted future with ever more automobiles. To gain freedom, we need creative utopias. We need models of a future city in which life will be more human, models of a social and economic structure in which there is less oppression and violence. Could the utopia of the biblical Year of Jubilee not become helpful for finding desperately needed alternative models to the present social and economic structures of both East and West?

Task 3: What might be a Jubilee celebration in our society, taking up the basic concerns of the ancient Jubilee legislation and translating them for today?

> If time allows, this question should be explored in small discussion groups which then report back to the plenary.

The Jubilee and the Holy Year

The celebration of the Holy Year in the Roman Catholic Church has its own history and was never simply a repetition of the biblical Jubilee. Yet the intimate relationship between these two celebrations was clearly expressed in the fifth chapter of the "Bull of Indiction of the Holy Year 1975." That chapter emphasizes the social dimension, and the following quotation aptly summarizes a Bible study on Leviticus 25:

> The ancient origins of the Jubilee as seen in the laws and institutions of Israel clearly show that this social dimension is part of its very nature. In fact, as we read in the book of Leviticus, the Jubilee Year, precisely because it was dedicated in a special way to God, involved a new ordering of all things that were recognized as belonging to God: the land, which was allowed to lie fallow and was given back to its former owners, economic goods, insofar as debts were remitted, and, above all, man, whose dignity and freedom were reaffirmed in a special way by the manumission of slaves. The Year of God, then, was also the Year of Man, the Year of the Earth, the Year of the Poor, and upon this view of the whole of human reality there shone a new light which emanated from the clear recognition of the supreme dominion of God over the whole creation.
>
> In today's world also the problems which most disturb and torment mankind — economic and social questions, the questions of ecology and sources of energy, and above all that of the liberation of the oppressed and the uplifting of all men to a new dignity of life — can have light cast on them by the message of the Holy Year.

The critical question for a truly ecumenical celebration of the next Holy Year is whether or not such a translation of the biblical Jubilee for the contemporary world will become the central affirmation.

A footnote in the *Jerusalem Bible* clearly summarizes the social and economic character of the Year of Jubilee, but then concludes with the sentence: "Transposed on a spiritual level, the Holy Year or the Year of Jubilee of the Church gives to Christians periodically the occasion of a remission of their debts towards God." Is such a transposition to the spiritual level legitimate? All depends on the meaning one gives to the term "spiritual." The Bible calls us to what one might describe as "spiritual materialism." The spiritual is not opposed to the economic. God's Spirit embraces both soul and body, both mental and social structures of society, such intangible things as words and thoughts as well as such very tangible things as the fields we cultivate and the metals we mould. In this sense the biblical institution of the Year of Jubilee has always been on a spiritual level, because it was always a response to God's ownership over the whole of land and all people. Such a truly spiritual — and therefore all-embracing — celebration must not be replaced by a Holy Year in which the main accent lies almost exclusively on the relationship between the individual soul and God.

The theologically based social and economic demands of the biblical Jubilee arise out of the festive and expectant mood of its celebration. The Jubilee received its name from the Hebrew word *yobel*, which means the ram's horn used as a trumpet. The *yobel* in this case was not a trumpet of the judgment but a trumpet announcing a great festival of liberation. The accent of the biblical Jubilee does indeed not lie on repentance, penitence, and indulgences but on joy, jubilation, and shouts of gratitude of all those who finally found liberation. Moreover, the prophet speaking in Isaiah 61 did not look backwards to the restoration of an ancient Israelite custom; he looked forward to the Messiah who would initiate the true Year of Jubilee.

This Messiah has come. He has proclaimed the truly ecumenical Holy Year and invited us to his feast.

If possible, the study ends with the playing of a joyous trumpet melody and a festive meal.

5 GOD AND THE POWERFUL

The biblical search for wisdom

The main part of this material was prepared for a Bible study in Fontaine-
bleau, France, in May 1975, at a consultation of top executives of multinational corporations with delegations from the Roman Catholic Church and
the World Council of Churches. Later rewritten, it became the second of four
Burgmann College lectures at the Australian National University in Can-
berra (March 1976) and was repeated at the 1976 summer school of Princeton
Theological Seminary. It is this text which is published here.

This material has been used several times for participatory Bible study.
Enablers will find here enough background material for a participatory
study. Members of the group should have a worksheet with the texts of Proverbs 22:17-23, the Egyptian wisdom sayings of Amenemopet I, 9-II, 6 (cf.
below, p. 99), and 1 Corinthians 1:18-25. The study would start with *Task 1*
where participants are asked to write down three proverbs from their own
cultural heritage and to examine the style and subject matter of such traditional proverbs. This leads to a discussion of the literary milieu, style, and
main subject matter of the biblical wisdom literature. In *Task 2* the participants would be asked to compare Proverbs 22:17-23 with the Egyptian
wisdom sayings of Amenemopet, and to discover what is specific for the
biblical proverbs. Having acquired some understanding of Old Testament
wisdom literature, participants would be asked in *Task 3* to compare 1 Corinthians 1:18-25 with what they have learned about the wisdom literature in the
Old Testament. How has Jesus taken up, continued, and transformed the Old
Testament wisdom teaching according to this Pauline text? The study could
end with *Task 4*, asking participants to make new proverbs expressing the
New Testament wisdom teaching.

Towards midnight on September 17, 1961, a small airplane flying from
the war-ridden Congo crashed in Northern Rhodesia (now Zambia). When
the wreckage was found, almost all passengers had died. Among them was
one of the most powerful men of our generation, Dag Hammarskjöld, the
secretary general of the United Nations. This untiring international civil
servant was killed — accidentally or intentionally — during one of his
many missions for peace.

Dag Hammarskjöld came from among the powerful. His father had been Swedish Prime Minister. He himself had continuously worked among the powerful of this earth — politicians, decision-makers in finance and industry, the most influential artists. Through his personality and his function, he wielded an enormous moral and political power.

When the news of Hammarskjöld's death reached the world press, few knew that almost ten years earlier this man had surrendered his whole being to the biblical God. Later his intimate journal, *Markings*, was published. Then it became clear where this powerful man found the source for his untiring efforts for peace, despite all the opposition, slander and resignation he met.

Four months before his death Dag Hammarskjöld made an entry in his diary describing how the biblical God broke into his life. Hammarskjöld showed his usual restraint in speaking about his faith. His is the most hesitant — and perhaps for that reason the most convincing — description of a Christian conversion that I know.

> I don't know Who — or what — put the question, I don't know when it was put. I don't even remember answering. But at some moment I did answer *Yes* to Someone — or Something — and from that hour I was certain that existence is meaningful and that, therefore, my life, in self-surrender, had a goal ... (*Markings*, p. 169).

A word from God for the powerful

What was the claim the biblical God made on Dag Hammarskjöld, the claim he wants to make on all the powerful of this world? Was there a word from God for the Pharaohs, kings, and military commanders of ancient times; is there one today for presidents, prime ministers, directors of large newspapers, radio, and TV stations, top executives in multinational corporations and trade unions, or for the secretary general of the United Nations?

Such powerful people face difficult decisions. Seldom can they make a clear-cut decision between the good and the evil. At best life for them is an endless series of responsible compromises in the midst of highly complicated economic and political facts. They seem to be shaping a new humanity and a new earth with their decisions. At the same time they know something of the burden of Atlas, carrying the whole weight of heaven and earth. Caught up in the power struggles of our time, can they really expect any help from the God revealed in such an old book as the Bible?

Indeed the Bible is very old. Its most ancient parts go back to the second millennium before Christ, when the Israelite tribes were still nomads, struggling for survival in the desert. The most recent come from the last decade of the first century after Christ's birth, when the clash between the Christian church and the Roman empire began and persecutions had started. Obviously these texts were written long before the industrial revolution. In the books of the biblical library we read of no multinational corporations, no energy crisis. We cannot expect concrete answers to the particular questions the world confronts us with today. But we *do* meet in the Bible the tough questions of human existence, of personal and social ethics, of economic and political power struggles.

When the Israelite tribes had settled in Palestine, they had soon to face questions of military defense and of strained relationships between rich landowners and poor peasants. For such situations the early prophets spoke and the priestly legislators wrote. Large parts of the Old Testament were written later, when the Israelites had become a distrusted minority of displaced persons and slaves. The questions they faced were ones of suffering, of personal and national identity. In the New Testament we enter the world of power politics. When Jesus was a boy the Jewish resistance movement began to fight against the military occupation of Palestine by the Roman legions. His life and the environment of the earliest church were marked by the vicious circle of armed resistance evoking cruel repression — which we know so well from our own time. Paul's letters were written to prepare congregations which probably consisted largely of slaves and migrant labourers for martyrdom. The Bible thus does address itself to people who meet the hard questions of human suffering, of work and money, war and peace, legislation and exploitation.

Is there any word from the biblical God for the human predicament of the powerful? Certainly there were prophetic words of judgment; for example those of Nathan facing David with his passionate plea for justice and his announcement of divine punishment (2 Sam. 12). And there were words of forgiveness pronounced by priests who had offered the sin offerings and could on that basis proclaim divine atonement (Lev. 16). All of us, especially the powerful, need to look at our human predicament through the eyes of prophets and priests.

But there is a third biblical perspective which is probably even more relevant for the powerful of this earth. It is the so-called wisdom-literature, a part of the biblical literature which has been much neglected in the church's teaching. In recent years biblical scholars have rediscovered the importance of this perspective, both in the Old and the New Testaments. Its most succinct expression is found in the Old Testament books of Proverbs and Ecclesiastes, but its point of view also marked the early history-writing in the time of Solomon, especially the oldest creation story of the Bible (Gen. 2), some of the psalms, and the book of Job.

Biblical wisdom literature began almost three thousand years ago in the royal courts of David and Solomon in Jerusalem. There were of course also wise men and women in the villages, and this rural wisdom marks the style of Amos' prophecy for instance. Some of these sages were summoned to act in the royal courts as counselors to the king, his military commanders, and the administrators of the political and commercial enterprises of the kingdom (1 Kings 3-5). The social setting is important here. One could almost say that as long as the Israelites were poor and powerless, they could live by faith alone. But then Jerusalem began to command the trade-routes from Egypt to Mesopotamia, from Arabia to Greece. Solomon had developed an impressive import and export trade, a strong army, and clever diplomacy with neighbouring states. The ruling class became wealthy and powerful and had to cope with an increasing cultural and religious pluralism. The powerful had to make far-reaching decisions. Therefore they sought wisdom, and the biblical God spoke to them not only through priests and prophets, but especially through the sages.

Sayings of wisdom

What is the main theme of this wisdom perspective on the human predicament? The sages say little or nothing about the great themes of the prophets and priests — election, covenant, salvation. When they speak about God they see him as the Creator rather than the Redeemer. Their main theme is *life* here and now, with its earthly joys and sorrows. They raise questions of survival, of a foolish and a wise style of life, of the attainment of abundance and quality of life.

The oldest part of the book of Proverbs is chapters 10-31, which contain various collections and transcriptions of advice given by wise men to the powerful at the royal courts. This counsel includes such matters as how busy decision-makers can maintain bodily health and a clear mind. Physical and mental health are indeed important parts of life, but quality of life means much more. It has also to do with the choice of the right friends and especially of a loving wife; for, as the sages say:

> It is better to live in a corner of the housetop
> than in a house shared with a contentious woman (25:24).

An abundant life can include material wealth, and wisdom literature does not romanticize poverty or show patience with the lazy ones:

> A slack hand causes poverty,
> but the hand of the diligent makes rich (10:4).

Yet wealth does not automatically lead to fulness of life.

> Better is a little with righteousness
> than great revenues with injustice (16:8).
> Better is a dinner of herbs where love is
> than a fatted ox and hatred with it (15:17).

Often these Proverbs confront the wise with the foolish. There is a deep conviction that only true wisdom and righteousness lead to a full life:

> In the path of righteousness is life,
> but the way of error leads to death (12:28).

Yet this is exactly our problem: how do we know what is right and what is wrong, what is wise and what is foolish? How did the sages at the royal courts know? The sages knew that we never face a totally dark or bright situation, but usually seek our way in a grey fog where good and bad are mixed together. Wisdom thus means patiently sorting out what leads to life and what to death. But how did the wise men and women go about it? There were four steps in this process of discernment.

First of all they simply observed what happened around them, accumulating empirical knowledge of what is right and wrong. They started with the facts — whether these facts pleased them or not. Looking at what happened to the farmhands of rich Palestinian land owners they saw that

> The fallow ground of the poor yields much food,
> but it is swept away through injustice (13:23).

Yet not only injustice struck their eyes. They observed also that

> One man gives freely, yet grows all the richer;
> another withholds what he should give,
> and only suffers want (11:24).

In their observations of the facts of life the sages took a long view. They were not fooled by the appearances of the moment. They saw that

> A righteous man falls seven times, and rises again;
> but the wicked are overthrown by calamity (24:16).

Second, the sages did not claim to have a monopoly of wisdom. They learned wherever they could. Wisdom is not sectarian. In the book of Proverbs we find for instance a long passage (22:17-23:11) which has striking parallels with the probably much older Egyptian *Teaching of Amenemopet*. Perhaps the Old Testament sages simply took over, shortened, and edited these Egyptian wisdom sayings; perhaps both Amenemopet and they had learned it from a common older source of wisdom. There is indeed much wisdom outside the Bible and outside the Jewish-Christian faith.

Third, in observing the facts of life and learning from the wisdom of other cultures and religions the Old Testament sages discerned a certain order in life, certain causes and effects. They did not systematize the results of their observation into a natural law, but they did dare to make some tentative generalizations about this order in life. They saw, for instance, that integrity lasts longest:

> The integrity of the upright guides them,
> but the crookedness of the treacherous destroys them (11:3).

They noticed especially what good or bad consequences the wise or foolish decisions of the powerful had in the affairs of society:

> By the blessing of the upright a city is exalted,
> but it is overthrown by the mouth of the wicked (11:11).
> When the wicked rise, men hide themselves,
> but when they perish, the righteous increase (28:28).

Fourth, the wise did not transform what they had come to see into the authoritative codes, norms, and laws as the Priests did. Nor did they ever proclaim: "Thus says the Lord," which is the typical language of prophets. They were too much aware of the limitations of human knowledge:

There is a way which seems right to a man,
but its end is the way to death (16:25).

Despite such limitations, the sages did not remain silent. They became advisors to the decision-makers, teaching them by reasoning. They did not appeal to any special outside authority. Their appeal was to the facts of life, observed with a long-term perspective in mind.

What has been said so far seems no more than down-to-earth common sense, sometimes a bit naive, sometimes with glimpses of deep understanding. Is there any difference between this empirical biblical wisdom and the much older wisdom literature in Egypt and Mesopotamia, or the wisdom one finds in the twentieth century, whether among old people in African villages or among specialists in personnel management in the Western industrial world? There is in fact more to it.

The source of wisdom

Nobody looks at the facts of life without conscious or unconscious presuppositions, hidden or professed confessions of faith. What was the basic point of view, the basic creed of the Old Testament sages?

One statement occurs more often than any other in the biblical wisdom literature. With minor variations, it is said five times that "the fear of the Lord is instruction in wisdom" (15:33; cf. 1:7; 9:10; Ps. 111:10; Job 28:28; cf. Sirach 1:11-20 and many other passages from intertestamental wisdom books). In the Old Testament the term "fear of the Lord" may simply mean obedience to the divine will. Yet it also has overtones of "commitment to God," "confidence," "trust in God." This particular source of biblical wisdom has four important consequences for discerning what is good and what leads to a full life.

First, the ethics of biblical wisdom is not the self-righteous moralism of those who conform to ethical codes and obey imposed laws. It is rather the fruit of a spirituality, the outcome of a deeply responsible attitude. It consists of a life which responds to the God who created earthly realities, in whom the sages put their trust. Many of the psalms and large passages of the book of Job are moving expressions of this wisdom spirituality.

Second, the fear of God and the trust in the Creator which was intimately related to it give the sages a new attitude towards the earthly realities they observe. They do not simply describe the facts of life but confront these facts with what Hendrik Kraemer called biblical realism. This means that the sages take account not only of the present state of creation, but also of the will and purpose of the Creator. A good example of this is the editorial work the sages did on the same wisdom sayings as the Egyptian Amenemopet. Already in the initial exhortations to listen to the teaching, which are parallel in the Egyptian and biblical texts, the Old Testament sages inserted a reminder of the purpose of all wisdom teaching: "that your trust may be in the Lord" (22:19a). The Egyptian text then continues:

> Guard thyself against robbing the oppressed
> and against overbearing the disabled.
> Stretch not forth thy hand against the approach of an old man,
> nor steal away the speech of the aged.

The passage from Amenemopet simply enumerates one imperative after another. The Israelite sages added references to a legal institution ("the gate") and indicated the motive for the imperatives:

> Do not rob the poor, because he is poor,
> or crush the afflicted at the gate;
> for the Lord will plead their cause
> and despoil of life those who despoil them (22:22f).

Here we see an intimate link between the wisdom literature and the prophetic preaching of the Old Testament. The fear of the Lord linked with the trust in the Creator motivate action and lead to responsible discernment, judgment, and decision.

Third, the same trust also liberates human beings from the crippling fears and fundamental anxieties of life. The sages abandoned to God this fundamental anxiety about the ultimate outcome of their actions and the final destiny of this world. Thus they were freed to act, from step to step. The clearest example of this is King David. After the famous prophecy of Nathan had revealed to him God's purpose with his kingship (2 Sam 7:8-12), he was free to act in the here and now, deciding and fighting, sinning and praying. He was neither as Prometheus who wanted to live without the gods nor as Atlas who thought that he must carry the whole burden of heaven. This attitude of reverence and trust is the basic expression of faith in the Old Testament, the conviction that depite all outward appearances God "has the whole world in his hands" as the well-known spiritual affirms. God's design is unshakable. Such faith and trust mark all those who live according to the wisdom spirituality.

Finally, trust in God is a response to God's faithfulness and his trust in human beings. Indeed, in the Old Testament wisdom literature human beings are essentially seen as those who have been entrusted with the creation. Therefore the sages advised the kings and all people to take up this challenge of stewardship over creation, to explore the world, to work with creation so that full life may develop for all:

> It is the glory of God to conceal things,
> but the glory of kings is to search things out (25:2).

In the creation story of Genesis 2, which is strongly influenced by this wisdom perspective, the earth is pictured as a desert which can flower and bring forth life only if the Creator gives rain and if man tills the ground (Gen. 2:5). Man is thus seen as the co-creator with God, the trusted steward of all the human and material potentialities of this earth.

Wisdom incarnate

The sages at the courts of David and Solomon were a bit too optimistic about the human ability to be responsible stewards of this earth and to cope with the far-reaching decisions involved in this vocation. As a matter of fact, later sages, like the author of Ecclesiastes, were much more sober, even pessimistic. They were deeply aware of the ambiguity and even the futility of all human search for the fulness of life. They doubted that human attempts would ever be able to make this earth a place of justice and joy (Eccl. 1). In the time between the Old and the New Testaments, the sayings of the sages became more and more combined with apocalyptic visions of cosmic catastrophes (see the book of Daniel and such intertestamental writings as the book of Baruch). According to these later sages God took a horrible risk by entrusting this earth to men and women such as we are. Thus the sages looked for a new intervention of God in history.

Christian believers affirm that precisely such a new divine intervention has happened in the life and teaching, death and resurrection of Jesus of Nazareth. What was Jesus' attitude to the Old Testament wisdom tradition? How did the early church see the relationship between Jesus and the wisdom tradition? Several New Testament scholars have explored this question in depth, but a few things can be confidently affirmed after even a cursory reading of the New Testament with this question in mind.

Jesus often taught like a wisdom teacher. Matthew especially shows him to us as such in his gospel, for example in the parables of the wise and the foolish stewards (24:45-51; 25:14-30) or of the wise and foolish girls (25:1-13). Jesus' sayings have the same vivid and illustrative flavour as Old Testament proverbs: a typical example is the end of the Sermon on the Mount, where Jesus compares the one who listens to his teaching and acts on it to a wise man who builds his house on the rock while the foolish build on sand (Matt. 7:24-27).

What distinguishes Jesus' wisdom teaching from that of the Old Testament sages is a great sense of urgency. According to him the moment of truth and ultimate decision has arrived. One might say that the ethics of the book of Proverbs is very much an ethics for penultimate realities and decisions, such as questions concerning the wise or foolish use of our health and our wealth. The ethics of Jesus, however, challenges us to face the ultimate realities and decisions: What is the meaning of our life, the final purpose of this earth? "What will it profit a man, if he gains the whole world and forfeits his life?" (Matt. 16:26).

What is this true life? How does wisdom become visible? Here is another important difference between the Old and the New Testaments. For the earliest wisdom literature it was human conduct which revealed both wisdom and foolishness. In the later Old Testament wisdom sayings, however, a tendency developed to visualize wisdom as a person. Thus the theological preface to the old wisdom sayings of Proverbs (ch. 1-9), written relatively late, pictures wisdom as a woman who invites us into her house so that we may have communion with her (Prov. 9:1-6). Highly sexual language is sometimes used in the wisdom literature written during the second and first centuries B.C. (for example Sirach 24:19-22). In another intertestamental writing personified wisdom also appears as a manifestation of God, especially of his glory and creative power:

> Wisdom, the fashioner of all things, taught me....
> She is a breath of the power of God,
> and a pure emanation of the glory of the Almighty ...,
> a spotless mirror of the working of God (Wisdom 7:22ff).

In the New Testament this personalized wisdom is sometimes identified with Jesus (Matt. 11:19; John 1:1-18, which does not however use the term "wisdom"; 1 Cor. 1:24f, 30). To follow his way is to be on the way of wisdom. For the Old Testament sages the true source of wisdom was what they called "the fear of the Lord," trusting the Creator-God and being responsible to him. In the New Testament this becomes much more explicit: the source of true wisdom is communion with Jesus. It is not laws and codes that let us discern what is ultimately good and evil but, as the apostle Paul wrote, our conformity with the mind of Christ (Phil. 2:5), our following the way of Jesus. Even more strongly than the Old Testament wisdom literature, the gospels and Paul's letters propose an ethic which is not a slavish following of rules, but the outcome of a spirituality, of a "renewed mind" (Rom. 12:2).

In the New Testament the search for wisdom finally narrows down to the question of what is the mind and the way of Jesus? The answer from the gospels is clear: it is the mind of loving self-giving for others, it is the way to the cross. Whether we like it or not, whether we accept it or not, this apparently foolish wisdom of the cross belongs to the centre of the New Testament. It is at the very heart of Jesus' teaching: "Whoever would save his life will lose it, and whoever loses his life for my sake will find it" (Matt. 16:25).

This New Testament understanding of wisdom was most radically stated by the apostle Paul when he wrote to the Christians in Corinth. In their spiritual enthusiasm they wanted to base their faith on human wisdom. They boasted of their belief in the risen Lord and forgot Christ's crucifixion. Challenging all faith which bypasses the cross, Paul wrote:

> We preach Christ crucified,
> a stumbling block to Jews and folly to Gentiles,
> but to those who are called, both Jews and Greeks,
> Christ the power of God
> and the wisdom of God (1 Cor. 1:23f).

Paul knew that God's weakness at the cross is stronger than human power, God's folly of the cross is wiser than human wisdom.

A practicable ethics?

In search for wisdom we come to stand face to face with the crucified Christ. The powerful of this earth will not forever need to play the role of

Prometheus and Atlas. There is a third figure in between, who shows the way in the human search for wisdom.

This is exactly what Dag Hammarskjöld experienced when he surrendered himself to the biblical God. He met God in the shape of the crucified Lord, the one who sacrificed his life for others and thus opened a way out of the vicious circle of greed and violence. It was the passion narrative of the gospels, together with the psalms, that Hammarskjöld read and meditated on most often in the Bible. He knew that surrender to the biblical God implies readiness to go the way of the cross:

> I came to a time and place where I realized that the Way leads to a triumph which is a catastrophe, and to a catastrophe which is a triumph, that the price for committing one's life would be reproach, and that the only elevation possible to man lies in the depth of humiliation (*Markings*, p. 169).
> The price you must pay for your own liberation through another's sacrifice, is that you in turn must be willing to liberate in the same way, irrespective of the consequences to yourself (*Markings*, p. 163).

The search for wisdom ultimately reaches the cross. Hammarskjöld, who held what was called "the most impossible job in the world," learned that for the powerful there is only one way: the way of self-sacrifice.

Can this New Testament wisdom ethics really be practised in the ecclesiastical, economic, and political power struggles of today? Could it become the ethics for churches and multinational corporations, the ethics for US and Soviet politics? I guess the answer is "No!" Yet perhaps the question is wrongly put. Sometimes we must do what seems impossible. The really decisive question is not whether this ethics is practicable, but whether our present world situation does not *demand* such an impossible ethics of personal and corporate self-giving and sacrifice.

If one listens to the predictions of the Club of Rome and other perceptive observers of the tides of our time, one gets a truly apocalyptic vision of our human predicament on this spaceship called Earth. I am not competent to decide whether the members of the Club of Rome are really wise and prophetic men and women. If they are, then the Old Testament wisdom ethics of the Proverbs is not good enough for our situation, nor is it good enough simply to seek a code of ethics for maintaining an honest *status quo*. We must then think much more radically; and the seemingly unrealistic New Testament wisdom ethics would indeed be more realistic to our present world situation than all our talk about the hard fact of economic competition and political power struggles.

The real question to ask is not whether the New Testament wisdom ethics looks practicable. The real question which all of us must answer is the following: How can the impossible become practicable? How can we make at least a few first steps towards an ethics of sacrifice within the present power structures?

6 GOD AND THE POWERLESS

The biblical search for justice

Substantial parts of the following material have been used in many groups as an introduction and conclusion for Bible studies on the prophecy of Amos, on the social legislation in Deuteronomy, on the *anawim*—passages in Zephaniah, on Psalm 22, Jeremiah 20:7-18, and Isaiah 53. On other occasions a summary of the Old Testament parts of the following material has been used as an introduction to studies on such New Testament passages as the first Beatitude (Matt. 5:3/Luke 6:20) and the credal statement in 2 Corinthians 8:9.

The form in which this material appears here is a shortened version of the third Burgmann College lecture (cf. introduction to previous study).

Too often we speak about the poor and the powerless in their absence. To help us recall their presence among us on this earth we will let some of these powerless people look at us and question us through the work of some artists.

Five slides are projected, with brief commentaries. The works of art I have used are these:

1. Zatkine's monument commemorating the bombing of Rotterdam. The poor and powerless are people in war zones, who know only destruction and hatred. Desperately they try to protect themselves from the fire falling from the skies.

2. Ernst Barlach's sculpture of a Russian beggar. All over the world there are victims of oppression, people without faces. Society has forced them into situations in which they lose their human dignity and their right to speak — whether it is among blacks in Southern Africa, deprived of basic human rights through the unjust legislation of a government which claims to be Christian, or among the people hidden away in psychiatric clinics by the repression of an authoritarian government, as happens in the Soviet Union, or among men and women tortured in the prisons of Latin American military regimes.

3. Takeji Asano, woodcut of a blind woman. Powerless are those who suffer from illness, like this woman crying out for eyesight. Millions of illiterate people are exploited outcasts in our society, as are the physically and mentally disabled, the dying.

4. Käthe Kollwitz, lithograph of a mother and hungry child. The hungry ones who somehow survive far below the minimum standards for life are reduced to utter poverty and powerlessness. Thousands of people know daily the horrors we see in this lithograph — the utter incomprehension in the eyes of the child and the misery of a mother who has no bread to give.

5. Erdmann-Michael Hinz, Cain. Finally, we must not forget the misery and helplessness of those who suddenly realize that they have missed the purpose of their life, that they are hollow men and women, playing meaningless roles imposed on them, living in idle motion, as one sees it in the face of this Cain, who realizes in the moment of truth after murdering Abel what he has done.

Two responses to the cries of the powerless

What is our attitude towards these poor and powerless of this earth? We can of course attempt to ignore them. We can try to close our eyes to their unspeakable suffering, close our ears to the cries of pain and anger shouted at the doorsteps of our private lives. Yet how much longer can we continue to shut ourselves off from the misery of this world?

For many centuries such indifference to the poor and the powerless has been challenged by individuals and groups in all continents. The most common response to the reality of human misery is that of compassionate service. The Red Cross is probably the agency most commonly associated with this first response. Christian missions also have a long record of initiating charitable activities — opening homes for the blind and the deaf, pioneering in education and medical care for the poor, initiating development in rural areas and social work in city slums.

That kind of service is continued by many international organizations. In the World Council of Churches, this service among the powerless involves more staff members and more money than any other aspect of the Council's work. Emergency programmes for areas of natural disasters and war are organized, refugees are resettled, and service teams sent into poverty-stricken areas. Money, food, and clothing are collected and large rehabilitation schemes initiated. This is one way of relating to the poor and powerless.

Since Karl Marx wrote his *Communist Manifesto* a second way of dealing with the worldwide scandal of poverty and the exploitation of the powerless has grown in strength: the poor are organized and encouraged to ask not for charity but for justice. They refuse to remain the object of service activities. Instead of struggling to get the rich and mighty to do more *for* them, they themselves initiate political action for a transfer of power. In poverty they have discovered the power of the powerless. Today it is not only Marxists, but also many Jews and Christians and believers of other faiths or secular ideologies who stand on the side of the poor and struggle with them to break out of the vicious circle of poverty. This lay behind the World Council of Churches' organization of its Programme to Combat Racism, and it explains why many people are calling for a new economic order.

Where does the biblical God stand in this search for justice? Must those who follow him make a choice between these two ways of relating to the powerless? Is the biblical God with those who respond with compassionate service or is he on the side of those who join the struggle of the powerless for a transfer of power? Or might there be a third relationship to the powerless which goes deeper than either of these two? We will examine some biblical evidence with these questions in mind.

Prophetic protest and legislation

The first thing we must say is that the Bible does not romanticize poverty, powerlessness, or weakness. It is important to emphasize this because there has always been a tendency in Christian spirituality to despise physical health, the human body, the material things of this world, including power and riches. This tendency comes more from Greek thinking than from the Bible.

Before the Babylonian exile the Israelites thought of God's blessing essentially in terms of material wealth, many children, large harvests, health and a long life, peace in their own land and victory in war (cf. Deut. 28:2-6). This "biblical materialism" must not be too quickly "spiritualized." *Shalom*, that all-embracing peace and wellbeing which the biblical God promises, affects the whole person, all of society, and the entire cosmos. We must not too quickly reduce it to "peace of mind" and the "salvation of souls." This biblical materialism continued in the New Testament; Jesus healed the sick, transformed water into wine at a marriage feast, and promised God's kingdom which is nothing less than a new heaven and a new earth. Significantly, the Bible ends with the great vision of Jewish and Christian hope:

> I saw a new heaven and a new earth ...
> I heard a loud voice from the throne saying,
> "Behold, the dwelling of God is with men.
> He will dwell with them, and they shall be his people,
> and God himself will be with them;
> He will wipe away every tear from their eyes,
> and death shall be no more,
> neither shall there be mourning, nor crying nor pain anymore,
> for the former things have passed away."
> And he who sat upon the throne said:
> "Behold, I make all things new" (Rev. 21:1-5).

This positive evaluation of health, joy, and even material wealth, this totality of *shalom* which is the will of the biblical God, implies a very specific attitude towards those who are poor, ill, oppressed, and utterly powerless. In the ancient Mesopotamian societies contemporary with the Old Testament believers, illness and poverty were seen as a fate, a punishment from the gods, or as a sign of the human inferiority of the poor, sick, and powerless. The writers of the Old Testament, by contrast, saw miserable poverty and powerlessness first of all as a scandal. It indicated to them that the wealthy, who had been entrusted with God's blessing, were not fulfilling their trusteeship according to God's will. The Israelite believers never forgot that this whole earth and all its riches are God's possession (Ps. 24:1-2), and that man's status in this world is that of a steward. The human trustees of God's creation must use and administer the gifts entrusted to them according to the will of the divine Creator and owner. Because many powerful Israelites forgot their trusteeship, a scandalous poverty and exploitation of the powerless began to develop even among God's elect people. This situation became acute when the Israelite tribes entered Canaan and gradually changed their nomadic style of life to that of landowners and city-dwellers.

At that moment the biblical God revealed himself as the defender of the poor. Through the prophets of the eighth century B.C. — Amos, Hosea, Micah, Isaiah — he chastised the hypocrisy of the rich who brought fat calves to be sacrificed on the altars of Bethel and Gilgal but in fact worshipped their wealth and oppressed the poor.

> Thus says the Lord:
> "For three transgressions of Israel, and for four,
> I will not revoke the punishment;
> because they sell the righteous for silver,
> and the needy for a pair of shoes,
> they that trample the head of the poor into the dust of the earth,
> and turn aside the way of the afflicted!" (Amos 2:6-7).

The prophetic protest shaped the whole legislation of the book of Deuteronomy:

> To the Lord your God belong heaven and the heaven of heavens, the earth with all that is in it.... The Lord your God is God of gods and Lord of lords, the great, the mighty, and the terrible God, who is not partial and takes no bribe. He executes justice for the fatherless and the widow, and loves the sojourner, giving him food and clothing. Love the sojourner therefore; for you were sojourners in the land of Egypt (Deut. 10:14, 17f).

This new, updated edition of the Mosaic law made a strong call for compassion towards the poor and the powerless. Within the boundaries of Canaan, the Mosaic law therefore fully supports the first response to poverty we mentioned, that of generous charity and compassionate service.

But Deuteronomy goes far beyond mere charity. The second response to scandalous poverty and powerlessness, that of social and political action and change, is rooted in part in the Israelite legislation of the seventh and sixth centuries B.C. Not only the rights of the powerful but also those of the poor are being legally defended. The laws give directives on how to order society with justice. Rich landowners are legally obliged not to harvest the whole of their fields, so that the poor may glean the rest (Deut. 24:19-22). Part of the tithe must be given to poor immigrants, orphans, and widows (Deut. 14:28-29). The same legislation orders the landowners to give a regular daily pay to the hired labourers (Deut. 24:14-15). It severely forbids lending money at interest to Israelites (Deut. 23:19-20) as well as exploiting the poor through the perversion of legal practices (Deut. 24:17-18).

It was probably just before the Babylonian exile that such ancient Israelite customs as the Sabbath Year and later the Year of Jubilee were legally fixed in the holiness laws (Lev. 25, cf. Exod. 23:10-11; Deut. 15:7-11). Although these laws were never fully enforced, they remain remarkable documents of the search for justice, especially if one evaluates them in their own historical setting and compares them with the social situation of the ancient Middle East (cf. study II/4).

Jesus and the powerless

What was the attitude of Jesus to the poor and powerless of his time? How did he take up the Old Testament's call for generous compassion and its concern for structures of justice?

The first thing that becomes clear in reading the gospels is that Jesus *saw* the poor and powerless, *heard* their outcry, and opened his heart to them. There is a kind of compassion with closed eyes which gives generously to alleviate "poverty" but never dares to look at poor people. Jesus did not give in such an uninvolved way. He noticed the misery of lepers at the roadside and of a tax collector who was a rich collaborator with the Roman oppressors. He even had eyes for the children at a time when children had no status at all in society. Therefore the poor, the ill, and the despised came to him. He did not reject them; on the contrary he invited them: "Come to me, all who labour and are heavy laden, and I will give you rest" (Matt. 11:28).

The Greek words used in this saying refer to people who do heavy slave labour. Many of those who came to Jesus must have been exploited farmhands of the rich landowners, the so-called "poor of the land" who had to struggle day and night for the survival of their families. They had no time to observe all the Sabbath laws. Therefore they were despised both by the rich Sadducees and the rigorous Pharisees. According to Matthew's testimony Christian mission actually began as a spontaneous response of Jesus' compassion as he faced the scandal of poverty and powerlessness: "When he saw the crowds, he had compassion for them, because they were harassed and helpless, like sheep without a shepherd" (Matt. 9:36). Jesus therefore sent out his disciples on a mission of healing to announce the coming kingdom where there would be no more poverty, oppression, and perdition.

Yet the ministry of Jesus does not stop at compassion. As in the Old Testament there is a development beyond charity to the search for justice. Luke's account of Jesus' first public teaching is significant in this respect. During the synagogue worship on a Sabbath morning in Nazareth Jesus read the great prophecy in one of the last chapters of the book of Isaiah. It announces that God's anointed will come with the power of God's Spirit:

> to preach good news to the poor ...
> to proclaim release to the captives ...
> to set at liberty those who are oppressed,
> to proclaim the acceptable year of the Lord
> (Luke 4:16ff; cf. Isa. 61:1f).

At that point Jesus interrupted his reading of the Old Testament passage — which goes on to announce the "day of vengeance." It is as if Jesus wanted to put the accent on the last part of his quotation: "to proclaim the acceptable year of the Lord." This "acceptable year of the Lord" is almost certainly a reference to the Year of Jubilee. It is therefore probable that Jesus understood his whole ministry to be the initiation of a new Year of Jubilee, the true and final one. This implies a fundamental change with respect of land-ownership. It implies liberation from slavery and remission of debts and initiates a time for rejoicing and praising the Lord.

God's "anawim"

With all this we have not yet mentioned the most amazing and radical way of the biblical God to deal with the scandal of poverty. If we want to follow Christ we must not only go beyond charity to the search for a just society. We must go beyond this human justice to something even deeper, something for which it is difficult to find the right word. One might call it "divine justice," the "victory of the cause of God," "*shalom*," or simply "love" — if we are ready to fill this much-abused term with the meaning the crucified Lord has given it.

Before commenting on this third and deepest response to poverty and powerlessness we must state clearly that it does not cancel out either compassionate service or the struggle for justice. Rather, we must see it as a spirituality and motivation which enables us to go on doing compassionate service even when the sources of human compassion have dried up, and to stay involved in the struggle for justice even when our human hopes for success have been shattered. This spirituality lets us take the first and the second ways to the end, and usually means self-sacrifice.

This particular spirituality, which had the deepest impact on Jesus and the early church, developed only gradually in the course of Israel's spiritual journey. Often it is called the spirituality of the *anawim*. This Hebrew term has been translated "the humble," "the meek," "the poor," but none of these grasps the full meaning. Often it is used together with other Hebrew terms which are used almost interchangeably, especially *ani, rash, dal,* and *ebiōn*. Originally all these terms simply referred to social and economic poverty and dependency. They designate those who are low and dependent (*ani, anaw*) in contrast to those who are wicked and brutally violent. Or they point to the economically poor (*rash*) in contrast to rich. They refer to the weak and powerless (*dal*) in contrast to the high and mighty; or to the miserable one, the beggar, somebody who suffers innocently (*ebiōn*) in contrast to those in positions of economic and social privilege. Often these shades of meaning overlapped, and the terms tended to be seen as synonymous. But in the late seventh century B.C. *ani* and *anawim*, and later also *ebiōn*, received a new and deeper meaning.

It was probably the lonely and little-known prophet Zephaniah who first used *anawim* in this qualitatively new sense. His prophecies are generally dated around 630 B.C., that is towards the end of what is called the dark age of Judah. The majority of the population of the Northern Kingdom of Israel had been deported to Assyria, and the small remaining Judean kingdom had lost its political freedom. Under the influence of the powerful Assyrian empire Israel was rapidly losing its cultural and religious identity. In the temple of Jerusalem sacrifices were offered to the gods of Canaan and Assyria, while the rest of the land was full of witchcraft. Corruption marked the king and his ministers, the priestly class, and even the official prophets.

Then the Scythians, fearful hordes of warriors from Central Asia, invaded the Assyrian empire and swept over Palestine. It is possible that Zephaniah discerned in this historical event a sign of the end, a sign of God's judgment. He therefore addressed a radical message of judgment to the leaders in Jerusalem:

> Her officials within her are roaring lions;
> her judges are evening wolves
> that leave nothing till the morning.
> Her prophets are wanton, faithless men;
> Her priests profane what is sacred,
> they do violence to the law (Zeph. 3:3-4).

God's traditional agents among the covenant people — the kings, priests, prophets, and sages — had failed. Was there any hope left?

Zephaniah saw a dim hope only for those and through those who usually don't count, namely the *anawim*. These poor and humble ones would become the chosen servants of God. The inhabitants of Jerusalem are told:

> I will remove from your midst
> your proudly exultant ones,
> and you shall no longer be haughty,
> in my holy mountain.
> For I will leave in the midst of you
> a people humble (*ani*) and lowly (*dal*).
> They shall seek refuge in the name of the Lord,
> those who are left in Israel;
> they shall do no wrong
> and utter no lies ... (3:11-13).

While economic and other kinds of poverty remained a scandal for Zephaniah, he began to see dimly a possible transformation, in which the *anawim* could themselves become instruments for the victory of God's cause. His advice must have sounded enigmatic to the Israelites of the seventh century:

> Seek the Lord, all you humble/poor (*anawim*) of the land,
> who do his commands;
> seek righteousness, seek humility/poverty (*anawa*);
> perhaps you may be hidden
> on the day of the wrath of the Lord (2:3).

Many of those who first prayed the psalms learned this spirituality of the *anawim* in their struggle of prayer. Job is another person who deeply incorporated that new and deeper meaning of the term *anawim*. The Old Testament passages which express this spirituality most deeply are the servant songs of the unknown Prophet of the Babylonian exile, especially the famous poem in Isaiah 53. The first one who fully incorporated the new vision of Zephaniah, however, was none other than Jeremiah. He called himself an *ebiōn* (Jer. 20:13), and it is in his prayers and confessions (11:18-12:6; 15:10-21; 17:14-18; 18:18-23; and 20:7-18) that we see most clearly the self-understanding of the *anawim*.

Like Amos and Isaiah in the eighth century, Jeremiah denounced the high and mighty because they did not put their trust in the Lord and therefore selfishly exploited the poor. For a time he probably made common cause with the Deuteronomic reformers who elaborated a just legislation (Jer. 11:1-8). When King Zedekiah — probably in connection with a Sabbath or Jubilee Year — had proclaimed liberty to the Hebrew slaves only to see the powerful take them back, Jeremiah publicly exposed this hypocrisy and proclaimed "liberty to the sword, to pestilence, and to famine" (Jer. 34:17). Yet all this pleading for passionate service and all this involvement in the struggle for justice yielded no results. Jeremiah was accused of treason, imprisoned, misunderstood, derided and abandoned even by his friends. Total powerlessness marked his life: "I was like a gentle lamb led to the slaughter" (Jer. 11:19).

Yet this "lamb" did not passively submit. A holy anger broke out of this "meek" one, and he looked forward to God's vengeance upon the wicked (Jer. 11:20; 15:15). However, his misery was even deeper than that caused by outward enmity and powerlessness. His whole faith and hope were at the point of breaking. He struggled with fear and doubts, reaching the decision to desert God's cause (Jer. 20:9). He even cursed the day of his birth (Jer. 15:10f; 20:14ff). Then, like the Israelite who first prayed Psalm 22, Jeremiah finally threw himself into the arms of his incomprehensible God. He could no longer turn to his own power and prestige nor to the help of friends. He could only look to God and stretch out his empty hands. "To thee have I committed my cause" (Jer. 20:12).

There is in this "poor of the Lord" no resignation to the state of the world, no submission to the fate of poverty, oppression, and misery, none of the apathy (*apatheia*) so highly prized by Stoic philosophers. Jeremiah did not simply become an Atlas, steadfastly carrying the weight of heaven on his shoulders, nor was the passion of his prayers that of a Promethean revolt against God. He did not seek a proud self-reliance or simply a transfer of power.

> One of the best visual interpretations of such an Old Testament "poor of the Lord" is a small clay figure which the East German sculptor Erdmann-Michael Hinz, then only sixteen years old, modelled a few months before his untimely death. (Project a slide of this sculpture on the screen.) Hinz called it "the praying beggar": it is a young man who looks up to heaven in utter misery and holds up his disproportionately large hands with a passionate gesture. These hands are empty. (Project a slide with a close-up of the hands.) The beggar is one of the many people who, lacking any human hope or resources, either fall into deep despair or throw themselves utterly into the hands of God. This beggar has nothing any more to give. Yet exactly such a scandalous poverty and misery can be transfigured into the radical power of love. Those with empty hands have no charity to give. They can only give themselves. It is from such *anawim* that we can learn how to give generously. They can teach us the way of compassionate service.

As the spirituality of the "poor of the Lord" developed further, the vindications of the *anawim* themselves became less central. It was seen more clearly that what is ultimately at stake is the cause of God himself, *his* justice, peace, and reign, the ultimate victory of *his* design. This led to the insight of the necessary vicarious poverty and suffering of God's servant (Isa. 53). From such *anawim* we must learn the cost and the aim of all struggles for liberation and justice.

Jesus and the powerless

The ultimate image and incarnation of the "poor of the Lord" is Jesus nailed on the cross. Words fail as we stand facing him.

> Let us therefore try to see him through the eyes of two contemporary artists. (Projection of a slide with the crucifix by the Peruvian Indian sculptor Edilberto Merida, followed by silent contemplation.) He is the one who "emptied himself, taking the form of a servant ... and became obedient unto death, even death on the cross" (Phil. 2:6ff). Of him the early Christians confessed, as Paul reminded the Corinthians: "Though he was rich, yet for your sake he became poor, so that by his poverty you might become rich" (2 Cor. 8:9). (Projection of a slide with the majestic crucifixion mural painted by the Cameroonese artist Engelbert Mveng, followed by silent contemplation.) From the cross he gives his benediction with outstretched hands. From there he shows the way through and beyond compassion, through and beyond struggles for human justice, to God's all-embracing peace. Utterly powerless on the cross, the crucified Lord wins God's cause.

7 THE COMING OF THE CHRIST

Messianic hopes and Christ's incarnation

The worksheets and script for this study are designed for a two days' retreat during Advent, but individual steps in this process can easily be omitted or singled out as independent shorter studies. The worksheets on "Messianic expectations" and "The coming of Christ" should be copied for distribution to the participants at the appropriate time. The woodcut of Asano should also be available, either as a slide or enlarged as a poster.

The hopes by which we live

Nobody can live without hope. Without it people fall into a despair, which may in extreme cases lead to suicide. One finds this insight not only in the Bible: the Greek philosopher Plato (fourth century B.C.) noted that human existence is shaped by what we hope and how we hope. One good way to know one another is to reflect together about our hopes and the expectations we discern among our neighbours and friends.

Task 1: Think of three friends, neighbours, or colleagues, and try to describe what these persons hope or fear: their short-term provisional hopes and their ultimate hope, as well as the despairs which threaten their lives.

After each participant thinks about this individually, reflections on present-day hopes and anxieties in the milieu of the participants are shared in small group discussions.

An alternative way to stimulate reflection about current hopes is to place before group members a collection of evocative photographs, taken from illustrated magazines or especially prepared for this method of "photo-language." Each participant chooses two or three photographs which seem best to express the prevalent hopes or anxieties among his or her friends, neighbours and colleagues. In small groups the participants then tell one another why they have chosen these particular photographs and which hopes or fears they see expressed in the images.

By reflecting about the hopes and anxieties of our friends, neighbours, and colleagues we have in an indirect way already touched the hopes by which we ourselves live and the despairs which sometimes make life almost unbearable. For none of us is an island. The prevalent hopes and fears of our environment mark us strongly. Nevertheless, each of us is unique. Each of us has also very personal hopes and anxieties. These are too intimate to discuss openly with people we do not know very well. But Advent is the right time to reflect about the intimate hopes and anxieties which help or hinder us to live. We cannot simply hide behind the hopes and fears of our time and milieu. Nor can we take over the biblical hopes and expectations in an uninvolved and totally objective way. Our own hidden anxieties must be overcome by them, and our own intimate hopes must be transformed by them.

Task 2: Make a silent inventory of your most intimate anxieties and hopes, both your short-term fears and expectations and your ultimate anxiety and hope.

> The results of this individual meditation should not be shared with the group. However, the retreat programme must allow for free time during which participants who wish to do so may talk about their fears and hopes with somebody whom they deeply trust, and the arrangements for such pastoral opportunities should be announced.

The hopes of the Israelites

The book of Job illustrates a revealing conflict of hope. Job's pious and well-meaning friends had a doctrine of hope which they preached incessantly to the complaining and despairing Job: "The hope of the godless man shall perish" (Job 8:13). "Is not your fear of God your confidence, and the integrity of your ways your hope?" (Job 4:6). The doctrine was clear cut: only those who feared God and lived according to his commandments could have a true and lasting hope. If Job despaired, that was evidence of his godlessness.

But Job's experience pointed to the fallacy in that doctrine. Although he had indeed feared God and lived a just life with full integrity, everything in which one hopes had been taken away from him: earthly possessions, children, true fellowship with his wife and friends, and finally even his health (Job 1-2). "My days are swifter than a weaver's shuttle," he complained, "and come to their end without hope" (Job 7:6). "My hope has he (God) pulled up like a tree" (Job 19:10).

Job's friends had become self-righteous by insisting on their own faith and hope — which was a faith in their faith rather than in the God who alone gives hope. To preach such a hope, based on the integrity of your own life, is not consolation but self-righteous judgment. Job, however, learned to hope against hope. In the midst of the ruins of his former hopes he finally discovered that neither our human capacity of hoping nor the integrity of our life can become the anchor of true hope. Nothing except God himself can be the content of our hope. Job no longer hoped for something, but for someone, the living God.

Such a conflict of hopes characterizes the whole history of the people of Israel. Job's way from human hope to despair and then to hope in God alone is a parable of what the Israelites had to struggle through again and again.

We can observe two main tendencies in the Old Testament articulations of hope. The first is related to the Exodus and Sinai-tradition, in which hope means essentially the expectation that the God who had led the people out of slavery would manifest himself again and establish his kingship over his people. The decisive period of Israel's history lay in the past, and the expectation was in the first place a hope for the restoration of this "canonical" period, when God himself was king, when he led his elect people in his wars and provided them rest and peace in the land which he had promised them.

The second tendency of hope among Israelites originated in the anointing of David as king over all Israel and his establishment in Jerusalem around 1000 B.C. This second type of expectation is less oriented to the re-establishment of a past situation, because around the figure of David and the subsequent Davidic kings the hopes for the coming of a personal Messiah crystallized. It is this second tendency within Israelite hope, that of the messianic expectations, which we are going to study.

Changing images of the Messiah

Throughout their history the Israelites maintained that it was God alone who would establish his kingdom. This is true for both the hope related to the Exodus event and that centred on the messianic king. The expected era of salvation is pictured either as the rest which God gives after a new Exodus or as the messianic era after the coming of the Messiah. Both visions of the coming age describe it as a time of all-embracing *shalom*, not only peace within the hearts of the people, not only peace among the nations, but peace embracing the total creation and manifesting itself in a harmonious living together of all creatures. In fact, it will be nothing less than a new heaven and a new earth (cf. Ps. 85; Isa. 11:6-9; 66:22).

In post-biblical Judaism the expectation of the coming of a personal Messiah became a generally accepted part of faith and worship. The fifteenth of the eighteen benedictions used in synagogue worship includes a petition "to let the shoot of David ... blossom quickly," which is a prayer for the coming of the Messiah. Just before the closing prayer in each Passover celebration the cup of Elijah is filled with wine, the door is opened, and the family rise from their seats, for according to an old legend Elijah, the forerunner of the Messiah, will come on a Passover night. The assembly may then sing the song of the martyrs: "I believe with perfect faith in the coming of the Messiah, and though he tarry, nevertheless, I do believe!"

Still, hope for the coming of the personal Messiah never played a very important role in Jewish faith. In Jesus' time all Jews hoped for the establishment of God's kingdom, but only certain groups among them expected the coming of the Messiah. However, the figure of the Messiah had become vague, because it combined too many contradictory traits.

Task 3: Visualize the figure of the Messiah according to the Old Testament and intertestamental texts (paragraphs 1-3 on the worksheet). Read these texts and then "paint" in words the portrait of the Messiah.

> The worksheet on "Messianic expectations" is distributed, and the group is divided into three subgroups, each taking one of the three paragraphs, and subsequently reporting to one another in the plenary.

The portrait of the Messiah changed in the course of centuries from the Davidic king to the expected new David, who is still an earthly ruler but whose kingship takes on cosmic dimensions, and finally to the priestly Messiah who — through the figure of Aaron — is depicted in the book of Sirach with all his splendour:

(God) clothed him with superb perfection,
and strengthened him with the symbols of authority,
the linen breeches, the long robe, and the ephod.
And he encircled him with pomegranates,
with very many golden bells around about,
to send forth a sound as he walked ... (Sir. 45:8ff).

Despite some variations, the picture of the Messiah had thus far remained quite distinctive, so that people could be expected to recognize him when he came. But in the second and first centuries B.C. the image became blurred. Heightened messianic expectations led to combinations of the traditionally expected Messiah with other figures in the Old Testament, and the classic messianic texts were read together with other Old Testament passages which also referred implicitly or explicitly to a coming Saviour.

> At this point the enabler reads and comments on paragraph 4 of the worksheet.

Not all these texts and figures were amalgamated in a composite portrait. Some groups in the time of Jesus held strictly to the hope of the Messiah as the new David or as the messianic priest. Others looked for various combinations of the classic Messiah with some of the texts and figures mentioned in the fourth paragraph of the worksheet. The situation was confused; hopes were contradictory. And nobody expected the Messiah in the form in which Jesus incarnated him.

A shocking Messiah

We can hardly imagine how difficult it must have been for Jesus' contemporaries, even those who had become his disciples, to see in him the Messiah. We have tried to visualize the figure of the Messiah as he appears in the messianic texts of the Old Testament. Now we will look at another figure — a woodcut by the Japanese artist Takeji Asano. Although it does not portray the Messiah, perhaps in looking at it we can experience some-

thing similar to what those people in the first century felt who gradually discerned in Jesus the Messiah.

| A slide of Asano's woodcut is projected or an enlarged poster of it shown.

Task 4: Let the figure on this woodcut speak to you.
a) What do you see?
b) Which persons or texts in the Old Testament does it evoke for you?
c) Which incidents in Jesus' life and which sayings and gestures of Jesus does it evoke?

First the whole group contemplates Asano's woodcut silently. Then the enabler asks the three questions in order, soliciting spontaneous short responses to each by group members. Group members may see different things here: a spiral which is pressed together; somebody crying in the dark; a woman praying for eye-sight (Asano actually made this woodcut when his wife was in danger of becoming blind); somebody who feels God-forsaken despite the presence of God's eye. Old Testament figures and texts which will probably be mentioned are Job, Jeremiah, the one who first prayed Psalm 22, the suffering servant of Isaiah 53; New Testament scenes from Jesus' life which come to one's mind include the prayer in Gethsemane, scenes of healing, the whole drama of passion.

Our experience looking at Asano's woodcut is probably comparable to what the disciples felt when they hesitantly began to confess Jesus as the Messiah: first a lack of comprehension and even shock; then recollection of figures and passages in the Hebrew scriptures which they had never related to current messianic expectations; finally a deep change in their understanding of who the Messiah is and what his ministry was to be.

Gradually the disciples and the early church confessed Jesus as the *suffering* Messiah, the "Christ crucified," who was indeed a scandal to the Jews and folly to Gentiles, as Paul wrote (1 Cor. 1:23).

Shocking as this new way of understanding the Messiah was, the early Christians did not reject the Hebrew scriptures and the hopes of the Israelites. In these scriptures they found new key texts for understanding that way of Jesus which they at first had not been able to understand — texts like Psalm 8, Psalm 22, Isaiah 53, Isaiah 61, Zechariah 9, and Daniel 7. Later, when the gospels were written, rereading the Hebrew scriptures in the light of Jesus' messiahship had already become the standard way for Christians to do Bible study. In fact, the gospels not only witness to the new way of God's action in Jesus Christ, but they also show the deep continuity between the hopes of the Israelites and the life, death, and resurrection of Jesus. It is to this that we now turn our attention.

The coming of the Christ

At Christmas we usually tell a very eclectic version of the coming of Christ. It is therefore important to listen to the witness of all four evangelists and to become attentive to all the details in their testimony.

Task 5: Without referring to the Bible, try to remember what the four evangelists tell us about Christ's coming.

> Since people have very different levels of biblical knowledge, this task would be embarrassing for many people to tackle alone. The enabler should propose that small subgroups deal with this question, before the whole group tries to reconstruct from memory what the evangelists tell about Christ's coming. The result will probably be a mixture of Luke's and Matthew's accounts with an occasional recollection of John's prologue.

Not surprisingly, we have reconstructed from our memories especially the words recited and incidents portrayed in Christmas pageants. Yet the actual texts of the four gospels are much richer and have deeper significance.

Task 6: Read aloud with divided roles and then record Matthew 1-2 (subgroup A), Luke 1 (subgroup B), Luke 2 (subgroup C), and the prologues to Mark (1:1-13) and John (1:1-18) (subgroup D). Then listen to the recordings and answer these questions: Who are the main persons which appear in your reading? Describe the scene before your eyes as you listen to the reading. Where does the action take place? What changes of localities or perspectives occur? What Old Testament figures and passages are quoted or alluded to in your passage? What image of the Christ arises from your reading (titles, attributes, etc.)?

> Recording a dramatic scripture reading takes time, and up to two hours must be provided for this task. If the group is too small for four subgroups

with enough voices each, omit subgroup D and in the introduction to Task 6 comment briefly on the passages from Mark and John, using the relevant paragraphs on the worksheet "The coming of the Christ" (this worksheet must not yet be handed out, however). If recorders are unavailable, subgroups can still do the dramatic reading and then answer the questions on the basis of the printed text.

When the work of the subgroups is completed the worksheet "The coming of the Christ" is distributed. The enabler reads this worksheet in a plenary session and members of the subgroups may then share with one another still other discoveries they have made which are not printed on the worksheet.

Christ, our hope

We started with a reflection on the hopes by which we live. Having come to know something of the hopes of the Israelites and their changing images of the Messiah, we have now listened to the testimony of the evangelists. The Messiah has come in Jesus; a strangely disconcerting Messiah in the form of the suffering servant who is nevertheless confessed as the fulfilment of Israelite hope.

He did not fit the expectations of his contemporaries. Does he fit ours?

Task 7: If we confess that Christ is our hope, what light does this throw on our own hopes and anxieties? Write an act of worship (a praise or a confession of faith, or a song of hope, or a petition and intercession or a prayer of dedication) on the basis of the insights gained.

This can be done by each member separately; or different subgroups can be asked to prepare one of the above mentioned acts of worship, which are then brought together in a closing celebration.

8 SALVATION: HOW DO YOU SAY IT TODAY?

A series of radio talks

> The following is the script for six Lenten talks broadcast over the National Broadcasting Corporation of New Zealand during the weeks before Easter 1979. I was asked to translate seven theological key-terms for a broad contemporary public. I have included them here for three reasons. First they show how stories from the Old and the New Testaments are intimately related with one another and how they are linked up with our own life stories. Second, they attempt to translate abstract theological concepts into the biblical way of doing theology, namely telling what God has done in human history. Third, they use a typically biblical manner of communication — combining and mixing language and music, stories and songs.
>
> Study enablers may want to use some of these short talks for a series of devotions, introducing periods of silence. Alternatively, this material could be used with a choir as short introductions for learning to sing the spirituals mentioned in the script.

Salvation

Have you ever been locked in a closet? Have you been caught in a tightly limited space without being able to escape, like a prisoner in a narrow cage? Then you certainly remember the relief you felt when the door was finally opened and you could freely move again.

If you have ever been through such an experience you know perfectly well what "salvation" means. As a matter of fact, you have experienced salvation in the most literal sense possible. For in the Hebrew language, in which the Old Testament was originally written, the verb "to save" means "to provide open space for the oppressed."

The word "salvation" is first used in the Bible in connection with a political liberation. More than 3000 years ago some tribes of the people of Israel were forced into slave labour in Egypt. They had to build garrison towns for the army of the mighty Pharaoh Rameses II. Ancient mural paintings found in Egypt show Israelite labourers at work, carrying heavy stones while being cruelly beaten by slave drivers.

You may remember the story: how these Israelites cried out of the depth of their oppression, how their God called Moses and sent him to Pharaoh, and how the Israelites finally received salvation. That means that they were given room to move, out of the prison of slavery into the open space of the desert. There they found not only space to live in but the space God lives in. They called it his covenant — one could almost call it a marriage between God and them — and it knitted them together as one people.

Through the centuries this story of liberation has been told from one generation to another, first among Jews but now for almost 2000 years by Christians also. This story has become a powerful inspiration for all oppressed people. Many of you know the spiritual which sums it up in a few telling words:

> When Israel was in Egypt land,
> Let my people go.
> Oppress'd so hard they could not stand,
> Let my people go.

Did you notice that striking description of the opposite of salvation? "Oppress'd so hard they could not stand." The Israelites had no space to be upright, they were crushed down by the burden they were forced to carry. Yet then God sent Moses, and the recurring chorus of that spiritual proclaims:

> Go down, Moses,
> Way down in Egypt land,
> Tell ol' Pharaoh,
> Let my people go.

If we want to understand the meaning of salvation, we ourselves must become part of this story. When slaves sang this spiritual in the southern United States in the nineteenth century, they identified themselves with the Israelite migrant workers in Egypt. For them "Pharaoh" was no longer that ancient Egyptian emperor Rameses II. Pharaoh had taken the appearance of the white slave masters. The "promised land" was not Canaan, but the northern states, where slavery had already been abolished. In a different situation of oppression they cried out to the same God as the Israelites did. They hoped that he would send a new Moses, that he would liberate them, that he would save them.

> At this point the recording of "Go down, Moses" as sung and trumpeted by Louis Armstrong, is played.

This trumpet opens up space and therefore becomes a symbol for what salvation means. It not only opens the space by which prisoners can move out into freedom; it also opens the space, heaven, from where God reaches down and makes a marriage covenant with his people.

Like the Jews black slaves in America expected the coming of a new Moses. They hoped for a new act of liberation, a total salvation from all that constricted them and made them less than human. Since the New Testament sometimes describes Jesus as such a new Moses, it is not astonishing that most of the music of these slaves is about the saving power of the life, death, and resurrection of Jesus. The talks which follow will use some of these mighty songs to help teach the meaning of other great Christian words.

Judgment

The talk begins with the singing of the spiritual "Go down, Moses" and the trumpet sound.

Louis Armstrong's trumpet announces the liberation of Israelite migrant workers from their slave labour in Egypt. This indeed is salvation to set the oppressed free, to open up space for a full life with one another and with God. But there is another side to this story of salvation: the trumpet which proclaims release to the captives announces judgment to the oppressor.

Frankly, "judgment" is not a word I like. Too often, the proclamation of divine judgment has been misused in Christianity. Talk of hell fire makes people afraid. The bad news of God's judgment has sometimes been preached first, as if to open people's hearts by fear to receive the good news of God's salvation.

I do not believe that this corresponds to the Christian message. But do not misunderstand me. I am not proposing to drop the word "judgment" and its biting reality from our lives. In reaction against hell-fire sermons, some Christians have gone too far in the other direction, preaching the good news of God's liberating love without any reference to judgment. I'm OK, you're OK, everything's OK. But this is simply not true. No rose-coloured glasses must hinder us from seeing that the way in which people, nations, social classes, and races live together is definitely not all right. There is no salvation possible without judgment. We can be set free only if something within us and around us is being broken. Liberation has its price. The other side of salvation is judgment.

Let me illustrate this again with the words of the spiritual. In the song which retells the story of liberation from Egyptian slavery, good news for the oppressed Israelites is bad news for Pharaoh, the oppressor.

Thus said the Lord, bold Moses said:
Let my people go;
If not I'll smite your first-born dead,
Let my people go.

And as this song of salvation goes on, a famous sign for judgment appears, namely darkness:

When Israel out of Egypt came,
And left the proud oppressive land
O, 'twas dark and dismal night
When Moses led the Israelites.

The saving event happened on a "dark and dismal night." An old Jewish story tells that while Moses was leading the jubilant Israelites into freedom, God himself wept because their liberation implied judgment over the oppressor; it meant the annihilation of Pharaoh's army. We cannot escape from the fact: good news for the poor is, at least initially, bad news for the rich.

There is another salvation story in the Bible which speaks of sudden darkness and links liberation with an act of judgment. This happened at Golgotha. The evangelist Mark tells us: "It was nine o'clock in the morning when they crucified him ... At noon the whole country was covered with darkness, which lasted for three hours ... With a loud cry Jesus died" (Mark 15:25, 33, 37).

The political and religious establishment had condemned Jesus. They thought that *Jesus* was being judged when he hung on the cross and when sudden darkness covered the whole earth. They did not recognize that in fact their own pride was being broken and their own faults were being paid for.

Some women who had followed Jesus stood from afar looking at what happened. They knew that the sudden darkness pointed to the judgment coming over the whole world. They knew that things in the world and in their own lives were not "OK". They knew that there is no salvation without the breaking and the setting right of all that is wrong.

This same deep knowledge is movingly expressed in another spiritual, which asks again and again: "Were you there?" The response is: "Sometimes it causes me to tremble, tremble, tremble."

> Were you there when they crucified my Lord?
> Were you there when they pierced him in the side?
> Were you there when the sun refused to shine?

If you want to know what judgment really means, you must learn to sing and live this song.

| During the last paragraphs the spiritual "Were you there?" is played at a
| low volume. Then the volume increases and the song concludes the talk.

Justification

| The spiritual "Were you there?" is played and the volume is gradually
| turned down to give way to the spoken word.

We listened to this spiritual to help us understand what "judgment" means. In order to liberate one must break the bondage. In order to save one must judge. The good news for the oppressed is bad news for the oppressor. Salvation and judgment are intermingled in the story which tells about the liberation of the Israelite tribes from slavery in Egypt, called the Exodus. There is the same light and darkness in the story of Christ's suffering and death. That is why the black slaves in nineteenth-century North

America trembled, trembled, trembled, when they contemplated through their hymns what happened when Christ died.

And yet the salvation story of Jesus' crucifixion is not exactly the same as the salvation story of the Exodus. When Moses led the Israelite tribes out of slavery, it was upon somebody else that God's judgment fell, on the Egyptian Pharaoh, on his people and land. When Christ died on Golgotha, however, the judgment fell on Jesus himself, the new Moses. *He* paid with his agony and death the price of our liberation. Therefore we can now go beyond that dark reality of judgment. We can rediscover and live what "justification" means.

Usually we use this difficult word "justification" when we have a bad conscience. We feel accused, whether by others or by our own conscience, and we try somehow to justify our acts. You probably know people among your neighbours or in your family who live with a chronic bad conscience, a constant feeling of shortcoming. Such people feel compelled to justify themselves before their own conscience, before their colleagues and neighbours, perhaps even before God. But constant self-justification leads to a horrible unrest in our lives, because we never quite make it. Whatever good deeds we do, however hard we try, the sense of shortcoming remains.

At this point we must listen to the question of the spiritual: "Were you there when they crucified my Lord?" For the crucifixion of Jesus opens up for us a totally new meaning of what justification is all about.

It is no longer *we* who have to justify ourselves. It is no longer *we* who need to save ourselves. There on the cross is the one who carries our burden, who paid the price for our liberation. He also frees us from the compulsion to justify ourselves. There is no more need for it, because in what happened at Golgotha we meet a God who has an amazing and radical way of setting things right.

God does not overlook what is wrong with us and our society. Nor does he come as the angry and accusing prosecutor to judge the world. His way to set things right is told us by John the evangelist in these famous words:

> For God loved the world so much that he gave his only Son, so that everyone who believes in him may not die but have eternal life. For God did not send his Son into the world to be its judge, but to be its saviour (John 3:16-17).

So we are justified by God, just as we are, with all our shortcomings. It is as if someone to whom you owed a great deal of money came and tore up the bill before your eyes and said: "I have paid for you. You are free, without any conditions, without any strings."

The black slaves in the United States knew how to respond to this amazing way of God's dealing with what is wrong with us and with our world. In their hymns they sang praises and shouted thanks. Sometimes they used the words of a song which was in fact written by a former white slave-trader. This hymn, "Amazing Grace," was sung with such fervour by black congregations that it is often mistaken as a spiritual. Its words are strongly marked by a piety which is typical of the revival movements of the 1800s. Personally I am not particularly fond of this language. Nevertheless, it is a genuine response to God's justification of people such as we are.

> Amazing grace, how sweet the sound
> That saved a wretch like me.
> I once was lost, but now am found,
> was blind, but now I see.

The talk ends with a recording of this hymn.

Sanctification

The hymn "Amazing Grace" is played, gradually giving way to the spoken word.

This famous American revival hymn, written by a former slaver-trader, is a spontaneous response to what happened when Jesus died. Filled with wonder the singer recalls the amazing way in which God had set right what was wrong in the world. He describes the impact of Jesus' death on the believer's life:

> It soothes his sorrows, heals his wound,
> And drives away his fear.

But then at the end the singer asks:

> Must Jesus bear the cross alone
> And all the world go free?
> No, there's a cross for ev'ryone
> And there's a cross for me.

This intimate link between the crucifixion of Jesus and the cross that each of us has to carry brings us to the heart of the word which we want to understand in this talk — "sanctification."

"Sanctification" is like the words "saint," "saintliness," "sanctify." Hearing these words, you may perhaps imagine a halo around a face which looks so holy, so spiritualized, so otherworldly that we can hardly recognize ourselves in it. And yet in the New Testament all members of the church are called "saints." Consider for example those quarrelsome Christians in Corinth — the rich among them so insensitive to the poor in their midst; some apparently leading immoral lives, slanderers, drunkards, thieves (1 Cor. 6:11). Not exactly the kind of company one would seek. Nevertheless, the apostle Paul speaks about them as the "saints." He addressed them as "the church of God in Corinth, sanctified in Christ Jesus, called to be saints" (1 Cor. 1:2).

Obviously "sanctification" in the Bible must mean something quite different from the way we use it in ordinary talk. We usually link holiness with special qualities somebody has gained after tremendous moral efforts. But in the Old Testament holiness means first of all to be separated from the common, to have a special relationship with God. That means in a New

Testament perspective those who are related to Jesus Christ, those who follow him and share his way and life.

Perhaps you can now begin to see the intimate link between Jesus' crucifixion and our sanctification. On the one hand Jesus' death makes it possible for us to love God in the way he intended and therefore makes us holy. Holiness is thus first of all a free gift which we receive without doing anything. But justifying us, God also sanctifies us.

On the other hand there is also a more active manner of remaining in communion with God and thus on the road to sanctification. The deepest way of doing so is indicated in the challenge Jesus made to his disciples: "'If anyone wants to come with me,' he told them, 'he must forget self, carry his cross, and follow me'" (Mark 8:34). To be sanctified means to participate in God's costly love for the world. The call to holiness means that we become active participants in what happened when Jesus was crucified, in that astonishing climax of what God has done in human history. For our own sanctification cannot be isolated from God's purpose of a sanctified world. The song is correct: there *is* a cross for everyone, there *is* a cross for me.

To carry a cross is never easy. In one of the most moving spirituals, the black American singers who are on the road of sanctification confess:

> Nobody knows the trouble I see ...
> Sometimes I'm up,
> Sometimes I'm down,
> Sometimes I'm almost to the ground....

But this hymn ends with a jubilant "Glory, hallelujah!"

> During the last sentences the spiritual "Nobody Knows" is sung in the background; the talk is concluded with it played in full volume.

Resurrection

> A recording of the concluding verse of the spiritual "Nobody Knows" is sung to begin the talk.

Isn't it strange that a song which speaks about all the "troubles here below" ends with the shout: "Glory, hallelujah!"? Those who first sang that song did indeed know trouble all around. They were slaves in the southern United States. To be beaten up, even to hang on a tree, was nothing extraordinary for them. It has been said that these slaves understood the story of Christ's suffering and death not only with their minds but also with their hurting backs. Out of their own experience they could understand it much better than those who sit on easy chairs. Why then shouts of joy and thanks in the midst of this suffering? Can joy come out of pain? Can life arise from death?

Yes, it can. This is the strange truth of "resurrection," the word we want to understand in this talk.

But how do we speak about the resurrection? Have you ever noticed that the gospels report practically nothing about that mysterious event when Jesus rose from the dead? There are long descriptions of what happened when he was crucified. Many people actually saw it: the women who followed him from Galilee, the passers-by, the soldiers who nailed him on the cross. Nothing like that can be said about the mysterious event of his resurrection. True, Matthew reports about that earthquake-event when Jesus' tomb was opened and the guards fell on the ground as though dead. But the tomb was already empty. Some women and disciples later met the risen Lord, but the actual event of resurrection was seen by nobody.

A veil of mystery hangs before this crucial scene in which joy came out of pain, life out of death, when the impossible became possible. Perhaps I can best describe it in the following way: the crucifixion was an event of history happening in the midst of history, probably on April 7, A.D. 30. The resurrection of Jesus happened within history, but it was not a normal event of history. Rather the end of history was anticipated. The reality of God's kingdom appeared in the midst of our present earthly realities. And so the range of our normal human possibilities exploded.

The resurrection is like a bomb which explodes and shatters the limited space and time of ordinary lives. Have you ever noticed in the biblical accounts of Easter how people suddenly began to run? The women who had come to embalm the body run into the town to tell the disciples. The guards of the tomb run into the town in order to tell the religious authorities. The two deeply disappointed disciples who were returning home to Emmaus suddenly run back to Jerusalem after the risen Lord has met them.

To believe in the reality of resurrection means to live with a bomb in your hands. A dangerous life, because the most unlikely things can happen. It means challenging the final fact of all human life, namely death. It means singing "Glory, hallelujah!" in the midst of the troubles here on earth.

Beginning on that Easter morning, attempts were made to stop so disturbing and revolutionary a message from going out into the world. The religious authorities gave money to the frightened guards, bribing them to tell a lie: "His disciples came during the night and stole his body" (Matt. 28:13). A little later Jesus sent out his disciples with quite another message: "I will be with you always, to the end of the age" (Matt. 28:20).

This is the choice before us: to participate in the mission of a lie or in the mission of the living Christ. Shall we proclaim that death is the end, or do we dare to believe and proclaim that Jesus' death was the decisive victory, that God's kingdom comes?

In the midst of their troubles the American black slaves dared to become messengers of the resurrection. Because they believed that Jesus has risen from the dead they eagerly looked out for that other morning "when the stars begin to fall," when the trumpet sounds and the nations are risen from the dead.

You'll hear the Christians shout.
To wake the nations under ground
Lookin' to my God's right hand,
When the stars begin to fall.
My Lord, what a mornin',
My Lord, what a mornin',
My Lord, what a mornin',
When the stars begin to fall.

This spiritual is sung softly in the background, with the volume turned up to conclude the broadcast.

Redemption and atonement

The end of the spiritual "My Lord, what a mornin'" is sung.

American blacks sang this song of hope when they were still bound in slavery. Having come to know Jesus they hoped for what seemed impossible: that they would be liberated in all aspects and that they would be at peace with God and with one another, even with their slave masters. Thus their spirituals often sing about the reality which we want to explore in this talk — the reality of "redemption" and "atonement."

Perhaps I can best explain what "redemption" means by telling about the translation of this word into an African language. A team of Bible translators working among the Bambara tribe in West Africa simply could not find the right translation for the concept of redemption. Finally they described the meaning of the biblical term to some older village folk and asked them how they would say in their own language, "God redeems us." They answered: "That is very easy. You simply have to say: 'God takes our heads out of the chain.'" At first the translators did not understand, but then the village folk explained: "Our forefathers told us how the slave-traders used to come and catch strong young Africans. Their heads were put into iron rings, connected by a long chain. In this way the traders walked their victims through the African villages down to the coast. But sometimes it happened that a village chief would recognize one of his relatives in this sorry caravan to slavery. He would pay a price for the liberation of this person and then his head was literally taken out of the chain."

This is exactly what redemption means. Things and people tend to become alienated. They are used for purposes foreign to their true destiny. To be redeemed means that such alienated objects and persons regain their rightful place because somebody has paid the price of release. Redemption is thus originally a commercial and juridical term. The Bible applies it to what happens in the relationship between God, human beings, and the enslaving powers of this world: people who have become enslaved to evil powers (and each of you can fill in here your own particular slavery) are redeemed; they gain back their rightful place as God's free children. In the Bible there is no speculation at all about to *whom* the price of redemption must be paid. It becomes quite clear, however, who it was who paid the price.

This brings us to our second difficult word, "atonement." I can best explain this term too with a story. Ever since the Israelite tribes had been rescued from slavery in Egypt, they had a longing to be *at one* with their liberating God. (Notice that the original form of the English word "atonement" is actually "at-one-ment"). Yet how could the Israelites be at one with their God when so many members of the covenant people broke the love relationship with him? An ingenious way was found to re-establish each year that love relationship.

On the so-called Day of Atonement a goat was brought before the solemn assembly of the people. Listen now to what Aaron, the high-priest had to do:

> Aaron shall put both his hands on the goat's head and confess over it all the evils, sins, and rebellions of the people of Israel, and so transfer them to the goat's head. Then the goat is to be driven off into the desert by a man appointed to do it. The goat will carry all their sins away with him into some uninhabited land (Lev. 16:21-22).

Now you know where the word "scapegoat" comes from. This ritual of the Day of Atonement perhaps reminds you of the story we remember very especially during Holy Week. The goat carried the whole guilt of the people into the desert and died in place of the people and for the sake of the people. The early Christians understood the death of Jesus in a similar way.

Therefore they confidently approached God in their worship with the petition: "*Kyrie eleison*" — "Lord, have mercy upon me!" For they knew that "Christ has died for our sins," as they confessed in the words of one of the oldest Christian confessions. Praise was therefore the main tenor of their worship, shouts of joy like this "glory, hallelujah!"

> Here follows the singing of a "Glory, hallelujah!" by a large choir to conclude the series of Lenten talks.

9 THE SHEPHERD AND THE SHEEP

A parable of Jesus

The main part of this study was originally used in a one-day meeting with pastors and elders in French-speaking Switzerland. A debate had been going on about what should have priority in the church's work: spiritual upbuilding of congregational life or missionary outreach to those outside the church. I was asked to lead a work session on the priorities within the church's life; and this parable study formed the central part of the meeting.

In the following script this material has been adapted for a more general learning situation. I have often used it as the first study in training courses for Bible study enablers because it immediately raises some fundamental questions about the ways in which Jesus taught, about the process of tradition and redaction of Jesus' teaching in the early church, and about the role which the addressees and their context play in interpreting the biblical message.

It is important that the participants do *not* know beforehand which parable will be studied; and in the course of the study copies of the worksheet on "The shepherd and the sheep" must be distributed.

The language of parables

Jesus did not teach by abstract reasoning, but by telling stories. He used a very special kind of story, the parable. This was not his invention. Jewish rabbis before and after him taught in a similar way, and even in the Old Testament we find some parables. Listen to one of these.

2 Samuel 12:1-10 is read dramatically using different voices for the narrator, Nathan, and David. This reading should either be recorded beforehand and played back or rehearsed in advance by three members of the group.

Task 1: Reread this passage and write down what it teaches about the style of parables and the way they function.

After a period of individual study participants exchange their discoveries with their neighbours and then share them in plenary discussion. The following points are usually made.

It is important to notice who tells the parable to whom. In this case it is the prophet who tells the king. Equally important is the concrete situation for which a parable is told, in this case David's serious but still hidden sin. This situation is not confronted immediately and challenged directly. Instead Nathan tells a story whose link with the situation gradually appears. In such parable stories there is often something odd which deviates from the normal pattern, a sudden turn in the expected course of things, an astonishing reversal of roles or unexpected results. In this case one expects that the rich man would slaughter one of his many ewe lambs for his visitor, yet he grabs the one and only beloved ewe lamb of the poor man. Parables also involve the hearers. In this passage David actually interrupts Nathan with an angry judgment, which turns out to be a judgment on himself. Nathan had no need to explain the message, he simply could say: "You are the man!"

Because of this special nature of parables, it is important to let them speak for themselves. They are open-ended, and we must let them *evoke* meanings rather than try to *fix* the meaning once for all by saying things like "The whole point of the story is ..." Especially Jesus' parables are not simply illustrative material but have this evocative character. "The Kingdom of God is like ..."

Memory and manuscript

We now turn to one of the best-known parables which Jesus told. Since parables are not in the first place texts to be read and explained, but stories to be remembered and told, we will do an exercise of memory.

Task 2: Close your Bibles and write down from memory Jesus' parable of the lost sheep which went astray. How does it begin? How does the story proceed? How does it end? Do not omit or add any details; simply write down the text as you remember it. After reconstructing the story itself, try to remember to whom Jesus told this parable and in what context it appears in the New Testament.

> This exercise can only be done with groups who have some biblical knowledge. As this varies greatly within every group, it is essential that this "reconstruction" of the text be done in teams of two or three, not individually (this would be too threatening for many participants). After about ten minutes of teamwork the group as a whole is asked to reconstruct the text of the parable, the addressees, and the literary context, still with Bible closed. Alternative versions will emerge which may lead to debates, though my experience suggests that most participants remember Luke's version of the parable best. Some may remember or guess that the parable is recorded twice. After this exercise participants will be eager to read the actual text, and at this point the worksheets with the synopsis of Matthew 18:12-14 and Luke 15:3-7 are distributed.

Although our common effort has succeeded in reconstructing the text of the parable fairly well, our memory is quite obviously not good enough. We need what the French call an *aide-mémoire*, a "help for memory," in the form of a manuscript.

As the worksheet shows, the parable is recorded twice, once in Matthew and once in Luke. In order to discover the similarities and differences it is useful to look at a "synopsis", which places the two versions side by side in parallel columns.

Task 3: Answer the following questions on the basis of a synoptic study of this parable: (a) What is similar and what is different in Matthew's and Luke's versions of this parable? (b) What are the key terms in the texts and its literary context in Matthew's and Luke's versions? (c) Who are the addressees according to Matthew and according to Luke? (d) In what literary context did Matthew and Luke respectively place this parable? What can this context contribute to our understanding of the parable's message? (e) How could you describe the style and purpose of the parable in Matthew's and in Luke's version?

> The task can best be done in subgroups, half of them examining Matthew version (and comparing it with Luke's) and the other half examining Luke's version (and comparing it with Matthew's). When most subgroups have finished their task these groups teach and correct one another in a plenary discussion. Most of the following discoveries will then be reported.

A story for different occasions

Although this parable story is essentially the same in both versions, a careful examination reveals many variations. In Matthew Jesus begins with a direct question to the hearers: "What do you think?" The hearers' active participation in discernment and judgment is sollicited. Luke's version also begins with a question, but it is more a rhetorical question presupposing the agreement of the hearers and forming part of the story itself. According to Matthew the sheep "goes astray" (vv. 12bc, 13), ninety-nine are left on the "mountains," and the question remains open whether the shepherd will actually find the one who went astray ("and *if* he finds it," v. 13). According to Luke, however, the sheep is "lost" (vv. 4bc, 6), the ninety-nine are left "in the wilderness" and the shepherd searches "until he finds it" (v. 4).

The difference between the mountain and the wilderness must not be overemphasized. In Palestine the two designate the same locality. But it is possible that these topographical indications have theological meanings. In Matthew's gospel mountains play an important role; and the term "wilderness" in the New Testament sometimes recalls the people of Israel's stay in the wilderness. It is significant that nothing is said about a sheepfold for the ninety-nine. The shepherd takes a great risk in leaving them unprotected on the mountains or in the wilderness.

The difference between Matthew's "going astray" and Luke's "being lost" is important. Their consistent and twice-repeated use marks them as key terms, whose full significance is seen if one observes to whom the parable is told and the literary context it is set in. Matthew 18 brings together incidents and teachings concerning the life of the church. Jesus addresses himself to his disciples, who wanted to know who is the greatest in the kingdom of heaven (18:1). He answered this question first with a significant gesture (a child in the midst of them, vv. 2-4) and a teaching in which the child becomes the metaphor for "the little ones" (cf. vv. 6, 10, 14). These little ones — another key term for Matthew — are weak members of the church, sheep who went astray, brothers and sisters who sinned (cf. vv. 15-20), who must be "won back" (v. 15) and be forgiven many times (vv. 21-35). In Jesus' teaching according to Matthew the possibility of lostness is not excluded. The shepherd searches but may not find the one who went astray (v. 13; cf. v. 17). In this case the sheep is indeed lost or perished (v. 14).

Luke has put the parable in the context of a meal (14:1ff) and a discussion of the messianic banquet (14:15ff). This led to a consideration of the conditions for discipleship (14:25ff), to Jesus' attraction of "tax collectors and sinners" (15:1) and a polemic question of the "Pharisees and scribes" (15:2). It is in this context and to this double audience — the multitude of sinners on one side and the Pharisees on the other — that Jesus told the three parables about the sheep, the silver coin, and the son, all of which were lost and found (cf. 15:6, 9, 24). The lost sheep here is not a church member who went astray, but a metaphor for the sinners who do not feel righteous but need repentance (cf. Luke 18:9-14).

The second half of the parable displays typical differences between Matthew's and Luke's versions which confirm the two tendencies observed so far. Matthew's ending for the parable is abrupt. The shepherd rejoices more over the one who was found than over the ninety-nine who never went astray. In his heart there is a special love for the weak. In this he resembles the Father in heaven whose "will" is that the little ones do not perish. The "will of the Father" is a favourite expression in Matthew's gospel, which insists on God's commandments. In the fellowship with his disciples Jesus is here seen as the teacher. The parable is written in a didactic style and with a strong pastoral concern for the weak in the Christian fellowship.

According to Luke's gospel Jesus embroidered on the story of the parable. The shepherd lays the sheep on his shoulders. Joy (a typical key term in Luke and Acts) flows over from the shepherd to his friends and neighbours and even into heaven. The parable has also a double accent and effect, corresponding to its double audience. For the judgmental and self-righteous Pharisees it has a cutting edge: God, whose special favourites they believe themselves to be, rejoices over converted sinners more than over them. For the multitudes of sinners, on the other hand, the parable becomes a missionary invitation and truly good news: the shepherd searches until he finds them. Those who ordinarily do not count become the occasion for a feast, and even in heaven there is rejoicing about them.

What did Jesus say

Some may find all these differences between Matthew and Luke disturbing. But to "harmonize" the two versions or make a mixture of both of them would not take seriously what is actually written. What then is God's word and message for us in this parable? Is Matthew or Luke nearer to the original situation? Even if we believe that we must listen to both, the question remains: What did Jesus originally say?

> It may be that no members of the group are in fact disturbed by this question — in which case it need not be raised. The comments which follow may then be treated as optional input if time allows. However, if the question is asked or if the enabler senses that members of the group are worried by it, a short plenary discussion of this-subject will be necessary.

The divergences here between Matthew and Luke have been explained in four different ways — each providing a different answer to the question of what Jesus actually said.

1. Jesus may have told the parable twice, once as a teaching for his disciples (as Matthew records it) and once as a missionary invitation for the multitudes of sinners and a reprimand to the Pharisees (as Luke reports). The two evangelists would in this case have had access to two different traditions, whether oral or already written, transmitting the memory of two different occasions. No one can disprove this explanation, but few scholars accept it.

2. Some may argue that Matthew's report is the older and more accurate one, on the assumption that Matthew the gospel-writer is to be identified with Jesus' disciple Levi/Matthew, which would make his account an eye-witness report. However, in the first gospel itself the author is never identified with the apostle Matthew; and the earliest report about the origin of this gospel (from Papias, around A.D. 135) is not clear at all. Some scholars believe that the first version of Matthew's gospel, now lost, was written in Aramaic or Hebrew. Such a lost version could indeed have been the earliest gospel written. However, it is almost certain that the present Greek version of Matthew depends on Mark's gospel and was not written before A.D. 80. All of Matthew 18 deals with questions from the church of the second generation, and it is thus unlikely that the present form of Matthew's rendering of the parable reports what Jesus actually said.

3. Another explanation of the divergences starts with the Lucan account. The whole setting of the parable in Luke does indeed remind the reader of the many other occasions when Jesus was challenged by the Pharisees and in turn challenged them, and when sinners and tax-collectors sought Jesus' fellowship. Also the main message of Luke's version fits in well with what we know about Jesus' proclamation. It is thus possible that Luke's account of what Jesus actually said is the more accurate one. Nevertheless, several of Luke's favourite terms are used in his version; and it is unlikely that Jesus would have told three similar parables in succession as is now reported in Luke 15.

4. Equally — perhaps even more — probable is the explanation that Jesus originally told the parable of the shepherd and the sheep in a setting similar to that reported by Luke. The main message communicated by Jesus through the parable may have especially emphasized the "foolish"

love of God, whose heart goes out to those most in need. Such love dares to take tremendous risks. The memory of Jesus' words was then taken up into the oral tradition, but soon received different accents in Jewish-Christian and Gentile Christian circles. Both Matthew and Luke would in this case have had access to already interpreted versions of the original sayings of Jesus. Each evangelist in turn edited the context and the text of this passage in such a way that Jesus' parable spoke most clearly to the needs and questions of the churches for whom his gospel was written. They did so in the firm conviction that God's Spirit and the presence of the risen Lord guided them in their work of transmission and accentuation of Jesus' words.

If this fourth explanation of the divergences between Matthew's and Luke's versions of the parable is correct, we have here a classic example of how the early church "worked" with Jesus' sayings. "God's word" never existed in a vacuum nor can it be kept safe in a timeless vacuum. From the beginning it was spoken into a concrete human situation. Already before the gospels were written, the early church transmitted the words of God not simply by repeating them, but by reaccentuating them for new human situations. The evangelists continued this process of tradition and accentuation. By the same token we would not be taking God's word seriously if we were simply to repeat it without attempting to discover where it hits, judges, heals, and guides us today in our own human situation. Our accentuation of God's word will not have the canonical authority which that of the evangelists has, but it is as necessary for us as it was for the churches to whom Matthew's and Luke's gospels were addressed.

What do we hear today?

Task 4: Which among the biblical emphases do you in your environment need most? Do you, in the first place, hear and tell the parable as the message of God's "foolish" love, as Jesus may originally have told it? Or is there at present more need to hear and tell of Jesus' missionary proclamation and invitation to conversion and the feast addressed to the multitude of sinners, as Luke told it? Or do we rather hear and tell the story in the way Matthew did, as Jesus' pastoral exhortation to his disciples to care for the little ones in their own fellowship, the sheep who went astray? Or must we today hear and emphasize especially Jesus' reprimand which, according to Luke, he addressed through this parable to self-righteous Pharisees?

> These questions can best be discussed in small groups leading up to a general discussion.

The answers to these questions will obviously vary according to the human situation in which we find ourselves and our evaluation of this situation. None of the emphases mentioned may be dismissed arbitrarily because we do not like them or because at first sight they seem irrelevant. Nor should we make a mixture of all these accents and thus avoid the special message or cutting edge in each of them. The divergences between the two accounts of the parable found in the New Testament not only allow but invite us to search for God's special word addressed through this parable to us in our own situation today.

Both Matthew's and Luke's versions have been included in the New Testament canon. Sooner or later we have to listen to all the biblical accentuations, though one may remain more timely for us than another. With a view to this, Task 5 is suggested as homework.

Task 5: Make a new hymn on the parable of the shepherd and the sheep. Take a popular melody from your culture, or compose a "catchy" tune yourself. Tell the story of the parable in a four-line chorus, to be repeated after each verse. Then translate the different biblical accentuations of the parable into separate verses, but use language and imagery that communicate easily in your culture.

10 FOLLOW ME

A meditation on Mark 2:13-17

> In the following script the method of "fantasy journey" is used for biblical meditation. This method can be followed only in a quiet place. It is also important for an atmosphere of mutual confidence to exist among the members of the group and the enabler. The actual meditation — the journey — will only take fifteen or twenty minutes, but enough time must be allowed for both the introduction to the text and the period of debriefing. For introducing the text it would be good to prepare a worksheet with the parallel accounts of Mark 2:13-17, Matthew 9:9-13, and Luke 5:27-32, and footnotes on the customs officers and the Scribes and Pharisees.

The actors and the scene

Among the first episodes of Jesus' public ministry, told in the gospels, are the stories about how Jesus called his disciples. We are now going to meditate on the call of Levi.

Task 1: Read Mark 2:13-17 and make a list of the persons we meet and the places where the story takes us.

> This quick examination of the text is done individually. The group as a whole then discusses briefly the actors and the scene of the story. The enabler adds the following details if they are not mentioned by members of the group.

The Roman empire was divided into many customs districts, often not larger than the former city-states. If someone brought goods, say, from Caesarea Philippi to Jerusalem, he had to pay duty on them several times. From the New Testament we know that there were customs offices at the entrances to the city of Capernaum and in Jericho. The Roman administration leased customs districts to the chief customs officers who made the best offer. Zacchaeus, who climbed a tree to see Jesus, was such a rich chief customs officer in Jericho (Luke 19:1-10). The chiefs in turn leased each of the several customs offices in their districts to those subordinate officers who offered most. Levi was such a minor customs official.

Customs officers were deeply despised and mistrusted among Greeks, Romans, and Jews. Nobody likes to pay taxes and duties; moreover, the Roman system invited corruption and exploitation. Fees were fixed by law at about 2-5% of the estimated value of the goods. But in order to pay the lease and make a profit the customs officers had to overtax the value of the goods and collect higher fees than prescribed. The greed of many officials aggravated the problem. As a result, customs officers were considered to be robbers.

The Jews had two more reasons to avoid all social contact with customs collectors. As collaborators with the Roman occupying power, they were considered traitors to the Jewish people. Furthermore, they were reputed to be ritually unclean because of their constant contact with Gentiles. Therefore they were looked upon as sinners and counted together with prostitutes. A pious Jew would never enter the house of a customs officer, and if a tax collector were to enter his house, it would have to be ritually cleansed.

The expression "the scribes *of* the Pharisees" (v. 16) occurs only in this passage (and several ancient manuscripts read "the scribes *and* the Pharisees"). Scholars disagree whether there was actually a distinction between the two. Some believe that among the Pharisees there were experts in the writing of Torah scrolls and legal documents, who formed a distinct leadership group. More likely the term "scribe" simply explains what all Pharisees were, namely a highly respected class of scholars who taught the oral law as well as the written law. They made new regulations about what is clean and unclean, how to observe the Jewish festivals, how to keep the Sabbath, how to explain the scriptures, and in general how to live in this life with a view to the divine retribution in the life after death. As such the Pharisees wielded great power.

The context of the passage makes it clear that the scene of this story is the shore of the sea of Galilee and the city of Capernaum. Mark's version does not make clear in whose house the meal took place. "His house" in Mark 2:15 could well refer to the house where Jesus usually stayed in Capernaum, that of Peter's mother-in-law (cf. Mark 1:29ff). Yet the parallel text in Luke (5:29) makes it clear that Levi's house is meant ("Levi made him a great feast in his house"). Jesus used to teach either from a boat to the crowds gathered on the shore of the Sea of Galilee (Mark 4:1b) or — as in this passage — while walking on the shore of the lake (cf. Mark 1:16 and 4:1a). Let us visualize this scene.

> If any members of the group have visited Palestine invite them to describe the scenery in this area. If there are no "eyewitnesses" present, some pictures or slides of the Sea of Galilee are shown by the enabler or a group member asked beforehand to do so.

Preparation for the journey

We could study the account of Levi's calling by using the synopsis and comparing Mark's account with those of Matthew (9:9-13) and Luke (5:27-32). Careful analysis would show that Mark probably combined two stories which originally may have been transmitted separately (Mark 2:13-14 and Mark 2:15-17). We could then discuss what Mark wanted to teach his readers about Jesus and about themselves by telling this story.

But the accounts of the call to discipleship not only solicit theological reflection but challenge readers on a deeper, existential level. We will therefore try to participate in the story by meditation. In our imagination we visit Levi, the customs collector, on that memorable day. In a moment we will close our eyes and take a journey.

All of us will probably experience this journey differently. You may want to remain an outside observer who simply looks at what Jesus does and how Levi reacts. Or you may want to identify with Levi himself. Some of you may not come along at all; others may follow the story up to a certain point and then stay there or drift from there; still others will live that whole memorable day together with Levi. Perhaps one or two of you will fall asleep. This is perfectly all right, and no one should be uneasy about it. There are occasions when such exercises of meditation strike some participant as manipulation. If one of you begins to feel like this, please open your eyes and stop the journey for yourself without disturbing others.

First find the most comfortable position on your chair, or sit or lie on the floor if you like. - - -

> The sign of three dashes indicates a pause in this script.

Now stretch your body, feel the tension in your legs, arms and back, then relax. - - - Become aware of the details of your breathing: the air which enters your nose and mouth, the movement of your chest and diaphragm as you breathe in and out. - - - Now close your eyes and keep them closed during the whole meditation, so that you see with your inward eyes. - - -

The journey
We are making a journey.

> The enabler now leads the participants, in their imaginations, to a natural spot known to most or all of them. This may be a river bank, a forest, a hill, a lakeshore or the like. The descriptive sentences which follow must then be adapted to the place chosen.

Let us first go to the nearby river and sit down at its bank. - - - See in your imagination the water which runs over the stones. - - - Hear and smell the river. - - -

Now we go still farther, over lands and seas, until we reach Galilee. We also travel in time, across centuries, to that day when Levi was called. - - - As we come nearer that place and time we hear the flute and drum of two Israeli shepherds. - - -

> Music is very dimly heard, but grows in volume. For this meditation exercise, quiet melodies played by a flautist are best. I like to use a short excerpt of a recording of the Israeli "shepherd's dance" played by Hillel and Aviva, from the the record MMS-90; but other short recordings of flute music can serve as well. After about one minute the music fades away.

Here is the house of Levi, the customs official. It is the large house of a wealthy man, and the time is early in the morning. - - - We go into the house. Levi sits alone at the breakfast table. His Edomite slave serves him, but the two do not talk together. - - -

Levi eats. - - - At the same time he calculates. - - - How much money must still be collected this month for paying the lease for the customs office? How much profit can be expected? Levi calculates.

Now he stands up, puts on his coat, and steps out of his house. - - - He walks through the main street of Capernaum towards the south entrance of the city. - - - Nobody greets him. People get out of his way. Levi knows many of them. Here comes the merchant who once tried to smuggle gold, which Levi then confiscated. There stands the fisherman who always complains that Levi overtaxes his catch of fish. And over there walks one of those Pharisees who never carry any goods with them, never pay any customs, and nevertheless speak evil of all tax-collectors, counting them with thieves and sinners. Levi knows most of them. And they all know Levi. But nobody greets him, not even the children. They all avoid him. Alone he walks to the customs house east of Capernaum to do another day's work. - - -

Now it is afternoon. Levi has calculated that he will soon have collected enough fees to pay for the monthly license. From then on all will be pure profit, and the late afternoon traffic is still to come. Just now it is the afternoon when very few people come in or go out of the city. - - -

Here comes a group. Levi looks up from his calculation. He recognizes them from afar: it is that rabbi Jesus of Nazareth, who has recently begun to teach along the seashore. Levi knows some of his followers — Simon and Andrew, John and James, all fishermen. They used to pay a lot of tax when they brought their daily catch to the first market of Capernaum. But they no longer carried any taxable goods, and their teacher of course had nothing at all. - - -

As the group approaches, Levi signals them to pass through. - - - Again he concentrates on the balance sheets, checking the entries once more. - - -

Suddenly Levi becomes aware that the steps have stopped. - - - He senses that somebody is looking at him. - - - He looks up, and looks right into the eyes of Jesus. - - -

There seems to be a long silence. - - - Then Jesus says to Levi: "Follow me!" - - -

Levi stands up, leaves the balance sheets and his money. He joins the many who follow Jesus. - - -

It is towards evening. Levi has invited Jesus and his followers to a feast in his house. And Jesus has accepted the invitation. Unaware of the ironic smiles of passers-by, Levi runs home. Once there, he helps his Edomite slave to prepare the feast. He sends invitations also to the customs officers of the northern and western gates of Capernaum. - - - Then he hears them coming: Jesus and his followers. Two prostitutes and some other outcasts

from Capernaum society enter Levi's house. All sit down for the feast with wine and tasty food. - - -
The house is full of talking and laughter. Never has Levi experienced such a joy. - - -
Jesus has invited him to sit on his right side. - - -
Those who pass by on the street see how Jesus is eating with sinners and tax collectors. A scribe comes up and asks some of his disciples: "How can your master do this?"
Jesus hears the question and says: "Those who are well have no need of a physician, but those who are sick; I came not to call the righteous, but sinners."

> After a short silence the music played at the beginning of the journey is heard again and then gradually fades out.

Reflection and prayer

> After the music has faded away, the enabler helps the participants return from the journey. This may take several forms, and it is up to the enabler to choose the most appropriate one. Here are three suggestions.

We have come back from our journey. We are back here in this room, in our own time. Open your eyes slowly, stretch, and look around.

> 1. The enabler may suggest that the participants take a walk, either alone or with a friend, and reflect about the meditation. Those who wish may gather after half an hour to discuss together the experience of the meditation and the insights gained.
> 2. Or the group may remain together and the participants share, first with their neighbours, then in plenary discussion, reflections about three questions: (a) How did you experience the meditation through this imaginary journey? (b) What have you learned about Jesus and yourself? (c) Reread Mark 2:13-17 and describe how the meditation has helped or hindered the right understanding of this text.
> 3. Or the members are asked to continue the meditation on Levi's calling by responding to this passage in the form of a written prayer. After an appropriate time the meditation ends with a period of prayer, during which some of these new prayers are prayed aloud.

11 THE HEALING
OF A DEAF-MUTE

Mark 7:31-37

> This study was prepared for a 1971 ecumenical seminar in Geneva for the training of Christians working among the deaf. The script has been slightly expanded in order to allow for more group participation. To facilitate this, it is advisable to prepare a worksheet reproducing the extra-biblical healing stories below, the parallel texts of Mark 7:31-37 and Matthew 15:29-31, and the text of Isaiah 35:5-6.

What would you do if you were a deaf-mute living in the first century of the Christian era?

You would know what to do today — at least if you lived in one of the countries where aid to deaf and mutes has been organized. You might have little hope for recovery, but at least you could find people and institutions who not only have specialized knowledge, but also the necessary love and patience to help you live with your infirmities and communicate with others. Yet if we want to understand the meaning of the well-known healing miracle in Mark 7, we must not jump too quickly into our present time. We must first attempt to understand this story of the deaf man with a speech defect in the setting of the first century.

We shall approach the study of Mark 7 from four different angles, which complement and correct one another. Each has its own particular contribution and danger.

The first approach sees the healing miracle in the setting of the Graeco-Roman world of Jesus' time. This can help us appreciate more fully Jesus' incarnation. He was not an alien from another world, but a man of his time, speaking its language and using its signs and symbols. But this must not mislead us into thinking that Jesus was simply a popular miracle worker of the first century.

The second approach examines the Old Testament background of Mark 7. This can help us see the extent to which Jesus' words and deeds, in fact his whole life, were marked by the spirituality and expectations of his people. Yet this must not blind us to the radically new word and deed which came into world history through Jesus' life and passion.

The third approach makes a distinction between the old tradition of this healing story and later redaction of the story, some of which may have been made by the evangelist Mark. This will help us understand better Mark's particular witness to Jesus. But Mark's theology, however interesting it may be, is not an end in itself. We believe in Jesus Christ, not in Mark's or Paul's or John's conception of Christ.

The fourth and most existential approach examines what Jesus' meeting with the deaf-mute can teach us about our encounter with deaf and mute people today, and asks what our own experience in this matter can contribute to our understanding of the text. The new light this sheds on the text may reveal facets of meaning which have escaped the learned exegetes with all their scholarship. But there is a danger here that our concern for deaf and mute people and their infirmity might distract us from the main focus of this passage. As we shall discover, Mark did not include this healing story in his gospel to teach us about the predicament of deaf and mute people or about healing methods. He wanted to show us Jesus.

Healing in the Hellenistic world and in the New Testament

Let us go back to our opening question: What would you do if you were a deaf-mute living in the first century? First of all, you would feel extremely lonely and miserable. Not only would there be very little hope that you could ever be healed, but you would also be an outcast from society.

The literature about healing miracles in the Graeco-Roman world is extensive. There are many stories of the healing of lame and blind people. One finds curiosities such as the healing of Cleo, a woman who was pregnant for five years and then gave birth to a four year old boy. But I have not found a single story of the healing of a deaf-mute.

A few extra-biblical accounts of the healing of a mute are known, but most of these date from after the time of the gospels. One is found in the rabbinic writings. A rather amusing one occurs in the legends about Christian saints, especially those of Cosmas and Damian. A third comes from the sanctuary of Epidaurus and tells about a dumb boy: "He came to the sanctuary seeking to recover his voice. As he was presenting his first offering and performing the usual ceremony, the acolyte who bears the fire (for the sacrifice) to the god turned and said to the father of the boy, 'Will you promise, if you get your wish, between now and the end of the year to bring the offering you owe as a fee for the healing?' At once the boy cried out, 'I promise!' The father was greatly astonished, and told him to say it again. The boy said it again and was made whole from that moment" (F.C. Grant, *Hellenistic Religions*, p. 57).

This was one of the things a deaf-mute could do in Jesus' time: go to the temple of Epidaurus, the Lourdes of the ancient world. Perhaps you would have seen one of the healing gods, most likely Asclepius, in a dream. He would have ordered you to go to Epidaurus. Since dreams were considered very important in those days, you probably would have followed this order, taken all the money you had, and traveled to the temple. There you would find many other sick people, gathering around the resident priests and physicians. You would have to submit to a rigorous diet, do exercises, take cold and warm baths, as well as mud baths. Above all, you would have to sleep in the temple and await a further dream in which the healer god would tell you what to do in order to be healed. Perhaps after a few days, weeks, or months you would indeed have another vision of Asclepius, who would show you which drug to take or which rite to perform and what to pay. The next morning you would do so and would be healed. Before leaving the temple you would probably request one of the artisans living near the temple to make a votive tablet to commemorate your healing and honour Asclepius. Several of such votive tablets have in fact been found in Epidaurus.

Another possibility would be to find what was called a *theios anthropos* (the Greek expression for "divine man"). Certain great men were believed to have a special healing power granted them by the gods. A famous example of this is described by the Roman historian Tacitus. It concerns the emperor Vespasian after his victory over the Jews in A.D. 70. Waiting in Alexandria for good winds to return to Rome, Vespasian visited the Serapis temple, where the following incident took place:

> One of the common people of Alexandria, well known for his loss of sight, threw himself before Vespasian's knees, praying him with groans to cure his blindness, being so directed by the god Serapis, whom this most superstitious of nations worships before all others; and he besought the emperor to deign to moisten his cheeks and eyes with his spittle. Another whose hand was useless, prompted by the same god, begged Caesar to step and trample on it.
> Vespasian at first ridiculed these appeals and treated them with scorn; then, when the men persisted, he began at one moment to fear the discredit of failure, at another to be inspired with hopes of success by the appeals of the suppliants and the flattery of his courtiers: finally, he directed the physicians to give their opinion as to whether such blindness and infirmity could be overcome by human aid. Their reply treated the two cases differently; they said that in the first one the power of sight had not been completely eaten away and it would return if the obstacles were removed; in the second case the joints had slipped and become displaced, but they could be restored if a healing pressure were applied to them. Such perhaps was the wish of the gods, and it might be that the emperor had been chosen for this divine service; in any case, if a cure were obtained, the glory would be Caesar's, but in the event of failure, ridicule would fall only on the poor suppliants.
> So Vespasian, believing that his good fortune was capable of anything and that nothing was any longer incredible, with a smiling countenance and amid intense excitement on the part of the bystanders, did as he was asked to do. The hand was instantly restored to use, and the day again shone for the blind man. Both facts are told by eyewitnesses even now when falsehood brings no reward (*Annals* IV, 81).

Task 1: Compare the account of the healing of a deaf man with a speech defect in Mark 7:31-37 with these two extra-biblical healing stories. What are the most striking similarities and differences between these accounts from Epidaurus and about Vespasian and the biblical healing story?

> If worksheets have not been prepared, it will be necessary to reread the two extra-biblical accounts after reading Mark 7:31-37. The participants are asked to reflect first individually, then to exchange discoveries with their neighbours. This leads up to a general discussion, during which most of the following observations will probably be made.

Jesus appears in Mark 7 as a *theios anthropos*, a "man favoured by god" who therefore had the power of miraculous healing. In his time many people considered him as such. Those who brought the deaf-mute to Jesus approached him in the same way as the blind man who went to Vespasian in Alexandria. According to the gospels' testimony Jesus was of course much more than a miracle worker; but in his love for the people he responded to their expectations, even to the extent of appearing like a worker of miracles.

In the healing of the deaf-mute Jesus even used methods quite commonly known from Jewish and Graeco-Roman accounts of healing: the laying on of hands, the touching of the diseased organ by the healer, the use of spittle, the accompanying prayer and use of foreign words, and to a lesser degree the separation of the patient from the crowd. Moreover, the form in which Mark tells the story conforms to the way healing miracles were generally reported in the Graeco-Roman world. They begin with the exposition, telling about the illness and the events leading up to the miracle. Then the healing miracle is reported with an emphasis on what the healer says and does. Finally the result of the healing is recorded with information about what the healed person does and how the spectators react.

The so-called form-critical school in biblical exegesis has strongly emphasized this similarity of form between biblical healing miracles and the extra-biblical healing stories. Some exegetes have gone so far as to suggest that many biblical accounts of healing do not go back to events in the life of Jesus but are rather Christian adaptations of this type of miracle story. Some believe that the miracles actually happened but that the evangelists consciously chose the well-known contemporary pattern for telling the healing story. Others think that the emphasis on the particular form in which the New Testament healing stories were written has been overplayed in modern exegesis. They point out that there is an inherent pattern or structure in telling about events of the same type, whether it is healings, catastrophes, or marriage festivals. Case studies in medical textbooks, for example, are universally reported according to the same pattern, but no one concludes from this that they are inventions which have nothing to do with real patients.

The differences between Mark 7 and the Graeco-Roman healing stories are at least as striking as the similarities. First, the healing does not happen by the power of just any god — Asclepius, Serapis, Dionysus, or one of the many other healing divinities then worshipped. According to the gospels, healing is always given by the power of the one God, the God of Abraham, Isaac, and Jacob, the God who called Jesus of Nazareth "my beloved Son."

Second, the extensive description of the healing process in Mark 7 and the use of external means such as spittle are an exception in the healing stories of the gospels. Only in two other gospel passages — the healing of the blind man in Bethsaida (Mark 8:22-26) and the healing of the blind man at the pool of Siloam (John 9:1-12) — is explicit reference made to external means of curing. In the healing miracles in the gospels Jesus did not use any such means. His presence, word, and touch sufficed. Several exegetes have thus suggested that Mark 7 is a Christian adaptation of an extra-biblical healing story, and that Matthew and Luke, recognizing this, did not take over this particular passage from Mark in their gospels. However, one can also argue that Jesus in fact used external means of healing in the case of blind, mute and deaf people not because this was also done in Epidaurus, but because these particular infirmities made such external means desirable.

Third, nothing is said in Mark 7 or any of the other gospel healing accounts about payment for the cure. This is in striking contrast to many extra-biblical healing stories, in which the price to be paid has a prominent place in the story.

Fourth, many miracle workers of the Graeco-Roman world — for example, the famous Apollonius of Tyana — made a frequent show of their healing powers. Unlike them Jesus sought no publicity. He charged the one healed and all those present "to tell no one."

Finally, it is important to note that at the end of Mark 7:31-37 an Old Testament text is referred to, namely Isaiah 35:5-6 (compare also Isa. 29:18). There may even be an echo of Genesis 1:31 ("and behold, it was very good") in the closing verse of Mark's story. These references point to the particular meaning and purpose of the New Testament healing miracles, which cannot be discovered merely by comparison with extra-biblical sources. We now proceed to examine the Old Testament background of this passage and its function within the whole of Mark's witness to Jesus.

The Old Testament background: illness and health in the ancient Near East

In the ancient Near Eastern world there were different attitudes towards human suffering and death. The old Mesopotamian Gilgamesh Epic teaches that

> When the gods created mankind,
> Death for mankind they set aside,
> Life in their own hands retaining. (Table X, col. 3)

According to another Mesopotamian epic, the story of Atrachasis, the gods decided to send famines and epidemics among people because "the noise which men made had become so excessive that their turmoil made the sleep of the gods impossible." When these measures did not achieve their end the gods decided to send the flood.

Homer had a higher view of human suffering. In the *Iliad*, Helen says to Hector:

> If Zeus has given both of us a hard fate,
> it is in order that future generations
> may sing about us (VI, 357-8).

Later the authors of Greek tragedies and classical philosophers explained suffering as fate.

Another type of ancient Near Eastern literature sees suffering as the result of evil powers or as the consequence of sin. As such, suffering could be combatted by magic and medicine. In ancient Egypt this combination between medicine and magic was highly developed. This dualistic view of history as the struggle between good and evil forces became the milieu out of which Hellenistic philosophies grew. Healing and salvation were no longer seen in terms of our bodily, earthly existence in this world. Plotinus, the founder and main representative of neo-Platonism, despised his body as the mortal prison of his immortal soul. Healing for him meant death, the liberation of the soul from the prison of the body.

Traces of all these conceptions of suffering are found in the Old Testament, but the main emphasis lies elsewhere. The biblical God is the creator of the universe and of human beings. A person is therefore seen as a whole, an indivisible unity of body and soul animated and directed by God's spirit. What God wants is health, wholeness of life, *shalom.*

Refusing to accept a dualistic world-view, the believers of the Old Testament maintained that there is only one God who rules everything. "Does evil befall a city, unless the Lord has done it?" (Amos 3:6). Illness too comes ultimately from God, paradoxically from the God who wants health. Most Old Testament writers thus considered it a riddle, a scandal. Job's friends failed in their human wisdom to help him accept his suffering. They explained his misfortune as a penalty for sin, as a divine discipline and teaching, or as the testing of the righteous; and they advised him to accept his suffering with patience and submission to God. But Job rejected all such human wisdom and maintained that his suffering was a scandal — and he was vindicated as the truly pious one!

Because the believers of the Old Testament could neither deny the reality of suffering in their lives nor explain it with human wisdom, they threw themselves into the arms of God and pleaded with him to give them health. One of the most moving examples is the prayer King Hezekiah of Judah wrote after he had recovered from a serious illness:

> I said, In the noontide of my days I must depart;
> I am consigned to the gates of Sheol for the rest of my years.
> I said, I shall not see the Lord in the land of the living;
> I shall look upon man no more among the inhabitants of the world.

Hezekiah then described his illness, acknowledging that it came from the Lord. He concluded his psalm:

Lo, it was for my welfare that I had great bitterness;
but thou hast held back my life from the pit of destruction,
for thou hast cast all my sins behind thy back.
For Sheol cannot thank thee, death cannot praise thee;
those who go down to the pit cannot hope for thy faithfulness.
The living, the living, he thanks thee, as I do this day;
the father makes known to the children thy faithfulness.
The Lord will save me, and we will sing to stringed instruments
all the days of our life, at the house of the Lord (Isa. 38:10-11, 17-20).

For a long time the believers of the Old Testament had no hope for resurrection and a life after death. Nor did they believe in the immortality of
the soul, because in the Old Testament life is seen as a whole. When the
body decayed human life ended. One could hope to live on only in one's
children and children's children. There are some traces of the development
of a belief in the resurrection of the dead among the Israelites, but it is only
in Jewish apocalyptic literature in the centuries immediately before and
after Christ that it was clearly expressed. In Jesus' day Pharisees and Sadducees still quarreled about this question.

Very early, however, the hope for a coming messianic age developed
among the believers of the Old Testament. Isaiah could console his contemporaries, who had lost hope because of wars, sufferings, and catastrophes, by pointing to the coming future messianic peace and wholeness:

Then the eyes of the blind shall be opened,
and the ears of the deaf unstopped;
then shall the lame man leap like a hart,
and the tongue of the dumb sing for joy.
For waters shall break forth in the wilderness,
and streams in the desert;
the burning sand shall become a pool,
and the thirsty ground springs of water (Isa. 35:5-7).

In this prophetic vision and elsewhere in the Old Testament healings
were seen as signs of the coming cosmic re-creation. They foreshadowed
and anticipated the messianic age.

Task 2: What can we learn from the above information about illness and
health in the ancient Near East and the Old Testament to help us understand the healing story in Mark 7:31-37? Why is Isaiah 35:3-7 at least indirectly quoted at the end of Mark's account?

> Participants reflect on these questions in small groups. In the plenary dis-
> cussion the following points will then be made by participants and the study
> enabler.

It is no accident that Mark indirectly quoted the passage from Isaiah at
the end of his account of Jesus' healing of the mute with a speech defect.
This link with the Old Testament adds three essential new insights to our
understanding of Mark 7.

First, Jesus was steeped in the Old Testament belief that illness and suffering are a scandal, which should not exist. He was angry with illness which deprives human beings of the wholeness of life, of *shalom*. To him salvation was never something merely "spiritual," something apart from bodily health. Jesus therefore heard the plea of the father who came with his son possessed by an evil spirit: "Have pity on us and help us!" (Mark 9:22). Mercy as a motive for healing should not be overemphasized, however. In the four healing stories reported in John's gospel mercy plays no role at all. It is more prominent in Luke and Matthew, but in Mark mercy is not the prime motive for healing. In the 26 healing stories in the gospels (not counting the parallel accounts of the same story), Jesus took the initiative only five times, and he never attempted to heal all the sick in any one place. For instance, on the occasion described in John 5:3ff, he healed only one man among "a multitude of invalids, blind, lame, paralyzed."

Second, Jesus' extraordinary healing power indicated to the Jews of his time that he was somehow related to the messianic age. This is why Jesus charged the healed man "to tell no one," because during that early period of his public ministry he did not want to be known as the Messiah (see also Mark 1:44; 5:43; 8:26). His "hour" had not yet come. Mark especially emphasizes this "messianic secret," but it is also in his gospel that, despite Jesus' charge to keep silent, those who are healed and those who have witnessed these healings do not hold back the wonders they have seen. "The more he charged them, the more zealously they proclaimed it" (7:36b, cf. also 1:45). Jesus' messianic authority cannot be hidden.

This leads to the third and most important new insight arising from the Old Testament background of Mark 7: Jesus' healings are understood as signs of the coming kingdom. They are manifestations of his messianic authority. Here is the fundamental difference between the accounts of healing in the gospels and the extra-biblical healing stories. When Jesus heals, he anticipates the kingdom, he affirms hope, not only for the healed person but for the whole world. This healing of one deaf man with a speech defect is a first fruit of the coming healing of all deaf and mute. The healing stories of the gospels are therefore essentially future-oriented. They are like decisive battles in a war which is still going on but which has already been won. They "portray" the coming kingdom.

With these remarks we have already moved in the direction of a theological understanding of Mark 7. Let us now continue by asking what particular message the evangelist Mark wanted to communicate by his redaction of this healing story.

Mark's special emphasis

In order to find the particular point in a given gospel passage, it is helpful to compare it with accounts of the same or similar events in other gospels. In the case of Mark 7:31-37 there is no direct parallel. Although Luke probably knew the gospel of Mark, at least in its original form, he did not take over this particular healing story as he did with many others. Matthew has only summarized Mark's account.

> If a worksheet with the synopsis of Mark 7:31-37 and Matthew 15:29-31 has been distributed, the enabler refers the participants to it, so that they can verify the following affirmations on the basis of the two texts.

A comparison between Mark's account and Matthew's summary shows the following interesting points.

First, Mark placed the healing in the mainly non-Jewish region of the Decapolis, while Matthew situated it in Galilee. Jesus' itinerary as indicated by Mark is an impossible one. It does not reveal a geographical recollection but a theological intention. Several interpreters believe that the mute with a speech defect was not a Jew and that Mark wanted to emphasize already here the universal nature of Jesus' mission. By contrast Matthew has strictly limited the ministry of the earthly Jesus to the Jews, with world mission, according to him, beginning only after the resurrection (Matt. 28:16-20). The actual text of Mark 7:31 does not state that the deaf-mute was a non-Jew, and it is therefore risky to build the above-mentioned hypothesis on this text. (It finds more basis in such texts as Mark 5:1-20 and 7:24-30). Moreover, there are exegetes who think that in Mark's mind the region of Decapolis belonged to the region of Galilee.

A second characteristic difference between Mark and Matthew is the fact that Mark tells the healing extensively in several verses, while Matthew merely summarizes it in one verse and puts it together with other healings (Matt. 15:30). Mark was in fact much more interested in healing stories than Matthew. He devoted about 20% of the verses of his gospel to tell the thirteen healing stories he records; Matthew used 9% for fourteen healing stories in his much longer gospel; only 8% of Luke's gospel are used for telling seventeen healing stories; John recorded only four healing stories, for which he used 5% of his gospel.

Mark's special emphasis on miracles already appears in his account of the beginning of Jesus' public ministry. After having called the first disciples, Jesus went into the synagogue of Capernaum and taught; this immediately led to the first healing event, the exorcism of an unclean spirit (Mark 1:23-27). This story ends with those present exclaiming: "What is this? A new teaching! With authority he commands even the unclean spirits, and they obey him." Jesus taught not only with words but also with miracles. However, he refused to perform spectacular signs (cf. Mark 8:11-13). According to Mark 13:22, only false Messiahs and false prophets needed to show such "signs and wonders" and their purpose was to deceive people. Jesus' miracles remained ambiguous, open to misunderstanding. Some of the scribes even interpreted his healing power as demonic: "He is possessed by Beelzebul, and by the prince of demons he casts out the demons" (Mark 3:22).

Nevertheless, despite the persisting ambiguity of the miracles, Jesus the Messiah taught through words and deeds. As the Lord, he could not tolerate the presence of demonic powers. The miracles in Mark's gospel are manifestations of God's holy anger against satanic wiles. This is especially true for the exorcism stories, and perhaps the healing of the deaf-mute can also be considered as such. The expression "his tongue was released" (v. 35) may be an allusion to the ancient idea that the tongue of mutes is fettered by demonic powers, so that only exorcism can "release" it. The use of a foreign word perhaps points in the same direction; it is known that Christian and non-Christian exorcists used such foreign words in their ritual.

We have already discussed the charge "to tell no one" and the fact that it was immediately disregarded. One of the characteristics of Mark's gospel is this emphasis on secrecy with regard to Jesus' Messiahship before the cross, coupled with the testimony that nevertheless the authority of the Messiah broke through his incognito.

This comparison between Mark's and Matthew's accounts of the healing of a deaf person with a speech defect has highlighted some of the important theological affirmations in Mark's gospel, but we have not yet discovered the particular teaching in this passage. For that we must examine where the story is placed in Mark's gospel and ask why it is placed there. It is in this redactional arrangement of individual stories and sayings that one can most clearly discover the theological intention of the evangelists.

According to Mark 7:14, Jesus called the people to him and said: "Hear me, all of you, and understand." This plea for understanding of what Jesus does and says goes right through the whole of Mark's gospel. After the miraculous feeding of five thousand, told in Mark 6, the disciples still did not understand who Jesus was. Mark makes this quite explicit: "They did not understand about the loaves, but their hearts were hardened" (v. 52). Their lack of understanding continued. After his plea in Mark 7:14, Jesus told a parable, but the disciples were as unperceptive as ever. This led Jesus to exclaim in disappointment: "Then are you also without understanding?" (7:18). Mark then records that Jesus went to Tyre and Sidon, cities inhabited mainly by non-Jews. It is there that a Syrophoenician woman — a Greek — had a glimpse of who Jesus really was. The disciples who had lived with Jesus and seen his miracles did not understand. Yet, a total outsider came to him and vaguely perceived his messianic authority. "He could not be hid" (7:24ff). It is immediately after this event that Mark tells the story of the healing of the deaf-mute which ends with the exclamation of the crowd: "He even makes the deaf hear and the dumb speak!"

Task 3: What did Mark want to emphasize by putting the healing story in the literary context just described?

> This question is discussed in the plenary and the enabler completes and sums up as follows:

The disciples are the deaf and mute! They do not understand. Their ears must be opened, their tongues must be released. Their eyes must be made fit to see again, as Mark shows later through the story of the healing of a blind man (8:22-26). With these two healings Jesus anticipated what he would do after his resurrection, namely help the disciples (and all the readers of Mark's gospel) finally to understand who the Christ is.

On the basis of an examination of these facts, a detailed study on Jesus' miracles in Mark's gospel states about this passage:

> For Mark the basic significance lies in the fact that Jesus lets the dumb hear and the mute speak. Here, in a symbolic way there is an anticipation of what Jesus will do for his disciples and all the faithful after his resurrection (cf. 9:9). He overcomes the hardening of the hearts (6:52; 8:17), the blindness and muteness of the people referred to already in Ezekiel 12:2 and Jeremiah 5:21. In 8:18 Mark alludes in the discourse of Jesus to the Old Testament complaint of Ezekiel 12:2 and Jeremiah 5:21, and he characterizes the disciples as the blind and the mute. Both the healing of the deaf-mute (Mark 7:31-37) and the healing of the blind (8:22-26) must be understood in this way (K. Kertelge, *Die Wunder im Markusevangelium*, pp. 160f).

Most exegetes agree that these two healing stories have essentially the same message, and that the story of the healing of the blind man thus ends Mark's account of Jesus' public ministry, after which he begins his way to the cross. But one can also argue that the way to the cross already begins with the story of the healing of the blind man. In the first part of his gospel, then, Mark shows that the disciples did not understand that Jesus was the Messiah. They could neither hear nor confess the good news that the Messiah had come; and this is most drastically expressed through the symbolic healing of the deaf-mute. In the second part Mark shows that the disciples have now heard the good news and can even confess it (compare Peter's confession in 8:29 — "You are the Christ"), but by their partial understanding they misunderstand Jesus. They still cannot see him as the suffering Messiah (cf. 8:31-33). This blindness to the good news that Jesus is ready to go the way to the cross and to suffer vicariously for the world, this illness of the misunderstanding of Jesus' ministry must be healed. Therefore Mark put the symbolic healing of the blind man at the beginning of the second part of his gospel.

Healing today

Deaf and mute people reading the above theological interpretation of Jesus' healing miracle would certainly not be content with it. Mark's use of the story may have a salutary effect on Christians and non-Christians who think that they can hear and speak and see, but who in fact are deaf, mute, and blind with regard to the good news of Jesus Christ. But with this the factual deafness and muteness of present deaf-mutes are not healed. Can Jesus not heal us today in the same very concrete manner as when he taught in Galilee?

We cannot escape this question. Indeed, we must ask the deaf and the mute of today to help us understand more deeply the meaning of this particular healing story. The following are some notes of a sermon preached by Denis Mermod to deaf and mute and re-translated from the sign language into written language.

Many of those who hear find it difficult really to understand this story. They say: Jesus performed a miracle. Yes, they are right, Jesus has in fact performed a miracle. But they do not understand why Jesus made these gestures with his hands, his spit, his eyes, and with the sigh.... We — we understand perfectly well! Jesus loves and understands the deaf. He takes him aside, away from the crowd where one cannot understand. Then Jesus makes a mime: The ears are obstructed? They will hear again! I will take my word and put my word into your mouth; so you will be able to speak! I will pray to God (the eyes lifted to heaven), so that he will send his Holy Spirit (the sigh). Then I say to you: "Be opened," with a word which you can easily read on my lips (in Aramaic): "Ephphatha." Jesus was the first teacher for speaking to the deaf! He immediately understood them. He did not speak much or speak very quickly, but he clearly indicated what he wanted to do, with his hands, and with a word that is easy to read from the lips.

Here and there these sermon notes may be questionable from the point of view of strict exegesis. But this sermon has the merit of bringing us back from later theological interpretations of the healing miracle to the person of Jesus when faced with a deaf-mute. And here we are being challenged by a miracle, a healing which even for today's medecine is impossible.

Task 4: Can the deaf and mute people of today be healed by Jesus' power? What has our study of Mark 7:31-37 taught us about this question?

> If time allows, this question can best be discussed in small groups. The enabler can then conclude with some such short remarks as the following.

I have no clear-cut answer to the question we have been discussing. But our study of Mark 7 allows us at least to make the following five assertions.

First, those who are deaf and mute or suffer from any other kind of illness need not passively accept their illness. With Job — and against the "wise" counsels of his friends — they may protest and struggle with God in seeking healing from him. Deafness and muteness is a scandal, something which should not exist, something which seriously threatens the whole purpose of human life.

Second, the healing of one deaf-mute as a sign and anticipation of the wholeness and all-embracing salvation of the coming kingdom strengthens our hope for the future healing of all illnesses and infirmities. Mark 7:31-37 must not be preached in the first place as a remembrance of something which once happened, but as an affirmation of hope: "He has done all things well; he even makes the deaf hear and the dumb speak."

Third, we can point to the remarkable history of Christian care for those who are deaf and mute. The story of Mark 7 has indeed made history: it is at the origin of the growing concern for and help to those who must carry the heavy burden of this infirmity. The promise in this story must continue to incite Christians to participate not only in the care for the deaf and mute but also in the medical struggle to allieviate and if possible heal them.

Fourth, deaf and mute people can help those not marked with such infirmities to discover a deeper and fuller meaning of life. They can teach us to communicate not only with words but with meaningful gestures. But above all they can cure us from the superficiality of too many words and the shallowness of a life which has no expectancy. The presence of deaf and mute people among us is a parable of the coming kingdom. It is a negative parable insofar as they show us who think we can hear and speak that in a profound sense all who do not seek the kingdom are deaf and mute. It is a powerful positive parable if deaf and mute are indeed healed or at least enabled to enter into communication with the surrounding creation, with fellow human beings and with God.

Finally, we cannot preach that now Jesus will heal all those who have to carry illnesses and infirmities. But we can and must preach that Jesus can make possible what for humans seems impossible. He has healed a deaf-mute, and as the living Lord he can still accomplish such a miracle if he so desires. Above all we can and must proclaim that Jesus has shown a way in which illness, suffering, and death can even now be not only a scandal, but become meaningful: namely, the way to the cross, the way of suffering for others.

12 WHO DO YOU SAY
THAT I AM?

Mark 8:27-35

This script consists of the edited and integrated notes for two studies originally prepared for a world consultation on "New Trends in Laity Formation," held in Assisi in September 1974 and organized jointly by the World
Council of Churches and the Vatican Council of the Laity. At least three
hours should be available for this study. For a shorter study, several subsec-
tions can be omitted. Or the script can be divided up to provide material for
two or three studies.

The worksheet on "Who do you say that I am?" is handed out at the
beginning.

"Don't act like a parrot — just reciting what you say you believe! We've
heard enough creeds as it is — Christian, Marxist, Humanist, whatever.
And then we see the gap between your preaching and your practice. I want
to know about the faith you actually *live*. What makes you tick?"

This outcry from a teenager close to me is a familiar one in the world
today. Indeed, it expresses my own deep longing. To be sure, the "how"
questions of the faith remain important: *How* do I live my faith in everyday
life? *How* can the church become a worshipping, serving, and witnessing
community? *How* do we teach Christian faith today? But behind these
"how" questions lies a much more fundamental quest: *What* do I believe?

Many people today — and I include myself — can no longer take Christian faith for granted. As a result, one hears much talk about a "crisis of
faith." Yet the crisis is only a side effect. At the heart of the matter is a
search for belief that is real; and the basic question goes beyond "How do I
live my faith?" to "What is the faith for which I am ready to live and die?"
And we cannot answer the question simply by repeating the classical Christian creeds.

Many of these creeds were excellent statements of Christian faith in the
first or fourth or sixteenth century. We must treasure them as a precious
heritage and learn from them. Yet they are not statements of faith for the
here and now. Nor can we answer the question with vague generalities like
"belief in God," "co-humanity," "liberation," "the Christian utopia."

Sooner or later in our quest for faith we will have to answer the question of Jesus of Nazareth: "And you — who do you say that I am?"

What do people say?

According to the passage we are going to study, Jesus asked his disciples: "Who do people say that I am?" (Mark 8:27). The answers given sound very Jewish: "John the Baptist; and others say, Elijah; and others one of the prophets" (v. 28).

The earliest written answers by non-Christians to Jesus' question are interesting. One comes from the Roman historian Tacitus. (*ca.* A.D. 55-120). Mentioning the persecution of Christians under the emperor Nero, he remarks, almost parenthetically:

> Christus, the founder of the name, had undergone the death penalty in the reign of Tiberius, by sentence of the procurator Pontius Pilatus, and the pernicious superstition was checked for a moment, only to break out once more, not merely in Judaea, the home of the disease, but in the capital itself, where all things horrible or shameful in the world collect and find a vogue (*Annals*, XV, 44).

Another first-century historian, the Jewish writer Flavius Josephus (*ca.* A.D. 37-110) gave a famous testimony, which has almost certainly been "Christianized" by later editors. A probable reconstruction of his original remarks runs as follows:

> About this time (i.e. after two disturbances among the Jews) there lived Jesus, a wise man. He was one who wrought surprising feats and was a teacher of such people as accept the truth gladly. He won over many Jews. ... When Pilate, upon hearing him accused by men of the highest standing among us, had condemned him to be crucified, those who had in the first place come to love him did not give up their affection for him. ... And the tribe of the Christians, so called after him, has still to this day not disappeared (*Antiquities*, XVIII, 63f, as reconstructed by C.K. Barrett).

Testimonies by outsiders are often helpful for understanding a person's character. Not that such outsiders are necessarily objective, but even so they may point to basic facts in that person's life which have been overlooked or taken for granted by those intimately involved. Even the biases and obvious misjudgments of such outsiders can be helpful for reaching a truer understanding of a given person or event.

Task 1: How do the observations, judgments, and misjudgments of Tacitus and Josephus help us understand more deeply who Jesus was? How do these earliest non-biblical testimonies about Jesus compare with what people are saying today?

> After a moment of individual study, participants share their discoveries with those sitting next to them. This leads to a general discussion, which the enabler summarizes and complements, including the following points.

One thing both Tacitus and Josephus emphasize is that Jesus was the victim of a violent death. He was executed, and Josephus specifies that this happened by crucifixion. Both historians mention the role of Pontius Pilate in the judgment. Jesus died after a political trial. Tacitus does not mention the enmity of the Jewish authorities against Jesus or the religious trial alluded to by Josephus and recorded by the gospel writers.

With all the prejudice of an educated and civilized Roman, Tacitus sees in Jesus the barbarian founder of a "pernicious superstition." Josephus, a Hellenized Jew, judges more positively. He recognizes the wisdom and the astonishing converting power in the life of Jesus. Neither of them mentions Jesus' resurrection. In fact there were no eyewitnesses to the event of resurrection. None of the gospel writers attempts to describe it. They tell about meetings of the already risen Lord with his disciples, and Matthew mentions the empty tomb, but not one of them ventures an account of how the mysterious event itself occurred. (The often wrongly interpreted passage of Matt. 28:1-7 describes the opening of the already empty tomb.) The first actual description of the resurrection event is in the apocryphal gospel of Peter (mid-second century), which the church rightly excluded from the biblical canon. In one sense, the silence of Tacitus and Josephus concerning the resurrection may be more "biblical" than many later dogmatic statements by Christians who have described the resurrection in such a manner that its veil of mystery is torn. Still, Tacitus and Josephus must clearly be regarded as outsiders. For them Jesus was a dead man, a person of the past, not a living presence. They do not confess together with the church universal that Jesus is now the risen Lord who judges and redeems the world and guides his people in its mission.

Although neither Tacitus nor Josephus knew anything about the resurrection, both acknowledge that the movement started by Jesus continued. Tacitus does so with great irritation; Josephus only states with amazement that the tribe of Christians has not yet disappeared. How much more astonished would they be if they saw us now, people of all continents and races still struggling with Jesus' question many centuries after the mighty Roman Empire itself ceased to exist.

What Tacitus and Josephus wrote about Jesus is representative of what many outsiders think about him even today: the founder of a new religion, a great, astonishing, and irritating man, a prophet or a madman, an admirable revolutionary or a pathetically naïve idealist, someone who in a way impossible to understand has caused millions of people to believe in an illusion. So people thought then and still think today. But what about Jesus' disciples and the early church? Did they really know him?

The answers of the first Christians

Long before the gospels were written and the earliest Christian creeds formulated, the disciples had to answer Jesus' question: "But who do you say that I am?" Peter answered it by assigning to Jesus a title: "You are the Christ" (Mark 8:29).

The given name "Jesus-Joshua" contains a message: it means "the one who saves." But in its search for the true identity of Jesus the early church assigned a whole series of other titles to him as well:

— *Messiah* (the Hebrew equivalent of the Greek title "the Christ") means the anointed messianic king.

— *Son of Man* can simply be a synonym for "man," but is also used as a designation for the persecuted prophet (Ezekiel is called "son of man" some 87 times). Many scholars think, however, that this title should most often be understood on the basis of a few texts in the apocalyptic writings of Daniel and Enoch in which "Son of Man" designates the supra-human judge who will come together with his people and bring history to its end.

— *Son of God* is a title whose New Testament use must be understood on the basis of such Old Testament texts as Psalm 2, where God calls the elected king his son.

— *Son of David* refers to the expected political Saviour who will re-establish the earthly kingdom of David.

— *Lord* is a title used for God in the Old Testament. In Jesus' time it had become the foremost title of the Roman emperors.

— *The Just One* is a title the Old Testament gives to those who obey God's will and thus often have to suffer, but whom God will vindicate.

— *Servant of God*, a title used by the great unknown prophet of the exile (Isa. 40-55), may originally have designated the remnant of the people of Israel, or a prophet or a saviour whose expected coming would inaugurate the messianic age.

— *Saviour* is a title already hidden in Jesus' Hebrew name; it was also used by Roman emperors, who liked to call themselves the saviours of the world.

— *New Adam* is a title indicating the one who comes to restore true humanity. It also played an important role in Jewish and Greek religious speculations and expectations of the first century.

This list (which could be continued) shows how the early Christians groped to understand the person and mission of Jesus and how they confessed him to their contemporaries in different situations. Not all titles were used by all believers. Jewish Christians preferred such titles as Messiah and Son of David, while Christians from pagan backgrounds tended much more to speak of Jesus as the Lord or the Saviour. The different titles thus reflect different spiritualities and varying missionary situations.

Task 2: Which of the above titles most clearly expresses your own faith and that of your church? Which title do you think would be the most meaningful witness to Jesus among non-Christians in your own culture today? Could you for a missionary testimony assign new titles to Jesus? If yes, which ones?

> Participants first discuss these questions with their neighbours, leading up to a general discussion. Concluding this discussion on titles the enabler may want to make some observation along the following lines.

If these questions are being discussed in an interconfessional and international group of Christians many different answers will be given. What is a meaningful title for some, expressing the very core of their understanding of Jesus, may be a meaningless term for others. What in one situation may be a challenging confession simply gives rise to endless misunderstandings in another. Many Christians may find that none of the above titles speak in an existential way, and they will continue the early church's search, calling Jesus "the liberator" or "the true human" or something else. This diversity of titles and the ongoing search show that each confession remains one-sided and is linked with a particular situation of confessing. Moreover, every discussion about Jesus' titles will sooner or later conclude that it is impossible to witness to Jesus by titles and verbal creeds alone. Jesus is not an abstract truth, but a living person who was called to go a specific way and who calls us to follow him in the adventure of Christian faith.

That is why the early church not only assigned titles to the risen Lord but also began to collect the oral tradition about his life, death, and resurrection. The passion stories were the first to be established. Soon sequences of miracle stories, as well as collections of Jesus' words and accounts of his teaching, were orally transmitted. The conversation between Jesus and his disciples near Caesarea Philippi falls into this last category. The form in which Mark has put it into writing has a catechetical flavour: through questions and answers old and new teachings are communicated.

What did actually happen?

In the time of Jesus all of Palestine was in religious and political turmoil. In A.D. 6 the emperor Augustus had incorporated Judea into the Roman Empire. He immediately asked Sulpicius Quirinus, his legate in Syria, to conduct a census so that he could tax the population of this newly annexed area. That started a Jewish resistance movement which ultimately led to the Jewish War of 66-70. Josephus writes that in A.D. 6 a certain Judas the Galilean "incited his countrymen to revolt, upbraiding them as cowards for consenting to pay tribute to the Romans and tolerating mortal masters, after having God for their Lord" (*Jewish War*, II, 18).

At that time religion and politics were intimately interwoven. Judas' movement, claiming the promised land of Palestine for God, fought violently to cleanse it from both the Romans and the Jewish ruling class, who collaborated with the occupying power. This led to intensified guerrilla warfare and severe repressions by the Roman legions. Thousands of rebels were crucified (Josephus called them "bandits," using the same Greek word the gospels apply to the two men crucified with Jesus). In this chaotic atmosphere fervent expectations arose among the Palestinian Jews. The words of the prophets and the visions of the apocalyptic writers were studied and memorized. For many the general waiting for the advent of the messianic age began to be crystallized into an expectation of the coming Messiah, the Son of David, who would liberate the people of Israel and re-establish the kingdom of David. This was combined with apocalyptic expectations concerning the Son of Man, a super-human judge who would bring history to its end and establish God's kingdom. The library of the Jewish sectarian community of Qumran, which was discovered in the Judean desert in 1948, contains many striking examples of such religious-political expectations of that time.

In such a situation Jesus' question was extremely dangerous and explosive. "Who do people say that I am? Who do you say that I am?" Perhaps that was why Jesus led his disciples away into the region of Caesarea Philippi, which was mostly populated by Gentiles. For the subject was definitely not one to be discussed publicly among Jews. The people in Galilee, both the fanatic, subversive rebels and informers for the Romans, were only too eager to hear and spread rumours about a new Messiah.

The conversation near Caesarea Philippi probably did not happen exactly as it is written in Mark's gospel. When the evangelists reported this incident several slightly different oral accounts of what had actually been said must have been in circulation. Only Matthew mentions Jesus' declaration to Peter that he would be the rock on which the church will be built (Matt. 16:17-19). Luke omits Jesus' sharp admonition to Peter which Matthew and Mark record (Matt. 16:22-23; Mark 8:32-33). John transmits the essence of the teaching of Jesus near Caesarea Philippi, but he places it in quite another context (John 6:66-71). The so-called confession of Peter is rendered by each writer in a different way:

"You are the Christ" (Mark 8:29).
"You are the Christ, the Son of the living God" (Matt. 16:16).
"The Christ of God" (Luke 9:20).
"You are the Holy One of God" (John 6:69).

How can such differences be explained? Perhaps the easiest way to understand this is to remember what happens when we ourselves tell about an incident which occurred several years ago. We search in our memory to reconstruct the facts, yet it is difficult to avoid forgetting or adding some details. We may clearly remember a word which was spoken then or an incident which occurred, but we tend to add details from events which happened or words which were said on similar occasions. We also accent our story differently according to the people with whom we speak and the circumstances in which we are speaking. The story goes back to the same memory of historical events, but it is told differently by different people and on different occasions.

This is exactly what happened during the period of the oral transmission of the words and deeds of Jesus. Many of these oral traditions are based on good historical memory. Yet around this core of memory details and words from other traditions about Jesus gradually accumulate. Moreover, the early Christians did not pass on such oral traditions with an archivist's interest, so as to maintain the source material for later historians. Rather the stories were told for liturgical, missionary, catechetical, and apologetic purposes. In fact, the early Christians did not envisage that these traditions would later be written down and collected in a book. For them the oral tradition was a treasure to be used for celebration, preaching, and teaching, which meant that the stories transmitted were differently accentuated in response to various occasions and settings.

What is the original nucleus of the incident which happened near Caesarea Philippi? Carefully examining Mark 8:27-35 from a purely literary point of view, one discovers several breaks in the flow and structure of this story. If one considers also the verses Mark 8:36-9:1, which belong to this passage, the impression grows even stronger that the present text of Mark is a composite of a nucleus with additions. For instance, the addressees of Jesus' words change several times. According to verses 27 and 31 they are the disciples; in verse 33 Jesus looks at his disciples but speaks to Peter only; in verse 34 the disciples are addressed together with the multitude.

Different hypothetical reconstructions of what was actually said during that conversation have been proposed. Some suggested that in the actual events Jesus' reaction in verse 33 followed immediately what is now commonly called "Peter's confession" in verse 29. Even without such speculative reconstructions one can detect in the present form of Mark's account what originally might have been the meaning of Peter's confession.

Task 3: On the basis of the contemporary expectations in Palestine, as described above, explore what "Peter's confession" originally may have meant.

> After individual study and exchange with neighbours some participants comment on this question, after which the enabler sums up as follows.

In the context of the religious and political expectations in Palestine Peter's "confession" appears in a new light. Usually we understand it as a decisive breakthrough to an accurate understanding by the disciples of their master's mission. But it is more likely that Peter misunderstood Jesus, seeing in him the expected national, religious-political Messiah, the one who would liberate Israel from Roman domination. This, according to Jesus, was a satanic temptation, a grave misunderstanding of his mission. He rejected being such a Messiah/Christ. Therefore his harsh retort: "Get behind me, Satan! For you are not on the side of God, but of men."

If this was what really happened near Caesarea Philippi, we can no longer make an easy distinction between the disciples and the people, between "us" and "them," between Christians and non-Christians. More often than not we think what people in general think. We cannot take our faith for granted. If Peter and the disciples misunderstood Jesus so basically, how much more are we in danger of misunderstanding him again and again. The disciples did not understand. Mark emphasizes this throughout his gospel, and Matthew often testifies that the disciples were people of little faith. To be on the side of God, to think God's thoughts, to think and act from the point of view of God's coming kingdom is an adventure no one can undertake lightly. Yet it is exactly such people with little understanding and little faith, people like the disciples and like us, whom Jesus calls into his service.

The new teaching

Having examined how non-Christians and the early church answered Jesus' crucial question, and having tried to understand what Peter originally meant with his "confession," let us turn to what Jesus wanted to teach his disciples according to Mark 8:27-35.

To understand this passage we must know something about the wider context of Mark's gospel. Mark was probably the first to combine various oral and perhaps already written sources about Jesus' miracles and teachings, linking them with an old tradition concerning Jesus' passion and resurrection. In so doing he invented a new literary genre — the gospel, the good news about Jesus Christ. It is generally assumed that he wrote his gospel for the church in Rome, probably between A.D. 62 and 72. At that time the title Messiah had been Christianized. The Christ was no longer associated with the expected political liberator of Israel, but with the figure of a righteous Lord and Saviour for the whole world. Many Christians actually began to associate this risen Lord with the vague notion of a Hellenistic divinity, and Jesus had therefore become for them an unhistorical eternal being without a recognizable face. In their spiritual enthusiasm Christians of the Hellenistic world strongly emphasized the fact of resurrection, so much that some of them claimed that they themselves had already been risen with Christ (cf. 2 Tim. 2:18).

Earlier the apostle Paul had to correct such an enthusiastic resurrection faith. In his letters he did so through polemical argument. Mark however taught the church simply by telling the story of the earthly Jesus. He presented him as the healer who was much more than a miracle worker. Above all he emphasized Jesus as the teacher.

Task 4: Observe the teaching method of Jesus in Mark 8:27-35. What is the particular new teaching in this conversation, and which verse is therefore the key one?

> After individual reflection participants exchange their findings with their neighbours. Then the enabler solicits some contributions to the plenary discussion and sums up in some way such as the following.

Jesus begins with what is already known. He asks first what people say about him. This question had obviously been discussed often among the disciples, and they have many answers ready (vv. 27-28). Jesus then proceeds to a more personal question. The disciples must have already reflected on this question, too, perhaps even privately exchanging opinions on it. Yet now Jesus himself raises the point. Peter, as usual the spokesman of the disciples, gives the answer.

In the time when Mark wrote and when the title Messiah no longer had the narrow national political meaning, this answer was not wrong. Indeed, Jesus is the Messiah, the expected Lord and Saviour of the whole world.

According to Matthew's gospel Jesus acknowledged this confession of Peter with a blessing and a great promise. According to Mark and Luke he simply charged the disciples "to tell no one about him." Such an order of secrecy appears often in Mark. By this insistence, Mark probably wanted to show that no one can understand the person and mission of Jesus without also seeing him as the crucified and risen Lord. To speak about Jesus without his passion inescapably means to misunderstand him.

Having re-established what is already known and having led the disciples to confess openly what they secretly thought, Jesus begins with the new teaching. Until then he had taught essentially through parables (Mark 4:33-34), but now he begins to speak "plainly" (Mark 8:32). In this new teaching he shows in what an astonishing way he has come to be the Messiah and the Son of Man. The key verse of the passage is indeed verse 31. Verses 27-30 form the introduction to it, and verses 32 and following show the disciples' reaction and the implications of the new teaching. After Peter's confession the disciples had shown no astonishment. After the amazing new teaching in verse 31, the disciples begin to react, again through their spokesman Peter. Nothing in the expectations of the Messiah then current had prepared them for Jesus' shocking revelation. Not even the song of the suffering servant of God (Isa. 53) was understood that way by the Jews of Palestine. No wonder Peter reacts and becomes the devil's advocate. What Peter asks Jesus to do was exactly what the devil had suggested in the temptation story: avoid the way to the cross and be a triumphant Messiah! Therefore Jesus rebukes Peter with the same words with which he had sent the devil away (Matt. 4:10). Yet he adds the significant order: "Behind me!" Here already may be a hidden call to discipleship leading to the cross.

The quest for true selfhood

The implication of the new teaching is one of the hardest sayings in the gospels: "If any man would come after me, let him deny himself and take up his cross and follow. For whoever would save his life will lose it; and whoever loses his life for my sake and the gospel's will save it" (vv. 34-35). Jesus speaks here about a subject much debated today: identity and selfhood. Critical observers of our time have said that the deepest illness of people today is their crisis of identity. In order really to heal persons and societies this alienation must be recognized and overcome. People, women, men and children, social classes, races, and cultures must find their own identity, their selfhood.

Task 5: What can we learn from Jesus' teaching in Mark 8:34-35 about the present quest for identity and selfhood?

> This question can best be discussed in small groups. In a retreat setting it can lead to a period of self-examination, ending with an act of worship, in which the elements of confession of sin, petition, and commitment will predominate. Alternatively, the following concluding remarks can be made.

Jesus does not preach a gospel of self-realization. He struggles against alienation and proclaims liberty to the captives (Luke 4:16-22), yet he does not think that if we have reached personal and cultural identity we will be saved. Our deepest alienation does not come from being dominated by other people or foreign cultural patterns. It comes from being turned in on ourselves, from wanting to assert ourselves and thus beginning to use both the things of this world and our fellow human beings for our own purposes. To this type of human thinking and human selfhood Jesus throws a radical challenge.

The most true and profound human identity is found not through self-realization, which too often degenerates into self-seeking, self-assertion, and finally aggressiveness. Those who really seek a faith that is worth living and dying for cannot consider the fulfilment of their own aspirations as the highest good. Paradoxically, true self-realization always includes self-transcendence. True liberation always means submission as well. "Not what I will, but what thou wilt" (Mark 14:36). It is the cause for which I live and for which I am ready to die which decides what I really am. It is the will to which I submit which marks my identity.

Yet Jesus did not teach with such general philosophical statements. He was much more specific: "Whoever loses his life for my sake and the gospel's will save it." The cause in whose service we find our true human identity is the person of Jesus and the gospel he announced and lived. To believe and serve this cause is not simply a matter of creeds. It implies a way, the way of the cross.

13 LET THE CHILDREN COME TO ME

Mark 10:13-16

The evangelists witnessed to Jesus in a narrative way, by telling stories. One effective way to understand and communicate the meaning of biblical texts today is thus that of a story. This script is the last part of a narrative exegesis which I have used in small and large groups in quite different cultural settings. Although audience participation here takes the form of listening, the degree of participation has generally been high, because the story and its telling reached both the mind and the heart, the intellect and the emotions of the hearers.

Study enablers can use this story as an introduction to group discussions. Questions like the following could be assigned to different discussion groups, which could afterwards teach one another in a plenary session:

(1) What did you learn from this story about the importance of children? Compare what people in your own environment say about the importance of children with the reasons for which Jesus singled them out by his words and gestures.

(2) What did you learn from the story about education? Examine Jesus' reversal of pedagogy and discuss its implications for life in the church and in your families and neighbourhoods.

(3) What did you learn from the story about conversion? Who was being converted and what were the reasons for this process of conversion?

The story is based on what we know about early Christian worship and about the position of children in the ancient Greek, Roman, and Jewish world. Most of the characters, their words, and actions can be documented from the Bible and ancient literature. The setting is inspired by an archaeological discovery made under the church of St. Clements in Rome: the meeting place of an Eastern mystery religion, the brotherhood of Mithras, was found side by side with an early Christian house-church.

The narrator of the story is a Roman legionary Gallus, who belongs to the brotherhood of Mithras. He has just come back from the Jewish war in Palestine where he took part in the siege and capture of Jerusalem in A.D. 70. In the first part of the story he tells how these events aroused his interest in that other Eastern religion — the Christ-people. He then recalls his attendance at a house-church meeting in the home of Rufus, an outstanding Roman Christian. There he also met Herodion, a Jewish Christian who knows much about rabbinic teachings, Philologus, a learned Greek slave who is the teacher of the sons of a Roman senator, a group of illiterate slaves from the Roman market, and Alis, a Christian widow from Upper Egypt.

During that house-church meeting the episode told in Mark 9:33-37 had been read from Mark's gospel. There was discussion of how these words and gestures of Jesus should be understood. Was Jesus insisting in a good rabbinic way on the importance of being like diligent *school*children, who are to become examples for the quarreling disciples (as Herodion proposed)? Was he speaking about children in a figurative way, in fact referring to the believers, God's children (as Philologus and Rufus maintained)? Or were Jesus' words and gestures to be taken literally, referring to real, ordinary children in whom Christ and indeed God chose to be present (as Alis believed)?

All this happened more than a week ago.

I did not intend to go back to their assembly though Rufus had cordially invited me to do so. After all, I belong to the brotherhood of Mithras. For Roman legionaries this is a much better fellowship. Our initiations may be harsh and cruel, fit only for men, and our liturgies top secret; yet there are moments when we reach ecstasy and are no longer ourselves but truly become inhabited by the invincible Mithras. Moreover, time just does not allow for belonging to a whole lot of Eastern religions, especially since we as legionaries must also do something for the official cults of Rome and the emperor.

Yet, despite all this, I went back to Rufus' house yesterday evening. You will laugh when I tell you why.

I simply could not forget the gestures and words of their Jesus concerning children. A strange thing has happened to me. I have suddenly begun to observe children here in Rome!

I am not married, and I have never had anything to do with children. The job of a Roman legionary does not lend itself to family life. Women, whenever we need them, can be found anywhere, but children are just not my affair.

Nevertheless, over these last few days my eyes have been opened. I have noticed all the boys and girls around us: those who play noisily in the marketplaces, the boys being led to school by their tutors, and the hungry and mutilated children whom the beggars of Rome use for getting money. And wherever I have seen a child I have been reminded of the Jesus about whom these people of Christ talk so much, of what he said and did. That is why I went back to the Christian assembly in the house of Rufus.

There were roughly the same people present as last week. At first the Egyptian woman was not there, but she came in during the hymn which concluded the opening prayers. She was holding a crying child in her arms, a thin and poorly-dressed girl under three years old.

After the hymn there was a moment of silence, which made the child's wailing all the more embarrassing. I heard the venerable Herodion whispering to his neighbour: "Does she think this is a nursery for crying babies?" Others looked with none too friendly eyes in the direction of Alis and the child.

The people of Christ have apparently the custom of telling one another about what has happened during the week. I was struck by this the first time I was among them. Some told of those who were ill. Others told about special joys and sorrows they had experienced. Still others brought greetings and news from assemblies of Christ-worshippers meeting elsewhere.

When this exchange of news started last evening, the Egyptian woman handed over her little brat to a neighbour. Fortunately the child had fallen asleep. Alis asked to speak, and told the assembly that she had reflected further about the Lord's word concerning children. True, children could refer figuratively to those who believed in Christ. Yet she was convinced that the word of Jesus has also to be taken literally. Therefore she had now welcomed into her home one of the many children exposed on the streets of Rome. Of course she could not provide this child with rich clothes and much food, but at least she could give her a deep motherly love and protect her from abuse.

Alis' information led to a heated discussion. Many spoke about the evil practice of "exposing" unwanted children. When a child is born here in Rome, it is laid before the feet of its father. If he takes it up into his arms, and thus acknowledges it, the child will be reared. But if the father refuses to do so, the child will be exposed. If these exposed infants do not soon die, they later become male or female prostitutes.

"Do you know what I heard recently?" asked Philologus with great indignation. "Nowadays some of the beggars of Rome are collecting exposed infants and deliberately maiming them. These starving and ailing children with shortened limbs, broken joints, and curved backs are exhibited in order to evoke pity; thus they can be used for begging. No wonder one sees so many mutilated little creatures in Rome. Others, apparently, are collecting exposed infants in order to use their brains and marrow for medical and magical purposes!

"In Greece things were better organized. Take Sparta for instance. There it wasn't the father's decision to rear or expose the child. All new-born babies had to be brought to the elders of the city, who examined each child. If it was well-built and sturdy they would order the father to rear it. If it was sickly or weak it was disposed of at a chasm-like place called Apothetae. Of course, I do not agree with this procedure, but at least it was more reasonable than the practice of child exposure here in Rome. And the Spartan elders were convinced that life which had not been well equipped for health and strength by nature was of no use to itself or to the state."

This long explanation obviously irritated the venerable Herodion. When he finally got the floor he stuttered. According to him, it was near blasphemy to speak about a "good" or a "bad" way of exposing children. Child exposure was totally evil, a grave sin against God, blessed be he. The Jews had always thought so and therefore never followed that horrible practice of doing away with new-born infants.

No, children were a precious gift from God. Did we not remember the great promise in the psalms ... and there came a quick swell of Hebrew, which translated something like:

> Children are a gift from the Lord;
> they are a real blessing.
> The sons a man has when he is young
> are like arrows in a soldier's hand.
> Happy is the man who has many such arrows.

Of course, children had to be disciplined so that they came to know the Torah and obey God's will.

Only — and at this point Herodion looked in the direction of Alis and the child — he wondered whether it was permissible to bring crying children into the holy assembly of the church of God. According to Jewish custom it was only from their thirteenth year that boys were allowed to participate fully in the synagogue worship.

"This," he concluded, "seems to me a good practice, which we Christians would do well to preserve."

Herodion had not noticed that during his last words the eyes of the Egyptian woman filled with tears. Without even asking to speak, she suddenly stood up and took out of her dress a letter written on a dirty piece of papyrus. With tears running down her cheeks, she said: "Brothers and sisters, now I must tell you something which I have never yet dared tell anybody.

"When I was a girl of sixteen my parents gave me to be married to Hilarion, a poor labourer in Upper Egypt. We lived together for only a few months, and then my husband had to go to Alexandria to find work. For a long time I heard nothing of Hilarion; and I was pregnant. So I went to the village scribe to send my husband a letter and ask for news. Months passed. Then, shortly before I gave birth to our child, the reply came. Here it is — I have carried it with me all these years:

> Hilarion to his sister Alis, very many greetings. Know that we are still in Alexandria. Do not be anxious. As soon as we receive our pay I will send it to you. If by chance you bear a child and it is a boy, rear him. If it is a girl, cast it out....

Alis could not speak any further because of her tears. Then she said in a barely audible voice, "It was a girl, our child. And what could I do but expose her? My husband never came back from Alexandria. Later I heard that he died of the plague. But I still carry his letter with me. And for many years I also carried the heavy burden of my guilt, the guilt of exposing, killing my own dear child. When I began to believe in Jesus I told him in my prayers about this great sin. He has forgiven me and taken my burden on himself. By his blood I am cleansed and freed from my guilt.

"Then last week Jesus spoke to me and to all of you — yes, to us here, not only to his disciples. He told us about the children and what we must do. So I understood what my task was. I have taken this poor, rejected child into my arms and welcomed her into my home."

Her voice was no longer hesitant nor veiled with tears. Something like a holy anger broke through in what she said: "Our Lord has put a small child in the midst of his disciples and taken it into his arms. How then can you hinder my daughter from coming into his presence?"

The atmosphere in the assembly of the people of Christ was leaden, like the heaviness before a storm, like the stillness before a hurricane. The Egyptian woman continued to stand there, looking around with eyes of fire. Then the quiet voice of Rufus was heard: "Thank you, sister Alis. We have heard you. And to show you and all of us that our Lord Jesus has also heard you, I am going to read now a passage in Mark's testimony which normally we would not have read until three weeks from now."

Rufus turned over the leaves in Mark's volume until he found the passage. There was all expectation in the room, and there was not the least bit of movement when he began to read.

> Some people brought children to Jesus for him to place his hands on them, but the disciples scolded the people. When Jesus noticed this, he was angry and said to his disciples: "Let the children come to me, and do not stop them, because the kingdom of God belongs to such as these. I assure you that whoever does not receive the kingdom of God like a child will never enter it." Then he took the children in his arms, placed his hands on each of them, and blessed them.

Nobody spoke or moved after Rufus had finished reading. Then one of the illiterate slaves from the market began to sing a beautiful hymn very quietly. One, two, and ever more voices joined in. Finally there was a mighty choir. They sang something like "Hallelujah!", and I felt that there were almost tears in my eyes.

I do not know any more of what happened in that assembly. I do not even know when and how I came back into my room last night. I could not sleep a moment, for again and again I heard the story which Rufus read and the words which Alis spoke.

If only this were really true, that we can receive God's kingdom, the salvation of our souls and bodies, just like a child which begs with empty hands! If this were true, I would not need to seek higher levels of initiation in the brotherhood of Mithras. Mithras slaughtered the bull for the select few. But their Christ sacrificed himself and gave his life for all, even women and children.

If this were really true, that we are cleansed, by his blood all of us, not only the highly initiated but people like Alis and like me — why then do I still go to the mysteries of Mithras?

I still do not know for sure what to think about that Jesus from Galilee. But one thing is certain. Next week I will return to the house of Rufus and attend the assembly of Christ's people.

14 JESUS AND POWER POLITICS

Mark 10:42-45

Originally prepared for a seminar of Asian student leaders in October 1972 in Tozanzo, Japan, this material has been adapted for use with many very different groups. In the present form it presupposes a work period of at least three hours, but it can easily be divided into two or three shorter sessions. The process will be helped by providing participants a worksheet with the short descriptions of Sadducees, Essenes, Pharisees, and resistance movements (cf. below pp. 172f) and a synopsis of Matthew 20:25-28, Mark 10:42-45, and Luke 22:25-27.

An open question

What is our Christian responsibility in power politics? Politics is the art of letting different people, different interest groups, different social classes live together in relative justice, peace, and security. It has to do with facing the tensions caused by the conflicting powers and goals which exist in every human society, in order to find and realize the most responsible compromise. Sooner or later one has to confront the difficult question of enforcement by the threat or use of physical violence, either to safeguard a relatively just and peaceful state of affairs or to reverse an obviously unjust situation. In connection with this use of violence the question of Christian participation in power politics becomes most acute.

Christians today do not agree on what stance they should take with regard to the use of violence. A short look at early church history can be quite revealing — and humbling — in this connection.

New Testament authors sometimes described the right conduct of Christian believers in military terms. Paul exhorted the Christians in Rome to "cast off the works of darkness and put on the armour of light" (Rom. 13:12). The ancient church continued to see its life and mission as a military service under Christ the *Imperator.* The Latin word *sacramentum* originally referred to the military oath a Roman soldier made upon entering the army; the church took it over to designate baptism. In the second century Tertullian, the son of an officer in the Roman garrison of Carthage, wrote to persecuted Christians: "We were called to the warfare of the living God in our very response to the sacramental words" (*Ad Martyras, III*). When St. Sabas was asked by his parents to become a military chaplain in the company his father commanded, Cyril reports that he answered: "I am a soldier in the company of God and I cannot abandon his army. Those who want to press me into desertion I can no longer call my parents."

The early Christians thus could not conceive that anyone could at the same time be a member of *militia Christi*, the army of Christ, and a soldier in the Roman legions. Early Christians were strict pacifists. Nevertheless more and more soldiers in the Roman army became Christians. Many died as martyrs; others tried to live a Christian life within the ranks of the army. It was in and through the Roman army that the breakthrough from the pagan and anti-Christian Roman empire to the Christian state of Constantine and Theodosius took place.

During the last great persecution under Diocletian many Christian soldiers and officers died as martyrs. This left a deep impression. In 311 the emperor Galerius granted tolerance to the church. A year later Constantine gave his army a banner with the monograph of Christ, under which they were victorious against Maxentius. In 313 the church was granted full religious freedom, which brought about a quick change in its official attitude. The very next year, at the Council of Arles, the church radically revised its theoretical pacifist attitude, and in Canon III it ruled that "those who in times of peace throw their weapons away shall be excluded from the eucharist." Military desertion because of Christian faith was now not only disapproved but punished by excommunication. Military saints were proclaimed, and developments began which led eventually to the crusades, "holy" Christian wars. Ever since there have been Christians who took a pacifist stance and Christians who said that in the struggle for justice and peace violent means could be used as a last resort.

Task 1: Debate the question of what biblical arguments can be found for a pacifist stance and what biblical arguments rather allow for "just war" or "just revolution."

> Divide the participants into an even number of groups, half of them arguing on the basis of biblical evidence for a pacifist stance, the other half arguing on the basis of biblical evidence for the use of violence as a last resort in the struggle for justice and peace. After sufficient time for preparation, the groups meet for debating. The enabler then sums up with comments like the following.

There are no easy answers to the question under debate. Isolated biblical texts and incidents can be found for justifying either stance. In the Old Testament the "holy wars of the Lord" stand in tension with the promises of peace by this same God. Great warriors like Samson and David cannot easily be seen together with the figure of the suffering servant in Isaiah 53. In the New Testament the familiar words of Romans 13:1-7 to the effect that as God's servant the ruler "does not bear the sword in vain" are in tension with the Jesus who ordered Peter to put away his sword (John 18:11). Many other prooftexts have been put forward. Not that there is a complete balance! One must be blind not to miss the major emphasis on a nonviolent struggle for justice and peace.

One thing does become clear through such a debate. It is not fruitful to quote isolated biblical verses as prooftexts for a pacifist or non-pacifist position. The biblical texts must be seen in their cultural and historical contexts and in the light of the major affirmations of the whole biblical revelation. The Bible must not be used as a quarry from which we mine a "biblical basis" for our own convictions and stances. We must be wary of "prooftexts" for what we already know. What is needed are clues to suggest new lines of inquiry and open up new perspectives. The Bible indeed provides us with such "clue-texts" and "clue-events" which help us to think and act from a new angle, to see God's point of view, when we are faced with open questions such as that of the use of violence and the Christian participation in power politics. Above all it testifies to a "clue-person," Jesus, who again and again astonishes us by showing us a way we often do not want to go, but which leads to fuller truth and life.

Jesus and the religious-political parties of this time

In A.D. 6, when Jesus was still a boy, Judea was incorporated into the Roman empire. This led to the beginning of the violent Jewish resistance movements and to the vicious circle of armed rebellion and cruel repression. Violence escalated, leading to the disaster of the first Jewish War (A.D. 60-70). What religious-political tendencies and "parties" existed among Palestinian Jews? What were the political options for Jesus and his disciples?

Most Palestinian Jews were victims rather than protagonists in this situation. *Children* did not yet count in society. *Women* had little or no place, and, if mentioned at all, it is usually as the wives or concubines of the powerful. Some charitable work among the victims of conflict is ascribed to them. Jewish writings of that time tell of the "merciful women of Jerusalem," who offered drugged wine to those who had been condemned to death and were on their way to execution. The majority of Palestinian Jews belonged to *"the poor of the land."* They were simply too poor to become religiously and politically active. Under the burden of heavy taxes village folk could not survive if they kept the full Sabbath laws, and so the Jewish religious authorities despised them. Many were so indebted to landowners that they could not risk any political activity. Still others were ostracized and excluded from the Jewish community, because they had become *collaborators* with their Roman masters.

Nevertheless, the situation of oppression was not accepted passively. Four religious-political tendencies in the Palestinian Jewish community of that time struggled in various ways for change. It would be wrong to call them either religious groups or political parties. Religion and politics could not be separated, and therefore one can speak more accurately of religious-political tendencies and groupings.

> At this point the participants are divided into four groups (Sadducees, Essenes, Pharisees, and resistance movement). If worksheets with the following short sketches of the four "parties" have been prepared, these are distributed. Task 2 is announced, and after the comments on each "party" are read, the members of that group are encouraged to ask questions of clarification and further information to help them identify with their role. The enabler must be prepared for such questions. If possible, a better alternative is to ask four participants ahead of time to do some preparatory reading on one of the four "parties" and to act as "specialists" in their respective groups.

The *Sadducees* were wealthy and staunchly conservative members of old Jewish families, from whom the high priests and elders were recruited. In religious matters they opposed every innovation, for instance the oral law and belief in the resurrection of the dead which the Pharisees propagated. In their style of life, however, they were open to the influences of the Hellenistic world. Their political hope was for a this-worldly religious/national state, centred on the temple of Jerusalem. Their privileged economic position depended on the temple tax, and also their socio-religious status was intimately related to the normal functioning of the temple. They were no friends of the Romans, who had to dismiss one high-priest after another, but to safeguard the continuation of the temple worship they reluctantly collaborated with the occupying power.

The *Essenes* probably split off from the priestly circles in Jerusalem. In order to safeguard a rigorous sanctity and obedience to the law they withdrew into the desert. The community of Qumran, whose library (the Dead Sea Scrolls) was discovered in 1947, was certainly a part of this Essene movement, but other groups of Essenes must have lived as fraternities in Palestinian cities. Their political hope envisaged an apocalyptic victory of the sons of light over the sons of darkness. Therefore they hated both those Jews who did not accept their rigorous piety and the Romans, who did not acknowledge the biblical God as their Lord. Instead of submitting to either the official Jewish religious authorities or the Roman government they hoped for the coming of the Messiahs — a military one who would lead the sons of light in their battle, and a priestly one who would rule over the faithful. Meanwhile they lived in a strict monastic life of men only. Their "rule of community" prescribed that they had "to seek God ... to love all that he has chosen and hate all that he has rejected; to keep far from all evil and cling to all good works; to act truthfully, righteously and justly on earth." Their daily life was marked by several daily ritual washings, a fraternal meal for full members, the sharing of goods, and a continuous study of the scriptures (the scrolls found near Qumran included not only copies of the Hebrew scriptures but several Essene scriptural commentaries).

The *Pharisees* can best be characterized as a highly respected and influential scholar class which championed the authority of the twofold law. Whether all Pharisees were scribes or whether the scribes functioned as the leading group among the Pharisees is still a matter of debate. Next to the written law of the Hebrew scriptures they set the oral tradition of unwritten laws. They began to "build a wall around the law" by adding many new prescriptions and prohibitions for all of life, not only matters of temple, synagogue, and family worship and details of the celebration of religious festivals, but also questions of property and matters of commercial, criminal, and family legislation. Unlike the Sadducees and priestly class, their life was not centred on the temple in Jerusalem, but on the many local synagogues and the schools attached to them. Some Pharisees lived in great poverty, others gained their livelihood in ordinary occupations, but all were interested in the study and teaching of scripture and leading a pure and obedient life. Characteristic for the Pharisaic movement was the internalization of the twofold law and the belief in the resurrection of the dead. Their hope for salvation lay therefore not in a this-worldly Jewish state, but in eternal life for all those who in this life remained law-abiding.

Finally, from A.D. 6 onwards there was a growing Jewish *resistance movement*, triggered by the Roman annexation of Judea. Its members struggled violently against both Jewish collaborators and the Roman occupying power itself. The Jewish historian Josephus wrote about it: "A Galilean, named Judas, incited his countrymen to revolt, upbraiding them as cowards for consenting to pay tribute to the Romans and tolerating mortal masters, after having God for their lord" (*Jewish War*, II, 118). The movement was probably split into several competing groups, the most important being the *Sicarii* (so called because they carried a *sica* or dagger) and the *Zealots* (that is, the fervent or fanatic ones). Some historians think that the name Zealot covers the whole resistance movement, but the party of Zealots probably did not come into existence until the first years of the Jewish War. The Sicarii fought violently for God's reign in the Holy Land, and they sometimes became the champions of the poor. Josephus writes about their capture of Jerusalem in August 66 as follows: "The victors burst in and set fire to the house of Ananias the high-priest and to the palaces of Agrippa and Bernice; they next carried their combustibles to the public archives, eager to destroy the money-lenders' bonds and to prevent the recovery of debts, in order to win over a host of grateful debtors and to cause a rising of the poor against the rich, sure of impunity. The keepers of the Record Office having fled, they set light to the building" (*Jewish War*, II, 426b-427). The Zealots struggled violently for the cleansing of the temple with a view to realizing the priestly utopia of Ezekiel 40-48. The motivating power for the whole resistance movement was the apocalyptic expectation that the political Messiah would soon arrive and lead them in their struggles.

There must have been considerable overlap and mobility between these groups and tendencies. Josephus tells in his autobiography that he himself came from a priestly family and was a priest, that he was initiated into the community of the Essenes, later became a Pharisee, and during the Jewish War acted as an officer of Jewish rebels in Galilee, who must have had some relationships with the Sicarii and Zealots. Finally he became a collaborator with the Romans and spent the latter half of his life as a friend and confidant of the Roman emperor's family. This shows that many options were open for a dynamic Palestinian Jew!

Task 2: Take up the role assigned to your group, and try to identify with it as deeply as you can. Then prepare for a debate on the following questions:

(a) Could you accept Jesus as a member of your group? If no, why not? If yes, why and under what conditions?

(b) Could you accept Jesus' disciples into your movement? Give reasons for your answer.

(c) Could you accept the present Christian churches (if you would have known them) into your movement?

> After a sufficient period of preparation the participants gather in plenary. The members of each group sit together, the "Sadducees" opposite the "Pharisees," the "Essenes" opposite the resistance fighters. Either the enabler or someone who has prepared the role ahead of time takes the part of the advocate of Jesus and the disciples. The advocate solicits entry of the Jesus movement to each of the four "parties" in turn. This leads to a debate, ideally not only between the advocate and the members of each group in turn, but also among the four different groups themselves. Through this process the enormous religious and socio-political tensions of Jesus' time and environment will be experienced, as will Jesus' position in the midst of this power politics. Insights gained can then be summarized, either after each round of debate or at the end, as follows.

Jesus was clearly no Sadducee. Nor were any of his disciples, although one of them, probably John, may have had some relationship with the Sadducee families (cf. John 18:16). It must be acknowledged, however, that the church throughout its history has often played the role of the Sadducees, willingly or unwillingly collaborating with the powerful of this world in order to safeguard its religious liberty.

There are some striking similarities between some words of Jesus and some of the affirmations and institutions in the Essene movement. Several of Jesus' disciples had first been disciples of John the Baptist, who probably knew the community at Qumran although he himself was not an Essene. Despite these parallels and a possible link with the Essenes through some of his disciples, Jesus clearly did not belong to that movement. He had women in his company, a collaborator with the Romans was one of his disciples, and Jesus preached love not hate.

Jesus' contemporaries probably considered him a Pharisaic rabbi. There are indeed striking parallels between some early Christian affirmations and the teaching of Rabbi Hillel, a contemporary of Jesus. Several Jewish authors of our time have shown how strongly Jesus and the early church, especially Paul, were rooted in Pharisaic thinking. The image of the Pharisees painted in the New Testament is indeed one-sided and polemical. This polemic against the Pharisees can be interpreted as an indication that Jesus was in fact very near to the Pharisaic movement. Yet again, he certainly was no Pharisee. He had not been the disciple of a rabbi and he did not despise the "poor of the land." His attitude to the law was much more radical than that of the Pharisees. He did not build a hedge around the law but penetrated to its centre, the love of God and our neighbours.

Today it is sometimes affirmed that the movement of Jesus had great affinity to the Jewish resistance movement of that time. Several passages in the gospels could indeed be so interpreted: Jesus cleansed the temple; some of his disciples carried weapons and were perhaps formerly members of the resistance movement; Jesus said that he came to throw a fire on this earth. Above all, Jesus was not stoned by the Jews but condemned by Pontius Pilate to die by crucifixion, the typical execution of rebels in first-century Palestine; and he in fact died between two such rebels. Both Jesus and the Sicarii announced that the kingdom of God was at hand. The violent struggle for the coming of this kingdom must indeed have been a temptation for the disciples and perhaps for Jesus himself. Yet he chose the more radical way of self-sacrificing love. Moreover, his mission could not be restricted by Jewish national/religious expectations.

Jesus' teachings and the way he went must have irritated the members of all four religious-political tendencies in Palestinian Judaism. Most of his time Jesus lived among the poor of the land. The majority of his disciples and followers came from among these poor. Yet the mysterious event on the mountain of transfiguration had shown clearly that Jesus was not simply one of the poor, but a king incognito, who had become poor in the fulfilment of his mission. What was this mission in a world of conflict? The teaching transmitted in Mark 10:42-45 and its parallels in Matthew and Luke indicates some of its central characteristics.

Jesus' strategy

Not long after Peter had confessed Jesus to be the Christ near Caesarea Philippi (Mark 8:27ff), two of the disciples who had been together with their master on the mountain of transfiguration (Mark 9:2ff) came to ask Jesus for a favour.

James and John wanted the privilege of sitting at his right hand and left hand side when he would be enthroned in his glory (Mark 10:35-37). They coveted the place of Moses and Elijah, having still not understood that the way to the glory leads through the elevation on the cross, through the baptism of death. Without realizing it, James and John were in fact asking to be elevated on the crosses at Golgotha on the right hand and left hand of Jesus. They would indeed become martyrs, as Jesus announced to them in a hidden way (v. 39); but for the moment all they were interested in was the privileges. "And when the ten heard it, they began to be indignant at James and John" (v. 41).

This situation happens often in my own family: one or two of the children — or sometimes their father — want to enjoy a privilege. Hearing about it, the others become irritated. The atmosphere grows full of tension and potential conflict. Unless the mother interferes and accomplishes a ministry of reconciliation there will be family warfare. The same thing happens daily in our societies, in the living together of different social classes, racial, and ethnic groups. On a larger scale, it marks the relationship among rich and poor nations: some ask for favours and grab privileges. The result is international tension, an explosive situation, and sooner or later war.

How does Jesus deal with such a situation of conflict, so typical of the political power struggle? Before examining his strategy, we should notice the somewhat different ways in which the evangelists have reported this incident.

> If the participants have a worksheet with the synopsis of Matthew 20:25-28/Mark 10:42-45/Luke 22:25-27, and if time allows, they should themselves discover the similarities and differences. Reflecting about the specific testimony of Mark, as compared with Matthew's and Luke's accounts, they teach one another. If no synopsis is available or time does not allow for such a synoptic examination, the enabler describes the context of Mark 10:42-45 and the particularities of Mark's account as follows.

Mark and Matthew place this teaching at the time when Jesus and his disciples "were on the road, going up to Jerusalem" (Mark 10:32), when Jesus had told his disciples for the third time that he would have to die (Mark 10:32-34). Immediately after the passage under consideration the passion story begins. Luke places a similar teaching in the middle of the passion story, namely during the Lord's Supper when Judas Iscariot had already betrayed Jesus (Luke 22:3-6), when the words of institution had been spoken (22:14-20) and a dispute arose among the disciples (22:21-24), just before the announcement of Peter's betrayal (22:28-34). It may be that Jesus made the same point twice, once on his way up to Jerusalem and once during the Lord's Supper. More likely the account of Mark/Matthew and that of Luke both go back to the same memory of an actual teaching, reporting different oral traditions concerning the circumstances of this teaching. In all three accounts the setting is a situation of conflict among the disciples.

There are only minor textual differences here between Mark and Matthew. The passage appears in the same literary context, although according to Matthew it was the mother of James and John, not the two disciples themselves, who made the request for a place of honour. In the text itself Matthew makes two small but significant omissions and one significant change of words. He simplifies Jesus' saying in Mark 10:42, speaking simply about "the rulers of the nations" rather than "those who are supposed to rule over the nations." (Many translations have "Gentiles" instead of "nations;" the Greek term can mean either, but the context suggests the more general meaning "nations" or "people.") In the same verse Matthew changes "*their* great men" to "*the* great men," a change sometimes overlooked in modern translations. Where Jesus says according to Mark 10:44

that those who want to be the first among the disciples must be "slave of all," Matthew has "must be your slave." In Mark's version Jesus thus places himself at a greater distance from the supposed rulers of this world, relativizing their power, while calling the disciples to become servants, slaves of *all*. Matthew's version can be read more smoothly, but his editorial work loses some of the sharpness of Jesus' words. Moreover, he emphasizes the service relationship within the church.

In Luke's version Jesus uses a rather different terminology and imagery, but he teaches essentially the same thing. The reference to the one who serves at table (22:27) is of course suggested by the context into which Luke has placed this saying of Jesus, the Lord's Supper. The most striking difference in Luke's account is his omission of the theological interpretation of Jesus' death. Scholars still debate whether Jesus himself explained his coming death as a "ransom for many," or whether this is the church's interpretation, later attributed to Jesus. This interpretation, recorded in Mark 10:45b, comes very near to the earliest Christian creeds (for instance, 1 Cor. 15:3b). Ransom can be understood either in the Old Testament context as an offering for the redemption of someone or in the Hellenistic context as a price paid for liberating slaves. It may also simply have the general meaning of "liberation" or "redemption." For Hebrew thinking "the many" does not mean a majority excluding a minority, but could almost be translated "for all," or more accurately "for the multitudes."

Task 3: Faced with a typical situation of tension, what does Jesus do and say according to Mark 10:42-45? Describe and discuss each of the steps of Jesus' strategy.

> This task can best be done in small study groups, though not the same four groups which earlier identified with the four "parties" — or the role-play may continue. The groups should be told that there are more than two or three steps to be discovered in this text. Afterwards the groups teach one another in the plenary. Most of the following points — and perhaps other new ones — will probably be mentioned.

Jesus is sensitive to the existing tension. He does not say that such tensions should not exist among his disciples and therefore avoid bringing them up. Nor does he cover this unpleasant affair with a cloak of charity. He avoids speaking separately with the two who coveted the privilege or with the ten who were grumbling, but brings the affair in the open and presumably gathers all the disciples around him.

When they are gathered, Jesus does not immediately raise the concrete issue of tension. He raises the special case into the realm of more general affairs, probably in order to prevent an immediate clash between the hotheaded disciples. In his teaching he often proceeded in this way, for instance, by making a point through the use of a parable. Here he speaks first about the broad issue of power politics and appeals to something on which they all agree: "You know that ...."

In his description of power politics Jesus shows himself a realist. He acknowledges the existence of powers, but he does not say that power is neutral. He knows that the use of power again and again degenerates into force. The teaching in Mark 10 therefore stands midway between the famous passage in Romans 13, where the powers and their legitimate use of force are positively evaluated, and Revelation 13, where the ever-present demonic perversion of power is revealed. In Mark 10:42 Jesus simply establishes the fact: in the world there are rulers. This in itself he does not challenge, but he sees that rulers have a tendency to rule from *over* the people and hand their government *down*. The great ones "exercise authority from above downwards." This Greek verb is found nowhere else in the New Testament or any other Greek literature that has survived, and it may well have been coined for the occasion.

Seeing the facts as they are, Jesus goes on to evaluate them. The "high up" authorities may act as absolute rulers. They may like to appear as benefactors (as Luke's version suggests). Yet Jesus clearly shows the relativity of their power: "the so-called rulers," "those who are supposed to rule," "their great men." To say such a thing in the Roman Empire, where the emperors declared themselves to be divine lords, was extremely dangerous. No wonder Jesus was not going to die a natural death but would be condemned to be executed.

Jesus is a realist, yet he does not resign himself before the hard realities of this world. He thinks and acts in accordance with the realism of God's kingdom, and thus challenges the disciples not to conform to these hard realities: "It shall not be so among you!" (v. 43). Earlier, during the conversation near Caesarea Philippi, Jesus had challenged his disciples not to think what people think, but to think what God thinks (Mark 8:33). This echoed the very beginning of Jesus' message: "The time is fulfilled, and the kingdom of God is at hand; repent and believe in the gospel" (Mark: 1:15). His message is inextricably linked with a call to conversion, a new way of thinking, a reordering of priorities.

In his call to conversion Jesus appeals to a basic human yearning: "whoever would be great among you ..."; "whoever would be first among you ...." Contrary to what often happens in a misguided Christian spirituality, he does not curb the human wish for excellence. Later, the apostle Paul would not be less zealous and demanding after his call than before, but his search for excellence would take another direction with new priorities. Similarly, Jesus does not say that we should become "humble" in the unbiblical sense of this word, that we should feel very modest and not seek what is high and excellent. He acknowledges our yearning for excellence, but directs it towards a new goal: servanthood as a conscious and free choice; moreover, in freedom "you must be slave of all" (v. 44). His clue for breaking through the vicious circle of oppression and rebellion in the human power play points to a way which we do not want to go.

Yet Jesus is not naive. He does not think that by changing people one has already changed the structures of society. Nor does he assume that if the structures are changed a new humanity and a new society would almost automatically be born. The challenge to conversion is addressed to a particular group of people, the disciples. No fewer than three times in this short text the expression "among you" appears. Who are they? According to the social, religious, and political structures of first-century Palestine they were an impossible group. How could a former collaborator with the Romans live together with people who may formerly have been members of the Jewish resistance movement! How could somebody known in high-priestly families live together with people from among the poor of the land! Immediately linked with Jesus' challenge to current ways of thinking is his creation of a new community which by its very existence challenges the structures of conflict in this world. Into the sick body of society he inserts a cell of healing, composed of agents of reconciliation and animated by a spirit of service. The greatest political action of the church in the world is its being the church — if indeed it manifests that humanly speaking impossible group which contains and reconciles in itself the tensions of the world.

What such a spirit of service and reconciliation means Jesus does not teach by words alone. The teacher becomes the pioneer. His basic teaching is his way to the cross. To overcome destructive conflict, to reconcile in the deep sense of this word, costs nothing less than the gift of one's own life.

The confession of faith in v. 45 states even more: the pioneer on the way to the cross is the redeemer. He gives "his life as a ransom for many." This central affirmation of the gospels does not exempt the disciples and the church of all times and places from following the steps of Jesus' strategy. But on this way of discipleship, believers need not march with the grim seriousness of moralists and militants who think that everything depends on their effort. The pioneer has gone to the end of the road. He has paid the price of liberation even for those who stumble with the first step.

With this teaching Jesus has not given us a political programme. To the controversial question about the use of violence no clear answer is provided. This text certainly challenges the oppressive use of violence by those in power. But some might argue that in a situation of institutionalized, oppressive violence the way of servanthood will, as a last resort, imply the sacrifice of a good conscience by taking up arms and being ready to pay the price of killing and being killed for the sake of others. Many others will protest against such an interpretation. The question remains open, and the debate is still on.

Nevertheless, Jesus as the "clue-person" has indicated a basic strategy. In each place and time we must now attempt to discern what this strategy implies for living in the hard realities of power politics with the realism of God's coming kingdom. What does it mean for members of an exploited majority or for a dominating minority? How can an ordinary citizen or someone entrusted with much political and economic power follow this strategy? The spirit, goal, and cost of it are clear. That the church's main political mission is accomplished by *being* Christ's church is equally evident. Yet action programmes and policies have to be discerned on the spot.

15 THIS IS ... DO THIS

The institution of the Lord's Supper

This script was prepared for a May 1978 seminar in Montevideo, Uruguay, which brought together an equal number of Protestant and Roman Catholic lay people and ministers/clergy. Although this study's particular interpretation of the eucharistic words, elements, and gestures has been put to the test with other groups, I would be grateful for critical responses as I am still not certain that the interpretation proposed is valid. The worksheet on "The Lord's Supper" should be copied for distribution after Task 1 has been completed.

The celebration and its explanations

A Bible study on the meaning of the Lord's Supper in a group of Protestants and Catholics risks splitting the group from the outset. Although a high degree of consensus about the significance of the church's eucharistic celebration has been reached in recent ecumenical consultations, the division of Christians is still most painfully experienced when we remain separated at the table of the Lord. Even if interconfessional groups anticipate the celebration of a common eucharist while remaining members of separated churches, the meaning of the Lord's Supper is a question that must still be faced.

One might say — quite correctly, of course — that the Lord's Supper is a great mystery which cannot be explained and which must be received in faith. Yet according to the biblical testimony faith is never something exclusively emotional. Faith calls for and leads to understanding, at least partial understanding.

I like to participate in eucharistic celebrations, whether in Orthodox, Roman Catholic, or one of the many Protestant churches. In such celebrations I experience that my faith is being built up and that I am inserted into a community of believers from all ages and continents. In this celebration I as a member of the church militant on earth today can become a contemporary of the great acts of salvation, the Exodus and the death and resurrection of Christ in the past and the coming messianic feast in the kingdom.

However, as soon as the meaning of the Lord's Supper is explained by Orthodox, Roman Catholic, Lutheran, Reformed, or other theologians, their discourses leave me ill at ease and confused. Some of these theological explanations — from those of the church fathers down to the most recent ecumenical statements — I simply do not understand. And what I understand seems to me to be removed both from the Jesus whom I have come to know in the gospels and from the concrete struggles of faith in everyday life.

I am not denying that the classic Orthodox, Catholic, and Protestant interpretations have been meaningful for many Christians in former centuries and remain so for believers today. I simply have to acknowledge that these interpretations do not speak to me, they do not warm my heart or nourish my faith. The same thing might be true today for many Christians around the world.

Is it possible that after almost twenty centuries of theological reflection about the mystery of the eucharistic feast we could find today a new level of meaning in the few biblical texts which report the institution of the Lord's Supper? Our several doctrinal teachings about this theme are strongly marked by patristic, medieval, Reformation, and counter-Reformation debates about the natures of Christ, various theological statements on the ways of salvation, and diverse understandings of the church and its ministries. Can a new study of the eucharistic texts in the New Testament free us from this long tradition of disagreements and give us all a fresh glimpse of the Jesus who told the parables, healed the sick, called us into discipleship and went the way to the cross? Debates and consultations on the Lord's Supper have often concentrated so one-sidedly on interconfessional differences and the search for an interconfessional consensus that the vital — and for ordinary church members much more important — relationship between the eucharistic celebration and the struggles of faith in everyday life has become marginal. Can a Bible study on the Lord's Supper make this link more evident?

With these questions in mind we will first try to reconstruct out of our memories what the New Testament authors actually report about the institution of the Lord's Supper.

Task 1: Close your Bibles and in teams of two or three write down what you remember about the following questions:

(a) When and where did the institution of the Lord's Supper take place?

(b) What were the meaningful gestures Jesus performed during that institution?

(c) What were the sayings which Jesus spoke during the celebration?

When most teams have completed their task, the group as a whole attempts to reconstruct from memory the context, the gestures, and the sayings. Many will probably remember that the institution of the Lord's Supper is reported somewhat differently in different gospels and by Paul. There will almost certainly be more agreement about the gestures than about the sayings. Before making a more thorough examination of the four texts of institution (Matt. 26:26-29; Mark 14:22-25; Luke 22:15-20; I Cor. 11:23-26) the enabler sums up and complements what has been said about the time and place of the institution of the Lord's Supper.

According to Mark, Matthew, Luke, and Paul the institution of the Last Supper took place in the evening of the night when Jesus was betrayed. Judas' decision to betray his Lord (Matt. 26:14ff; Mark 14:10; Luke 22:3ff) happens before the institution. So does the designation of the traitor in the first two gospels (Matt. 26:20ff; Mark 14:17ff) while according to Luke it takes place after the institution (Luke 22: 21ff). All three evangelists place the announcement of Peter's denial after the institution and preceding the struggle of prayer and capture of Jesus in Gethsemane.

John writes only indirectly about the Lord's Supper (John 6 and 13), and his whole chronology of the Passion week differs from that of the synoptic evangelists. Whether the institution of the Lord's Supper took place during a Passover meal (as the reports about the preparation of the meal in Matt. 26:17ff; Mark 14:12ff; Luke 22:7ff suggest) or whether it was a meal "before the feast of the Passover" (as John 13:1f reports) is still a matter of debate.

According to Mark and Matthew the institution took place "as they were eating" (Mark 14:22; Matt. 26:26). According to Luke, the institution consists of gestures and sayings in connection with a first cup and the bread at the beginning of or during the meal, while a second cup is mentioned "after supper" (Luke 22:17ff, 20; so also 1 Cor. 11:25). Some old manuscripts of Luke omit vv. 19b and 20, but the longer text is probably the original one.

The meal took place in Jerusalem, in the large upstairs room of a guest-house, to whose owner two of Jesus' disciples were led by "a man carrying a jar of water" (Mark 14:13ff). This place of the Last Supper is traditionally located on Mount Zion in Jerusalem. Near this place ancient ritual baths and cisterns similar to those found in the Qumran settlement in the Judean desert have been excavated, as well as the "door of the Essenes" in the city wall of Jerusalem of the time of Jesus. On the basis of these excavations and a study of available literary sources a German archaeologist has proposed that in Jesus' time there was an Essene settlement on Mount Zion. Perhaps, he has suggested, the Lord's Supper took place in the guest-house of that settlement. This would presumably explain why a man and not a woman (as current in the Near East) was carrying water. It would also shed new light on several passages in Acts as well as on certain similarities between the Lord's Supper and the Qumranite meal of fellowship.

More important than such guesses about the time and place are the actual gestures and sayings of Jesus during the institution of the Last Supper.

At this point the worksheets with the synopsis of the four texts of institution are distributed.

Task 2: Compare the four accounts of the institution of the Last Supper, first with regard to the gestures, secondly with regard to the sayings of Jesus.

> This task is done in the small groups which worked on Task 1 together. In the plenary discussion afterwards participants will make most of the following observations.

The sequence of gestures in all four accounts is almost the same: Jesus took bread and blessed or gave thanks for it. Then he broke it and gave it to the disciples, following up this series of gestures by a saying. Then he took a cup (note that Luke speaks of two cups, one at the beginning and one at the end of the meal) and gave thanks for it. Mark and Matthew then add that he gave the cup to the disciples. All the reports conclude with an indication that Jesus addressed a saying to the disciples. As we shall see, this common emphasis on the gestures of Jesus and this almost total agreement with regard to gestures in the four most ancient testimonies about the Last Supper are important.

Both series of gestures are accompanied by sayings. Here the various accounts show considerable differences. In the saying concerning the bread Matthew follows Mark, adding only "eat" to the "take," probably a liturgical expansion of the Markan text. Luke and Paul start immediately with "This is my body," adding the explanation "which is (given) for you" and the commandment to "do this in remembrance of me." The saying concerning the cup differs even more. Again one notices parallels between Mark and Matthew on the one hand and Luke and Paul on the other. The first pair records: "This is my blood of the covenant which is poured out for many," Matthew adding the theological specification "for the forgiveness of sins." The second pair records: "This cup is the new covenant of my blood," and Luke adds "which is poured out for you." Only Paul has a second commandment to "do this ... in remembrance of me." The first two evangelists then report with minor but typical differences Jesus' word that he will not drink of the fruit of the wine until the kingdom comes. Luke has a similar saying in connection with the first cup, while Paul explains that by celebrating this meal "you proclaim the Lord's death until he comes."

One should add to these different traditions concerning the sayings of Jesus the Christian eucharistic formula — certainly very ancient — in 1 Cor. 10:16: "The cup of blessing which we bless, is it not a participation in the blood of Christ? The bread which we break, is it not a participation in the body of Christ?"

Event and liturgical traditions

Scholars generally acknowledge that the various sayings of Jesus reported in the four accounts on the Last Supper are already strongly marked by the different ways of understanding and celebrating the eucharist in the ancient church. There is clearly a considerable difference between the tradition which Mark and Matthew received and incorporated into their gospels and the tradition found in Paul's letter. On the whole, Luke follows Paul's tradition, but he may have had access to still another tradition concerning the Lord's Supper. Various proposals have been made with regard to the probable milieu of these two or three liturgical traditions, but these proposals contradict one another. Behind and within these various traditions the original words (theologians would say *ipsissima verba*) of Jesus certainly lie, but since no consensus has been reached about what Jesus originally said it is dangerous to base discussions on the meaning of the eucharist exclusively on these various traditions or on this or that hypothesis about what his original words were.

It is much more probable that the four New Testament accounts actually report the original gestures (*ipsissima facta*) of Jesus. Additional evidence for this is found in the account in the last chapter of Luke of the meeting between the risen Lord and the two deeply disappointed disciples going to Emmaus. Jesus spoke to them on the way, but they did not recognize him until he sat with them and broke the bread: "When he was at table with them, he took the bread and blessed, and broke it, and gave it to them. And their eyes were opened and they recognized him" (Luke 24:30f). It was due to the gesture of breaking bread and giving it to them that the disciples finally recognized him.

This passage clearly reflects the eucharistic practice of the early church. The emphasis strongly lies on the breaking of the bread. It is not surprising then that in Acts the eucharistic meals of the early church are not described by the words of institution but according to the basic gestures of the breaking of the bread (cf. Acts 2:42, 46; 20:7).

The nearest parallel in John's gospel to the account of the Last Supper (John 13) is totally centred on a series of equally significant and exemplary gestures. Nothing is said there about the elements of the meal, but John reports that during the Last Supper Jesus washed the disciples' feet. He then explained this meaningful gesture as a *hypodeigma*. This term, which plays an important role in the letter to the Hebrews, means a fully representative sign and example. Moreover, Jesus ordered the disciples to continue to "do this," to repeat this deeply significant gesture. Exactly the same words ("do this") are used here as in Luke's and Paul's accounts of the Last Supper.

Such meaningful gestures remind us of the prophetic acts of Old Testament prophets. We should also be aware that in areas of oral tradition gestures are an extremely important means of communication, and words are usually accompanied by gestures. Jesus lived in such a culture of oral tradition, and his pedagogy consisted not in writing books and pamphlets, but in telling parables and doing significant acts, which stay in the memory.

The process of interpretation

There is no doubt that during the last common meal with his disciples Jesus communicated with gestures and words a great message to them. It had to do with his ministry and death as well as with the coming kingdom.

The disciples probably did not at first fully understand the meaning of this last solemn message, just as they did not at first understand the meaning of Jesus' crucifixion.

They transmitted to the early church what they remembered of Jesus' gestures and words, the gestures having obviously been imprinted much more deeply in their memory than the words. In the light of Jesus' crucifixion and resurrection and in the confidence that the risen Lord and the Holy Spirit would guide them, the believers of the early church began then to search the Jewish scriptures for clues to understand this last solemn message of the earthly Jesus.

The diagram on the worksheet shows how this process of interpretation may have proceeded. In addition to the eyewitness reports about what happened during the Lord's Supper, four main clues were found in the Scriptures of the Old Testament and a fifth one may have come from the religious environment of the church in Judea. We have no way of ascertaining whether or not Jesus, during his lifetime or during the Last Supper, gave some of these clues to the disciples.

The first clue is undoubtedly that of the Jewish Passover. Whether or not the Lord's Supper was in fact a Passover meal is of secondary importance: even if it happened on the evening before Passover, its link with that central Jewish feast would have been obvious to Jesus and the disciples. Yet it would be wrong to interpret the meaning of the Lord's Supper exclusively on the basis of the Jewish Passover. Jesus' gestures and words recall similar ones in the Passover liturgy, but this link is never especially emphasized. The accent lies on the new meaning given by Jesus. Even in the famous text where Paul states that "Christ, our paschal lamb, has been sacrificed" (1 Cor. 5:7), no direct link with the Lord's Supper is made. Nevertheless, the Passover and therefore the commemoration of the Exodus event belongs to the frame of reference of the Lord's Supper. The text of Exodus 12:21-28 and similar Old Testament prescriptions concerning the Passover (cf. Exod. 13:6-10; Deut. 16:1ff), as well as the whole Exodus story, are not actually quoted, but they certainly were in the mind of the early church. The commandment in Paul's and Luke's versions to "do this in remembrance of me" especially points in this direction. In their Passover feast Jews become contemporaries of God's great act of protection during the Exodus; in their Lord's Supper feast Christians become contemporaries of God's great acts of protection and of liberation in the life, death, and resurrection of Christ.

A second clue is that of the covenant sacrifice. In this case the relevant Old Testament texts may actually be quoted in Mark's and Matthew's versions of the institution (Mark 14:24; Matt. 26:28). According to an ancient account of the making of the covenant at Sinai (Exod. 24:3-8, from the so called Elohist source), Moses says after the peace offering, the public reading of the book of the covenant, and the blood ceremony: "Behold the blood of the covenant which the Lord has made with you in accordance with all these words" (v. 8). Still other sacrificial passages in the Old Testament were probably evoked in the minds of the early Christians, for example, the sin offerings, the day of atonement, and perhaps also the passage on the servant of God who gives his life for the many. Such covenant sacrifices functioned as a second frame of reference for understanding the Lord's Supper. The versions of Jesus' saying about the bread in Luke 22:19 and 1 Corinthians 11:24 ("given for you") and the specification in the saying concerning the blood in the three gospels ("which is poured out for many/you"), especially the extended version in Matthew 26:28 ("for the forgiveness of sins"), point in this direction. Just as in their covenant renewal festivals and temple offerings the Israelites were re-established as partners in God's covenant with them, so the early Christians experienced the celebration of the Lord's Supper as a re-establishment of the intimate communion between Christ and them.

A third clue was found in the prophetic promise of the new covenant. Again, the relevant Old Testament text is actually quoted, or at least alluded to, when (according to Paul's and Luke's versions) Jesus speaks about "the new covenant in my blood" (1 Cor. 11:25; Luke 22:20): "Behold, the days are coming, says the Lord, when I will make a new covenant with the house of Israel, and the house of Judah ..." (Jer. 31:31-34; cf. 32:38-40). The Lord's Supper was celebrated in the frame of reference of this hope. Just as the Qumranites claimed that they were the community of this new covenant, so the early Christians affirmed that in Christ this particular promise was now fulfilled.

A fourth clue for understanding the Lord's Supper was the prophetic promise of the coming messianic feast. "On this mountain the Lord of hosts will make for all peoples a feast of fat things, a feast of wine on the lees.... He will swallow up death for ever, and the Lord God will wipe away tears from all faces, and the reproach of his people he will take away from the earth ..." (Isa. 25:6-8). Such visions of the messianic feast were current in the time of Jesus. The two sayings in connection with the first cup in Luke as well as the concluding saying according to Mark and Matthew (Luke 22:16, 18; Mark 14:25; Matt. 26:29) clearly refer to this messianic feast. The Israelites looked forward to this feast, and the early Christians actually anticipated it when they celebrated the Lord's Supper with great rejoicing, "with glad and generous hearts, praising God" (Acts 2:46f).

In the days of Jesus the expected messianic meal had become the model for the daily solemn meal of fellowship in the Essene community of Qumran. The messianic feast is there described in an appendix to the community rule. The Jewish historian Josephus also describes the Qumranite meal as follows:

> After this purification, they assemble in a private apartment which none of the uninitiated is permitted to enter; pure now themselves, they repair to the refectory, as to some sacred shrine. When they have taken their seats in silence, the baker serves out the loaves to them in order, and the cook sets before each one a plate with a single course. Before meat the priest says a grace, and none may partake until after the prayer. When breakfast is ended,

he pronounces a further grace; thus at the beginning and at the close they do homage to God as the bountiful giver of life (*Jewish War*, II, 129ff).

The rule of the community itself stipulates that "when they set the table for a meal or prepare wine to drink, the priest is first to put forth his hand to invoke blessing on the first portion of bread and wine."

Bread and wine were the main elements of this meal, at which only the fully initiated could participate. As the members of Qumran community strengthened their fellowship through sharing a common meal, so the early church deepened its fellowship with Christ, who had table fellowship with tax collectors and sinners. It strengthened the community among the members by the sharing of the one bread. "Because there is one bread, we who are many are one body, for we all partake of the one bread" (1 Cor. 10:17; see also the warning in 1 Cor. 11:17-22, 27-29).

These four clues for understanding are not an exhaustive list. Certainly, the remembrance of the meals the risen Lord shared with his disciples (Luke 24:30, 36ff; John 21:12ff; Acts 1:4; 10:40f) also played an important role. Gentile Christians may have taken up into their celebrations elements of holy meals in the mystery religions of the Hellenistic world. Jewish Christians probably patterned their celebration according to common Jewish meals, and they also remembered the gift of manna with Moses' saying: "It is the bread which the Lord has given you to eat" (Exod. 16:14ff; cf. John 6:49f). What is important to notice is that the four New Testament accounts of the institution of the Lord's Supper already used different combinations of clues, and therefore a variety of liturgies and theologies of the Lord's Supper developed.

As this process of interpretation has continued throughout the centuries, a large theological library has been written about the nature of the relationship between the words of institution and the eucharistic elements. How can the bread become the body of Christ? How is the wine or the cup related to the blood of Christ? Does this mystery happen through the *epiclesis*, the prayer for the Spirit to come down on the elements and the people? Does it happen through a process of "transubstantiation," whereby the elements of bread and wine are actually transformed into the body and blood of Jesus; or a process of "consubstantiation," whereby the body and blood of Jesus are contained within the elements of bread and wine? Or are the sayings of Jesus to be understood symbolically? If so, what is the exact meaning of "symbol" in this case? Does it simply function as the sign for the body and blood of Christ, or are these elements symbols in the strong sense of this word, making present the body and blood?

In this whole literature concerning the relationship between the words of institution and the eucharistic elements Jesus' words in John 6:48-59 play an important role. This passage can indeed function as a basis for relating the words of institution almost exclusively to the element of bread (and by implication also of wine, cf. John 6:53ff). It must be recognized, however, that this passage stands within the context of Jesus' teaching about the bread of life (John 6:35ff) and leads up to the sayings: "It is the spirit that gives life, the flesh is of no avail; the words that I have spoken to you are spirit and life" (John 6:63).

In the time of the Reformation the debate centred essentially on the verb "is" in the sentences: "This is my body" and "This is my blood" or "This cup is the new covenant in my blood." In the original Aramaic, which Jesus presumably spoke, this word "is" almost certainly did not occur. If Jesus pronounced this saying he simply said: "This: my body"; "This: my blood/the new covenant in my blood."

However profound such varied traditional eucharistic theologies may be, it is doubtful that Paul, the evangelists, and even the earthly Jesus would have understood them. Philosophical notions like "substance," which play an important role in these theologies, are foreign both to the New Testament and to many people today. This does of course not mean that such eucharistic theologies do not communicate deep truths: theology need not simply repeat biblical affirmations with biblical terminologies. It is on the contrary called to restate the truth of Christian faith for each new given time and culture. However, if such theological statements no longer speak to people living in a changed world, it is time to go back and search again for the original meaning of biblical testimonies.

The search for the original meaning

In the traditional eucharistic theologies attention is almost totally concentrated on the sayings of the institution and on the elements of the meal. Both in our exercise of recalling the accounts of the Lord's Supper from memory and in our subsequent synoptic study of these accounts, we have seen the importance which Jesus' gestures play in the institution of the celebration. On the basis of this observation we must re-examine the relationship between the sayings, the gestures, and the elements of the Lord's Supper.

Task 3: "This is my Body"; "This is my Blood/this cup ...." What does the "this" refer to in these two sayings about the bread and wine/cup? Explore different possibilities and their implications for the understanding of the Lord's Supper.

> After a moment of individual reflection the participants share with their neighbours the insights gained. After a plenary discussion on this task the study enabler sums up and complements the various contributions.

The spontaneous response of most Protestants and Catholics is to relate the "this" to the elements of bread and wine. Members of the Orthodox Churches may react somewhat differently. Protestants and Catholics will probably still not totally agree about how the elements of bread and wine become the body and blood of Christ or how the risen Lord is really present in the celebration of the Lord's Supper. However, both have taught and generally assume that the "this" refers in the first place or exclusively to the elements.

This generally accepted reading of the sayings of institution creates a grammatical difficulty in the Greek text. "This" (*touto*) is in the neuter form while "bread" (*ho artos*) is a masculine. One might object that the neuter form *touto* is assimilated to the following "body" (*to sōma*), which is neuter in Greek, but *touto* generally refers backwards and not forwards. One might possibly translate: "What this bread is, is my body;" or one might make the body the subject: "My body is this." But both these proposals are highly questionable. If the authors intended a clear link between "this" and "bread" they would state: "This bread is ..." (*houtos ho artos estin ...*). In the saying about the blood/cup the same difficulty does not occur, because in Greek both "blood" and "cup" are neuter.

It would obviously be irresponsible to reject the traditional interpretations simply on the basis of this grammatical difficulty. But the emphasis we noted earlier in all four accounts on the gestures of taking, blessing/thanksgiving, breaking, giving, and explaining makes the almost exclusive concentration on the elements even more questionable. Moreover, in Paul's and Luke's versions the "this is" (*touto estin*) leads to the parallel commandment "this do" (*touto poieite*), where the "this" certainly refers to the whole of the Lord's Supper and not simply to the elements.

On the basis of these observations a few Protestant and Catholic theologians propose the following understanding of the original meaning of the Lord's Supper: The "this" refers back to the whole sequence of gestures in connection with the bread and wine/cup, which are interpreted by the sayings of the institution. The great message Jesus imparted to his disciples is as follows:

Once again, during the last supper with his disciples, Jesus has summed up in a prophetic act and word his whole ministry and prefigured his sacrificial death. In the Semitic languages "body" refers to the concrete bodily existence and "blood" refers to life. Both terms designate the whole person seen from two different points of view. In making the gestures of receiving, blessing/thanksgiving, breaking, and giving Jesus explains: "This is me, this is my life."

The acts of eating and drinking the broken bread and poured-out wine, which have become the material tokens of the person and life of the crucified and risen Lord, emphasize the intimate communion between the Lord and the believers and the believers among themselves. Moreover, they emphasize the "for you," the "poured out for many" of the whole life and death of Jesus. His body was indeed broken and his life poured out for the salvation of the world. In the most literal sense Jesus thus proves himself to be "the bread of life," as John testified.

Yet this celebration immediately leads to life in discipleship: "Do this!" Understood in this way, the Lord's Supper is also the prelude for Christian life and in certain times and situations the prelude to Christian martyrdom. In this celebration we have to learn the basic gestures of our Lord. Just as we have to be transformed in order to conform with the mind of Christ (Rom. 12:2; Phil. 2:5ff), so we have to enter into a life in which we are willing to be broken and ready to be poured out. So Christ taught us during the last supper with his disciples. The commandment to "do this" refers then not only to the eucharistic celebrations, which are to be continued in all places and times, but equally to the eucharistic life of the church of all ages and continents.

16 THE HOUR OF TRUTH

Mark 15:20b-41

The following confrontation play on Mark's account of the crucifixion of Jesus was first conducted in a training seminar with Protestant pastors in Colonia Valdense, Uruguay, in May 1978. It has been repeated with groups in other cultural and political situations. These later studies have sometimes included a more extensive look at the crucifixion accounts, for example, examining the oral (and perhaps already written) sources the evangelists used, or studying the Old Testament background of these accounts, or making recorded dramatic readings of the crucifixion accounts in the four gospels, followed by a synoptic study, or with art meditation. Two hours are needed for the confrontation play with its three parts of identification, confrontation, and debriefing.

The death of Socrates and of Jesus

There have been many descriptions of the death of two persons of antiquity — the Greek philosopher Socrates and Jesus of Nazareth.

Socrates "was a man of great independence and dignity of character," writes the ancient historian Diogenes Laertius. He added a saying of the philosopher which could well become a motto in our modern consumer society: "Often when Socrates looked at the multitude of wares exposed for sale, he would say to himself, 'How many things I can do without!'" Socrates' whole life was a search for truth. He was convinced that it was worse to commit injustice than to suffer from it. He fearlessly defended the laws over against the city government when it became lax in enforcing them. This did not please the Athenian authorities, and in 399 B.C. he was condemned to death. The death warrant is revealing: "Socrates is guilty of refusing to recognize the gods recognized by the state, and of introducing other new divinities. He is also guilty of corrupting the youth. The penalty demanded is death" (Diogenes Laertius, *Socrates*, II, 24f, 40). Thus Socrates was ordered to drink a cup with poison, and he refused to escape from prison when some of his disciples had made this possible by the unlawful means of bribery.

Socrates' most famous pupil Plato describes the dignified death of his master. Socrates spent the last hours of his life in philosophical conversations with his disciples. He sent away the women and children, for he did not want to hear their wailing, and he forbade his disciples to cry or to pity him. He also took a bath and put on clean clothes. Then, when his hour came, he calmly drank the poison and serenely died with the conviction: "I am just."

Throughout the centuries this beautiful death of Socrates has won the respect and admiration of cultivated men and women. How different is the death of Jesus! Let us listen to how the evangelist Mark described it.

> At this point a recorded dramatic reading of Mark 15:20b-41 is played. If none is available, a participant who is a skilled reader and has been asked to prepare this reading, presents the text.

Execution by crucifixion was probably invented by the Persians, later adopted by Alexander the Great and the Phoenicians, and finally taken over by the Romans. They used it to punish revolting slaves, temple robbers, and deserters.

In Palestine crucifixion became the typical way for Roman authorities to execute Jewish rebels, and historians report mass crucifixions both before and after Jesus died on the cross. Death by crucifixion was such a horrible torture that the Roman law forbade the punishment of a Roman citizen in this way. Those condemned to be crucified usually had to carry the cross bar to the place of execution themselves, sometimes with an inscription of their death-warrant hanging around their neck. Then they were undressed and scourged, if this had not happened already, and their arms were bound or nailed through their wrists on the cross bar. With the bar they were pulled to the top or a groove near the top of the pole of the cross, which was already standing. Their feet were then bound or nailed to the cross pole. Usually they sat on a piece of wood sticking out from the middle of the pole. At great suffering they could thus remain upright and continue to breathe. Only when they became too weak to keep upright — and this could last up to two days and nights — or when the bones of their legs were broken, would they finally die of suffocation.

It is in this way that Jesus died. No wonder that his crucifixion was and remains a scandal, not only for people in general, but also for Christian believers. In order that we cease to speak too glibly about the cross and face that scandal, which is at the heart of Christian faith, we will now attempt to be present at that fateful event. It happened on a Friday noon, just outside the ancient walls of Jerusalem, probably on April 7, A.D. 30. We will try to identify as much as we can with the groups of people who were actually present at the event. Later we will *not* perform a passion play, but will imagine that representatives of these different groups met by chance that evening, and we will see what happens.

Identification — confrontation — debriefing
Task 1: Reread Mark 15:20b-41 and list the persons we meet.

> After the list has been made, the group is divided into five subgroups. Roles are assigned by having each subgroup draw a small folded sheet on which one of the roles is inscribed. It does not matter if the role of women is to be played by men, or the role of chief priests or soldiers by women. The subgroups are: (1) The passers-by and bystanders, one of whom identifies with Simon of Cyrene and another with the person who brought the sponge full of vinegar; (2) the soldiers, one identifying with the centurion; (3) the chief priests and elders; (4) sympathizers with the two rebels, who were cruci- fied together with Jesus (the rebels themselves could obviously not be present at that chance meeting in the evening); (5) the women who followed Jesus.
>
> If the participants know very little about the social, religious, and political situation of first century Palestine, the enabler or a participant who has pre- pared beforehand will have to give some background information (cf. above pp. 158ff and 171ff).

Task 2: Reread Mark 15:20b-41 in your subgroup from the point of view of the people you are assigned to prepare. Identify as much as you can with this role. Avoid speaking about "they," but say from the beginning: "We, as passers-by ...;" "We, as Roman soldiers ...;" etc. Do *not* make a script for what you are going to say in the subsequent confrontation with the others present at Jesus' crucifixion, but examine the two following ques- tions: (a) What did we feel, think, do, and say before, during, and after the crucifixion of Jesus? (b) How did we relate to the other groups present and to Jesus before, during, and after his crucifixion?

> After a half hour of identification in subgroups the enabler calls the group together — even if some have not gone far in their process of identification. Meanwhile the chairs in the main meeting room have been arranged in five groups, with a large sign giving the identity of each group. The "soldiers" should be seated so as to confront the "sympathizers with the rebels," and the "priest scribes" confront the "women" and "passers-by." A single chair for the study enabler stands between the groups of the women and of the passers- by. It is important that there be no break between the period of identification of roles and the period of confrontation which now follows. As soon as all are seated, the enablers says:

We are now in Jerusalem. It is the evening of Friday, April 7, A.D. 30. I am a pilgrim from Alexandria, and it is only late this afternoon that I arrived in Jerusalem for the religious festivities. Now I hear that today some people were executed just outside the walls of this holy city and that some strange things happened. You were apparently present. Tell me what happened.

> There may be an awkward silence at first, but the enabler must not mod- erate the debate. The less he or she intervenes the better. If the confrontation is dominated for a long time by two or three subgroups, the enabler may draw in the other subgroups by direct questions, but he or she must stay in the role of the Jewish pilgrim who wants to know what happened and who is

intrigued by what is told and therefore desires to know more about that Jesus of Nazareth.

Such a confrontation can arouse deep emotions. Once I had to separate the soldiers and the group of sympathizers with the rebels, who had begun to hit one another. Once, in a police state, the sympathizers with the rebels refused to speak. When I wanted to draw them into the debate, they sent me a written message indicating that they could not speak as long as the soldiers were present. I sent the soldiers on an errand, and only then did the "rebels" speak. Once a participant broke out in tears, no longer able to bear playing the role of a self-righteous scribe.

While remaining the inquiring pilgrim, the enabler must nevertheless carefully watch all participants and if necessary stop the confrontation should it become unbearable for a participant. One way of discharging a too tense atmosphere is to stop the play for a moment and ask: "Does anyone want to change roles?" Usually no one will actually change positions, but the mere possibility of doing so safeguards the participants from identifying too intensively with the role.

The confrontation must not be continued too long (twenty to forty minutes is usually best), and the enabler must find the right moment to stop the exercise, preferably immediately after a hesitant confession by a "woman" or the centurion.

When the group reassembles after this break, the identification signs must have been removed, chairs arranged in a large circle if possible, and the participants invited to sit next to people who played different roles from theirs. Otherwise the debriefing will almost inevitably revert to a continued confrontation.

Task 3: Reflect on the two following sets of questions: (a) What have you experienced during the confrontation play both in the period of identification and the actual confrontation? Was there a change in your attitudes and emotions? How did you relate to the other groups present at Jesus' crucifixion? (b) How have you related to Jesus in the various phases of the identification and confrontation? What new things have you learned about Jesus and the first Christians through this exercise?

If the group is large, the discussion of these questions should take place in smaller study groups, each of which includes members of all five subgroups. However, the whole group may want to stay together so that all have a chance to ask further questions to people who made particularly intriguing remarks during the confrontation.

The testimony of Mark

Through such a confrontation play we have experienced the event of crucifixion more with our emotions than with our intellect. It is therefore important to turn back now to the biblical text in order to check and if necessary correct our experience by a careful rereading of Mark's testimony.

Task 4: Reread Mark 15:20b-41 with the following questions in mind: (a) What details of Mark's testimony did we overlook in our confrontation play? (b) What particular message does Mark want to communicate through his crucifixion account?

> After a period of individual study the participants exchange discoveries with their neighbours and then contribute to a general discussion. If some of the following points have not yet been made in this discussion, the enabler may want to mention them in the conclusion.

It is important to notice the Old Testament passages directly quoted or alluded to in this account. Details of Psalm 22 appear no fewer than three times: The initial cry of god-forsakenness: "My God, my God, why hast thou forsaken me?" (Ps. 22:1/Mark 15:34 in Aramaic, which is immediately translated); the mocking and wagging of the heads by bystanders (Ps. 22:7/ Mark 15:29); the division of the garments (Ps. 22:18/Mark 15:24). A passage from another psalm of lament is at least alluded to, where someone who is seriously ill complains: "My friends and companions stand aloof from my plague" (Ps. 38:11/Mark 15:40). Finally, still another psalm of complaint and praise, which has the same structure as Psalm 22, is quoted: "For my thirst they gave me vinegar to drink" (Ps. 69:21/Mark 15:36). There may be a reference to prophetic passages (e.g. Amos 8:9) in Mark 15:33. The quotation "he was reckoned with the transgressors" (Isa. 53:12/ Mark 15:28) occurs in verse 28 of Mark's account, which most modern translations correctly put in a footnote, since this verse, which does not occur in the most ancient manuscripts, is almost certainly a copyist's later insertion into the Markan text from Luke 22:37.

This strong and one-sided evocation of psalms of complaint and praise in Mark's (as well as Matthew's and Luke's) crucifixion account shows that the early church saw a profound analogy of the situation between the fate of Jesus and that of the Israelites who first prayed such psalms. Jesus was for them in the first place the suffering righteous one. There is a divine "must" in his suffering, but also the conviction that God will vindicate those who suffer for righteousness' sake. Mark emphasizes Jesus' agony and loneliness on the cross. The risen Lord, in whose power and authority Christians believe, is the one condemned by religious and political authorities, crucified between two political rebels, and required to endure the deepest agony. He does not intercede from the cross or console a rebel beside him or comfort his mother and a disciple under the cross, as two other evangelists report (cf. Luke 23:34, 43; John 19:26f). No confident prayer, no affirmation of achievement came over his lips when he died (cf. Luke 23:46; John 19:30). Not a dignified death following a bath, in clean clothes, during lofty philosophical discourses with friends, reassured by the conviction "I am just" — as Socrates died. Instead, a cry of prayer to the God afar, and finally simply the cry of death, strange for someone who dies of suffocation (Mark 15:34, 37).

Contrary to the two isolated texts in Mark 10:45 ("his life as ransom for many") and 14:24 (his blood "poured out for many"), Jesus' crucifixion is here not confessed as a sacrificial death for the atonement of the multitudes. Mark rather testifies to the great paradox that the messianic king should appear in such a state of helplessness, rejection, and condemnation: the "King of the Jews" (Mark 15:26) having a cross as his throne and thorns as his crown! Formerly he had healed others, even raised the dead and performed miracles, but now he refused to confound the mocking passers-by and chief priests by coming down from the cross and saving himself (Mark 15:29-32). His opponents seemed to be in the right: God had obviously abandoned him. The sudden darkness indicated judgment over him. Elijah did not come to take him down. He died helplessly with a cry; and that seemed indeed to be the miserable end of the story of Jesus.

Yet the chief priests and bystanders were blind. What appeared as Jesus' defeat was in fact his victory. The darkness had been the sign of judgment over those who had derided him. The curtain of the temple was torn when he died (Mark 15:38), signifying judgment over temple worship. The darkness only lasted until three o'clock in the afternoon (Mark 15:33), the hour of his death. When he died, light came back over the whole land. A miracle did indeed happen: "When the centurion, who stood facing him, saw that he thus breathed his last, he said, 'Truly this man was the Son of God!'" (Mark 15:39). While the religious authorities had remained blind to what really happened, a total outsider, a Roman centurion, *saw* something of the significance of Jesus' death.

What the centurion said (in the original Greek simply "son of God") was probably not more than: "This was a godly man, somebody favoured by the gods, who died so quickly and in this manner." The evangelist Mark, however, wants his readers to understand much more. He had entitled his gospel "The Good News of Jesus Christ, the Son of God" (Mark 1:1, though in some ancient manuscripts "son of God" is omitted). Then, at two crucial events of Jesus' life, God's voice solemnly declared "My beloved Son" — at baptism and on the mountain of transfiguration (Mark 1:11; 9:7). Now, at the climax of his gospel, Mark reports that confession again, this time publicly declared by a Roman. With his account of Jesus' crucifixion Mark therefore wants to encourage faith in the strangely hidden, but ultimately victorious king who is the suffering Messiah. The "women looking on from afar" (Mark 15:40f) are thus encouraged. So have the readers of Mark's gospel been strengthened in their faith ever since.

17 COME AND SEE!

Matthew 28:1-10

> This script and the one which follows were prepared for the large ecumenical assembly of Church Women United in July 1977 at Purdue University, USA. On two subsequent mornings a period of 75 minutes was set aside for participatory Bible study with over two thousand women on Matthew's account of Jesus' resurrection and the climax of Matthew's gospel. The worksheet "Come and see!" is to be used alongside the following text.
>
> Immediately before both sessions three women, representative of large sections and tendencies within the assembly, were asked to form with me a panel and at appropriate times to enter into a totally spontaneous conversation about the questions raised in the tasks mentioned. Their outstanding contributions greatly helped link the biblical text with the context of the mood and work of the assembly. Their spontaneity, humour, and graciousness made the study with this mass of people a very intimate and personal search for truth, not only for the panel members but also for many sitting in the huge hall.
>
> Another special feature of these experiments cannot be reproduced in words: after each study a dancer led all participants in responding with simple body movements to the main message of the text examined.

"Come and see!" That isn't as simple as it sounds. Although most of us have two more or less healthy eyes, this does not mean that we can see what really matters. I sometimes wonder whether we are not less and less capable of seeing because we are more and more bombarded with ever new images, symbols, and light effects. Through illustrated magazines and TV, through publicity posters and advertising pictures, through road signs and the symbols of our consumer society we all suffer from visual indigestion. We see — and yet we are blind.

Seeing the truth of the matter

Think of what has happened to human travel. Once men, women, and children knew how to walk, how to find their own way through fields and forests and small crossroads in old cities. They stopped here and there to pick up a remarkable stone they had seen, to greet a friend, or to console a crying child. Now on most of our travels, we are imprisoned in cars on the highways, guided by the road signs which dictate our speed and direction. Though we travel hundreds of miles we see little or nothing of all the human joys and sorrows, of all the beauty and misery of God's creation through which we hasten. Bombarded and moulded by thousands of visual effects, we are less and less able to see.

For seeing is not simply the passive consumption of what is visible. Seeing is a highly active, creative enterprise. The Swiss artist Paul Klee once wrote: "Art does not reproduce the visible, but it makes visible." Similarly one could say that to see does not simply mean to observe the surface of things, but to penetrate the invisible or rather to perceive the depth dimension, the significance of what strikes our eyes, to see the truth of the matter.

For such seeing we need the eyes of Jesus. Do you remember how he walked on the roads of Galilee? Here he sees a woman mixing some yeast with the flour. There he observes a sower scattering the seed on the plowed field. A little further he notices a woman searching for a lost coin. All these everyday happenings become parables of the kingdom for him. The visible evokes for him a reality which lies beyond the surface. He is neither a materialist, for whom the only things which exist are what can be touched and outwardly observed, nor is he a dreamer, who closes his eyes to the earthly realities and lives in a fantasy-world. It is in the midst of the hard realities of this world and time that he discerns parables of the kingdom.

We need such eyes to discover the signatures of faith, to perceive something of the mystery of resurrection. And so before we turn to the biblical text, I would like to do with you an exercise of seeing. The great German artist Käthe Kollwitz will be our teacher. Many of you have no doubt seen drawings and lithographs by that gifted artist who lived and worked in the slums of northern Berlin during the first half of this century. Let us see a few of her many self-portraits.

> At this point project on a screen slides of six self-portraits of Käthe Kollwitz, those of the years 1890, 1910, 1924, 1929, 1936, and 1943. If the equipment permits, use the procedure of gradual changeover by slowly superposing each slide over the previous one, which then fades away. In this way a "motion picture" of the aging and maturing face of the artist is shown on the screen.

Those who have eyes to see can discern in these six self-portraits the deep destiny, the long way of suffering which Käthe Kollwitz had to travel through two world wars, through fame and rejection. The portraits reflect what the artist saw happening in the world around her; and her very face has been shaped by it.

Now let us look at four aspects of the human reality which Käthe Kollwitz made visible through her art. Look at these four works of art with two questions in mind.

Task 1: (a) What aspects of reality does Käthe Kollwitz make visible by these four works of art? (b) Can you discern in this art work something of the reality of Christ's resurrection?

While the slides are projected on the screen the following short comments are made.

Slide 1: "Bread!" Käthe Kollwitz made this lithograph in 1924 during the famines in Austria and Russia. It served as a poster in the campaign for the hungry.

Slide 2: "Mother and child" (1916). One of many lithographs Käthe Kollwitz devoted to this theme.

Slide 3: A draft (1903) for a series of lithographs on the peasant war in sixteenth-century Germany, when exploited farmworkers and their families revolted against the landlords.

Slide 4: "Mother protecting her children." A lithograph created in wartime Berlin in 1942, under the rain of deadly bombs.

> While this same series of slides is projected a second time, the two questions of Task 1 are repeated for each slide. "What aspect of reality is here made visible?" "Can you discern in it something of the reality of Christ's resurrection?"
>
> Afterwards all participants are asked to exchange with their neighbours what they have seen, what the art works evoked in their minds, and whether something of the reality of Christ's resurrection was made visible to them. Then the panel members enter into a spontaneous discussion on the same questions, which is amplified by microphones through the whole assembly.

What happened on Easter morning

As we saw, the reality of Christ's resurrection is rather evasive, something to be dimly discerned rather than to be photographed and empirically described. No wonder the evangelists found it so difficult to communicate this mysterious event. The synopsis on the worksheet places the three accounts, by Matthew, Mark, and Luke, of what happened that first Christian Easter morning side by side.

Task 2: Examine this text and answer the following questions: What is similar and what is different between Matthew's and Mark's accounts? What is similar and what is different between Matthew's and Luke's accounts?

> Half of the group focuses on each of these questions. The panel is also divided into two teams of two for this task. After a period of individual study all participants are asked to share their insights with their neighbours. Then the panel members discuss publicly the similarities and differences noticed.

Summing up, we can establish the following major agreements and differences between Matthew on the one side and Mark and Luke on the other:

Time and place: Mark and Luke agree with Matthew about the time ("on the dawn of the first day of the week," that is early Sunday morning) and place (before the sepulchre or tomb).

The women: Matthew speaks of only two women, Mary Magdalene and the other Mary, presumably the mother of James. Mark adds a third one, Salome. Luke only uses the pronoun "they," which refers back to "the women who had come with Jesus from Galilee" (23:55). According to Mark and Luke these women came with spices to anoint Jesus' body, and Mark adds that they wondered who would roll away the heavy stone from the entry of the tomb. According to Matthew, however, the women simply come to "see" the sepulchre. For this seeing, Matthew uses a very special verb — *theorein*, which can best be translated "to be present, to look on and be involved in a solemn event," often a liturgical drama. The same verb is used twice in preceding passages, first for these same women who are present and look on from afar at the crucifixion (Matt. 27:55 and parallels) and later when they are present and look where Joseph of Arimathea laid Jesus in the tomb (Mark 15:47).

The opening of the tomb: According to Mark and Luke the stone was already rolled back when the women arrived at the tomb, and they actually went into the tomb but did not find the body. Instead they saw a young man (according to Luke two men) dressed in dazzling white clothes. Such emissaries are of course identical with "the angel of the Lord" about whom Matthew writes, but Matthew gives here a strikingly different account: only he had earlier mentioned the guard of soldiers who were supposed to watch the tomb (27:62-66). Now he tells about the great earthquake as "an angel of the Lord descended from heaven and came and rolled back the stone, and sat on it." He also relates that "for fear of him the guards trembled and became like dead men." We will come back to this peculiarity of Matthew's account of the Easter events.

The message of the angel: The message of the angel is roughly the same according to the three evangelists, although there are some significant nuances. Only Luke records that marvelous question: "Why do you seek the living among the dead?" And the angel there recalls one of Jesus' own predictions of his death and resurrection. All three record the central message: "He has risen!" but only in Matthew does the angel repeat this message. According to Matthew and Mark the angel commands the women to go and announce to the disciples — "and Peter," Mark adds — that Jesus will precede them to Galilee.

The reaction of the women: All three evangelists mention the women's fear and amazement, and in different words they tell how the women left the empty tomb. Matthew's wonderfully tense description says that "they departed quickly from the tomb with fear and great joy." According to Matthew and Luke, the women went to tell the disciples: but Mark has only this strange sentence: "They said nothing to anyone, for they were afraid." (According to the oldest available manuscripts this is in fact the very end of Mark's gospel. You can imagine that ever since theologians have wondered and written many dissertations about the perhaps lost true ending of that gospel!)

Matthew's testimony

Some of you might be taken aback by all these divergences in the gospel accounts of the Easter event. But whenever something tremendous and mysterious happens, you will soon have as many reports as there were eye-witnesses present. And do not forget that these accounts were written a good thirty-five to fifty-five years after the event. They do in fact reflect different memories and different interpretations of the Easter events. This leads us to the following questions:

Task 3: What is Matthew's specific testimony concerning Christ's resurrection? What does he actually tell us and what does he not tell us about the events on that Easter morning? Reread his account with this question in mind.

> After individual study and exchange with neighbours in the groups, the panel members discuss this question publicly.

Like the other evangelists Matthew does *not* give us a description of the resurrection itself. The women do *not* see Christ rising from the dead. When the tomb is being opened it is already empty. Jesus is not there, he has risen.

It is important to insist on this. While the event of the crucifixion was extensively described, while there were eyewitnesses at Golgotha, including the women who looked on from afar, the same thing is *not* true for the resurrection. The women are not invited to come and see the resurrection event itself, but the already empty tomb. Somehow the resurrection is another type of reality than the crucifixion. One might say that the crucifixion is an event of human history happening within human history. The resurrection, however, is an event of the end of times, an event from beyond history which has happened in the midst of human history on that first Christian Easter morning. Rightly the evangelists have not torn away the veil of mystery from this event. The resurrection must not and cannot be described empirically. It can only be hinted at through symbolic language.

All three evangelists write about the divine emissary with his dazzling white clothes. But Matthew clearly goes a step further in this symbolic evocation of what happened. He compares this coming of the angel with lightning. Then there is an earthquake. In his account of Jesus' entry into Jerusalem Matthew had already said that "all the city shook as in an earthquake" (21:10). In the account of the crucifixion Matthew alone of the evangelists wrote again about an earthquake and about the rocks which were split, the tombs which were opened, and the vision of the dead rising and appearing in the city of Jerusalem (27:51-53). Now, pointing to the event and significance of Christ's resurrection, Matthew again mentions an earthquake. The coming of a divine messenger, lightning, and an earthquake are all, according to the Old Testament, signs of a theophany, a manifestation of God himself. There are for instance striking parallels between Matthew's account of the Easter events and one of Daniel's visions (Dan. 10:5ff).

The first conclusion we can draw from these observations is that Matthew even more than the other evangelists sees in the resurrection a theophany, a manifestation of the presence of God. It is an event which breaks into the normal course of things, a breakthrough which creates unhoped-for possibilities, a happening which opens up our closed world and our small lives to transcendence. It is an anticipation of God's kingdom.

It may be that Matthew's account contains still another interpretation of the Easter event. Earlier we noted that only Matthew reports that soldiers were placed before the tomb to watch it. The verses just before the passage we are studying emphasize this securing of the tomb. The chief priest and the Pharisees had gone to Pilate to request a guard of soldiers. Pilate granted their request; and the very last verse before Matthew's Easter account reads: "So they went and made the sepulchre secure by sealing the stone and setting a guard" (Matt. 27:66). But then what happened? When the angel of the Lord appeared as lightning, when the earth shook and the angel opened the tomb, the guards trembled for fear of him "and became like dead men."

This sequence of events is quite familiar in the so-called miracles of liberation in ancient Greek and Jewish literature. The Greek author Euripides (484-406 B.C.) refers to similar phenomena in telling how the god Dionysos was liberated from prison. An even more striking parallel can be found in an ancient novel about Moses, written by the Alexandrian Jew Artapanos around 100 B.C. The New Testament itself also contains several miracles of liberation. When the apostles were in Jerusalem (Acts 5:17-25), an angel of the Lord opened the prison doors by night and liberated them despite all the sentries. Later, Peter was freed from his chains in a severely guarded prison by an angel of the Lord who shone like light (Acts 12:1-19). Paul was liberated from prison in Philippi (Acts 16:22-34), not by an angel but by a sudden earthquake.

When the gospels were written such miracles of liberation must have been a well-known literary pattern. It is therefore probable that the early church understood the resurrection of Jesus as such a miracle of liberation. Matthew has taken up this tradition and incorporated it into his Easter account. This fits in very well with the specific testimony to Jesus which Matthew gives in the whole of his gospel: he consistently shows us Jesus as the one who has power and authority to drive out demons, to heal the sick, to raise the dead, and to defeat Satan and death. In obedience to God's will, however, Jesus did not come down from the cross and save himself. Resisting this temptation, he died and was buried. But now, in a decisive miracle of liberation, God has raised him from the dead.

By taking up this special tradition Matthew comes very near to describing the resurrection event itself. But as we have seen he avoids doing so. He does not expand the liberation miracle by depicting the risen Christ coming out of the tomb. In awe he keeps the veil of mystery before that unfathomable event.

Not all Christians or later writers about the resurrection have shown a similar restraint. On the back of the worksheet is a fragment of an apocryphal gospel written in the middle of the second century. It is called the "Gospel of Peter" but of course was not written by the apostle Peter.

From verse 50 onwards, there is an Easter account which runs roughly parallel with the biblical Easter story. Later you can read this and see where there are parallels and where this unknown author of the second century has expanded the story. Much more interesting is the text immediately preceding this passage about the women at the empty tomb. Here we have indeed what you perhaps expected to find in the Bible, namely a description of the resurrection event itself. Let us hear it.

| A member of the panel reads verses 34-49 of the Gospel of Peter.

Task 4: How do you react to such a description of what presumably happened in the night from Easter Saturday to Easter Sunday?

| Participants share their immediate reactions to this passage with their neighbours, and then the panel members voice their reactions to this apocryphal dēscription of Christ's resurrection.

On the one hand, this passage from the so-called gospel of Peter is of course a dramatic story. Here the miracle of liberation is depicted as on a large canvas of Spanish Baroque art, or a Wagnerian opera: the loud voice from heaven, the stone which starts of itself to roll away, the superhuman angels who come out of the tomb with the risen Christ who is higher than the heavens but still weak from death, so that he must be sustained by the two angels. Then the cross which follows him and answers the voice from heaven and all the going and coming between the empty tomb and Pilate. It would not be difficult to turn this account into a good scene in a sensational motion picture about Jesus!

But that exactly is what disturbs and embarrasses me most about this account. It is written too much like a script for one of those bad-taste religious motion pictures which are sometimes produced in Hollywood. The veil has definitely been torn away from the mystery of resurrection. I am therefore thankful that the ancient church did not include such texts in the New Testament.

Like the women at the tomb, you and I are invited to come and see — but not such an otherworldly spectacle as the one described in the so-called gospel of Peter! The Easter accounts of the biblical gospels invite us to see the empty tomb and to contemplate its meaning. The signatures of resurrection are made visible only to those who first see the hard realities of this world: the passion, the crucifixion, the death — the hard realities which Käthe Kollwitz made visible in her art. And only if we learn to look at these realities with eyes of faith, may we here and there recognize traces of the risen Lord. Then we too will suddenly be full of "fear and great joy."

18 GO QUICKLY AND TELL!

Matthew 27:62-28:20

Details of the original setting for this script are provided in the introduction to the previous script. Again a panel of three women from among the
participants played an important role in the process of study. The appended
worksheet "Go quickly and tell!" must be used alongside this script.

"The women departed quickly from the tomb with fear and great joy."
The resurrection brings new space and new movement into our lives. In
fact, all the evangelists make an intimate link between Christ's resurrection
and our participation in his mission. In this Bible study we are going to
examine how Matthew relates mission to the resurrection in the climax of
his gospel.

The end of a book

The end of a book, drama, or motion picture is decisive. A good closing
page can save a mediocre story. A trivial closing scene can spoil a good
play. The last scene should, indeed, throw a new light on the whole story
and at the same time open up new visions and perspectives for life. This is
certainly the case for the ending of the four gospels.

Mark ends almost in the middle of a sentence. The women "fled from
the tomb ... and they said nothing to anyone, for they were afraid" (16:8).
Whether Mark indeed wanted to end his gospel so abruptly, or whether the
original closing paragraphs of his testimony have been lost, we do not
know. The present abrupt ending suggests to me that the gospel story has
not yet come to an end, that the readers are invited to stop being mere spectators in order to become actors in the story and like true disciples follow
Jesus on the way to the cross.

Luke ends his gospel with the risen Christ leading the disciples out of
Jerusalem and giving them his blessing. And "while he blessed them, he
parted from them" (24:51). The disciples then went back to Jerusalem
"with great joy, and were continually in the temple blessing God" and
waiting for the promised Spirit. Do you remember the unfinished worship

service in the temple of Jerusalem at the beginning of Luke's gospel? The officiating priest Zechariah had a vision during which he lost his speech, so that he could not give the benediction to the assembled worshippers (1:21-22). At the end of his gospel Luke returns to this liturgical setting, and it is the risen Christ who gives the benediction while he ascends to heaven. His benediction therefore falls on ever larger areas of this world. In a liturgical manner the coming world mission is foreshadowed. Indeed, in the Acts of the Apostles, the second volume of his gospel, Luke describes Christ's mission as an escalation of God's blessing from Jerusalem to Athens and to Rome, the cultural and political capitals of the ancient world.

John's gospel — if one includes the later postscript of chapter 21 — ends with a moving conversation between Jesus and Peter, in which Jesus asks three times: "Do you love me?" The gospel of John is indeed like a declaration of love: "God so loved the world that he gave his only Son, that whoever believes in him should not perish but have eternal life" (John 3:16). This is one of the major themes which runs through the fourth gospel, and like every declaration of love it leads up to that crucial question: "Do you love me?"

What about *Matthew*? In a moment we will examine how in the closing part of his gospel Matthew has interwoven three different traditions in an artful way, putting before the readers a decisive, final alternative. Yet in order to appreciate fully this ending of Matthew's gospel we must know a few things about the first evangelist.

Matthew and "mission" in the Old Testament

Matthew must have written some ten or twenty years later than Mark, probably in the period between 75 and 85 after Christ. In fact, he made a second, enlarged edition of Mark's gospel by using some additional sources, for instance a collection of "sayings of Jesus" which Luke has also used and some further material apparently known only to him. The most typical characteristic of Matthew, however, is his extensive use of the Old Testament. Matthew has fifty-two explicit Old Testament quotations, compared to sixteen in Mark, eighteen in Luke, and seventeen in John. Again and again Matthew shows his readers that "the law and the prophets" have been fulfilled: therefore with Christ there is not only a new beginning, but also deep continuity between the basic Old Testament affirmations and expectations and the authoritative teaching, life, death, and resurrection of Jesus.

The reasoning from scripture gives Matthew's gospel a "rabbinic" and a pedagogical flavour. The author may actually have been a converted rabbi, and the gospel was probably written for a church of Greek-speaking Jewish and Gentile Christians somewhere on the Syro-Phoenician coast, where church members still debated polemically with the Jews of the synagogue across the street. By showing how Jesus taught his disciples Matthew wanted to teach these Christians how to participate in Christ's mission.

Let us therefore now go into the school of Matthew and sit at the feet of this converted rabbi in order to learn how we must participate in Jesus' mission. In a genuinely Matthean manner we are first looking at some texts from the Old Testament which you can find on the worksheet and which tell us something about how the mission to the nations was conceived in Old Testament times.

Task 1: Read the Old Testament texts on your worksheet (Gen. 12:3; Isa. 2:2-3; Isa. 42:1-2, 4, 6b; Isa. 60:1-3). Then describe in your own words how world mission was understood according to these Old Testament passages.

> After a moment of individual study, participants share with their neighbours what they have discovered. Then the panel members enter into a spontaneous discussion about these Old Testament passages, this discussion being relayed to the audience by microphones and loudspeakers. This is summed up and complemented by the enabler as follows.

Strictly speaking there is no sending out, no mission in the Old Testament. True, Abraham and the people of Israel are called to become a blessing among the nations. However, the fulfilment of this task is not seen as involving God's elect people in going out, preaching and converting the nations. There are a few exceptions. Thus during the time of Jesus the Pharisees were involved in a converting, missionary activity (cf. Matt. 23:15). Yet the history of the Jewish people provides only a very few such instances comparable to Western Christian missionary expansion. By and large, in the Old Testament and in Jewish self-understanding ever since, the election to be God's people was not conceived of as an election for a mission, but rather as an election for a presence among the nations. One of the deepest Jewish thinkers of the twentieth century, Franz Rosenzweig, once said: "The mission of the Jewish people is not the proclamation of a message, but the procreation of a people." This Jewish presence among the nations receives its specific quality by three things: (1) worship of God; (2) obedience to his Torah (this Hebrew term is usually translated "the law," but this is misleading, because the Torah is rather "the will of the living God"); (3) the hope that in the messianic age all nations will come to Zion in order to worship and obey the true God. This coming pilgrimage of the nations to Zion is expressed for instance in Isaiah's prophecy, according to which many people shall come and say: "Come, let us go up to the mountain of the Lord, to the house of the God of Jacob; that he may teach us his ways and that we may walk in his paths" (2:3).

Matthew's understanding of mission

Matthew has taken up this Old Testament expectation. He affirms in his gospel that in Jesus the messianic age has come and that the pilgrimage of the nations to Zion has therefore begun. But for him Zion is no longer a mountain or a city or the temple; the destination of the pilgrimage of the nations has now become Jesus himself, who gathers his people from among all the nations.

This new and old understanding of mission already appears in Matthew 1 and 2. There all the great themes of Matthew's gospel are anticipated as in the prelude of a symphony: Jesus is presented as the "son of David, the son of Abraham" (1:1). His name "Jesus — Jeshua" is explained: Jeshua means the saviour, for — as Matthew adds — "he will save his people from their sins" (1:21). The main title given to Jesus in this initial chapter is "Emmanuel" and again Matthew adds the explanation "which means, God with us" (1:23). This Jesus came first of all to invite God's chosen people to the messianic feast, and it is important to notice that according to Matthew the earthly Jesus strictly limited his mission to the people of Israel. But already in his prelude Matthew indicates what is going to happen: when Jesus was born in Bethlehem the leaders of his people in nearby Jerusalem neither recognize him nor come to worship him (2:4-6). Moreover, before Jesus was two years old, he and his parents had to escape and become refugees in Egypt. Later they found refuge as persecuted migrants outside of Judea, in the border area of Galilee (2:13-15, 19-23), which Matthew calls the "Galilee of the Gentiles" (4:15). Yet in Bethlehem an amazing thing happened: while the Jews did not recognize their Messiah, visitors from the East came and worshipped him. These were *magi*, Oriental astrologers. In their own country, they may have been considered to be "wise men" but the Jews saw in them idolaters, pagans (compare Paul's evaluation of another such astrologer, Acts 13:6-12). Paradoxically, these most unlikely and most despised representatives of the Gentile world were the ones who initiated the expected pilgrimage of the nations in the messianic age!

This *coming* of the Gentiles to Jesus is further emphasized throughout Matthew's gospel. Think of the Roman centurion who comes to Jesus with his exemplary faith. Jesus himself exclaimed on that occasion: "Truly, I say to you, not even in Israel have I found such faith. I tell you, many will come from east and west and sit at table with Abraham, Isaac and Jacob in the kingdom of heaven" (8:5-13). There are several other instances of this coming of the nations. Then, however, a major policy change happens in God's missionary plan. This is most clearly seen in the way in which Matthew rendered the parable of the wedding feast (22:2-10, reproduced on worksheet). The same parable is told in Luke's gospel where it appears as a straightforward story with several details which Matthew did not deem it necessary to include (Luke 14:16-24). Instead of this, Matthew's version is highly theological, almost an allegory, a story in which each detail, not only the story as a whole, refers to special meanings and events beyond the story. In this case the parts of the allegory point to events and epochs of the salvation history. On the worksheet the most typical words and probable additions in Matthew's rendering of this parable are italicized. Here are Matthew's major points:

V. 2: In Luke's version the parable begins with "A man once gave a great banquet." In Matthew's version it is "a king who gave a marriage feast for his son," and the story is introduced as a parable of God's kingdom. This "king" is of course God, the son is Jesus the Messiah, and the marriage feast is the expected messianic banquet at the end of times.

Vv. 3-5: In Luke's version only one servant is sent out with the invitation, and Luke then reports in an anecdotal way all the excuses given by those who were invited. According to Matthew the king twice sends out a group of servants. The first group (v. 3) probably refers to the prophets of the Old Testament announcing the coming messianic banquet, while the second group (v. 4) is probably an allusion to what Matthew tells in chapter 10 — the commissioning of the twelve disciples to announce among the people of Israel that the kingdom of heaven is at hand.

V. 6: Only Matthew reports that those invited captured this second group of servants, "treated them shamefully, and killed them." This is probably an allusion to the persecution of the early church. According to Matthew Jesus had already announced this persecution when he sent out his disciples to the people of Israel (cf. Matt. 10:17-25).

Vv. 7-8: Only Matthew says that the king "sent his troops and destroyed those murderers and burned their city." This is probably an allusion to the destruction of Jerusalem in the year 70. Only in Matthew's version is the king's verdict pronounced: "The wedding is ready, but those invited were not worthy."

V. 9: This leads to a third sending out of the servants. It is typical that Matthew uses exactly the same word in this verse as he will use again in the so-called mission command at the end of his gospel: "Go therefore ..."

Task 2: We saw that the Old Testament teaches about world mission. Describe now the shift in God's missionary strategy which Matthew shows in his version of the parable of the wedding feast.

> After a period of individual study participants share their insights with their neighbours. Then the panel members discuss publicly the change of God's missionary strategy, and the enabler summarizes.

This parable of the wedding feast indicates a major shift in God's missionary policy. The original plan was that the elect people of Israel would recognize its Messiah and come to the messianic feast. This would trigger off the pilgrimage of the nations to the mountain of Zion. Yet only a few among the Israelites had accepted the initial invitation to become members of the messianic fellowship. Therefore Christ now sends out these disciples to invite the nations for the messianic feast. What was originally the task of the whole people of Israel is now accomplished by the risen Christ together with the learning community of disciples who gather around him.

The great alternative

Before we turn to the closing passages of Matthew's gospel, where this announced change of God's missionary policy becomes effective, I must tell you something about the style of Matthew's teaching. Recent studies on the first gospel have shown that Matthew has been strongly influenced by the Old Testament wisdom literature, for example, the book of Proverbs. Remember how in these Proverbs the reader is again and again put before an alternative so that he or she must make a decision. The way which leads to death is confronted with the way which leads to life. Wisdom is opposed to foolishness. In a similar way Matthew constantly sets alternatives before us. In the prelude to his gospel he confronts the mighty king Herod with the poor and helpless king Jesus (2:1-12). According to the sermon on the mount a choice must be made between the narrow and the wide gate (7:13-14). The wise man who builds his house upon the rock is put over against the foolish one who builds on sand (7:24-27). Similarly the destiny of the wise and foolish virgins (25:1-13) and the judgment as a separation of the sheep and the goats (25:31-46) are painted before our eyes. Many of these passages are found only in Matthew's gospel. It is dangerous to become a disciple in Matthew's school, because he challenges his listeners and readers again and again with an alternative and thus asks us to make a decision. This is especially true for the end of Matthew's gospel.

Let us see how he composed this climax of his testimony. At the end of the worksheet is a schematic presentation of the sources Matthew used and the way he probably put them together to make a dramatic whole.

Matthew obviously had three traditions at his disposal. Like Mark and Luke he knew about the women at the tomb and the message of the angel. This *synoptic tradition* is italicized in the middle of the worksheet. Matthew interwove it with part of a *first special tradition* which apparently neither Mark nor Luke knew. It begins with the request for a guard and Pilate's permission to watch the tomb and seal the stone before the sepulchre. This same tradition must then have included the story of how the angel of the Lord descended and rolled back the stone and how the guards trembled and became like dead men. The same tradition is continued in verses 11-15, which tell how the soldiers ran into the city and told the chief priests and elders what had taken place. This scene is strangely similar to that other gathering of the chief priests and elders when they gave money to Judas Iscariot to betray his Lord.

Interwoven with the synoptic material and the first special tradition is a *second tradition*, also apparently unknown to Mark and Luke, though John has a somewhat similar passage. When the women ran into the city to tell the disciples, the risen Jesus intercepted them and repeated the message of the angel. This second tradition is later continued by the report of how the disciples went to Galilee, where Jesus had preceded them. He waited on the mountain and gave them his final message.

Notice how Matthew has used these three traditions. Like an able movie producer he cut the story into several scenes and contrasted them in such a way that they build up towards a last great alternative. The main actors are the guards at the tomb and the chief priests and elders on the one side, the women and the disciples on the other. The risen Lord and the angel bring movement into both groups. After the awesome event of the opening of the tomb, two different types of messengers run into the city of Jerusalem. The women are intercepted by Jesus, so that — paradoxically — it is the Roman soldiers who first bring the message about what happened at the tomb into the city. Then in the last two scenes a twofold mission is described: on the one side that of the soldiers, commissioned by the chief priests and the elders; on the other side that of the disciples, commissioned by the risen Christ. It is hard for Christians today to imagine the suspense people must have felt when they heard or read for the first time this dramatic ending of Matthew's gospel. Let us listen to it.

A previously recorded dramatic reading of Matthew 27:62-28:20 is played.

Have you noticed that decisive and final alternative with which Matthew confronts us? Have you noticed how the mysterious event of resurrection leads to a twofold mission?

Task 3: Reread the two last scenes of Matthew's gospel, vv. 11-15 and vv. 16-20. Describe with your own words this alternative of two contradictory missions which are proposed to us.

After a moment of individual study participants exchange insights with their neighbours, and the panel members then discuss publicly the alternative of two missions. The enabler concludes.

This is the choice before us. The first alternative is to join the mission of those who were sent out with a lie. Our message is then that the body of Jesus was stolen at night by the disciples, that the story of Jesus has come to a miserable end with his crucifixion and burial, and that God is dead. The mysterious event of the resurrection will then not disturb our usual way of thinking and acting, our style of life. Our world will then remain a closed one. The course of things will go on as usual, without the breaking in of God's kingdom into history. Financially, this may even be profitable for us — as it was for the soldiers.

The second alternative is to become part of that other mission, though we may have doubts, as some of the disciples did when the risen Lord waited for them on the mountain in Galilee. Jesus did not begin to reason with these doubting disciples, nor did he say that because of their doubts they could not become agents of his mission. He sent them out like the third group of servants in the parable of the wedding feast. This mission is described in typical Matthean terms. Nothing is said about the proclamation of the gospel and conversion. Jesus speaks here rather about discipleship, the teaching of the nations, and their incorporation into the messianic community through baptism so that they too may know the Torah, the will of the living God, which Jesus has taught during his earthly life.

Christ's enthronement speech

Which of these alternative missions will you and I choose? If indeed we participate in Christ's mission, this climax of Matthew's gospel will speak to us in still another way.

Usually these last verses are called "the command to mission." A careful reading of the text shows that this is an inadequate title. The commissioning is only part of this closing passage. It is as it were put in brackets between two other affirmations. Immediately before the commissioning of the disciples we hear that all authority has now been given to the risen Lord. Throughout his gospel Matthew has shown Jesus as a person full of authority. The sermon on the mount, for instance, closes with the words: "The crowds were astonished at his teaching, for he taught them as one who had authority, and not as their scribes" (7:28-29). It is an authority to drive out demons and to forgive sins, even an authority to restate the Torah. Indeed, Matthew depicts Jesus as a new Moses, and shows how the messianic authority clashes with that of the Pharisees, high-priests, and elders. Yet now, by what had happened at the cross and the resurrection, "*all* authority in heaven and on earth" has been conferred on Jesus. In the Greek text of this closing passage the inclusive word "all" resounds no fewer than four times: *all* authority, *all* nations, *all* commandments, *all* the days.

The climax of Matthew's gospel has the form of a cosmic liturgy of enthronement: the new king is invested with all authority. Therefore the messengers are sent out to invite all the nations. And finally comes the king's enthronement speech. It is the shortest and most powerful ever pronounced: "See, I am with you always, to the close of the age." Remember the main title given to Jesus in the first chapter of Matthew: there he was called Emmanuel, which means God with us. Through his resurrection he has now become the universal Emmanuel, the God with us in all times and places. This is the great promise given to us if we follow the women and the disciples, and if we too go quickly and tell.

19 JOHN'S VISION OF CHRIST

An introduction to John's gospel

At the large interracial South African Congress on Mission and Evangelism, held in March 1973 in Durban, I led four Bible studies on how each of the evangelists proclaimed the gospel of Jesus Christ. The aim was not to analyze a single passage, but to sketch in broad lines the main characteristics of each gospel, especially its particular missionary orientation. The following script is an expansion of a presentation there using material from other introductions to John's gospel, especially the studies prepared for the WCC Consultation on the Church and the Jewish People (Jerusalem, 1977). This material can easily be cut down for shorter introductions to John's gospel; it can also be expanded further to become the script for talks and studies in a retreat, preferably at the time of the feast of transfiguration.

Coming from the gospels of Mark, Matthew, and Luke to the gospel of John is like entering another world. A good way to develop sensitivity for the language, symbolism, and imagery of John is to participate in the worship of an Orthodox Church. Indeed, no church tradition has been more deeply marked by John's testimony than the Orthodox. We will therefore first listen to two Orthodox choirs. The first hymn is sung after midnight at the very beginning of Easter Sunday, and as the cathedral choir of Athens sings this Byzantine tune you will hear the church bells announcing the day of resurrection. The words of the hymn are deeply Johannine:

> Day of Resurrection
> Yes, let us become light at the great feast!
> Let us embrace one another.
> We will call "brothers" those who hate us!
> For the resurrection's sake let us forgive everything.
> And thus we shall proclaim:
> Christ has risen from the dead,
> By death has he overcome death,
> And to those in the tombs he grants life.

A recording of this Easter hymn, the *Doxasticon*, is played. It is included on the record appended to the publication *Das Buch der heiligen Gesänge der*

> *Ostkirche*, ed. by E. Benz, H. Thurn, C. Floros (Furche Verlag, Hamburg, 1962). Record Philips W 1302 R, side 1, hymn 4b.

The second hymn has a Slavonic tune and is sung by the choir of the Russian Orthodox cathedral in Paris. It is a hymn which expresses well John's vision of what mission means. Its words are:

> God is present, recognize it, all nations and submit to him.
> For God is in the midst of us!
> Listen to him until the ends of the earth,
> For God is in the midst of us!
> Submit to him, you mighty ones,
> For God is in the midst of us!
> God, the mighty, the all powerful, the prince of peace,
> For God is in the midst of us!

> A recording of this hymn is also included in the record mentioned above, side 2, hymn 5.

After this prelude we are going to approach John's gospel from four different angles. First we will try to get a grasp of the whole testimony and attempt to see Jesus through the eyes of the evangelist. Then we will examine the origin and transmission of this particular testimony: Who is the author? To whom is the testimony addressed? Third, we will, so to speak, enter the theological workshop of John by using his peculiar vocabulary and listening to some of his great statements of faith. Finally, we will look at some works of art which have been deeply influenced by John's vision, so that we may learn from these artistic interpretations.

A Chinese print

Reading John's gospel is like looking at a Chinese print. In the forefront, one sees an everyday scene drawn very realistically — a water-carrier crossing a bridge or a sage meditating under a tree. Similarly John "paints" only a few scenes from Jesus' life, drawing them out with many details so that often they fill a whole chapter: the conversation with Nicodemus who had come at night, the meeting with the Samaritan woman at the well, and other such incidents.

Behind this foreground Chinese prints usually show a landscape with trees, mountains, a lake, or other natural scenery, as it were through a haze. Often a third dimension can be discerned, a horizon vaguely visible where heaven and earth meet. Similarly, there are deeper levels of meaning within and behind the scenes and sayings from Jesus' life which John reports. As if looking with X-ray eyes at the outward appearances, the evangelist penetrates them, uncovering one layer of truth after the other. One can therefore never fully grasp, rationally explain, and systematize John's highly evocative and symbolic language.

Paul reasoned with local churches and missionary opponents, thus starting an ongoing theological debate. Mark was the first to combine the passion story with what the early church remembered about the healings and sayings of the earthly Jesus, thus creating the new literary genre of the gospel. Matthew rearranged this whole gospel tradition in the form of a new Pentateuch (the first five books of the Bible which tradition assigns to Moses), so that the early church might learn to live with a better righteousness than that of the Pharisees. Luke compiled his two-volume narrative on the acts of the earthly Jesus and the acts of the heavenly Jesus as an "orderly account," showing how the history of salvation proceeded from one period to the other. He gave the church the sequence of the church year. John, however, has much more shaped the spirituality of the church, especially that of the Eastern Orthodox Churches. John's gospel invites prayer and meditation rather than intellectual analysis. It is a vision of Jesus rather than a story or an explanation of him. When the Greeks came to a disciple they did not ask: "Sir, tell us about Jesus and explain him to us." According to John's testimony they said: "Sir, we wish to *see* Jesus" (John 12:21). Like a Chinese print, John's gospel invites us to *see*.

What is the image of Jesus painted by John? If one concentrates on the beginning, the well-known prologue, the evangelist saw Jesus in the first place as the Logos in whom there was life and light and truth. In the first century the term Logos, which means "the word," evoked varied deep meanings: "In the beginning God created the heavens and the earth ... And God said" (John 1:1ff; Gen. 1:1f). God's creating and separating power has become incarnate in Jesus. In Psalm 119 God's Logos and God's Torah (that is the will of the living God, his statutes and laws) are used almost interchangeably. What that psalm sings about the law, we see now in Jesus: in him God's will has come to us in person (cf. John 1:17). Of wisdom it is written: "The Lord created me at the beginning of his work ... then I was beside him, like a master workman" (Prov. 8:22ff). For wisdom "is a breath of the power of God, and a pure emanation of the glory of the Almighty ..., she is a reflection of eternal light, a spotless mirror of the working of God and an image of his goodness" (according to the intertestamental book of Wisdom 7:25ff; cf. 9:1f). In Jesus — so the prologue of John's gospel affirms — we can see this divine wisdom as a human person among us.

Next to this strong emphasis on incarnation — "the Word became flesh" (John 1:14) — the fourth gospel places an equally strong emphasis on resurrection. Jesus is shown already during his earthly life as the risen Lord. He is painted not only as the one who, by incarnation, came from the heavenly Father, but also as the one who, by resurrection, returns to the heavenly Father.

What event in Jesus' life is therefore most central in John's testimony? Some scholars have suggested that it is the event of transfiguration. In the midst of his incarnation Jesus appeared on the mountain before Peter, James, and John as the risen Lord in his glory, the glory of the Son of God. This certainly is one of the major keys of understanding for John's vision of Jesus.

Task 1: Where has John in his gospel recorded the transfiguration, this key-story of his testimony? Reflect about the significance of what you discover.

After a short individual search the participants exchange with their neighbours their "discovery" of not having found the story at all, or of having found only various allusions to it, in John's gospel. This is then briefly discussed in the plenary, and the enabler sums up.

We are faced here with a riddle. While all other evangelists report the transfiguration (Matt. 17:1-8; Mark 9:2-8; Luke 9:28-36), John never tells this most Johannine episode of Jesus' life. Throughout his gospel one finds allusions to it, beginning already in the prologue. The scene of transfiguration is most clearly recalled in John 12, where one also finds an echo of Jesus' prayer in Gethsemane: "Now is my soul troubled. And what shall I say? 'Father, save me from this hour'? No, for this purpose I have come to this hour. Father, glorify thy name. Then a voice came from heaven, 'I have glorified it, and I will glorify it again' " (vv. 27-28).

In this passage John makes the Gethsemane scene transparent with the light of transfiguration. The same is true for the whole account of passion in the fourth gospel. Transfiguration was for John therefore not simply one among the many episodes in Jesus' earthly life, but the key for understanding the whole incarnation, work, death, and resurrection of Jesus as God's Son. He retold the gospel as one great transfiguration story.

It is as if John sits on the mountain of transfiguration and sees first the manifestation of God's glory in Jesus' signs among the Jews, Samaritans, and Greeks (John 1:19-12:50). Then, on a deeper level, he sees the manifestation of God's glory in the revelations and prayers of Jesus within the fellowship of his disciples (John 13:1-17:26). Many scholars would include in this second part the whole passion and resurrection story. However, since chapters 18-20 could as well be an immediate continuation of chapters 1-12 as of chapters 13-17, it is preferable to consider this section as a third major part, in which God's glory is seen to be manifested in Jesus' passion and resurrection.

Yet who is it who has seen and testified and written down? Like all the other gospels, the Chinese print of John's gospel has not been autographed. This leads to our second investigation.

The excavation of a tell

"Tells" are artificial mounds found in Palestine, which an untrained eye can hardly distinguish from natural hills. Archaeologists excavating the accumulated remains of ancient settlements which form the tell can reconstruct the successive stages in its development. In many ways John's gospel is like such a tell, with several layers of tradition placed on top of one another.

Clearly, the latest (probably the fourth) layer of tradition was not written by the evangelist. To it belongs chapter 21, which is an appendix added by the final redactors, members of what is sometimes called the "Johannine school." The beloved disciple is indirectly designated as the author of the gospel (John 21:24, cf. v. 20). The final redactors have also made the present arrangement of the material and some annotations (for example

John 4:2, 44; 11:2; 19:35). It is generally held that this final edition was made at the end of the first century in Asia Minor, probably for a church of mainly Gentile Christians for whom Jewish customs and festivals had to be explained.

The third level of the "tell" is the gospel as the evangelist wrote it in Greek, perhaps in a series of versions, the earliest at roughly the same time as Matthew and Luke wrote (ca. A.D. 75-85). At that time Jewish Christians were excluded from the synagogue (cf. John 9:22; 12:42; 16:2), which probably accounts for the strongly anti-Jewish statements found for instance in John 8. "Jews," at that level, become almost synonymous with what the other evangelists call the "scribes and Pharisees" or the undecided "crowd" or even "the world" which has rejected Jesus. Scholars disagree about whom this written form of the gospel was originally addressed to. Were they a Jewish-Christian church in Syria or in Asia Minor? Or had the passage from the Jewish milieu to that of the Hellenistic world already happened, all the more so because there was the "bridge" of a strongly Hellenized Judaism outside Palestine? Did the evangelist therefore write mainly for Gentile Christians immersed in the religious and philosophical melting pot of Asia Minor? This last hypothesis seems to me the most probable.

Digging deeper, one reaches the second level, that of the oral tradition. Indeed, what the evangelist wrote down must have been the result of three or four decades of oral teaching by a great theologian. It may be that the shift from Judea or Syria to Asia Minor occurred already during that period, and the translation of the gospel for a new cultural and religious milieu had to be accomplished. In the next section we will examine the language and thought of this theologian in more detail. But who was this theologian? Opinions diverge on whether he was the same person as the evangelist who later fixed the oral tradition in writing. Personally I think that this was indeed the case. Many identify this theologian-evangelist with John the Elder, about whom Papias wrote (ca. A.D. 135), and whom he distinguished from the apostle John, the son of Zebedee. Whoever this great theologian was, he had received the tradition of faith on which he meditated deeply from an eyewitness of Jesus.

That eyewitness, almost certainly the "beloved disciple," began the Johannine tradition. To use the image of the tell, he laid the most ancient layer of the first level of the mound. This brings us back to the time of Jesus' public ministry and the years immediately following his death. The fourth gospel never states that this eyewitness was the apostle John, the son of Zebedee. Strangely enough, it is only in John's gospel that the name of the disciple John *never* occurs! Whatever else that means, the eyewitness and beloved disciple wanted to remain anonymous. Was this founder of the Johannine tradition identical with the theologian who later shaped and taught this particular tradition of faith? And if so, was he also identical with the evangelist who still later fixed the gospel in writing? It was Irenaeus of Lyons who first stated, around A.D. 180, that this was actually the case. Probably the final redactors of the gospel also thought so (cf. John

21:24). On the basis of careful examination of the internal evidence in the gospel itself, many scholars today rather believe that the eyewitness and the theologian were two different people. However, this question will probably never be resolved.

More important than the name of the eyewitness is his initial testimony. He was a Jew who must have lived in Judea and possibly had close links with the temple worship in Jerusalem. "The other disciple" (John 18:15), who "was known to the high-priest," refers probably to the beloved disciple and thus to the founder of the Johannine tradition. His Judean "bias" emerges from the following statistics: 27 of the 40 main passages of John's gospel are situated in Jerusalem, 5 in Judea, only 1 in Samaria, and 6 in Galilee. This represents a quite different "gospel geography" from that of Mark and Matthew, both of whom emphasize the significance of Galilee in the life and mission of Jesus. It also differs from Luke, where roughly equal space is given to the account of Jesus' words and deeds in Galilee, Samaria, and Judea.

Eight of the nine important discourses of Jesus recorded in John's gospel take place in Jerusalem and one only in Galilee. While in the first three gospels 17 of the 22 recorded healing stories happen in Galilee, John reports only four healing stories, one in Galilee and three in Jerusalem. Clearly Jesus' life and ministry in Jerusalem and Judea are emphasized in the fourth gospel. Therefore the chronology is also different. According to John Jesus came to Jerusalem several times for religious festivals, and his public ministry lasted more than three years. John's dating of the events of Passion week differs from that of the other evangelists, perhaps simply because he may not have used the official Jewish lunar calendar but the older solar calendar which was also used by Jewish sectarian movements such as the community of Qumran.

The eyewitness and the theologian were convinced that "salvation is from the Jews" (John 4:22). Though 39 of the 71 occurrences of the term "Jew" or "Jews" have a pejorative sense, the designations "Israel" (4 times) and "Israelite" (once) always have the positive sense of bearers of God's promise and true heirs of the Old Testament heritage. The "tell" of John's gospel is indeed firmly built on the rock of the Old Testament.

At a first glance this is not obvious. There are indeed fewer Old Testament quotations and allusions in John's gospel than in the equally long gospels of Matthew and Luke (according to one generally accepted list only 27 quotations and allusions in John over against 109 in Luke and 124 in Matthew). Yet for John the Old Testament as a whole, not isolated fragments from it, formed the background and framework of the new revelation in Christ. In his few explicit Old Testament quotations, John often uses a prooftext method to show that this or that event or saying in Jesus' life "was to fulfil the scripture." More often, however, the Old Testament as a whole was for him a strong undercurrent for theological reflection. He confessed Jesus not only as the Logos but also as the "Messiah," the "king of

Israel," the "prophet" and — more often than in the other three gospels — the "rabbi."

The first three chapters of Genesis have shaped much of John's prologue, though they are never directly quoted. Abraham, Isaac, Jacob, and above all Moses are referred to. The whole gospel may have been patterned on Exodus. Jesus speaks in John's gospel as Moses speaks in Deuteronomy. Another Old Testament and Jewish tradition which certainly influenced the structure of John's gospel are the principal feasts of the Jews (Sabbath — John 5; Passover — John 6; Tabernacles — John 7-9; Dedication — John 10). The theologian reinterpreted the old gospel traditions in a similar way as the unknown prophet of the exile did with the tradition of the prophet Isaiah (Isa. 40-55). Even more important is the influence from wisdom literature (Proverbs and the intertestamental books Sirach and Wisdom of Solomon) on the style and content of the gospel.

This excavation of the tell of John's gospel, from the latest layer of the final redactors' work to its foundation in the Old Testament, has led to several important insights which must be kept in mind while reading individual passages from the fourth gospel.

First, these passages, which in their present form were written just before the end of the first century, have a long period of oral transmission behind them. It is thus important to study them not simply as written texts, but to read them aloud and to hear them.

Second, as many of these passages go back to the testimony of an eyewitness, they sometimes contain better historic reminiscences than the "older" gospels of Mark, Matthew, and Luke. Yet to concentrate too much on the question of the historicity of what is reported is to miss John's intention to let us see the depth dimensions of what happened.

Third, as the Johannine tradition of faith was transmitted orally and then in written form over sixty or seventy years, a shift took place from the Judean and perhaps Syrian Judeo-Christian milieu to the philosophical-religious milieu of Asia Minor. The tradition had thus to be reinterpreted. This was the work of the theologian John, whether he was the eyewitness/theologian/evangelist in one and the same person, or the eyewitness/theologian or the theologian/evangelist.

John the theologian

The ancient church called the author of the fourth gospel "the theologian." Among early Christians this title did not evoke the image of a learned professor of theology but rather of someone who serves the glory of God by reflecting and proclaiming God's revelation in such a way that it leads to prayer and commitment. This theologian's aim is well expressed in the last two verses of the gospel:

> Jesus did many other signs in the presence of the disciples, which are not written in this book; but these are written that you may believe that Jesus is the Christ, the Son of God, and that believing you may have life in his name (John 20:30-31).

Another aspect of a theologian's task is restating the gospel for a new time and environment. John has certainly done so in a most daring way. As a matter of fact, some circles in the ancient church were not certain whether John's gospel really should have a place in the New Testament. Should it be rejected as a book which did not genuinely witness to Jesus Christ? Should it be counted together with such apocryphal gospels as that of Peter? Had John really maintained the essential gospel tradition? Why did he not tell about the appearance of the risen Lord in Galilee? Why did the apostle Peter play such an unimportant role in his account? These questions were debated in the early church, and may help explain why the final redactors added the appendix of chapter 21, in which Peter is given the task of being shepherd of the church and where Jesus appears to his disciples in Galilee, testifying to the trustworthiness of the beloved disciple.

Christians of the ancient church who knew one or more of the first three gospels must have been bewildered when they first read John's gospel. So many of the traditional Christian key words are seldom or never used in this new gospel, terms like "God's kingdom," "righteous," "to proclaim," "to call," "to repent." Indeed, John invented a new Christian vocabulary, using new images and thoughtforms for witnessing to Christ. Many of these have their origin in the Old Testament and intertestamental wisdom literature. Other terms John certainly borrowed indirectly from Jewish sectarian groups like that of the community of Qumran and from the strongly Hellenistic Jewish philosopher Philo of Alexandria. Still other terms and concepts were probably borrowed from the Gnostic movememt, a religious philosophy and way of salvation which later developed especially in Egypt, but which perhaps already marked the time and milieu of the Christians for whom John wrote. John has thus taken up the language and thoughtforms of the new time and environment for which he restated the gospel. By doing so he proved to be a true theologian.

Here are twenty of John's key-terms, listed in the order of the Greek alphabet, comparing their frequency of occurrence with Matthew and Luke.

> The list on page 220 should either be prepared ahead of time for distribution to the participants or written clearly on a blackboard or flip chart.

Task 2: Try to speak Johannine language and write a paragraph beginning with the sentence: "John witnesses to Jesus ...." Use as many of John's keywords as you can to sum up what you learned of John's testimony so far.

> When most participants have completed this task ask some of them to read their Johannine summary of John's testimony.

It is of course not enough only to count words and then immediately draw theological conclusions from the statistics. One must weigh the meaning of these terms and hear them in the context in which they occur. Therefore we are now going to listen to some of the great passages from

Greek key word	English equivalent	Number of occurrences		
		John	Matthew	Luke
agapān, agapē	to love, love	43	9	13
alētheia	truth	25	1	3
ginōskein	to come to know	56	20	28
doxazein, doxa	to glorify, glory	41	11	22
zēn, zoē	to live, life	53	13	14
theōrein	to contemplate	24	2	7
Iēsous	Jesus	237	150	89
Ioudaios	Jew	71	5	5
kosmos	the world	78	8	3
krinein	to judge	19	6	6
martyrein, martyria	to testify, testimony	47	1	2
menein	to remain	40	3	7
oida	to know	85	25	25
horān	to see	31	13	14
patēr (used of God)	the Father	118	45	17
pempein	to send	32	4	10
pisteuein	to believe	98	11	9
tērein	to keep, to safeguard	18	6	0
phaneroun	to make manifest	9	0	0
phōs	light	23	7	7

John's gospel. These readings are chosen to show John's particular view of mission, namely the threefold sending of the Son, the Spirit, and the church. After a short summary of each of these three steps of mission, we listen to John's own testimony.

> The Johannine passages indicated at the end of each paragraph are played back from a previously recorded dramatic reading. Alternatively, divide the participants into three groups, each of which prepares for the recital of one of the series of texts.

1. Salvation is offered to all in Jesus Christ. For this the Father sent his Son into the world. Where he comes, a crisis happens. Yet those who believe in Jesus' mission of love are united with him. They are separated from the bondage of evil and receive true life. *John 1:1, 3-5, 14; 3:16-17; 1:9-12; 12:20-21, 23-25, 31-32, 44-46; 14:6.*

2. What Jesus has done on earth through his signs and words is only a beginning. Having given his life for the salvation of the world and thus glorified God, his mission is continued through the sending of the Spirit. *John 10:14-16; 14:16; 16:7, 33; 17:1-3.*

3. It is in the context of this growing harvest of the continuing mission of Jesus through the Spirit that the church too is sent into the world. Its calling

is to glorify God by witnessing to the truth in Christ, by being sanctified and bearing the fruit of love. *John 17:15-22; 15:5-10; 20:21-22.*

John restated the gospel tradition not in order to write a new, contextual theology. Nor was his primary purpose a polemical one, either against the Jews, the Hellenistic philosophers, or Gnostic teachers. There are polemic passages in his gospel, and he certainly wanted to correct the faith of Christians who were in danger of confusing the living Christ with laws or rituals or religious-philosophical ideas. However, the main purpose of the Johannine teaching lay probably elsewhere.

The very last scene reported in John's gospel is the meeting of the risen Lord with the doubting Thomas (John 20:24-29). Does Thomas perhaps represent the church for which John restated the gospel? In this case the main purpose would be a pastoral one. Jewish Christians who had been excluded from the synagogues and confused Gentile Christians in the religious-philosophical melting pot of Asia Minor were in a crisis of faith. Already facing sporadic persecutions, they wondered whether it was worthwhile to suffer for Christ. They doubted like Thomas. John therefore encouraged them to remain firm in faith, showing them the victorious Christ who fulfilled his Father's will by giving his life for his friends. "Blessed are those who have not seen and yet believe" (John 20:29). Christians of the last third of the first century could no longer see Christ and his signs with their outward eyes. But with the eyes of faith, on the basis of the testimony of a trustworthy eyewitness and as members of the worshipping church, they could confess: "We have beheld his glory, glory as of the only Son from the Father" (John 1:14).

The icon of God's glory

The word "icon" (from the Greek *eikōn*) is used in one of the apostle Paul's great sayings. He wrote to the Corinthians that "we all, with unveiled face, beholding (or mirroring) the glory of the Lord, are being changed (in Greek the same word is used as in the story of the transfiguration) into his likeness (*eikōn*) from one degree of glory to another" (2 Cor. 3:18). John could have taken this word of Paul as a motto for his gospel.

The Orthodox icons are paintings of saints, angels, Old Testament events, and especially key events of Jesus' life which one finds in all Orthodox churches and homes. These are not idols. Orthodox believers do not worship the icons but rather use them as helps for worshipping God. The icons remind Orthodox believers that our body and our whole life is destined to participate in Christ's transfiguration. More than that, the icons show that the things of this world, the whole creation, are to be transfigured to become a mirror of the glory of God, as Paul wrote.

"What the gospel tells us by words, the icon proclaims by colours and makes it present for us." This statement by an Eastern Church council shows the intimate relationship between the icons and the gospels, especially the gospel of John. A widely used Orthodox liturgical manual states: "In order to learn iconography and to understand an icon, pray to the holy

John." This advice could also be turned around: "In order to understand John's gospel, meditate on the icons." This we are presently going to do as a fourth and last approach to John's vision of Jesus.

The following text is spoken while the slides are being projected. Each paragraph should be preceded and followed by a moment of silent meditation. Reproductions of the icons used — or similar ones — can be found in most art books on Orthodox iconography. Van Gogh's 1888 painting of the sower is not as well known as his other paintings on the same theme. It is exhibited in the Van Gogh museum in Amsterdam, and a good colour reproduction of it appears in the Van Gogh volume of the *Time/Life* art book series.

1. *The icon of transfiguration by Theopane the Greek, end of 14th century.*
Formerly every Orthodox monk who devoted his life to painting icons had to begin his sacred art by painting such an icon of transfiguration. He had to learn at the outset that painting icons does not mean painting with colours, but with light. There are no shadows in the icons because the source of light comes from the transfigured persons and things. Meditating on such an icon, one is reminded of John's testimony: "We have beheld his glory, glory as of the only Son of the Father."

2. *The icon of Our Lady of Vladimir, Byzantine art from the early 12th century.*
There is much beauty in the face of Mary, yet not the natural beauty of Raphael's Madonnas but the beauty of a new creation, a transcendent beauty. Jesus is not the litte *bambino* we see in paintings from the Italian Renaissance. He is dressed in adult clothes and his face is serious and majestic. The child presses himself affectionately to his mother, and with one hand he reassures her. The basic geometric symbolism is very important in iconography. In this particular icon we find a high triangle within a rectangle: the triangle pointing to the mystery of the Trinity, which is inscribed here in the rectangle which symbolizes the world. "The word became flesh, and dwelt among us, full of grace and truth."

3. *The icon of the crucifixion by Master Dionisi, 1500.*
"God can do everything, except force man to love him," said the church fathers. This is why Christ had to be crucified. In Orthodox iconography the crucified Lord is never painted with realism in the midst of agony or as a spent and dead body. Death is seen rather as a deep sleep and the Lord on the cross maintains his majesty. "I see him crucified, and I call him king!" (Chrysostom). Golgotha becomes the place of the cosmic battle. The cross is the tree of life. At its foot one sees the skull of Adam. Symbolized by the first Adam, the whole of humanity is now cleansed by the blood of the second Adam. The cross reaches up to heaven. We are reminded of Christ's saying according to John: "I, when I am lifted up from earth, will draw all to myself."

4. *The icon of the empty tomb, end of the 15th century.*

None of the gospels describes the actual event of resurrection. In accordance with this biblical awe before the mysterious event of the resurrection, no icon exists which portrays the event of resurrection. What is shown is only the empty tomb with the two angels who tell the women that Jesus has risen: "Why do you seek the living among the dead?" (Luke 24:5). Even today in Orthodox countries, those who meet on Easter morning say, "Christ is risen," and they receive the spontaneous and joyous answer: "He is truly risen!" As in all icons, the colour symbolism is important: a patch of luminous gold (the colour of heaven) has split open the dark world of death. The angels are clothed in dazzling white, the colour of the divine world. From that world Jesus came and said: "I am the light of the world." "I am the resurrection and the life; he who believes in me, though he die, yet shall he live."

5. *The icon of the Holy Trinity, by Andrej Rubljew, 1415.*

This is the most famous icon. One must meditate on it for a long time to appreciate its deep symbolism and message. The episode told in Genesis of the three messengers who visited Abraham to announce that he would have a son and would thus be a blessing for the nations has become a symbol for the mystery of the Trinity. Abraham appears no more and the three angels stand in a cosmic landscape: the central angel — symbolizing the Father — is shown before the tree of life; the angel at his left side — symbolizing the Spirit — sits before the mountain of revelation from which flows the living water; the angel on his right side — symbolizing the Son — sits before the new Jerusalem. The three figures are in dialogue and form a perfect circle. Movement starts from the left foot of the angel representing the Spirit, passes through the central figure and comes to rest in the vertical position of the angel. Many words of the Johannine Christ come to one's mind as one meditates on this icon. In iconography convex lines signify the speaking, the revelation, while concave lines symbolize the listening, openness to revelation. Notice this interplay of revealing and receiving in the convex lines of the blessing arm in the centre and the receiving concave lines of the figure of the Son. He prayed "that they may all be one; even as thou, Father, art in me, and I in thee, that they also may be in us, so that the world may believe that thou hast sent me."

6. *The painting of the sower, by Vincent van Gogh, 1888.*

A Johannine painting: a tilled field with a sower in the foreground, fields with corn ready for the harvest in the background and above all the enormous dazzling sun on the horizon. Jesus responded to the Greeks' request to see him with the words: "The hour has come for the Son of man to be glorified. Truly, I say to you, unless a grain of wheat falls into the earth and dies, it remains alone; but if it dies, it bears much fruit."

> We are the field,
> and let us pray that we may be a well-tilled field,

ready to receive the word of salvation.
We are the grains,
and let us pray that we may be ready to die to our old self,
so that we may bear fruit.
We are called to be sowers,
and let us pray that we sow good seed.
But we always need the sun, the love, and the glory of God.
Lord, make us icons of your glory.

20 WHO IS THE CHURCH?

Acts 2

Much of the following material is adapted from the catechism drawn and written in 1953 for illiterate oral communicators in Central Celebes, Indonesia, described in the first chapter of Part I. I have since used similar exercises with groups in very different milieus, including highly literate cultures. The different steps of the following study can be taken separately for a series of relatively short meetings or together as a basic programme for a one-day session or a weekend. An expanded version of this script was used to make a cassette with introductions and conclusions for four Bible studies produced by the Pacific Conference of Churches, in March 1980.

Images of the church
What is the church? Where is the church? The usual way to answer such questions is with definitions or by pointing to a church building. But neither definitions of the church nor church buildings are found in the New Testament. The early Christians met in private homes. When they reflected about the reality and purpose of Christ's church, they spoke in images, just as Jesus did. Only twice is the term "church" used in the four gospels (Matt. 16:18; 18:17), but several times Jesus said to the group of disciples: "You are ...," using a word image rather than an abstract definition of what the members of his church are called to be. Similarly Paul and other New Testament writers used images rather than definitions to suggest who the church is and what its members are commissioned to do.

Task 1: Look for images for the church in the New Testament, and make a simple line drawing of each on a large sheet of paper. Select only such images which are used in the New Testament and which refer indeed to the members of the church (e.g., disciples, believers, a local church, etc.) and not to God's kingdom. You may use your Bibles to double check, but start by working from your memory.

This task should be done in groups of three to five people, provided with a large sheet of paper and felt-tip pens. Yet such tools, which may be too expensive, are not absolutely necessary. In Central Celebes we drew with our fingers in the sand at the seashore or with charcoal on wooden planks. This task can be presented in the form of a competition: Which group finds and draws most New Testament images for the church within half an hour? Afterwards all the large sheets with the images are put on the wall, or — to avoid duplication of the same image — members of each group are asked in turn to draw one of their images on the blackboard, until all the images found are drawn. Many of the following images and probably still different ones will have been found.

What we have before our eyes are only a few samples. One study on the images of the church in the New Testament lists no fewer than 96 different images. These include of course also minor variations within the same

Salt of the earth (Mt 5:13)

Light of the world (Mt 5:14)

Sheep of Christ (Jn 10)

Branches of Christ, the vine (Jn 15)

God's field (1.Cor 3:9)

God's building (1.Cor 3:9; cp Eph 2:20)

God's Temple (1.Cor 3:16; cp Eph 2:21f)

Christ's body (1.Cor 12:27; cp Eph 1:22f)

Letter from Christ (2.Cor 3:3)

Mirror of God's glory (2.Cor 3:18)

Ambassadors of Christ (2.Cor 5:20)

Household of God (Eph 2:19)

Christ's beloved (Eph 5:25-32)

Soldiers of Christ (2.Tim 2:5; cp Eph 6:11 ff)

Living stones (1.Petr 2:9)

family of images. This multitude of images has been given to us so that we may look at them, meditate on them, and learn from them.

Task 2: Consider these images for the church with the following question in mind: What do these images evoke in you concerning the life and mission of the church?

> After a moment of silent contemplation, participants are asked to comment spontaneously. If necessary, the enabler can sum up as follows.

Three things are especially emphasized in many of these images: First and foremost is the very intimate relationship between Jesus and the church. Without Christ the head, his body the church is dead. Without Christ the vine, its branches will wither away. Without Christ the shepherd, the sheep will be scattered. Without Christ the bridegroom, the bride will be mourning. The most important priority for the church is therefore to remain in this intimate communion with Christ. The question: "Who is the church?" can almost be answered with just one word: "Christ." Where he is, there is at least potentially the church.

A second emphasis in many of these images is the interrelationship within the church. Each member of the body needs and completes the other members. It is interesting that almost nowhere in these images do specially ordained ministers or priests play any role. There are of course many passages in the New Testament which do speak about the crucial role of the apostles as well as of other ministers, but in the images for the church the main accent lies on the whole people of God and its fellowship. Many living stones have to be put together to build the church. (How difficult it is to build with living stones!) The pilgrim people are held together by a common vocation, and God's family is united by the overarching divine love. A divided church has lost the fulness of grace. Who is the church? Not individual believers or ordained ministers, nor an impersonal institution, but the community of the believers.

Third, many of the images strongly emphasize the purpose of the church in the world. Our calling is to be the salt of the earth (not to build beautiful salt barrels and store as much salt as possible in them!). We are to be the light of the world, which means that we cannot preserve our being, but must be spent like a candle is spent when it burns. Our task is to be the letter of Christ, not an empty envelope but people with a message to be delivered. Who is the church? Not those who safeguard their spiritual treasures for themselves, but those who are ready to be spent for God's cause.

It would be interesting to examine critically our church budgets and church activities on the basis of these top three criteria: Do they foster the relationship between Christ and the church members? Do they lead to the growth of that fellowship where each one has something to receive and to contribute? Do they serve the essential purpose of the church in the world? However, we have perhaps asked too quickly what the images mean and what their implications are for our church life. By rationalizing them we have not let them speak long enough to our unconscious mind and emotions. It is therefore good to train our sensitivity for the symbols and images which are given to us today in our own environment.

Task 3: Take a walk around inside or outside the house or building where you are meeting. Look at nature and things created by human hands. Are there any new images for the church which perhaps speak more strongly to us today than the images found in the New Testament? If you discover such new symbols or material parables for the church bring them back into our fellowship.

> After such a search for new images the first part of this study can best be concluded with a period of worship, during which the group sits in a large circle. Participants who have found a new image share their token for the church and explain with two or three sentences what it reveals to them. This leads to thanksgiving, confession, intercession, and an act of commitment

The origin of the church

When and where did the church have its beginning? Many answers are possible. One could start with the call to Abraham (Gen. 12:1-3) or with God's covenant with the people of Israel at Mount Sinai (Exod. 19:1-6) or with the prophetic promise of the new covenant (Jer. 31:31-34). All these passages point to events in salvation history which are highly relevant for our reflection on the church. In this connection it must be emphasized that in the New Testament the church is never called the *new* Israel. Although a decisive new beginning in salvation history was made with Christ, there remains a deep continuity between the history of the people of Israel and the history of the church. It is therefore not wrong to look in the Old Testament for the origin of the Christian church.

Turning to the New Testament one could discover the church's origin in the calling of the first disciples (Mark 3:13-19) or in the decisive events of Christ's death and resurrection. More often, however, Pentecost is seen as the birthday of the church. Let us therefore discover what the Pentecost story reports about the origin of the church.

Task 4: Make a recording of a dramatic reading of Acts 2:1-47 with the voice of a reader for the passages which are not in direct speech, a voice for Peter, the voice of a lector for the Old Testament quotations, and voices for the bystanders and enquirers.

> If there are more than ten participants two or more groups should be formed. The reading can of course also be prepared for direct recital without recording, but for the following exercise of listening recordings are preferable. As soon as the recitals or the recordings are ready the participants gather for the next task.

Task 5: Listen to the recording (or recital) of the Pentecost story as if you had never heard the narrative of this event. During this first playback try to shut out as much as possible your own questions about the story or your reflections about its meaning: concentrate simply on the listening. After this first listening exercise, play back for a second time the recording of

Acts 2 (or make a second recital of this chapter), and now listen to the story with the question in mind: What does it report about the origin of the church? You may want to jot down catchwords as you listen.

> After the second listening exercise participants exchange their discoveries with their neighbours, leading to a general discussion about Pentecost and the origin of the church. Many details will be mentioned. The enabler need not repeat them in the concluding remarks for this second part of the study if they have already been clearly expressed in the plenary discussion.

The Spirit came when "they were all together in one place," yet it rested "on each of them" (vv. 1-3). The church is from its beginning universal, where languages from all the then-known world are spoken (vv. 4-11). This may be referring to the phenomenon of "speaking in tongues," known in Corinth (1 Cor. 14:6ff) and in the present-day charismatic movement, but more likely it is a symbolic language miracle which anticipates the later world mission of the church. While the church is gathered in one place, its presence is noticed outside and becomes public, a matter of amazement, a laughingstock, and a source of questions (vv. 12f).

This leads to the first Christian missionary proclamation. It does not start from an ancient biblical text, but takes its point of departure from an amazing event in the time and place of the hearers (v. 15). Then the sermon refers back to the scriptures to indicate clues for the understanding of what is happening in the present (vv. 16-21). This present new reality is intimately related with what Jesus of Nazareth has done and has suffered (vv. 22-23). It is also related to Christ's vindication, when God raised him up from the dead and exalted him at his right hand, sending the Spirit, as David already foresaw (vv. 24-35). The proclamation ends with a confession of faith in the form of a direct appeal to the hearers who have in fact already been involved with the destiny of Jesus: "Let all the house of Israel therefore know assuredly that God has made him both Lord and Christ, this Jesus whom you crucified" (v. 36). Such a missionary proclamation leads to conversion and baptisms (vv. 37-41) and a new kind of community life, marked by fellowship and joyous worship (vv. 42-47).

The most important message about the origin of the church which comes through in this story is the emphasis on the *mystery* of the church's origin. The church remains a thoroughly human body, where people speak, eat together, and sing, yet it is not the work of human beings. What created it are God's great deeds in Jesus Christ and the irruption of the Spirit's power which can only symbolically be alluded to as a mighty wind, as tongues of fire, and as a language miracle. Despite the many all-too-human realities within the church, it defies easy definition. It may seem to be dull and dead for a long time, and then suddenly comes again an irruption of that Spirit which gives new, amazing life.

How does one become a member of the church?

At the end of the story of Pentecost Luke states that "the Lord added to their number day by day those who were being saved" (v. 47).

Task 6: How does one become a member of the church according to Acts 2:36-38? Examine step by step the process of becoming a Christian as it is outlined in these verses and fix each step by a symbol or simple line drawing so that we see the process before our eyes.

> This task is done either individually or in groups of two or three participants. Then all together create a drawing with the different steps necessary for becoming a Christian. For this exercise a blackboard and chalk are far preferable to a sheet of paper with felt-tip pens. In this way different proposals for visualizing can be drawn, erased and replaced by new ones. The role of the enabler is to be the advocate both of the text and of the silent members of the group, so that no important detail is overlooked and that all participants can contribute. Some such drawing as the following then gradually appears on the blackboard. The small letters indicate the sequence of drawings. Individual signs may have changed several times (by wiping out a symbol already drawn and replacing it with a new one). The final drawing reproduced here with descriptive text following can only hint at the highly dynamic and dialogical nature of this learning process.

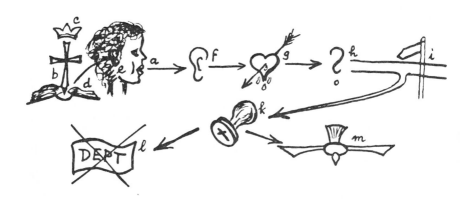

How does one become a member of the church? Our immediate answer may be "by conversion/repentance" or "by baptism." True, but Acts 2:36-38 enumerates many more steps which precede repentance and baptism. Where does the process start?

Somebody — in this case the apostle Peter — proclaims a message (symbol (a) is now drawn, the preaching mouth and the arrow symbolizing the message). There is no church without proclamation, but it is a very special proclamation, namely the one about Jesus crucified (b) whom God made Lord and Christ (c). Had there been no eyewitnesses of what Jesus did, no listeners to his words, no apostles called to be with him (at this point an eye and an ear are drawn at the right side of the cross, later to be erased), there would be no church today. We become members of the church if through proclamation we are inserted into a story which started a long time before us. It even started centuries before Christ — so Peter affirms in his proclamation — with what David and the Old Testament prophets announced (at this point a scroll is drawn at the left side of the cross, later to be erased).

However, Peter and the visionaries of the Old Testament have long since died. How then can we still come to know their testimony? Their witness was fixed in writing (at this point the scroll and the eye/ear signs are erased and replaced by the open Bible (d) under the cross). A succession of persons were commissioned to be the guardians and witnesses of this message which, throughout the centuries, was also spontaneously proclaimed by ordinary Christians (the preaching mouth is now completed to become the face of a witness (e) with an eye and an ear, and an arrow from the Bible to the ear). Without such ongoing missionary proclamation there is no church. Yet proclamation is not magic. The Spirit which was at work in Jesus, in the prophets and apostles, in the making of the Bible, and in the ongoing ministry of the church must also intervene in the ear and heart of new hearers.

We cannot become Christians without hearing the message (f), and this message must cut our hearts (g). The well-known symbol of the heart pierced by an arrow expresses exactly what happens when we become Christians: we fall in love. This love-story is that of a love with deep joy and fulfilment, because it responds to God's great love for us, which Christ came to declare and seal to the world. All those who have had the experience of falling in love with somebody know that then our past and present life becomes one great question mark (h): "What shall we do?" This question is addressed to people who suddenly have become "brethren" and certainly also "sisters." Confidence and fellowship have been created even before the inquirers are integrated into the new community! In this divine-human love-story, the answer to the question about what to do starts with an unpopular word: "Repent!" This literally means: change your thinking, walk in another direction (i).

Then comes a great, symbolic act, "symbolic" in the deep, sacramental meaning of this term: "Be baptized every one of you in the name of Jesus Christ!" It is both an eminently personal act ("every one of you") and an incorporating act into the community. Those who are baptized become in a real sense participants in the story of Jesus, members of his body and his people, part of that reality expressed in the manifold images for the church. In many texts of the church fathers baptism is described as an ordination for the ministry of being the church in the world.

Baptism can be visualized in different ways: a person immersed in water, or buried, or washed clean, or being integrated into a body or fellowship, or receiving the sign and seal of the cross (k), coming thus under God's special protection and command. Nothing is said in the text about the way in which people were baptized, or about whether it was only adult believers or also children of families who desired to become part of the Christian fellowship.

Two affirmations are made in connection with baptism. The baptized are promised the forgiveness of their sins (l) and the gift of the Holy Spirit (m).

The church is the fellowship of forgiven sinners, not of self-righteous moral heroes. And, once again, the link between Pentecost and the church is emphasized: the Christian community and its members do not stand by their own strength, but by the power of the Spirit who challenges the spirit of our time, the fashions and priorities of our environment.

There is no mechanical linkage between the ritual of baptism and the receiving of the Spirit's gift. Later in Acts, Luke tells about people in Samaria who were baptized but had not received the Spirit (Acts 8:15ff). He also tells about people in Caesarea who had received the Spirit but were not yet baptized (10:47f). Yet both cases were clearly considered as exceptions. As members of the church we may confidently count not only on the forgiveness of our sins, but also on the ever new irruption of the Spirit in our lives.

21 BIBLICAL PROCLAMATION AND POLITICS

Acts 17:1-10a

> The first part of this script, the exercise of story-telling, was prepared for a Bible study training seminar during the first Pacific Christian Youth Conference in Suva, Fiji, in January 1980. The second and third parts have been specifically written as an invitation to readers of this book to join in an attempt at creative writing and story-telling.

The telling of a story

The most common way of remembering, teaching, and proclaiming God's great acts is story-telling. This is true both for the Old and the New Testament. It remains true still today, especially in predominently oral cultures. If we want to be messengers of the biblical message we must learn the art of story-telling.

Task 1: Each participant chooses a partner and the two tell one another their favourite short story. While the one is telling his or her story, the other observes carefully how the narrator tells the tale. Then the roles are reversed. When both partners have told their short stories the two reflect together on what they observed and what they have learned about story-telling.

> The type of story used in this preliminary exercise must be chosen according to the cultural milieu of the participants. In Africa one can best suggest a short traditional story about animals. In the Western world it is often a favourite joke which is the best entry into the art of story-telling. In the Pacific it was suggested that each tell the other his or her favourite traditional story of how the islands were created. When most teams have finished their task some of the discoveries made are shared with all participants in a short plenary discussion. After this the enabler introduces the next task.

The stories we told one another we knew by heart. We have heard and told them so often that they have gradually imprinted themselves on our memories. Or it may be that this or that story is such a good one, that it tells about such striking characters and such astonishing turns of events, or that it contains such a memorable message that it sticks in our mind. Sometimes even a less impressive story gets fixed in our memories simply because it has been told so well.

We will now learn to tell one another a biblical story. It reports about events happening in the city of Thessalonica, the present Saloniki, northern Greece, when the apostle Paul first went there to preach the gospel. It is told in Acts 17:1-10a and we must first memorize it.

> Paul and Silas traveled on through Amphipolis and Apollonia and came to Thessalonica, where there was a synagogue. According to his usual habit Paul went to the synagogue. There during three Sabbaths he held discussions with the people, quoting and explaining the scriptures and proving from them that the Messiah had to suffer and rise from death. "This Jesus whom I announce to you," Paul said, "is the Messiah." Some of them were convinced and joined Paul and Silas; so did many of the leading women and a large group of Greeks who worshipped God.
>
> But the Jews were jealous and gathered some of the worthless loafers from the streets and formed a mob. They set the whole city in an uproar and attacked the home of a man called Jason, in an attempt to find Paul and Silas and bring them out to the people. But when they did not find them, they dragged Jason and some other believers before the city authorities and shouted: "These men have caused trouble everywhere! Now they have come to our city, and Jason has kept them in his house. They are all breaking the laws of the Emperor, saying that there is another king, whose name is Jesus." With these words they threw the crowd and the city authorities into an uproar. The authorities made Jason and the others pay the required amount of money to be released, and then let them go. As soon as night came, the believers sent Paul and Silas to Berea.

Task 2: Again form teams of two partners each and proceed in the following way:

(a) Read the story aloud to one another (4 minutes).

(b) Decide together how the story can be subdivided in three to five different episodes and give each of these episodes a short subtitle, using key terms which occur in the text of that particular episode (5 minutes).

(c) Memorize the sequence of subtitles and then read the story once again to one another, but add now from memory the subtitle before each episode (6 minutes).

(d) Tell one another the story without subtitles, first with one partner as narrator, speaking from memory, while the other checks the accuracy on the basis of the text; then reverse the roles (10 minutes).

> It is important during this task that partners do not speak about the story, but strictly concentrate on memorizing and telling it as it is written. One way to make certain that this rule is observed is to impose a strict time schedule for memorizing and telling. The enabler should encourage timid team members to recite with a loud and animated voice, regardless of what the other teams are doing beside them.
>
> The story can be subdivided into the following four episodes, though this is by no means the only subdivision possible: "Paul proves from the scriptures that Jesus is Messiah" (vv. 1-3); "Convinced converts and the reaction

of the jealous Jews" (vv. 4-5); "Accusation: trouble-makers who say that there is another king" (vv. 6-8); "Jason pays, while Paul and Silas escape" (vv. 9-10a).

Not only *what* we say communicates something, but also *how* we say it — our emotions and intonations, the speed and pauses, and the gestures we use. We will practise this with the two short passages that appear in direct speech from the story (v. 3b, vv. 6b-7).

Task 3: Try out in your teams various ways of reciting the words of Paul and of the jealous Jews in Thessalonica:

(a) Remember an occasion on which you have tried to convince an audience about the truth of something which was absolutely essential to you. Then say with the same feelings, intonation, and gestures Paul's statement in v. 3b: "This Jesus whom I announce to you is the Messiah."

(b) Remember a time when you have felt jealous because somebody took over the floor from you. With what tone and gestures did you speak — or would you have liked to speak — about this incident? Then say the words in vv. 6b-7 with the same deep feeling of irritation, jealousy, and accusation.

(c) Having practised the right way of speaking these two high points of the narrative, tell one another the story again. This time don't worry about remembering all the details and the exact wording (which is anyway only the wording of one among several good translations of the original Greek). Concentrate your whole attention on telling the story with the appropriate emotions and intonations, speed and pauses, gestures and facial expressions.

> At the end of this third task the enabler may call on two or three participants to tell (not to read) the story to the whole group.

If a story has been imprinted in our memories, it becomes part of our own life story. It begins to function as a small or large sector in the frame of reference in which we see and by which we measure everything that happens in our own lives. In Bible study we attempt to see our life's story in the light of the biblical story and vice-versa. In this way the two types of stories can illumine one another, and the biblical story gets a chance to have an impact on our lives.

Task 4: Examine during a moment of silent the following two questions:

(a) Did memorizing and telling the story recorded in Acts 17:1-10a evoke in your memory events in your life? If so, does the biblical story throw any new light on what you experienced personally or does your own experience help you to understand the biblical story?

(b) What does the incident in Thessalonica teach us about the political dimension of the Christian proclamation? Examine this in the light of your own involvement in public life as a Christian.

> If this study is essentially planned as an exercise in story-telling, Task 4 can be given as "homework." However, question 4b may make a continua-

tion of the study not only desirable, but imperative. The historical background of the story must then be examined and the text analyzed more carefully in order to discuss the delicate question of the relationship between preaching and politics. If such a continuation of the study is foreseen, Task 4b should be omitted. It will be replaced by Task 5 later in the study.

The context of the story

In Paul's time, Thessalonica was the capital of Macedonia. Located like an amphitheatre on rising terraces around a bay with an excellent harbour, the city was also the central point of the via Egnatia, the main road connecting Greece with Byzantium and Asia Minor, the first main thoroughfare built in the Roman empire outside Italy. Thus Thessalonica not only had great political and strategic importance, but also became an outstanding commercial centre, attracting many foreigners, including a large colony of Jews.

The settlement had been founded in the fourth century B.C. and in the year 42 B.C. it became a free city within the Roman empire, with its own city-authorities (Acts 17:6 and 8 correctly designate the members of this non-Roman town council as *politarchai.*) As a provincial capital Thessalonica was also the seat of a Roman proconsul, who represented the Roman senate and the emperor. At the time of this incident Claudius, who reigned from A.D. 41-54, was emperor of Rome. No doubt the proconsul watched with a careful eye all that happened in this key city, which had after all been the centre of the Macedonian revolt against the heavy yoke of Roman rule in 149 B.C. Thessalonica's record in the annals of Roman administration was not clean.

Paul came to Thessalonica in the year 50 during his second missionary journey. Shortly before that, an edict had been issued by Claudius, which the Roman historian Suetonius reports as follows: "Since the Jews constantly made disturbances at the instigation of Chrestos, he expelled them from Rome" (cf. Acts 18:2). It is quite possible that Chrestos refers to Christ, and that the disturbances in Rome were caused by Jewish-Christian controversies about the Messiahship of Jesus. The edict expelling the Jews from Rome is not typical of Claudius, who on the whole had no anti-Jewish policy.

Paul's arrival in Thessalonica also coincided with a meeting of the Roman senate in the same year, reported by the Roman historian Tacitus in his *Annals*. On that occasion not only was Claudius' successor, the ill-famed Nero, designated emperor, but it was also decided to grant Claudius after his death a fastidious state-burial. Like the great Augustus he was then to receive the *apotheosis*, deification. Some centuries earlier, when Alexander the Great came from Macedonia to Egypt and the East, he had been acclaimed as a son of the gods. Under his successors, the deification of rulers became a feature of the Hellenistic world. In the Eastern part of the Roman empire Roman emperors were therefore often worshipped as divine beings even before the official Roman imperial cult was established.

An inscription from about 9 B.C. publishes a letter of the proconsul to the cities in the provinces of Asia concerning the birthday of Caesar Augustus:

> *Whereas* the Providence which orders the whole of human life has shown a special concern and zeal and conferred upon life its most perfect ornament by bestowing Augustus, whom it fitted for his beneficent work among mankind by filling him with virtue, sending him as a Saviour, for us and for those who come after us, one who should cause wars to cease, who should set all things in fair order;
>
> *And whereas* Caesar, when he appeared, made the hopes of those who forecast a better future (look poor compared with the reality), in that he not only surpassed all previous benefactors, but left no chance for future ones to go beyond him, and the glad tidings (Greek *euangelia*) which by his means went forth into the world took its rise in the birthday of God ...
>
> *Resolved*, with Good Fortune and Well-being, by the Greeks of the province of Asia: The first day of the month of all the cities shall be the ninth day before the Kalends of October (23 September) which is the natal day of Augustus ...

Before their arrival in Macedonia, Paul and Silas had had traumatic experiences in Philippi (Acts 16:12-40). The third member of this missionary team, Timothy, was certainly also with them when they arrived in Thessalonica, although Luke saw no need to mention him in between the events reported in Acts 16:1-3 and Acts 17:14-15. The travel on the via Egnatia from Philippi to Amphipolis (some 48 km), from there to Apollonia (some 47 km.) and onwards to Thessalonica (some 57 km.) is mentioned only briefly. The team apparently headed quickly for the capital city of the province (Acts 17:1a) after leaving Philippi.

This hurry may not have been due only to Paul's mission strategy, according to which he started work in important cities rather than small towns and villages. Financial reasons may have been equally pressing. Paul and his collaborators were after all not backed up by a mission board, with a budget assuring regular payment of salaries and travel expenses. In his first letter to the Thessalonians he wrote: "Surely you remember, our brothers, how we worked and toiled! We worked day and night so that we would not be any trouble to you as we preached to you the Good News from God" (1 Thess. 2:9; cf. 2 Thess. 3:7-10). Moreover, we know from Philippians that several times the Christians in that place sent material help to Paul while he laboured in Thessalonica (Phil. 4:14-16). Quite possibly Paul found work as a tentmaker in the house of Jason, just as a year later he exercised that profession in Corinth at the home of Aquila and Priscilla, who had been expelled from Rome by the edict of Claudius (Acts 18:2-3). Thus Paul and his colleagues (perhaps Paul *for* his colleagues; cf. Acts 20:34) filled up the empty mission purse while doing missionary work.

The stay of the team in Thessalonica was certainly longer than "three Sabbaths" (Acts 17:2) suggests, probably several months. From Acts 13 onwards Luke usually reported only the foundation of a new local church and the beginning persecution which drove Paul and his collaborators onwards to the next city. Luke was not interested in the humdrum of earning one's livelihood and the slow building up of confidence necessary for all serious work of mission. He therefore mentioned only the last three Sabbaths, when Paul openly spoke about Jesus as the suffering and risen Messiah, which led to the dramatic events told in the story and the nocturnal escape of the missionary team.

This was not the end of the story. Worried about the situation in Thessalonica, Paul sent Timothy back from Athens to the capital of Macedonia for a pastoral visit (1 Thess. 2:17-3:5). In A.D. 51 Timothy returned to Paul, who had meanwhile proceeded to Corinth, bringing good news about the faith and love of the Christians in Thessalonica (1 Thess. 3:6-10). Yet there was also some bad news: Christians in Macedonia had suffered persecution by their own countrymen — this time not so much the Jewish colony as Macedonians themselves (1 Thess. 2:14; 2 Thess. 1:4). This did not worry the apostle unduly. He had already warned the new converts that Christians would have to suffer affliction, and he was now overjoyed to hear that they stood firm in the test of persecution. What worried him was their exaggerated enthusiasm with regard to the hope of the coming end of history. They were wondering what would happen to Christians who died before Christ returned. They also wanted to know when in fact Christ would return (1 Thess. 4:13-5:11; 2 Thess. 2). There was apparently a danger that such a concentration on the imminent end of history might lead to an immoral life: some considered the present state of affairs, with its rules and morals, as of no account any longer (1 Thess. 4:1-8). This exaggerated hope also led to social disruption: some became idle, ceased to work, and in their enthusiasm disregarded existing social structures (1 Thess. 4:11-12; 2 Thess. 3:6-13).

On the basis of this good and yet somewhat worrying news, in A.D. 51 Paul, Silas, and Timothy wrote from Corinth their first letter to the Thessalonians. This was not only the earliest letter of Paul but in fact the earliest Christian writing about which we know. Perhaps due to further news from Thessalonica the team sent a second letter from Corinth, some time in A.D. 52 or 53.

The making of a story

Having learned to tell the story of the events in Thessalonica and having seen something of the context of the story, we can now turn to the details and the significance of what is reported in Acts 17:1-10a.

According to his custom Paul used the Jewish synagogue as a platform to reach both the Jews and sympathizers and inquirers among the Greeks, the so-called "God-worshippers" (v. 4). He taught by quoting and explaining (in the original Greek: "by entering a dialogue with"), starting his arguments from the Jewish scriptures (v. 3). Some Jews — among them presumably Jason — were persuaded. Yet Paul's biblical teaching and proclamation made a greater impact among the Greeks, whether actually persons of Greek origin or non-Jewish immigrants who spoke Greek. Luke reports about "a large group" of such converts. Most of them were probably slaves, because only they had to do heavy manual work, and as was shown earlier, the question of work was soon to become a problem in that young church. Also "many of the leading women" became converts (v. 4). Several times Luke emphasizes the conversion of women, particularly those coming from prominent families (Luke 8:1-3; 10:38-42; Acts 13:50; 17:12). They were indeed going to play a key role in the life and mission of the early church.

This evoked the jealousy of the Jews (v. 5). The root for the word "jealousy" here is the same as that from which the term "Zealots" comes. During these years the religious-political resistance movement among Palestinian Jews was growing in intensity. The Jewish historian Josephus writes about Cumanus, who was Roman procurator in Palestine from A.D. 48-52, that an infuriated Jewish crowd once threatened him and that he therefore ordered a cruel repression in which thousands were killed. Under his rule many Jews, "emboldened by impunity, had recourse to robbery; and raids and insurrections, fostered by the more reckless, broke out all over the country" (*Jewish War* II, 238). Although we know of the later activity of such Jewish rebels in Egypt (*Jewish War* VII, 408ff), it is unlikely that the jealous Jews in Thessalonica belonged to such a militant group. They were either fanatics of the Pharisaic type, who at that time were trying to win converts (cf. Matt. 23:15), or deeply faithful Jews exasperated by Paul's heretical teaching about the Messiah, or simply members of the synagogue who had hoped to win the support and money of the influential women.

The jealousy led to the agitation, the city-wide uproar, the house-search, the accusation of a scapegoat in place of the mysteriously hidden culprits, the payment of a fine, and the nocturnal escape of the missionary team (vv. 5-10a).

Task 5: Examine what Paul actually taught and proclaimed in the synagogue (vv. 2-3) and what the accusers stated before the city authorities (vv. 6b-7). On the basis of this discuss the political dimension of Christian proclamation.

> This task can best be done in small study groups, leading up to a general discussion. The enabler sums up and complements the discussion in some such way as the following.

Paul did not actually preach a political sermon. Although among Palestinian Jews the title "Messiah/Christ" had a deeply political connotation (cf. above II/7 and II/12), Paul was not using it in this way. He did not speak about the Jewish Messiah in general nor did he call Jesus the "son of David" or "the new David" — which would immediately have had political connotations for the Jews. Nor did he designate Jesus as "the king", which would have had subversive overtones for Greeks and Romans.

What Paul did in the synagogue of Thessalonica was nothing more than Bible study, straightforward biblical teaching. He probably had turned to Old Testament passages such as the psalms of complaint and praise, for instance Psalm 22, which speaks about the righteous one who must suffer but will be vindicated by God. He may also have quoted the passage about the suffering servant in Isaiah 53. On the basis of such clue-texts he argued with the Jews about the divine "must" of suffering in the mission of the Messiah. He then showed them the amazing and at first shocking way in which Jesus of Nazareth was in fact this suffering, crucified and risen Messiah. Arguing from the scriptures about Jesus the Messiah was the typical way of mission among Jews and God-fearing Greeks within and around the synagogues (cf. Acts 2:14ff; 13:17ff). The teaching and proclamation was totally concentrated on Jesus the Christ, probably without any open or concealed political implications.

What the hearers heard, however, was a dangerously subversive proclamation, at least if we take their accusation before the city authorities seriously. Of course, the phrasing of their accusation may only have been a clever move to discredit the missionary team and force the authorities to take action, as the Jewish authorities in Jerusalem did in the case of Jesus before Pilate (John 19:12). Yet whether the accusers actually believed what they said or only pretended to do so, they did in fact state very clearly the political dimension of each true biblical teaching and proclamation. Literally they said: "Those who turn upside down the *oikoumene* (that is, the whole inhabited world), they have now come here. Jason has welcomed them in his house. They all act against the decrees (in Greek: "the dogmas") of Caesar, for they say that there is another king, namely Jesus!"

Paul did not actually say these things. It was the outsiders, not Paul himself, who claimed that the preaching of the gospel upsets the *oikoumene*. His aim was not to mount a political demonstration. At the critical moment he was not even on the scene, but was hiding or being hidden by fellow believers. No one who knows anything about Paul could accuse him of lack of courage or hesitancy to suffer together with Christ, but on this occasion he clearly felt that continuing the proclamation of the gospel had priority. Therefore he and his colleagues escaped at night and let others pay the price.

Like the early Christians as a whole, Paul did not confront Caesar's kingship with that of Christ in a provocative way. Jesus himself had avoided being made a king (John 6:15), and thereby missed a political opportunity, as some might say. Nevertheless, Jesus was later accused before Pilate: "We caught this man misleading our people, telling them not to pay taxes to the Emperor and claiming that he himself is the Messiah, a king" (Luke 23:2). Jesus' messianic kingship was thus felt to be a challenge to earthly rulers. The early Christians apparently tried to avoid this ambiguity. Instead of confessing the crucified and risen Jesus as a king they confessed him as the Messiah and/or the Lord, as Peter did in the final challenge of his Pentecost proclamation (Acts 2:36), and as the very last verse of Acts repeats again (Acts 28:31).

Yet despite this early Christian caution the political dimension of the biblical proclamation remained. When Paul and the early Christians con fessed Jesus as the Lord (*kyros*), they thought in the first place of the messianic king and Old Testament passages like Psalm 110:1. They saw in Jesus the God of the Old Testament at work. Therefore they called Jesus *kyrios*, the title usually given to God in the Greek translation of the Old Testament. Yet this confession, "*Iēsous kyrios*" which at first had no political intention, sooner or later came inescapably in conflict with the predominant political confession, "*kaisar kyrios*," "Caesar is the Lord." An ancient inscription celebrates for instance "Nero, the *kyrios* over the whole world."

In other times and circumstances Christians may be led to spell out the political implications of the Christian proclamation much more forcefully than Paul and the early Christians did. Yet they must make certain that their politics are rooted in the central Christian confession that the crucified and risen Jesus is the Lord. On the other hand, those Christians who want to make a neat separation between the "spiritual" and the "political" realms must learn from the Bible that a truly Christian proclamation always has also a political dimension.

Task 6: Write a short narrative — a "narrative exegesis" like the one presented above in II/13 — on Acts 17:1-10a. Use what you learned about the emotions behind the story when you told it, the background information given about the context of the story, and the insights you gained while examining the text of the story. Imagine for instance that in the winter of A.D. 50-51 the Roman proconsul (call him Fabius) writes a report to the emperor Claudius about some of the main events in Thessalonica during the past year. He still finds it difficult to make sense of what really happened when Jason was almost lynched, because the excited crowds could not find the real culprit.

To learn more about what educated Romans like "Fabius" thought about Christian preachers and their message, read the quotation from Tacitus' *Annals* quoted above in script II/12. Give your story a personal note by assuming that the wife of Fabius (call her Priscilla) was one of those leading women won over by Paul and that one of her slaves belongs to the Christians in Thessalonica. What happens when Fabius questions some of the city authorities, a leader of the synagogue, and Jason about what really took place? Intersperse your narrative with dialogues between Fabius and Priscilla. What did Fabius finally write in his official report? What did he himself actually think about this whole affair? Write this narrative not simply as entertaining fiction, but as a narrative way of communicating biblical faith.

22 THE RADICAL CURE

Galatians 5:16-24

> The appended worksheet on "The Radical Cure" was prepared for a May 1979 staff retreat of the World Council of Churches, during which two Bible studies on texts from Galatians were held. This worksheet served both as a general introduction to Paul's letter and as the background material for the first study, which dealt with Galatians 5:16-24. Groups which have much experience in Bible studies can probably use this worksheet without an enabler; less experienced groups may find the introductory and concluding remarks in the following script helpful.

Paul's angry letter

I would not like to have been Paul's secretary when he dictated his letter to the Galatians. He was angry. We can almost see him pacing up and down the room, gesticulating, sometimes ominously silent, then suddenly bursting out long sentences with a speed that a secretary could not follow.

Already the customary formula at the very beginning of the letter is interrupted by an argument: "Paul an apostle — not from men nor through man, but through Jesus Christ ...!" How could the Christians in Galatia doubt his apostolic authority and listen to the messengers of another gospel? So upset was Paul that — consciously or unconsciously — he omitted the first paragraph found in all his other letters to churches, namely the initial thanksgiving and blessing (compare Gal. 1:6ff with Rom. 1:8ff). Even in his letters to the troublesome and far from "saintly" Christians in Corinth, Paul started with thanksgiving (1 Cor. 1:4ff) and blessings (2 Cor. 1:3ff). But here, after the greeting, the letter begins immediately with Paul's astonishment and his question about what had led the Galatian Christians to become "deserters" of God. What had "bewitched" these "foolish Galatians" (3:1), that they were now about to "fall from grace" (5:4)?

We do not know for certain where to locate these Christians in Galatia. Since 25 B.C., the Roman province of Galatia had comprised not only the region of Galatia in the northern part of Asia Minor, but also Pisidia, Lycaonia, and parts of Phrygia, Isauria, and Pamphylia on the southern coast.

Some scholars assume that the recipients of this letter were the churches in the southern part of this province, which Paul had founded on his first missionary journey and revisited briefly during the second journey (Acts 13:13-14:28; 16:1). In this case the "Galatians" would be converts mainly from the Greeks and Hellenized Jews and Gentiles living in Pisidian Antioch and the cities of Iconium, Lystra, and Derbe in Lycaonia.

Much more probable is the hypothesis that the addressees were converted Celts (Gallians) who had migrated in the fourth and third centuries B.C. and now lived in the region of Galatia in central and northern Asia Minor. In the eyes of the Greeks they were barbarians, all the more so because several times these warriors from Central Europe had made common cause with the Romans against the Hellenistic princes of the coastal cities in Asia Minor. The process of Hellenization was curbed among them not only by Roman influences but also by the persistance of Celtic customs and religions. In Roman Gaul the old Celtic idols continued to be worshipped under another name. This was likely the case also among the Celts in Galatia, who probably mixed their ancient beliefs with Phrygian religions and the Roman emperor cult.

On this second missionary journey Paul fell ill when he passed through "the region of Galatia" (Gal. 4:13f; Acts 16:6). Nevertheless, he preached the gospel; and in this missionary proclamation he had to cross more difficult cultural frontiers than hitherto among Jews, Greeks and other Hellenized Gentiles. There were, however, converts, and a church began to grow which Paul visited again on his third missionary journey, "strengthening all the disciples" (Acts 18:23).

These Christians had received the Spirit, and the apostle reminds them several times of this fact. He even addresses them as "spirituals" (6:1). They were indeed running well, as Paul himself testifies (3:2-5; 5:7). A powerful experience of salvation and liberation was theirs with miracles being performed (3:5). They were a "new creation" (6:15). Yet after the initial period of spiritual enthusiasm, difficulties suddenly arose, leading, in the eyes of Paul, to an extremely dangerous crisis. We are not told how the apostle came to know about these difficulties. After a fruitful ministry in Ephesus he was facing serious trouble in that city (Acts 19:23-41). It was just then, either during his last weeks in Ephesus or already during his travel through Macedonia to Corinth, in the winter of A.D. 55/56, that he wrote his angry letter.

The problem of converted "barbarians"

Many commentators believe that the Galatian crisis originated with false teachers, either from within the community or from the outside, who came and misled the converts. In the growing literature about these false teachers, one scholarly hypothesis contradicts another. In fact, Paul only occasionally swipes at such false teachers but he never names them (1:6ff; 4:17; 5:10, 12; 6:12ff). His argument is with the Galatian Christians themselves, not with these elusive opponents. The aim of his letter was not polemic, but the apostolic-pastoral struggle for helping his beloved converts regain their belief in the crucified Lord and trust the Spirit which they had received. "My little children, with whom I am again in travail until Christ be formed in you!" (4:19).

The crisis of the Galatians can be documented over and over again from mission history in Africa, Asia, and the Pacific. Formerly, life had been strictly regulated by customs and laws, imposed by the closely knit life of the tribal communities and by the forces of nature, the stars, the seasons, and festive days. Then they heard the gospel of Jesus Christ and experienced that tremendous liberation of a life by grace alone, a life guided and growing by the power of the Holy Spirit. But gradually, after Paul had left them, self-seeking human nature began to assert itself. There were "trespasses" against God's will within the Christian community (6:1). Believers became frightened of the great Christian freedom. Were they not losing their salvation by such trespasses?

Paul was not present to answer this question. But probably at that moment teachers from within or from outside the community came with a ready-made answer. Despite all the learned studies of this subject, we will probably never come to know what they taught. But it is clear what the anxious Galatian Christians understood them to say: You are indeed in danger, if you follow "man's gospel" (1:11) — presumably that preached by Paul — whereby Christ is made "an agent of sin" (2:17). You will only be saved if in addition to your belief in the crucified Lord and the guidance of the Spirit you perform some legal prescriptions, especially circumcision (2:3; 5:2ff; 6:12ff) and observe certain days and feasts (4:10). These teachers probably also cast doubts on the authority of Paul. They based their teaching on the Jewish scriptures, showing that only in this way could the Galatians become "sons of Abraham" (3:7; 4:21ff).

In his passionate letter Paul first reestablished his apostolic authority (Gal. 1-2) and made his own confession of faith (2:19-21). Then he refuted these false teachers' interpretation of what it means to be "sons of Abraham" and gave his own Christian-rabbinical interpretation of the Old Testament teaching on this matter (3:6ff; 4:21ff). He showed that seeking salvation by way of the law — whether Jewish law or former Celtic customs — inevitably leads to perdition. However, Christ has become a curse for us, opening the new way of salvation by grace. The curse was thus transformed into blessing (3:10-14), and the history of salvation was thereby led to its decisive turning point (4:4-7).

Probably this was the first time that Paul stated here his famous doctrine of a life not by law but by grace alone, made possible by Christ's death for us. The crisis in Galatia became thus the occasion for the birth of one of the most precious theological reflections, although it is far from certain that the Galatians in fact understood the apostle's deep theology. Perhaps less than one year later Paul developed and clarified his thoughts on this subject when he dictated from Corinth the letter to the Romans.

From this centre of Pauline faith the argument of the letter to the Galatians then turns to the concrete problem of the converted "barbarians." They had a problem with their self-seeking human nature, which Paul designates with the Greek term *sarx*, usually inadequately translated by "flesh." In a nutshell, their question was: "How can we live in the flesh (*sarx*) according to the Spirit (*pneuma*) if we are always tempted to live according to the flesh (*sarx*)?"

The "flesh" and the Spirit

Paul's answer was a radical one. According to him it was impossible to solve the problem with our *sarx* by legal safeguards like circumcision (5:1-12). Freedom in Christ is certainly full of risks; nevertheless, we are called to freedom (5:13-15). No compromise is possible between the *sarx* and its whole series of "works" on the one side and the Spirit with its rich harvest, its "fruit" on the other (5:16-23). How then can we live in the *sarx* — which is the only possible way of living as human beings who are not disincarnate spirits, but children, women, and men of flesh and blood — but do so *according to the Spirit*?

Before we examine Paul's radical answer we should look at how the two key terms in Paul's exhortation are used in the Old and New Testaments: *sarx* and *pneuma*, "flesh" and "Spirit."

In the Old Testament human beings are seen as a psychosomatic unity. There is none of that dualism which sees the human as having a divine soul within a sinful body. We do not *have* a body, but we *are* an animated body (Hebrew *basar*). We do not *have* a soul, but we are an incarnate soul (Hebrew *nephesh*). Body/*basar* thus designates the whole human being, seen from the perspective of its bodily, corporeal existence. Soul/*nephesh* designates this same total human being, but seen from the perspective of its animation, its life. For Hebrew thinking it was therefore inconceivable to speak about an immortal soul which could go on living after the body had decayed. Nor was the body considered as a prison for a supposedly divine soul. Both the animated body and (to say the same thing from another angle) the incorporated soul were seen as part of God's good creation. Yet both have been corrupted by the self-asserting human revolt against God. In this life such self-destructive corruption could be halted only by letting oneself be guided by God's Spirit (Hebrew *ruah*). Hope for a life to come was at first solely based on procreation. Israelites lived on through their children and children's children. That is why one finds an essentially positive attitude towards human sexuality in the Old Testament. Only relatively late did another hope for a life beyond death arise in Hebrew thought: not the immortality of the soul, but the resurrection of the psychosomatic unity of the whole person. Sadducees, who did not accept such new teaching, and Pharisees, who stoutly defended it, were still discussing about this matter of resurrection when Paul was arrested and accused in Jerusalem towards the end of his ministry (cf. Acts 23:6ff).

In the New Testament this Old Testament view of psychosomatic unity in human life persists. The incarnate soul (Greek *psyche*) is not considered to be immortal, and the animated body (Greek *soma* or *sarx*) is not viewed in a pejorative way. In this life we are safeguarded from self-destruction if we let God's Spirit (Greek *pneuma*) guide us. In a few passages Paul speaks also about the human spirit — also using *pneuma* (cf. 1 Cor. 2:11). This human spirit is not divine, but at time has almost the same significance as *psyche* or *sarx* and sometimes designates the human self-consciousness. It functions, so to speak, as the antenna for being sensitive to God's Spirit, who is to guide the whole person. For the life to come the Christians accepted the Pharisaic hope in the resurrection of our whole person. Only gradually did the Hellenistic belief in the immortality of a disincarnate soul creep into Christian spirituality.

The term *sarx*, which means literally "flesh," translates in the first place the Hebrew term *basar*. It designates the creature before God, the corporeal person, often with an emphasis on its fragility. John could thus say that in Jesus the word (*logos*) became *sarx* (John 1:14). Paul quite often used the term *sarx* in this non-pejorative way, for instance in the expression "flesh and blood" (Gal. 1:16), or when he wrote about "the life I now live in the flesh" (2:20).

However, especially in his letters to the Galatians and to the Romans, Paul gave the term *sarx* still another meaning, and in this case a pejorative one. In such passages as Galatians 5:16-24 and Romans 8:5ff, *sarx* is opposed to God's *pneuma*. It then becomes an almost personalized evil power struggling against God's Spirit. This second, pejorative meaning of *sarx* characterizes sinful human nature abandoned to itself and therefore on the road to self-destruction. It does not affect the "body" more than the "soul." Paul states that we can and must "glorify God in our bodies" (1 Cor. 6:20), and conversely he speaks about a "fleshly thinking," a mind set on the things of the *sarx* (Rom. 8:5). Translators have always found it difficult to render this second meaning of *sarx* in modern languages and it is indeed not always possible to use the same word. The Revised Standard Version translates it literally as "flesh," which communicates something inaccurate — or nothing at all — to modern readers. The New English Bible often translates *sarx* in a misleading way as "our lower nature" (as if it were to be distinguished from a supposedly higher nature inborn in men and women). Today's English Version often translates better but too generally with "our human nature." A good translation, sometimes used in the Jerusalem Bible, is "self-indulgence."

While Paul and the New Testament thus reject an anthropological dualism, a splitting of the human nature into a bad body and a good soul, they do speak about a dualism of spiritualities. The source of guidance for our life can either be God's Spirit or our self-indulgent ego, either God's *pneuma* or the *sarx* in its second, pejorative meaning.

Paul was misunderstood very soon within the ancient church. His dualism of spiritualities was interpreted as an anthropological dualism.

Influenced by Hellenistic thought, Christians also began to consider the body as the prison of an immortal soul. This led to a totally unbiblical disdain of the body, of sexuality, and womanhood. Salvation was now sought through the liberation of the supposedly divine soul out of the body, and through its ascent out of this material world through the heavens into reunion with the divine beyond all bodily existence. Two so-called sayings of Jesus, found in the apocryphal Gospel of Thomas (*ca* A.D. 200), show how quickly such totally nonbiblical thinking misled many Christians from the second century onwards, especially Christians who adhered to the widespread religious philosophy and way of salvation commonly known as Gnosticism.

> Jesus said: "Woe to the flesh that depends on the soul; woe to the soul that depends on the flesh" (Saying 112). Simon Peter said to them: "Let Mary leave us, for women are not worthy of Life." Jesus said: "I myself shall lead her in order to make her male, so that she too may become a living spirit resembling you males. For every woman who will make herself male will enter the Kingdom of Heaven" (Saying 114).

Paul's radical answer

Paul's answer to the problem of the Galatians was neither a new form of legalism nor an escape from bodiliness. How to live in the *sarx* (in its first meaning, designating the bodily existence of human beings) without being guided by the *sarx* (in its second pejorative meaning)? Paul categorically responds: "Those who belong to Christ Jesus have killed the *sarx!*"

In order to understand this radical statement we must become sensitive to how Paul uses the Greek verbs. In Greek the *perfect* tense refers to a past event or action but at the same time conveying the continuing effect of this event or action up to the time of speaking. It is therefore as much a present as a past tense. The *aorist* tense (not found in English) refers to a past event or action seen as if telescoped to a point. It thus designates the starting point or the concluding point of the event or it sees the action, which may have lasted for a short or long time, as one single and compressed whole.

Task: Paul wrote to the Galatians: "Those who belong to Christ Jesus have crucified (*estaurōsan*, aorist active) the *sarx* with its passions and desires" (5:24). Examine the meaning of this bold affirmation in the light of the following texts. On the basis of these describe the main characteristics of a Christian spirituality as Paul taught it.

> "Christ redeemed (*exēgorasen*, aorist active) us from the curse of the law, having become a curse for us — for it is written, 'Cursed be every one who hangs on a tree' " (Gal. 3:13).
> "For I through the law died (*apethanon*, aorist active) to the law, that I might live in God. I have been crucified with Christ (*synestaurōmai*, perfect passive); it is no longer I who live, but Christ who lives in me, and the life I now live in the flesh (*en sarki*, here not the pejorative meaning of the term) I live by faith (*en pistei*) in the Son of God, who loved me and gave himself for me" (Gal. 2:19-20).

"Do you not know that all of us who have been baptized (*ebaptisthēmen*, aorist passive) into Christ Jesus were baptized into his death? ... We know that our old self (here not *sarx* but *ho palaios hēmōn anthrōpos* = "our old human being") was crucified with him (*synestaurōthē*, aorist passive) so that the sinful body (not *sarx* but *to sōma tēs hamartias* = "the body of the sin") might be destroyed, and we might no longer be enslaved to sin" (Rom. 6:3, 6).

"Far be it from me to glory except in the cross of our Lord Jesus Christ, by which the world has been crucified (*estaurōtai*, perfect passive) to me, and I to the world" (Gal. 6:14).

"My self-seeking love (*erōs*) has been crucified (*estaurōtai*, perfect passive)" (letter of Ignatius to Romans, 7:2; early second century).

Participants can best do this task first individually. Later they exchange insights with neighbours and then contribute to the general discussion. The following comments might be used by the enabler as a conclusion of the study.

Christian spirituality

Christian spirituality is totally centred on what God did for us in Jesus Christ. He has redeemed us; that is, he has paid the price for our liberation. The many aorist tenses in Paul's teaching and exhortations point back to those completed saving events in the past, which happened for us and in which we were involved. There are also the perfect tenses, usually in the passive voice, which point to the fact that what happened for us and to us in the past remains efficacious until today. According to Paul Christian ethics is not an ethics of the "must," of the works which we have to accomplish in order to become acceptable in God's sight and good in the eyes of our fellow human beings. It rather is an ethics of the "therefore:" because God has accepted us, we can now respond in freedom to his love. The fruit of the Spirit can now grow in our life (notice the opposition of the plural "works of the *sarx*" and the singular "fruit of the Spirit" in Gal. 5:19-22).

This Christian spirituality is intimately linked with what happened at Golgotha. The theology of the cross, which Paul outlined in Galatians 3 immediately led him to an ethics of the cross in chapters 5 and 6. "I have been crucified with Christ" (Gal. 2:20). This happened to us in baptism, where "our old self was crucified with him" (Rom. 6:6). Both the aorist passive and the perfect passive are used to characterize this decisive beginning of our Christian life as a completed event in the past which nevertheless maintains its actuality and efficacity until today. Paul therefore never tired of reminding Christians of the cross of Jesus and of their baptism, in which they became participants in the event of the cross. His ethics was a baptismal ethics, and his answer to the Galatians' problems was to call them back to their initial death and resurrection experience.

In Galatians 5:24, however, Paul did not use the passive voice which usually occurs in the reference to baptism. He stated that those who are in Christ have themselves crucified (aorist active) the *sarx*. They have put their own self-indulgent ego on the cross. They not only went passively through a death and resurrection experience in their baptism, but they actually wanted this to happen and therefore collaborated in their own death and resurrection experience. What Jesus asked of his disciples in his teaching near Caesarea Philippi (Mark 8:34-35), the Galatians had already done. Paul therefore reminded them of their conversion. He did not use that term. Rather he spoke about "those of Christ." In many other passages he specified this expression as meaning those who live in Christ and in whom Christ lives (cf. Gal. 2:20; Rom. 8:1). Christian spirituality is thus for Paul the outflow of this conscious initial search of intimate communion with Christ.

To be "in Christ" and to let "Christ be in us:" such a conscious search for intimate communion with Christ has often been called Paul's mysticism. This expression is accurate as long as one does not define the term "mysticism" generally as an at-one-ness with God in which the human person is, so to speak, dissolved in a divine world. Paul probably knew some such general mystic experiences. Almost certainly writing about himself, he once stated: "I know a man in Christ who fourteen years ago was caught up to the third heaven..." (2 Cor. 12:2ff). Yet it is not such general mystical experiences which are at the heart of Christian spirituality. No immediate, direct "sweet communion" with God, forgetting the hard realities of this world! The union is mediated and leads to struggles. Paul's mysticism remains strictly Christ-centred. Only through Christ — and, Paul insisted, only through the *crucified* Christ, by suffering together with him — can we have union with God. The immediate consequence of such a mediated union with God in Christ is the struggle of faith. Paul's mysticism leads to a militant ethics, yet this ethics does not degenerate into self-righteous activism. It remains rooted in Christ and is nothing but the outflow of the spirituality we have described, the harvest of the Spirit.

23 LITURGY AND LIFE

Ephesians 2:1-10

The following script and worksheet "Liturgy and Life" (Eph. 2:1-10) are the material of the first of a series of four Bible studies on Ephesians. The other three studies dealt with "One Lord, one faith, one baptism" (Eph. 4:1-6), "Different gifts, one ministry" (Eph. 4:7-12a) and "The purpose of it all" (Eph. 4:12a-16). The introductions and conclusions for these four studies are recorded on a 90-minute cassette, *A Plea for Unity*, released in 1980 by the World Council of Churches, along with a booklet giving information about Ephesians, suggestions for further reading, and instructions for Bible study enablers. The package also includes worksheets for the four studies.

Except for the added subtitles and some biblical references, the following text has been left exactly as it was spoken and recorded on the cassette. It is not a cassette for passive listening. On the contrary, it requires considerable study and reflection on the part of individuals or groups who use it. The worksheet "Liturgy and life" must be used alongside this script.

The concluding song on the baptismal hymn of Ephesians 5:14 was composed on the spot by Mrs Nicola Sutherland, during a study on the letter to the Ephesians at a training seminar in Auckland, New Zealand, in 1979.

[Flute]

Invitation to a journey

I would like you to make with me a journey in time and space. We are going to visit a small group of Christians in the first century after Christ. The place is somewhere in the Roman province of Asia, which formed part of the present Asia Minor. The provincial capital was the then flourishing Ephesus, on the coast, but there were also cities in the interior such as Colossae and Laodicea. This was a melting pot of the most varied people, cults, and cultures: Greeks especially in the coastal cities, Phrygians and other people from the East everywhere, with many Jews among them.

The Jews had actually won many adherents, especially as they propagated a Jewish faith which was open to Greek philosophy and Eastern mysteries. They competed with old Persian cults which attracted the masses because of their ecstatic processions and dances. The Greeks also had brought their gods and blended their worship with the fertility cults of Asia Minor. Remember the famous Artemis of Ephesus. Her temple was reputed to be the most marvelous of all the seven wonders of the ancient world. Ephesian silversmiths made big money by producing and selling miniature temples of Artemis. The book of Acts reports how they banded together, raised a mob, and almost lynched the apostle Paul, who had dared to say "that gods made with hands are not gods" (Acts 19:26). For two hours the mob cried with one voice: "Great is Artemis of the Ephesians!" (Acts 19:34).

Since this dramatic incident years had passed. From Ephesus the Christian church had spread into the interior of the province of Asia. Here and there, in cities first but gradually also in villages, believers gathered for worship, teaching, and mutual exhortation. From the end of the first century onwards these Christians would have to face persecutions. Many would have to make the difficult choice between apostasy and martyrdom. However, at the time when we are visiting them the persecution had not yet started. True, the Jewish Christians were being excluded from the synagogues. They therefore suffered a double discrimination: as Jews they were hated by Greeks and other nations and as Jewish Christians they now also lost the support of the intimate Jewish community. They should of course have found a new community within the Christian church, yet Jewish and Gentile Christians did not always see eye to eye with one another. Moreover, the new converts from among the Greeks and other nations were not yet firmly rooted in the tradition of the Christian faith. They therefore became an easy prey to all the popular philosophies and messages of salvation which were propagated by itinerant philosophers, by Jewish missionaries, and adherents of Eastern mystery religions.

No, it was not easy to be Christ's church in that melting pot of people, cults, and cultures. The Christians were confused and deeply divided.

God's family

It is such a group of confused and divided Christians that we are visiting. They gather in a home during the passion week. Once again they listen to that dramatic story of the last days in the life of our Lord: how Jesus entered the city of Jerusalem as the king of peace; how the crowd welcomed him and cried "Hosanna!" which means: "Give salvation! Give freedom!"; and how only a few days later presumably the same crowd cried "Crucify him!" Together they meditate on the meaning of Christ's death upon the cross. Then a Jewish Christian teacher stands up, takes a scroll from the holy scriptures of the Jews, that with the sayings of the prophet Isaiah. He reads a word which the biblical God addressed to his stubborn people: "I have seen his ways, but I will heal him.... Peace, peace, to the far and to the near, says the Lord" (Isa. 57:18f).

The teacher puts the scroll aside, repeats the text once again in order to imprint this promise on the memory of the assembled Christians. Then he applies the word from the Hebrew scriptures to both the cross of Jesus and to the situation of the divided congregation. Let us listen to what he says "It is Christ who brings us peace by making Jews and Gentiles one people. With his own body, broken at the cross, he has broken down the wall that had separated us and had made us enemies. You Gentiles by birth, you were far away from Christ. As foreigners you had no part in God's cove nant with his people. But now you have been brought near by the death of Christ. And you Jews by birth, you were near to him, but you became pris oners of your laws. Now, by his death, Christ has abolished your wrong use of the law, in order to create one new people out of the two races. By the cross he has united us into one body. That is the good news of peace for all of us — for you the Gentiles, who were far away from God, and for you the Jews, who were near to him! None is a stranger any longer. All are now fellow citizens with God's people and members of God's family" (free paraphrase of Eph. 2:11-19).

A baptismal service

A few days later we are again with these Christians in the Roman pro vince of Asia. They, of course, did not yet know the church year as we cele brate it now with the sequence of Easter, Ascension, and Pentecost. The whole period of fifty days after the resurrection was for them one great Pentecost, where the risen and exalted Christ and the gift of his Spirit stood in the centre of worship. Not just the day of Easter, but each Sunday was for them a feast of resurrection. It is on such an early Sunday morning in the period of Pentecost that we meet the Christians of Asia Minor again.

This time they do not gather in a private house. Outside the city they stand on the border of the river. The Jewish-Christian teacher has just reminded the assembled Christians that among Jews the Pentecost is the feast on which they remember how at Mount Sinai God gave them the law. "God took the people of Israel as his bride," continues the teacher. "At this time of Pentecost the covenant was established and at this time the cove nant vows must be renewed. It is important that we remember this today for through baptism these converts here are now incorporated into the covenant of God's love. But before we baptize them let me tell you a great mystery: God's plan is much more astounding than any of us can as yet grasp. He wants nothing less than 'to bring all creation together, everything in heaven and on earth, with Christ as head' (Eph. 1:10). And though we are here only a handful of Christians, we are called to be the body of Christ, of that Christ who is the supreme Lord over all things" (paraphrase of Eph. 1:22f).

After these words the new converts are baptized in the river, and as they join the community of the believers the whole assembly bursts out in shouts of joy and singing. There are psalms sung, with body movements and the clapping of hands. A jubilant mood takes hold of the assembled Christians and it is impossible to understand all their spiritual songs and prayers on a purely rational level. Yet out of this chaos of fervent voices suddenly arises a beautiful hymn, a baptismal hymn:

> Awake, O sleeper,
> arise from the dead
> and Christ shall give you light" (Eph. 5:14).

Baptismal exhortations

Let me make here a parenthesis. This hymn and the words with which we heard the Jewish-Christian teacher address the congregation are quoted from that deep meditation which in our Bibles is called Paul's letter to the Ephesians. Both the indication concerning the addressees and the identity of the author of this document are still debated in the scholarly world. Probably Ephesians was something like an encyclical, a circular letter addressed to Christian congregations in the Roman province of Asia. Was it the apostle Paul, who, during his last imprisonment at the end of his life wrote it? Or was it one of his disciples who wrote it, after Paul's death, in the name of the apostle?

The question about the author and the original addressees will probably never be fully solved. There is a much more important matter, however, on which scholars have reached a wide agreement and which is crucial for the right understanding of Ephesians.

This brings us back to the Christians in Asia Minor and their baptismal feast. The author obviously used much traditional material, formulas of early Christian worship. Moreover, many scholars have pointed to the fact that baptism is mentioned and several times alluded to in Ephesians. There are also more references to the action of the Holy Spirit than in most other letters of the New Testament. A good case can therefore be made for the assumption that much in Ephesians arises out of an early Christian baptismal service during the period of Pentecost.

If we want to understand the message of the encyclical we must learn to pray and sing it. Moreover, we must learn to live according to its spirituality. Liturgy and life are here intimately related. It would be wrong, however, to despise study and knowledge. To know God's plan of salvation is much emphasized in Ephesians. As an introduction to your participation in that particular liturgy and life I am therefore inviting you now to make a comparative study.

Task: If you look at the worksheet entitled "Liturgy and Life" you will find side by side two biblical texts. One is Paul's famous exhortation to the Christians in Rome where he reminds them of their baptism (Rom. 6:3-11). The other is an exhortation from Ephesians (Eph. 2:1-10). These are not easy texts. In the footnotes on the worksheet I have explained some of the difficult words and pointed to some nuances of the original Greek texts. The passage from Ephesians could very well have been part of what the Jewish-Christian teacher said to the converts who had just been baptized on that early Sunday morning in Asia Minor. Read this passage from Ephesians and examine it with the help of the explanatory notes. Then compare it with the passage from Romans. There are of course similarities between the two texts. Yet in order to grasp the special mood and message of Ephesians you should concentrate on the striking particularities of Ephesians if compared with Romans. After you have completed this comparative study you may want to listen to my short conclusions. For the moment stop the cassette-recorder. Shut me up and make your own exploration.

[Musical signal]

Liturgical anticipation

I would very much have liked to be with you and learn from you. You will certainly have noticed most of the particularities which I am now going to mention. If you discovered other things, please do not discard them right away simply because they will not appear in my summary. You may have seen the importance of details which I did not notice! Here then is my list of particularities.

Both passages refer to definite past events which led to a change of life. You probably noticed the frequent use of that particular tense of verbs in the Greek language which is called the "aorist" and which is explained on the worksheet. A decisive turning-point is being recalled. Believers have begun to live a new life. Yet this turning-point is differently accentuated. In Romans the main emphasis lays on the fact that believers have been baptized into the death of Christ, that they were crucified and buried with Christ so that they might begin to lead a new life. In Ephesians, however, not the death with Christ is emphasized. In their conduct before conversion and baptism the believers were already dead. It is just as the father said about his rebellious and repentant youngster in one of Jesus' parables: "This my son was dead, and is alive again" (Luke 15:24, 32). Similarly the author of Ephesians contrasts the death of the former life with the real life together with the risen Christ. The accent lies totally on God's life-giving, resurrecting activity. Remember the baptismal hymn which we heard: "Awake, O sleeper, arise from the dead, and Christ shall give you light."

Intimately connected with this first major difference is a second one, which appears clearly in the different use of the tenses of Greeks verbs. In his exhortation to the Romans Paul looks back to what happened in the past: Christ has died and in their baptism the Roman Christians died with him. Another past event is the resurrection of Christ. The believers' resurrection, however, remains a future event: "We *shall* certainly be united with him in a resurrection like his" (Rom. 6:5). A strong tension between the "not yet" and the "already" remains. Contrary to this the author of Ephesians made the following bold statement: God has "made us alive together with Christ ... and raised us up with him, and made us sit with him in the heavenly places" (Eph. 2:5-6). The future tense has disappeared and all verbs are in the past or present tense. The "not yet" is being swallowed up in the "already."

This second observation immediately leads to the third one. If one exaggerates a little, one might say that in Romans a horizontal time-perspective predominates while in Ephesians it is a vertical space-perspective. The believers do not look forward eagerly and hopefully to the times to come — as in Romans — but the future is anticipated and believers confidently know that, through God's grace, they now already participate in Christ's resurrection and ascension. The heavens are open to them. Though still attacked by the evil powers, they sit with Christ above the powers. Consequently the verb "to save" is twice set in the perfect tense: "We have been and we are now saved." Nowhere else in the New Testament does this verb appear in the perfect. It is mainly used in the present or future tense: "We are in the process of being saved" and "we will be saved." The hymns which the author of Ephesians quoted in his exhortation affirm much more: re-created in Christ we are nothing less than God's work of art! These are dangerous affirmations. Such exultant language of prayer could easily lead to arrogant triumphalism. Such a "liturgical eschatology" — that is an anticipation of the things to come in the experience of worship — could lead to an otherworldly and escapist spirituality.

Yet here it is important to make a fourth observation. Have you noticed how those exultant hymns in the Ephesian passage are twice interrupted by the sentences: "By grace you have been saved!" It is almost as if during the baptismal service which I described earlier the Jewish-Christian teacher interjected these reminders while the congregation was singing: "It is not *your* work and certainly not any righteous works which count. Therefore do not boast. All this is God's gift. He has set you on the way to a liturgy and life, for singing praises and participating in *his* good works."

From liturgy to life

We must take this exhortation seriously and act on it. I therefore end this study by suggesting two *tasks*:

First, memorize the early Christian baptismal hymn (Eph. 5:14). Make a melody for it. Sing it (preferably accompanied by interpretative gestures) and repeat it until it becomes a theme-song of your life.

Secondly, examine your daily life and try to detect what are your self-glorifying works which must be abandoned if you want to live your baptism. Examine also how in your daily life you can better participate in God's good works with a view to his purpose for the universe.

[Flute]

Awake O Sleeper

(c) Cantor   (A) = all in the congregation

24 THE HOPE IN US

1 Peter 3:15

> A few days after the end of the South African Congress on Evangelism in 1973 (cf. introduction to II/19) I visited a schoolteachers' course in Edendale, South Africa. Suddenly the director of this course turned to me, saying: "I heard that you often lead Bible studies in which everybody can participate in exploring the biblical text and reflect about it. Alas, in about five minutes we must conclude this course, but why don't you quickly lead us in such a Bible study?" Only a few had Bibles at hand, and the first of the five minutes had already begun. I am afraid we overspent the time allotted and the study lasted almost ten minutes. For better or for worse, this is roughly the way in which that "mini Bible study" was conducted.

You probably all know that during the last two weeks the large interracial South African Congress on Evangelism took place. Some of you may actually have attended that enormous rally in the stadium in Durban, where Billy Graham proclaimed the good news about Jesus Christ.

That is one good way of evangelism, and its results can be quite remarkable. There is another way of evangelism, however, which looks much less spectacular but whose results usually last longer. Let us discover it together.

Listen to the following passage in the first letter to Peter. Peter addressed it to ordinary men and women, many of them illiterate slaves, some people who had probably just been baptized: "Make Christ your Lord. Be ready at all times to answer anyone who asks you to explain the hope you have in you" (1 Pet. 3:15).

This verse is like a little window, through which we can see how early Christian evangelism took place. Peter warns the Christians that they must be ready for a conversation with their non-Christian neighbours and fellow workers. It is interesting to notice *who* begins to speak in this anticipated conversation. Listen once again to the passage and then answer the question: "Who begins to speak?"

> The text of 1 Pet. 3:15 is read again. Then the participants are asked to share in half a minute with the neighbours sitting beside them their answers

to the question. Almost invariably some will answer: "The Christians!";
others: "The non-Christians!"

"The Christians?" That is indeed what we expect. Usually we think of
evangelism in this way: Christians — especially those gifted for preaching
— go out and tell the non-Christians about the good news. The apostle
Paul certainly did exactly this, and since him there have been many great
missionaries and evangelists. In this passage, however, it is the non-Christians who begin the conversation. Peter warns the ordinary Christians that
they will be questioned and challenged by their non-Christian neighbours
and that they have to give an answer.

Do you remember what these non-Christian neighbours ask for information about? It is about the hope which Christians have. And Peter writes
that all these ordinary members of the church, even those who have just
been baptized, must always be ready to explain the hope they have in them.

Now turn to the person sitting next to you. Describe together, in your
own words, the other type of evangelism we discover in this passage. What
is the hope of the early Christians, and how is this hope related to the
telling of the good news?

> Participants talk with one another, trying to formulate what they have discovered about early Christian evangelism from 1 Pet. 3:15. If time allows, this
> will of course lead to a general discussion and a more thorough examination
> of the historical and literary context of the exhortation in verse 15.
>
> This exhortation forms part of a circular letter to the Christians dispersed
> in the five Roman provinces of Asia Minor, which was probably written by
> the apostle Peter shortly before his death. It is generally assumed that Peter
> died in the persecution of the Christians in Rome under the emperor Nero in
> A.D. 64. At that time there was as yet no general persecution of Christians in
> Asia Minor, although the believers had to suffer from occasional local disturbances and petty discrimination.
>
> For the literary context of the exhortation one must notice that the whole
> passage of 1 Pet. 3:13-17 exhorts believers to be confident in the face of
> persecutions, and that this is based on an Old Testament passage (Isa.
> 8:11-15), quoted in verse 14b. If time allows it is interesting to go back to that
> prophecy of Isaiah and then examine Peter's exhortation in the light of it.
>
> In a "mini Bible study", however, this further examination cannot be
> made. After 1-2 minutes of exchange with neighbours, the enabler must stop
> short the beginning exploration with some concluding remarks such as:

The hope of the early Christians was that Christ is Lord and that his
cause would win. This hope became visible in their daily life. Their priorities obviously differed from those of the people surrounding them. They
were even ready to suffer and die for that hope. Such a visible hope astonished or irritated their neighbours and colleagues. So questions arose, not
only friendly questions, but also accusations. Christians were summoned
before the judge. In a literal sense they had to make a defense of their hope.

In the early church evangelism was thus not only an organized activity
by especially gifted persons. It was much more the spontaneous and non-aggressive "gossiping of the gospel" by ordinary Christians in the course of

their daily life. And the secret of it all was the hope which had become visible in the life of the Christians.

This is therefore the key question for evangelism, as we go back into our daily neighbourhoods and jobs: "How today can our Christian hope become visible in our lives?"

If more time is available for this study, this last question should be first discussed in groups and then in the plenary. It can lead to a general examination of Christian hope. In a time like ours, when so much of industry, public life, and even church activity is being planned according to the forecasted future, Christians must dare to live under Christ's lordship and to act now already in the light of the coming kingdom, building signs of its coming. To plan according to the forecasted future ultimately means to remain a prisoner of past and present developments which are projected into the future. To live under Christ's lordship and to act according to the hope for the coming kingdom, however, leads to a totally different style of life, in which new acts and attitudes are possible, though in the eyes of the world these will often be seen as foolish behaviour. Such visible hope will astonish and irritate our neighbours and colleagues and give rise to questions. Then Christians — all of them, not only the theologians and commissioned evangelists — must be ready to bear witness to the hope by which they live.

25 SALVATION TO GOD

Revelation 7:9-12

This script is the last part of the second biblical presentation at the World Mission Conference in Bangkok, December 1972-January 1973 (see the introduction to study II/2). Under the title "The cost of salvation", the session started with a dramatic presentation of how church executives under the pressure of work often become insensitive to the crisis of their suffering fellow human beings — in this case to the moving complaint of an African in a society of institutionalized racism. This led to a study of the struggle of prayer which one finds in the complaints and praise of Psalm 22, and from there to an art meditation showing the victory of Christ's cross. At that point the introduction to the second main text of this presentation followed, the vision and hymns of Revelation 7:9-12. The script for this last part of the presentation is here printed in an expanded version to make it a study on its own.

Visual theology

In silence show a few slides of artistic interpretations of Jesus' crucifixion — for example, a Romanesque crucifixus, a Russian crucifixion icon, and an Ethiopian illumination showing Christ as the lamb above the cross.

The sculptors and painters whose passion art we have just seen help us think in images. This is a good introduction for understanding something of the visions and liturgies of the last book of the Bible, John's Revelation. For many of us twentieth-century Christians this Apocalypse is still a dark and closed book, though the very name given to this type of literature means the "lifting of the curtain," the "revelation" (*apokalypsis*).

The language and the strange and quickly changing imagery of visual theology are alien to people trained in descriptive technical language and abstract western thought patterns. Yet great photographers and cinematographers in our generation have helped some people grow new "antennae" for understanding apocalyptic imagery better. And the increasingly popular literature of "science fiction" often uses apocalyptic language and could well be called secular apocalypse.

However, the biggest difficulty we have in understanding John's Revelation does not arise from its form and its peculiar way of communication, but from the great difference between our life situation and that of its first readers. We sit in reasonably comfortable chairs. It is unlikely that many of us this week will become martyrs for Christ's sake — martyrs in the strong sense of this word, where blood flows.

Encouragement for martyrs

The Christians in Asia Minor, for whom this book was written around A.D. 95, lived in quite another situation. They had heard of cruel persecutions suffered by the Christians in Rome under the evil emperor Nero (54-68). Decades earlier their fellow Christians in Asia Minor had had to face harassment and occasional persecutions. Then a relatively quiet time for Christians had come under emperor Vespasian (69-79) and his son Titus (79-81).

Now the younger brother of Titus had ascended the throne, the emperor Domitian (81-96). Roman historians describe him as a cruel despot who, in the name of his procurators, issued circular letters with the announcement: "Our Master and our God bids that this be done." He was in fact an able, though severe administrator, and his biographers paint a darker picture of him than he deserves. But it is true that he made the life of Jewish subjects, and especially converts to Judaism, much more difficult than his predecessor had. Since Jews and Christians were still seen together in the eyes of many Roman administrators, the life of Christians too was precarious under the rule of Domitian. Contrary to what is often assumed, there were as yet no generalized persecutions of Christians in Asia Minor at that time. Nevertheless, believers already had to be prepared to pay the cost of discipleship by being exiled — like John on the island of Patmos — or even by martyrdom.

We get a glimpse of the situation as it developed from a letter written by Pliny the Younger, governor of Bithynia and Pontus, two provinces in northern Asia Minor. This letter was written in 112 to the emperor Trajan, but it refers back to events up to twenty-five years earlier:

> It is a rule, Sir, which I inviolably observe, to refer myself to you in all my doubts; for who is more capable of guiding my uncertainty or informing my ignorance? Having never been present at any trials of the Christians, I am unacquainted with the method and limits to be observed either in examining or punishing them. Whether any difference is to be made on account of age, or no distinction allowed between the youngest and the adult; whether repentance admits to a pardon, or if a man has been once a Christian it avails him nothing to recant; whether the mere profession of Christianity, albeit without crimes, or only the crimes associated therewith are punishable — in all these points I am greatly doubtful.
>
> In the meanwhile, the method I have observed towards those who have been denounced to me as Christians is this: I interrogated them whether they were Christians; if they confessed it I repeated the question twice again,

adding the threat of capital punishment; if they still persevered, I ordered them to be executed. For whatever the nature of their creed might be, I could at least feel no doubt that contumacy and inflexible obstinacy deserved chastisement. There were others also possessed with the same infatuation, but being citizens of Rome, I directed them to be carried thither.

These accusations spread (as is usually the case) from the mere fact of the matter being investigated and several forms of the mischief came to light. A placard was put up, without any signature, accusing a large number of persons by name. Those who denied they were, or had ever been, Christians, who repeated after me an invocation to the gods, and offered adoration with wine and frankincense to your image, which I had ordered to be brought for that purpose, together with those of the gods, and who finally cursed Christ — none of which acts, it is said, those who are really Christians can be forced into performing — these I thought it proper to discharge. Others who were named by that informer at first confessed themselves Christians, and then denied it; true, they had been of that persuasion but they had quit it, some three years, others many years, and a few as much as twenty-five years ago. They all worshipped your statue and the images of the gods and cursed Christ.

Pliny's letter goes on describing what the governor found out concerning the Christians, especially their cultic assemblies. As "political associations" were forbidden by imperial decree, he writes:

I judged it so much the more necessary to extract the real truth, with the assistance of torture, from two female slaves, who were styled "deaconesses": but I could discover nothing more than depraved and excessive superstition.

That is why Pliny asked the advice of Trajan: on the one hand he could not find much wrong with these Christians; on the other hand, their movement was growing in a disturbing way.

This contagious superstition is not confined to the cities only, but has spread through the villages and rural districts; it seems possible, however, to check and cure it (*Letters* II, 96).

In such a situation Christians in Asia Minor began to wonder whether Christ's cross had indeed been that victory which they confessed it to be in their creeds and eucharistic worship. Was it worthwhile to suffer and become a martyr for Christ?

This question they addressed to the venerable John, himself a victim of the beginning persecutions. He was exiled on the island of Patmos (Rev. 1:9). Whether this was the apostle John the son of Zebedee, or John the theologian, or an otherwise unknown prophet John, or John the elder (about whom the ancient Christian author Papias writes), we do not know. But we have the artfully constructed book of his messages and visions. After some hesitations the ancient church decided to include it in the canon of the New Testament. John wrote his message to be read aloud (Rev. 1:3), and he sent it to the churches of Asia Minor (Rev. 1:10) so that they might take courage as they faced martyrdom. Here is the main structure of what he wrote:

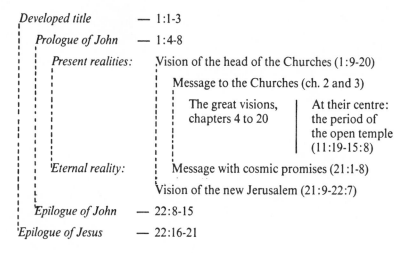

Developed title — 1:1-3

Prologue of John — 1:4-8

Present realities: Vision of the head of the Churches (1:9-20)

Message to the Churches (ch. 2 and 3)

The great visions, chapters 4 to 20 | At their centre: the period of the open temple (11:19-15:8)

Eternal reality: Message with cosmic promises (21:1-8)

Vision of the new Jerusalem (21:9-22:7)

Epilogue of John — 22:8-15

Epilogue of Jesus — 22:16-21

We will attempt to see only the beginning of John's great visions, listen to how he told it, and hear what he heard.

The door open to heaven

> After this I looked, and lo, in heaven an open door! And the first voice, which I had heard speaking to me like a trumpet, said: "Come up hither, and I will show you what must take place after this!" (4:1).

"Heaven" for John is not a space so far above the earth or a time so far beyond ours that it would be totally unrelated to what happens in human history. On the contrary, heaven is intimately related to our time and space, because it is that transcendent reality which embraces the whole human reality, which breaks open the closed earthly space and time and gives it meaning. What is about to happen on earth can be seen in heaven.

The first thing seen by John, as he is lifted up into heaven, is a throne, not a throne of Caesar in Rome, but that of the dazzling presence of God (4:3). Later he hears that "the Lion of the tribe of Judah, the Root of David" is also present and that this Lion has conquered. But when his vision becomes clearer, he sees the Lion appearing strangely in the form of "a Lamb, as though it had been slain" (5:5f).

John himself says that he received these visions "in the Spirit on the Lord's day" (1:10). It may well be that during a eucharistic service he suddenly saw what he was going to write down, for his visions are strongly marked by the words and hymns of the eucharistic liturgy.

In a moment we will listen to John's account of what he saw and heard. We will see the four living creatures which according to Ezekiel 1:4ff represent the forces of the whole universe (only later did they become the symbols of the four evangelists). We will hear the universe thus symbolized singing the *Sanctus* before God:

> Holy, holy, holy, is the Lord God Almighty,
> who was and is and is to come! (4:8).

Then, when Christ appears as the slaughtered Lamb and as the victorious victim, the *Benedictus* is prayed by the twenty-four elders, who probably symbolize the triumphant church in heaven, represented perhaps by the twelve prophets and the twelve apostles:

> Worthy art thou to take the scroll
> and to open its seals,
> for thou wast slain and by thy blood
> didst ransom men for God
> from every tribe and tongue and
> people and nation ... (5:9).

This vision of a heavenly Easter liturgy continues with the opening of the book with seven seals (6:1-8:1) and the hearing of the sound of seven trumpets blown by angels (8:2-11:18). This leads to the vision of the opening of God's heavenly Temple (11:19-15:8), from which come judgment (16:1-18:24) and praise (19:1-10). Then the heavens are fully opened bringing destruction to the evil world (19:11- 20:14) and finally the outlook on the new heaven and the new earth (21:1-22:7).

As the Lamb opens the seals, we will see the four riders on white, red, black, and grey horses going out into the whole world. This part of the vision is strongly influenced by the visions of Zechariah 1:8ff; 6:1-8. They symbolize the signs of the end of times (cf. Matt. 24:3ff). We will hear the martyrs cry: "How long before thou wilt judge and avenge our blood?" (Rev. 6:10), and we will see the kings and mighty of this earth hiding in caves from the coming judgment (6:15ff).

Then, between the opening of the sixth and the seventh seal, the vision will show us the church of the martyrs, worshipping "in white robes, with palm branches in their hands" before the throne in heaven (7:9). This is probably an allusion to the Feast of Tabernacles, when the Israelites entered the temple courts in procession, waving palm branches, and shouting: "Hosanna!", "Save us!" (cf. Ps. 118:25). Together with these worshippers from the Old and the New Testaments we will say the great blessing:

> Amen! Blessing and glory and wisdom and thanksgiving and honour and power and might be to our God for ever and ever! Amen! (7:12).

> At this moment a previously recorded dramatic reading of Revelation 4:1-7:12, with appropriate musical interludes, is played. At the end all participants join in the prayer of the great benediction (7:12).
> If no such recording has been made beforehand, and if the group is not too large, the participants can be asked to prepare such a reading and to listen to it. There will have to be the voice of John who reads all which is not in direct speech, the voices of the four living creatures (4:8b; 5:9f; 6:1, 3, 5, 7; 7:10, 12) and of the twenty-four elders (4:11; 5:9f; 7:10, 12), a single voice for one elder (5:5), the fifth angel (7:3), and finally the voices of the martyrs (6:10), the kings and mighty (6:16f), and the great multitude (7:10, 12).

In making such a dramatic reading it will be important not to spend all the time guessing what this or that strange image or saying may mean. If asked, the enabler can simply say: "I do not know." He or she will be in good company, for the best biblical scholars do not know either! In hearing a symphony of Beethoven one does not ask with each musical note what it means. Nor does one analyze each gesture or photographic detail of a film of Ingmar Bergman. What is important is the total impact of what is heard and seen.

Salvation ascribed to God

What we have heard and seen in this begining of John's vision is like a growing echo, like a rising wave caused by what happened on a Friday noon outside the walls of Jerusalem. The apocalypse indeed shows us the cosmic repercussions of the crucifixion of Jesus.

Salvation was wrought by the slaughtered lamb. Yet just before the great benediction there is an astonishing liturgical affirmation by the multitude from every nation, all tribes, people, and tongues: "Salvation belongs to our God who sits upon the throne, and to the Lamb!" (7:10). This is the translation of the Revised Standard Version. The original Greek text is shorter and has no verb, but simply states: "The salvation (to) our God ..." (a dative case without preposition).

Task: What is strange in this acclamation? What would we expect the universal church to confess?

> After a short moment of individual reflection participants exchange with people sitting next to them thoughts about the above questions. The enabler then solicits contributions for a plenary discussion. Participants may have discovered other versions of this liturgical acclamation in other modern translations, and the enabler should ask further questions to help the group reflect about the meaning of these various translations The study can be concluded with such remarks as the following.

There are different translations for the acclamation of the universal church. Today's English Version translates: "Our salvation comes from God ..." Similarly, the New American Bible renders the acclamation: "Salvation is from our God ..." This makes sense and certainly is true. But is it what John actually wrote? It is possible that the dative has a causative meaning ("Salvation by our God"). Yet in the immediately following benediction the same Greek construction appears with nouns ("Blessings and glory and wisdom," etc.) related to a dative case without a verb or preposition. All translations, also the two quoted above, render this in some such way as: "Blessing and glory ... be to our God."

The Jerusalem Bible and the New English Bible translate: "Victory *to* our God ..." This comes close to the original Greek, though something of the sting of this acclamation is lost by translating the Greek word otherwise rendered "salvation" as "victory."

Whether it fits our thinking or not, the correct translation almost certainly reads: "Salvation to our God and to the Lamb!" But what does this imply? Must God and Christ be saved? Must we and can we ascribe salvation to God and Christ?

The precarious situation of those for whom John wrote sheds light on these questions. These Christians had made God's cause their own. And now this very fact led them into suffering. All the world around them proclaimed that the Roman emperor was the Saviour, and Christians were asked to do the same. By any human standard it was Caesar, not their God, who wrought the victory. What Pliny later wrote to Trajan seemed to be correct: it would be possible "to check and cure this contagious superstition" of Christian faith, if not by persuasion then by persecution.

Anxious thoughts and doubts thus arose in the hearts of Christian believers in Asia Minor, doubts which have assailed Christians throughout the centuries whenever God's cause was contested and ridiculed. Is the God of Abraham and of Jesus not an illusion? There are so many gods! Is the hope for the coming kingdom not simply another wishful dream? There are so many dreams! Is the ultimate victory really God's?

For Christians faced with martyrdom, belief in God is neither a matter of course nor a matter of little importance. It is the most decisive matter. What is at stake for them is no longer their own predicament, the outcome of this or that human struggle or their own salvation. Like big gamblers they either quit the game or put all their stakes on one cause, namely the belief that the biblical God truly exists, that heaven (in the sense that was earlier described) indeed embraces our whole time and space, that Christ's sacrifice on the cross does indeed have cosmic repercussions, and that the salvation is God's.

John affirms this cause of God, not by proving God's existence with arguments, but by drawing the anxious churches in Asia Minor into the ongoing worship of the church of all ages, in heaven and on earth. This remains the great challenge of his Revelation: to join in a song of God's victory in the midst of doubts and apparently losing battles of faith:

> The strife is o'er, the battle done;
> Now is the Victor's triumph won;
> O let the song of praise be sung;
> Alleluia!

> Death's mightiest powers have done their worst,
> And Jesus hath his foes dispersed;
> Let shouts of praise and joy outburst;
> Alleluia!

> He broke the age-bound chains of hell;
> The bars from heaven's high portals fell;
> Let hymns of praise his triumph tell;
> Alleluia!

APPENDICES

Appendix A
METHODS AND TOOLS

Strictly speaking only two things are necessary for doing Bible study: a biblical story or text and a person — or preferably a group of persons — ready to be challenged, converted, comforted, and guided by what God communicates through the Bible. Additional aids may in fact become a hindrance, standing in between the Bible and the hearers/readers of today. Yet rightly used some methods and tools can help the process of study.

1. METHODS

The word method (from the Greek *methodos* or *methodeia*) could point to something pedagogically very significant, for the literal meaning of the Greek word is "going a way together with somebody." However, the only two occurrences of this term in the New Testament have a pejorative meaning: "clever devices," "craftiness" which leads to error, "wiles" of the devil (Eph. 4:14; 6:11).

This is a healthy warning for those who are fascinated by methods. It is the Holy Spirit, not the mastery of methods, which establishes communication. Methods can become channels or obstacles for the Holy Spirit. It is thus important to reflect about them and learn to use them.

Which method?

There is no one ideal method. Which one is best in a particular circumstance will differ according to the biblical story, theme, or text studied, the composition and the needs of the study group, the place of meeting, the time available, and the gifts of the enabler.

The scripts in Part Two followed a great variety of methods. But even this variety by no means exhausts all possibilities. Those trained in the structural analysis of stories and customs are presently applying this approach to Bible study. People trained in psychology use methods of psychological analysis for understanding biblical events and persons. Groups involved in revolutionary struggles and trained in the Marxist analysis of society are now applying the insights and methods gained there to the examination of the scriptures. Many more uses of drama, meditation, and body movement than those suggested in the preceding scripts have been explored. All such methods must be tested for whether or not they really serve the process and aim of Bible study as described in the preface of this book.

Some basic advice

"When you come together, each one has a hymn, a lesson, a revelation, a tongue, or an interpretation. Let all things be done for edification" (1 Cor. 14:26). This glimpse of the Christian community in Corinth and Paul's advice remain valid also for the experiment of Bible study.

Each person has something to contribute. Therefore Bible study is participatory and can best be done in groups. In large classes or assemblies, it is good to divide from time to time into smaller subgroups of 7-12 participants sitting in a circle. Such small group work takes much time. It requires a sufficient number of meeting places and people skilled in enabling others to do Bible study. Moreover, even in small groups the imposing and talkative members tend to stifle the contributions of the timid ones. The preceding scripts therefore often suggest that the enabler proceed in the following way, both in small groups and in large assemblies:

(a) Having introduced the study with the necessary information about the biblical passage and its context, put *a question or task* to the group. The question or task must be clearly stated and should not simply lead to a "yes" or "no" answer, but to exploring the biblical passage and/or its implications for today. If such a question or task is posed early in the study, it will break the monologue and set the pattern of participatory Bible study early. In the course of the study it is also good to take up a question raised by a participant and to submit it to the whole group in the same way as the questions/tasks posed by the enabler.

(b) Allow a short silence period (2-5 minutes, depending on the question or task) for *individual reflection.* This will restrain those who want to talk immediately. Not all people think with the same speed. Quick thinkers and reactors are often superficial, slow thinkers and reactors sometimes very deep. Give the latter ones a chance to think through the question or task and the former ones time for second thoughts.

(c) Follow up the period of individual reflection with about 5 minutes of *exchange*, during which those sitting next to one another share their thoughts and discoveries about the question or task. In almost any seating arrangement it is possible for two or three persons to talk together without having to shift chairs or go through the time-consuming exercise of dividing up into different groups. Since this procedure allows the timid and less eloquent participants to begin to formulate their discoveries, it prepares and encourages them to participate in the subsequent discussion. It also gives a chance to compulsive talkers to "let off steam" and may thus make them more ready to listen. It gives all participants the opportunity to communicate their discoveries to at least one other participant. If the listener reacts with enthusiasm, the statement made will almost certainly be brought into the general discussion; if the discovery is important but not yet clearly stated, the listener may help the explorer to state his or her discovery more succinctly; if the statement meets with blank incomprehension, the "discovery" may not have been a helpful one after all and it will probably not be brought in and burden the subsequent discussion.

(d) Have a period of *general discussion* in which as many participants as possible are encouraged to speak. For the moment allow divergent opinions to stand without comment. If the group is too large, the general discussion can be replaced by a carefully chosen panel of 3-4 members sitting with the enabler on the platform. If these panel members represent various "constituencies" in the assembly, the participants will soon identify with "their" speaker and thus indirectly participate in the panel discussion. The panel members must not be briefed beforehand about the questions/tasks posed, so that the panel discussion remains totally spontaneous (for examples of this procedure see the studies II/17 and II/18).

(e) After the general discussion the enabler sums up, possibly adding his or her own opinion (not as though it were the final truth, but only as a personal and, one hopes, well-informed conviction). Then the enabler continues the study by *leading up to a next question or task.*

This repeated sequence of input-lecture, question/task, silent individual reflection, exchange with neighbours, and general discussion usually allows for a high degree of participation, and the study can go on well over one hour without overtiring the participants. It is beneficial to alternate the more intellectual and analytical questions and tasks (those for the left hemisphere of the brain) with questions or tasks which mobilize the emotion and imagination (the right hemisphere of the brain), and with tasks which involve movement of the whole body.

"*Each one has a hymn, a teaching, a revelation, a tongue, or an interpretation.*" This enumeration of contributions may sound strange to modern readers, but it shows that the church in Corinth was not simply a discussion club. Nor should a Bible study group be.

(a) There is a place for a *hymn (psalmos)*. Most appropriate is the ancient *Veni Creator Spiritus* — "O Come Creator Spirit". This hymn and prayer should become the underlying melody and petition of all Bible studies. It is good to choose in addition a hymn — old or new — which relates particularly to the biblical passages to be studied. Even better is to compose and sing a really new song to the Lord. Indeed, there is no better way to fix for remembrance and rumination the insight gained in a Bible study than by making a new song. Hidden poets can be discovered in almost every group, able to put into evocative and rhythmic language the insights gained. Musicians are plenty, certainly those who can play an already existing popular melody, sometimes also those who can compose a new hymn or at least a sung response to spoken verses. And all over the world people like to sing, joining in the psalm singing, chanting, and shouting with joy of the church of all ages and continents. Moreover, where there is music there can also be movement, be it simple gestures, a procession, or a dance.

(b) There must be a *teaching* (*didache*) — and therefore also a willingness and curiosity to learn. The teaching must come in the first place not from teachers and other specialists, but from the biblical text or story. Therefore the reading and hearing of the text and story must never be omitted in Bible study. Part of receiving the teaching is actually learning how to read and listen to the passage under discussion. Those knowledgeable in ancient history or the biblical languages, those who have traveled in the lands of the Bible, or those who have done some preparatory reading for the study should be especially called upon. Yet everyone can contribute to this teaching, if only by asking a "stupid question" — which so often proves to be a very basic one.

(c) A *revelation* (*apokalypsis*) may happen — not always, but here and there it will appear. In the context of Paul's letter to the Corinthians this means a sudden prophetic insight, as for instance how in the cross and resurrection of Christ, the end, purpose, and goal of history have broken into our present history. Through such a revelation the closed and self-sufficient world of our lives and societies is opened to transcendence. Jesus would have said that it is through such a revelation that God's kingdom comes close by. Such insights which suddenly dawn on us during a Bible study are both fearful and joyful and they leave their deep mark on us.

(d) No wonder that revelations go together with *tongues* (*glossa*), that is speaking a language not addressed to human beings, but to God. It is like music without words, unintelligible to the human mind, yet somehow understood by the human heart. How could one speak otherwise where God's kingdom is at hand? Christians in Corinth limited this way of speaking to the phenomenon of glossalalia ("tongues-speaking"), as do some members of the charismatic movement today. But "tongues" can have wider significance, including such liturgical shouts as "kyrie eleison!", "maranatha!", "Abba! Father!", "hallelujah!", and all deep speaking from the heart, "the sights too deep for words" (Rom. 8:26), "the groaning of the whole creation," joined in by the church (Rom. 8:22f). Not all Bible studies lead to such a speaking to God, and when it happens it often does not become public but remains in the heart. This is good, and in accordance with Paul's own advice (cf. the whole of 1 Cor. 14).

(e) Wherever there is speaking in tongues in public, there must be *interpretation* (*hermeneia*), a translation of the words spoken to God into words spoken to human beings. In Bible study interpretation receives a still deeper significance. It means that the message of the biblical passage has to be translated for the here and now and applied to our own life situation. Unfortunately, most contemporary literature on "hermeneutics" is a philosophical-theological in-group discussion, difficult to translate for those who are not part of the discussion. But the *practice* of hermeneutics must in the first place be accomplished by Christian lay persons in the midst of their struggles of faith. It is a biographical and political enterprise rather than a literary and philosophical one. No experiment of Bible study is complete without challenging each participant to enter into this practice of existential interpretation.

"Let all things be done for edification." This is a good test for methods of Bible study. It is not the most exciting, nor the most modern — nor, of course, the dullest — method which is the best one, but those which best edify the church. Edification in the Bible does not refer to spiritual individualism, in which we edify ourselves with pious thoughts and words. An analysis of how the terms "edify" and "edification" are used in the New Testament yields rich insights for Bible study enablers:

(a) It is in the first place God or Christ who edifies, sometimes represented by his apostles or other ministers, and occasionally by the members of Christ's body who edify each other. In the process of Bible study the primary author of edification, Christ, must therefore stand in the centre, not the theological and didactic specialist nor the group and group dynamics.

(b) What is edified is the community of the church, its faith, hope, worship, witness, and service. Even when we study the Bible alone it must be done with a view to this community. We must be ready to let ourselves be built into that sometimes awkward fellowship of Christians.

(c) "Edification" is often used in contrast to "destruction." Faith and hope must be built up and not be destroyed. Yet in order to build on the right foundation, buildings on shaky or unsound foundations must be pulled down. In Bible study this pulling down and building up does happen. Thus the use of historical-literary analysis of a biblical text can be threatening to many (e.g. the work with the synopsis, as in script II/9, or the analysis of sources for the redaction of a gospel, as in script II/18). However, if such tools of critical scholarship are used in a pastoral way, they will help to find the right foundation. To participate in a biblical confrontation play (cf. II/16) or a meditation through fantasy journey (cf. II/10) can become an upsetting experience and should therefore only be done in a mutually supportive group.

(d) Edification is not an end in itself. It has to be done with a view to the proclamation of the gospel, and with a view to becoming instrumental for God's presence in the world. Therefore it is good to read the Bible together with the daily newspaper. Our eyes of faith are opened, so that we see not only the surface but also the signs of judgment and the kingdom in present-day events. It is also much healthier periodically to do Bible study in Christian service-teams or action-groups than to have continuous Bible study groups which do nothing else together. Nor should we forget that edification means to add new stones to the building, new members for Christ's body. As a young student I once asked the well-known Ceylonese evangelist D.T. Niles how I could keep my Christian faith alive. His answer was: "Be always in contact with at least one first generation Christian." This is also good advice for keeping alive a Bible study group. Try to include at least one member who is a seeker or one who has just become a Christian. Such a person will help you and the group to listen to the biblical message with new ears and to read the texts with new eyes. His or her questions will safeguard the group from settling down in complacent faith and in words without prayer and action.

2. LEADING QUESTIONS AND TASK ASSIGNMENTS

Questions and task assignments must be found which will help the group explore the meaning of a biblical passage and discover its message for today. (In the following I use the term "passage" to include a short text, a story, a whole book, or a theme occurring in a series of biblical texts.) For writing Bible study outlines and for preparing sermons and biblical talks, the following framework of questions and tasks might be useful. Many of these will not be appropriate for the particular group or occasion for which the preparation is done. Some of the questions and tasks presuppose so much biblical, historical, and theological knowledge that they are not applicable for many groups. Nevertheless, in most cases many will remain which are applicable. The art of Bible study enabling then consists in selecting the two or three questions and tasks which are the most helpful. Often it is advisable to divide the group and to assign a different question or task to each participant or subgroup, so that the participants can teach each other afterwards.

Three different types of exploration are being suggested: (a) The biblical passage must be given a chance to address us as it actually stands, whether we like it or not, whether it confirms or questions our faith, whether it seems relevant to our situation or not. (b) The study happens within the fellowship of the church of all ages and continents whose faith and conduct have also been guided by this scriptural passage; we should therefore explore what light is shed by the faith and life of the church on this passage and *vice versa.* (c) We have reason to study the passage with the expectancy that through it God may speak to us in our particular situation here and now; we therefore make this exploration as an experiment for discovering whether and how God puts his claim on us by this passage.

These three approaches are complementary and cannot be neatly separated, but it is advisable to keep all three in mind for each study. The exploration can start with any one of the three approaches. In several of the methods used in the scripts of Part Two, two or three are used simultaneously. Often the passage suddenly comes alive for us and our situation today while we are examining how it spoke to the first hearers in their time and context. Or we discover what we are asked to do here and now while we are rewriting the passage as a prayer. Or our eyes are opened for details in the passage only when we reread it with a view to finding out what it has to say for our relationship with our neighbours and colleagues.

What is in fact said, shown and written in the passage?

First contact with the passage: If the passage is very well known reconstruct it first from memory and then check the actual wording. If it is a short text copy it word by word. If it is a dramatic story, record it on a cassette. Read it and listen to it. Write down your spontaneous reactions to it: What pleases you? What shocks you? What do you not understand?

Analysis of details: Which words and expressions occur several times, correspond to one another, or oppose one another? What are the indications of time (tenses of the verbs, etc.) found in the passage? What indications does it give about the place of action and change of place during the action? Who are the actors (they can be persons, ideas, or things)? How do they become operative? What happens to them? Is it possible to subdivide the passage into several episodes? If so, give subtitles to each episode. If it is a gospel text, look for parallels in the other gospels. If there are parallels, use a synopsis for comparing them.

Seeing the whole: Try to see what actually happens in the passage, either visualizing it in your mind or making a diagram or simple line drawings. Does the end differ from the beginning? If so, when, where, how, and by which actor did the transformation come about?

Evocations: Are there words, images, and gestures in the passage which strongly evoke other passages in the Bible? What is their meaning? To which genre of oral tradition or literature does the passage belong (narrative, proverbial, catechetical, liturgical, etc.)? What implications does this have for understanding the passage? If it is an Old Testament passage, what New Testament passages are evoked — or *vice versa*?

Literary context: Examine what precedes and follows the passage in the Bible. What can you learn from this immediate context? Where is the passage placed in the biblical book from which it is taken? How does it confirm, complement, or correct what you know about the main emphasis and message of this book and its author? Do any extra-biblical literary documents of the ancient world come to your mind as you read the passage? Is there a connection between the two? If yes, do they have a common source? Has one influenced the other in form and/or content?

Historical context: Does the passage reveal anything about the social, economic, political, and religious background of the author and the first hearers or readers? The passage was produced by a community of believers or by an individual author for a community of believers: Who speaks to whom? What questions are raised and answered? Locate the probable place of the author(s) and addressees on the map of the Near East and examine when the passage was written. Then find out as much as you can about the general human situation in that place and time. Are there indications in the passage that an older oral tradition or written document has been reworked and reinterpreted for a new situation and time?

Feedback: Having done some of these explorations check whether your initial spontaneous reaction to the passage has changed. Have questions of understanding been clarified? Have new questions arisen? Is it still the same part of affirmation of the passage which pleases you or irritates you?

What is to be heard, seen and meditated by the church?
The passage and the church: To what aspects of the church's worship, community life, service, and witness is this passage most related? Give examples of how and where the passage is in fact quoted or misquoted. Make suggestions about when and where the passages should be especially kept in mind for guiding the life of the church.

Liturgical life: If the passage is a prayer, examine what kind of prayer it is and rewrite it in modern language. If it is not a prayer, try nevertheless to pray it. If the passage is a hymn, try to find a melody for it and sing it; if it is not a hymn, try to transform it into one. Examine what direct or indirect relationships exist between the passage and the sacraments: what light does it throw on the church's understanding and practice of baptism and the Lord's Supper and *vice versa*? Can the passage be expressed through a symbol or a significant gesture which could be used in worship? Try to transform the passage into a worship service. What structure and sequence of worship elements does it suggest? What kind of prayers, hymns, and liturgical gestures does it ask for? Divide tasks, prepare for it, and then celebrate the worship.

Teaching and confession of faith: What does the passage reveal about the biblical God? How and through whom does he act in creation and history? What does the passage have to say about the human predicament and the human vocation? Does the passage reaffirm, complement, or correct the traditional confessions of faith, e.g. the Apostle's Creed? Which of the major Christian confessions (Orthodox, Roman Catholic, various Protestant traditions) and which teacher (church father, Reformer, present-day theologian) most strongly emphasize what stands in the passage? In which continent and in which social, economic, political and religious situation does the passage speak most clearly and urgently? If the passage contains an insight of faith not found in your church's teaching and confessions, rewrite it in the form of a catechetical question and answer or a confession of faith, and seek an image (artwork, photograph, etc.) which communicates that particular new insight of faith.

Fellowship and mission: What does the passage teach about the life and mission of the church? What aspects of Christian community life are highlighted? How does your own local church compare with them? Write a paragraph for a Christian discipline which would help you and your church more fully to become that type of community. Which aspects of the Christian message are highlighted? Are they an integral part of your church's witness? Prepare a short message (in the form of a proverb, a parable, a dialogue or a three-minute radio talk) by which the particular message of the passage is communicated.

Rumination and meditation: If the passage is short, learn it by heart. If it is long, select a few central sentences and learn them by heart. Over a period of several days recall this memorized passage and discover how it sounds and what it says in different moments of your daily activities. Try to participate in the passage by means of a fantasy journey. Try to translate the passage into body movement (mime). Try to condense the passage into a one-sentence prayer and live with this prayer for several days.

How is God's claim put on us here and now?

Participation: Try to identify with one actor in the passage (for instance by taking part in a dramatic reading, through a role play, through a confrontation play, through full dramatic transposition of the passage for today's world, through a fantasy journey, or simply by retelling the passage from that actor's point of view). Then examine how you acted in this role and what it teaches you.

Confrontations: With the passage in mind read the daily newspaper and look through a popular illustrated magazine. How does the passage confirm, correct, or challenge the daily news? What images in the magazine make visible or hide what is communicated in the passage? What popular proverbs, slogans, songs, radio and TV programmes confirm or contradict the passage? If there is confirmation, discuss how the message could be stated more explicitly. If there is contradiction, draft in telegram style a protest on the basis of the passage. Try to figure out how the message of the passage could be communicated in a public place to passers-by through a prophetic act.

Self-examination: Examine your own initial reactions to the passage and those of your group. Why did the passage please you, irritate you, or leave you cold? To what fears and hopes of you or your group or social class does the passage speak? What call to conversion, judgment, promise, and encouragement are to be found in it for you and your group? With whom should you speak about how the passage relates to your life? Read and discuss the passage with a special person or group of people in mind, friends or enemies, people you like or people who irritate you. What does the passage have to say for your relationship with this person or group of people?

At the end of this framework of questions and tasks it is salutary to repeat that no methods can either create the motivation to do serious Bible study nor guarantee that the passage studied will come alive for the here and now. The biblical God is not at our disposal. He sometimes chooses to remain silent for long periods and to be a God from afar.

3. SOME TOOLS

No expensive laboratories are needed for experiments with Bible study. For most a good study edition of the Bible and a good measure of curiosity, endurance, and courage is enough.

Translations and study Bibles

Some of the old translations — for instance the King James Version — are excellent. However, since they were made not only has the English language changed substantially but also important old Hebrew and Greek manuscripts of the Bible have been found. The reconstructed original text from which modern translations are made therefore comes nearer to the original manuscripts of the Old and New Testament scriptures, none of which has been preserved. Moreover, during this century the theory and practice of translation have been reviewed and perfected.

It is therefore indispensable to work with a good modern translation. But which one? Personally — but this is a matter of taste — I usually turn to the *Good News Bible* (Today's English Version, published by the American Bible Society and Collins/Fontana, 1976) in order to read for myself whole books in the Bible or in order to read aloud to people who have little or no knowledge of the Bible and whose mother tongue is not English. I like the *New English Bible* (Oxford U.P., study edition, 1976) for reading in a worship setting. For actual Bible study, however, either the *Jerusalem Bible* (Darton, Longman and Todd, study edition, 1967) or the *Revised Standard Version* (study edition in "The Oxford Annotated Bible", Oxford U.P., 1962) are most appropriate.

Although special study editions of these modern translations are more expensive, the purchase of such an enlarged edition is highly recommended. They should include the Apocryphal/Deuteronomical books, maps of the biblical lands, a detailed chronological table showing how the biblical events and writings relate to the general history of the ancient Near East, short introductions to the different parts of the Bible and to each biblical book, cross references in the text and a certain amount of annotation. Any of the above-mentioned English study editions will do.

Sometimes it is good to use different translations in a Bible study group. However, one must then be careful that the discussion does not centre exclusively on the divergencies of translation. If there is little time available, it is better to provide participants with a *worksheet* with just one good version of the text, typed in a way which helps the process of study (e.g. with synopsis, with complementing texts from other parts of the Bible, extra-biblical texts, etc.).

A word of caution must be added with regard to Bible paraphrases such as that of *The Living Bible* (Tyndale House Publishers, Wheaton, 1971). These are *not* translations and should therefore not be used as a basis for Bible study. They can be helpful for current reading, however, or for discovering the topical meaning of a passage for today (cf. for instance the excellent New Testament paraphrases by J.B. Phillips).

For those who want to dig deeper and those who prepare study outlines or act as Bible study enablers some additional tools are helpful. A full discussion of this matter is found in F.W. Danker, *Multipurpose Tools for Bible Study* (Concordia Publishing House, St. Louis, 1960). The following list mentions only the most essential tools. The purchase of even these is rather expensive. Each local church or at least each church region should therefore gradually build up a small biblical reference library for its members.

Tools for examining the text

A *concordance* is a volume which lists all the words in the Bible (except the most frequent conjunctions and prepositions like "and," "of," etc.) and indicates all the passages where each occurs. Used critically this tool is not only helpful for finding quickly where a certain key-term is prominent, but it shows also how the same term is used with varying frequency and often astonishingly distinct meanings in different books of the Bible. Cf. for example, Nelson's *Complete Concordance of the Revised Standard Version* (New York, 1957).

Much of what can be found out by a critical and imaginative use of the concordance is summarized in *biblical wordbooks*. They contain short articles on the major biblical terms, indicating what connotations they have in the original language and what meanings they receive in different parts of the Bible. One must be careful not to apply all the meanings to the particular occurrence of the term in a given passage. Cf. for example, A. Richardson's *A Theological Wordbook of the Bible* (New York, 1950).

For the study of the gospels it is indispensable to have access to a *synopsis*, in which the corresponding passages of the first three or preferably all four gospels can be seen together on one page. The best available is that by K. Aland, *Synopsis of the Four Gospels*: Greek-English edition with text of Revised Standard Version (United Bible Societies, 1972).

There is a host of good *Bible commentaries* aimed at very different readerships. They are handy for quick reading about how one scholar understands a biblical book or one of its passages. For the same reason commentaries can be dangerous, because too often they become a substitute for one's own exploration of a passage. It is good to have for instance the thick one-volume *Peake's Commentary on the Bible* edited by M. Black and H.H. Rowley (London, 1962). There or in similar comprehensive exegetical works one finds enough references to commentaries on the different books of the Bible.

Tools for understanding the context

Much geographical, historical, economic, political and religious background information can be found in one of the many good biblical *encyclopedias* and *dictionaries*. Cf. for instance the illustrated *New Westminster Dictionary of the Bible*, edited by H.S. Gehman (Westminster Press, Philadelphia, 1970).

Some of the commentary series have also good *introductory volumes*. Cf. the paperback volumes of the Cambridge Bible Commentary: O.J. Lace (ed), *Understanding the New Testament* (Cambridge U.P., 1965); C.M. Jones, *Old Testament Illustrations* (Cambridge, 1971); E.B. Mellor, *The Making of the Old Testament* (Cambridge, 1972); O.J. Lace, *Understanding the Old Testament* (Cambridge, 1972).

Those looking for *primary sources* about the biblical context will find many of them in the paperback volumes of J.B. Pritchard (ed.), *The Ancient Near East*, Vol. I: An Anthology of Texts and Pictures (Princeton U.P.,

1973) and Vol. II: A New Anthology of Texts and Pictures (Princeton, 1975); H.C. Kee, *The Origins of Christianity: Sources and Documents* (Prentice Hall, 1973), or the good collection by C.K. Barrett, *The New Testament Background: Selected Documents* (London, 1961). An excellent introduction to first-century Palestine is also Josephus, *The Jewish War* (Penguin Books, 1972).

Appendix B
ACKNOWLEDGMENTS

The late Suzanne de Dietrich was the pioneer of the ecumenical redis- covery of the Bible. Her book *Le dessein de Dieu* (Neuchâtel, 1943) has been reprinted many times. Translated into a score of languages, it was one of the first "Protestant" books to be used extensively in Orthodox and Roman Catholic seminaries and other training institutions. An English edi- tion was published under the title *God's Unfolding Purpose* (Westminster Press, Philadelphia, 1960). Her other classic, *Le renouveau biblique*, in which she summed up the insights gained about the Bible and the ways of doing Bible study, was one of the first books ever published by the World Council of Churches, then still in the process of formation (in the series "Ecclesia Militans," Geneva, 1945; a totally rewritten and updated version appeared as *Le renouveau biblique, hier et aujourd'hui*, two volumes, Neu- châtel, 1969). To Suzanne de Dietrich, who opened the eyes of so many around the world to the Scriptures, the first acknowledgment is due.

My other great teacher in "biblical realism" was Hendrik Kraemer. He challenged me to reflect about questions of communication in a biblical, historical, and transcultural perspective, both in personal conversations and through his lectures on *The Communication of Christian Faith* (Phila- delphia, 1956). He also encouraged me to write the IMC research pamphlet on *The Communication of the Gospel to Illiterates*, based on a missionary experience in Indonesia (London, 1957).

Excellent information about the Bible is gathered in the three thick volumes of *The Cambridge History of the Bible*, Vol. 1: From the beginnings to Jerome, ed. by P. R. Ackroyd and C. F. Evans (Cambridge, 1970); Vol. 2: The West from the Fathers to the Reformation, ed. by G. W. H. Lampe (Cambridge, 1969); Vol. 3: The West from the Reformation to the present day, ed. by S. L. Greenslade (Cambridge, 1963). These volumes contain bibliographies for further study. Documents on the ecumenical dis- cussion of biblical authority and interpretation are gathered and intro- duced by E. Flesseman-van Leer (ed.), *The Bible: Its Authority and Interpre- tation in the Ecumenical Movement* (WCC, Geneva, 1980). Cf. also R. C. Rowe, *Bible Study in the World Council of Churches* (WCC, Geneva, 1969).

It would be impossible to enumerate and acknowledge the sources of specific biblical interpretations given in the scripts of Part Two. The main source was of course the biblical text, examined with the tools mentioned in Appendix A. Yet a good deal of reading in specialized exegetical studies went into the preparation of most of the scripts. I owe therefore a deep gratitude to a host of historians and exegetes. Although the presuppositions, methods, and results of much academic biblical scholarship are presently being questioned, I still believe that the study of the original historical milieu of the biblical affirmations as well as form- and redaction-critical studies of these affirmations remain essential if they are rightly to be understood.

I also believe that modern linguistics and a more fully literary analysis of the text as it stands (of which I know much too little) are important. All such studies are of course a typical enterprise of the Western analytical mind. They remain strongly marked by Western literary cultures, and none of them leads to a fully objective hearing, reading, and understanding of the Bible. Nevertheless, they offer a safeguard against arbitrary interpretations of the biblical message. Historical and literary studies of the Bible can no longer be done with an arrogant claim to be objective and universal, but they must not be belittled, for they form an important Western contribution to the ecumenical search for truth. Representing the many from whom I learned in this field of exegesis, I acknowledge here only the teachers and colleagues of the "Institut des sciences bibliques" at the University of Lausanne, in whose explorations I was privileged to participate.

It would be equally impossible to trace back the sources of the various less academic methods suggested in the scripts of Part Two. Some of them were "invented" on the spot, suggested either by the biblical passage under consideration or by a particular situation of the study group (and later I sometimes discovered that learned pedagogical treatises had already been written about such methods!).

First of all I want to pay tribute to the oral communicators in Luwuk-Banggai (Indonesia), who opened my eyes to the fact that the Bible is more than a book. Then there is a growing ecumenical fellowship of biblical communicators and Bible study enablers who learn from one another. Here are, almost at random, some among the many with whom I am on the way: P. Babin in France and H. V. Klem in East Africa, who explore questions similar to those discussed in Part One; Th. E. Boomershine in the USA, who applies the insights gained from studies on oral tradition to biblical memorization and story-telling; J. Bronk and friends in Holland, who introduced me to the possibilities of mime for understanding and communicating the biblical message; J. Esquivel and others in Latin America, who work with basis groups and discover the political implications of Bible study as they struggle for justice in an oppressive society; P. Fueter and his colleagues in the European Bible Societies, who face the challenge of the translation of the Bible beyond the print media; W. Hollenweger from Switzerland, who explores the "bodiliness" of Christian faith and the possibilities of narrative exegesis; C. I. Itty from South India, M. Rogers in Jerusalem, and P. Mases in Sweden, through whom I came to know something of the value of silent retreats and biblical meditation according to Eastern spiritualities; E. A. Nida and J. C. Margot, translation specialists of the United Bible Societies, who have contributed many new insights into biblical communication arising out of the theory and practice of Bible translation; E. Njau in Kenya and M. Takenaka in Japan, who helped me to see the importance of visual arts for biblical meditation; U. Ruegg and his colleagues in the Swiss working group for Christian adult education, from whom I learned the possibilities of the confrontation play; M. Th. Porcile-Santiso from Uruguay, who allowed me to participate in the rediscovery of the Bible among Roman Catholics and who introduced me to the irritating and stimulating studies of M. Jousse on the oral tradition; F. Tagoilelagi from Samoa and others in the Pacific, who in a friendly but persistent way defend the "lecture naïve" of the Bible; W. Wink in the USA, who helps us to look critically at the methods of historical-critical exegesis and to find another "paradigm" for Bible studies.

Origin of quotations

Old and New Testament texts as well as those from the Apocrypha are quoted from the *Revised Standard Version of the Bible*, copyrighted 1946, 1952, (C) 1971, 1973.

In the scripts II/8, 13, 21 and 24 the translation of the *Good News Bible: Today's English Version* (The Bible Societies, Collins/Fontana, London 1976, fourth edition) was used. In some isolated cases a more literal translation or a paraphrase were made from the original.

Permission has been granted to quote from the following sources:

The Loeb Classical Library (Harvard University Press: William Heinemann) Diogenes Laertius, *Socrates* (R. D. Hicks); — Josephus, *Against Apion* (H. St. J. Thackery); *Antiquities* (R. Marcus and A. Wikgren); *Jewish War* (H. St. J. Thackery); — Plato, *Phaedrus* (H. N. Fowler); Pliny, *Letters* (W. M. L. Hutchinson); — Suetonius, *Claudius* (J. C. Rolfe); *Domitian* (J. C. Rolfe); — Tacitus, *Annals* (C. H. Moore and H. Jackson).

Excerpts from "The Instruction of Amen-Em-Opet", transl. by John A. Wilson, and from "The Epic of Gilgamesh", transl. by E. A. Speiser in James B. Pritchard, *The Ancient Near East: An Anthology of Texts and Pictures*, ed. by James B. Pritchard (copyright (C) 1958 by Princeton University Press).

F. C. Grant, *Hellenistic Religions: The Age of Syncretism* (The Liberal Arts Press, Inc., Indianapolis/New York 1953).

Excerpts from *The Dead Sea Scriptures* in English translation, with Introduction and Notes by Theodor H. Gaster. Copyright © 1956, 1964, 1976 by Theodor H. Gaster. Reprinted by permission of Doubleday & Company, Inc.

The Mishnah, translated by Herbert Danby (1933), by permission of Oxford University Press.

New Testament Apocrypha, edited by E. Hennecke (Lutterworth Press, London 1963). *Acts of John* (K. Schäferdiek); — *The Gospel of Peter* (C. Maurer).

The Nag Hammadi Library, edited by J. M. Robinson (E. J. Brill, Leiden 1977).

The Passover Haggadah, edited by N. N. Glatzer (Schocken Books/Ferrar, Strauss and Young, New York 1953).

Howard Clark Kee, *The Origins of Christianity* (Prentice Hall Inc., Englewood Cliffs © 1973), *Orientis Graeci Inscriptiones Selecta* No. 458 (W. Dittenberger).

The Odes and Psalms of Solomon, edited by Rendel Harris and Alphonse Mingana, Vol. II (John Rylands University Library, Manchester 1920).

The Apocrypha and Pseudepigrapha of the Old Testament, edited by R. H. Charles (Clarendon Press, Oxford 1913), Vol. II, *The Testament of Levi.*

The Fathers of the Church (The Catholic University of America Press, Washington 1959, 1977). *The Didache* (Francis X. Grimm); — Saint Justin Martyr, *First Apology* (Th. B. Falls); — Saint Augustin, *Confessions* (V. J. Bourke).

Ancient Christian Writers (Newman Press, New York, and Ramsey, New Jersey) Egeria, *Diary of a Pilgrimage* (G. E. Gingras).

The Ante-Nicene Fathers, edited by A. Roberts and J. Donaldson (W. B. Eerdmans Publishing Co., Grand Rapids, Mi.). Tertullian, *Ad Martyras* (S. Thelwall).

The Nicene and Post-Nicene Fathers, edited by P. Schaff and H. Wace (W. B. Eerdmans Publishing Co., Grand Rapids, Mi.). Eusebius, *Church History* (A. C. McGiffert); — Chrysostomos, *Concerning Statues* (W. R. W. Stephens); — Gregory the Great, *Selected Epistles* (J. Barmby); — *The Seven Ecumenical Councils* (H. R. Percival).

A. Cochrane, *Reformed Confessions of the Sixteenth Century* (SCM Press, London 1966).

J. Calvin, *Institutes*, translated by H. Beveridge (W. B. Eerdmans Publishing Co., Grand Rapids, Mi., 1964).

D. Hammarskjöld, *Markings*, translated by L. Sjöberg and W. H. Auden (Faber and Faber, London 1964), reprinted by permission of Faber and Faber Ltd.

G. J. Cuming, *Hippolytus:* A Text for Students (Grove Books, Bramcote 1976).

K. Aland (ed.), *Synopsis of the Four Gospels* (United Bible Societies, Stuttgart 1972).

Other quotations are translations from the original made by the author. The scripts II/3, 4, and 12 are edited versions of Bible studies already published in the periodical *The Laity Today*, Nos. 19/20 (Rome 1975), and Nos. 21/22 (Rome 1976). They are published here in a revised version by permission of the Concilium de Laicis, Vatican City. The series of radio talks in script II/8 is published by permission of the National Broadcasting Corporation of New Zealand. The whole of the narrative exegesis on "Let the Children Come To Me" (II/13) was published under the title *"A Child? A Story for Adults"* (NCEC/WCC, Nutfield/Geneva 1979).

The woodblock "Give me eyes" on p. 116 is from Takeji Asano. First published in Masao Takenaka (ed.), *Living in Today's World* (Kansai Seminar House, Kyoto 1969).

The song on p. 256 is from Mrs. Nicola Sutherland, Auckland.

WORKSHEETS

Historical context

Worksheet II/3
The time of Jeremiah

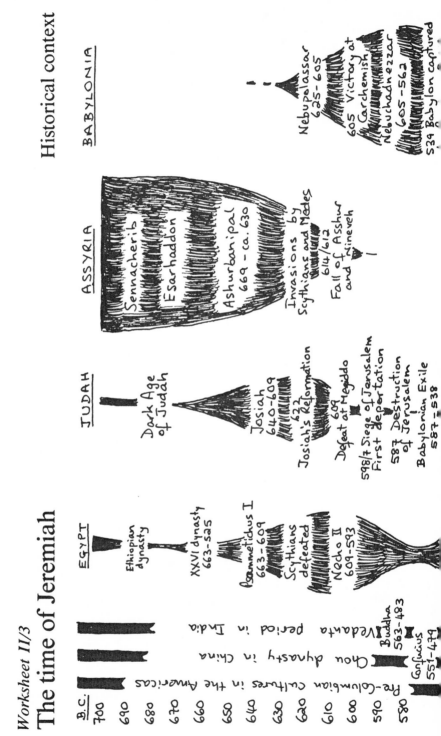

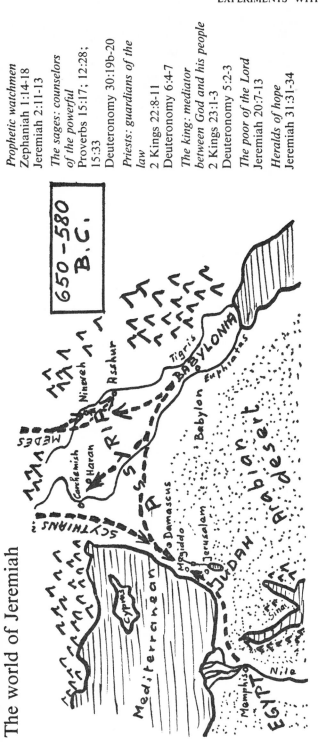

The world of Jeremiah

Prophetic watchmen
Zephaniah 1:14-18
Jeremiah 2:11-13

The sages: counselors of the powerful
Proverbs 15:17; 12:28; 15:33
Deuteronomy 30:19b-20

Priests: guardians of the law
2 Kings 22:8-11
Deuteronomy 6:4-7

The king: mediator between God and his people
2 Kings 23:1-3
Deuteronomy 5:2-3

The poor of the Lord
Jeremiah 20:7-13

Heralds of hope
Jeremiah 31:31-34

Task 1: Learn to recite with the right intonation and gestures your assigned scripture readings, e.g., those of the prophets, sages, priests, kings, poor, or heralds.

Task 2: How did Jesus — according to the testimonies of the New Testament — take up, continue, and transform the Old Testament ministry assigned to you?

Task 3: How can you today participate in the ministry assigned to you? Prepare a worship service with a prophetic word/act, a proverb of wisdom, a new piece of legislation, a covenant renewal ceremony, a prayer of the poor, and a vision of hope for today's world.

Worksheet II/7a

Messianic expectations
in the Old Testament and intertestamental times

Throughout its history the people of Israel have maintained that it is God, and he alone, who will establish his kingdom. This kingdom is described as the *all-embracing "shalōm"*, not only peace within the hearts of people, nor only peace among the nations, but a harmonious living together of all creation, human, animals and nature — in fact, nothing less than a new heaven and a new earth (cf. Ps. 85; Isa. 11:6-9; 66:22). Because of this centrality of God's kingship and this all-embracing vision of the end and purpose of history, the Jewish hope has centred much more on the coming of a messianic age than on a personal Messiah (from the Hebrew *mashiah*, Greek *Christos* = "the anointed").

If the Messiah is considered as coming from beyond some time in the future, one should rather speak of a messianic vacuum than a messianic expectation in the Old Testament. If, however, the Messiah is seen as the anointed one, it is possible to detect several deep changes in the Old Testament image of the Messiah.

1. When the Israelite tribes asked for an earthly king, in the eleventh century B.C., Samuel first resisted this demand (1 Sam. 8), but later he yielded and anointed Saul (1 Sam. 10). With *the anointing of David* the earthly kingship became an accepted institution. "Your house and your kingdom shall be made sure for ever before me; your throne shall be established for ever" (2 Sam. 7:16). This promise of Nathan addressed to David is the basic messianic text. Already Judah, a forefather of David, had received a similar promise from Jacob (Gen. 49:8-12). All Davidic kings were now seen as "God's Anointed". In 520 B.C. the last ruler from the family of David, Zerubbabel, was declared to be the Messiah by the prophets Haggai (2:20-23) and Zechariah (4:6-10; 6:9-13). The Messiah was thus seen in the first place as an earthly ruler, a political figure.

2. As one king after the other fell short of the ideal of messiahship the Israelites began to look out for *the coming of a new David*. Around 735 B.C. the prophet Micah blessed Bethlehem, the town of David: "From you shall come forth for

the one who is to be ruler in Israel" (Micah 5:2-4). At the same time Isaiah prophesied to the house of David: "Behold, a young woman shall conceive and bear a son, and shall call his name Immanuel" (Isa. 7:14). "There shall come forth a shoot from the stump of Jesse ... and the Spirit of the Lord shall rest upon him" (Isa. 11:1-12). "For to us a child is born ... and the government will be upon his shoulder, and his name will be called 'Wonderful Counsellor, Mighty God, Everlasting Father, Prince of Peace'" (Isa. 9:1-7). Similar prophecies are found in the oracles of Jeremiah at the end of the seventh century and of Ezekiel in the first half of the sixth century B.C. (Jer. 23:5-6; Ezek. 34:23-31; 37:24-28). This Messiah in the person of the new David was still conceived as a political figure inaugurating the messianic age. Such hopes were revived among the Pharisees in the first century B.C.: "Behold, O Lord, and raise up unto them their king, the son of David.... And he shall gather together a holy people, whom he shall lead in righteousness ..." (Ps. of Solomon 17:1-38). This hope was also strongly present among the Jewish rebels in the first century of the Christian era (cf. Theudas and Judas the Galilean mentioned in Acts 5:35-37).

3. *During and after the Babylonian exile* when the Davidic kingship had come to an end the second Isaiah hailed the Persian king Cyrus as "God's Anointed" (Isa. 45:1, about 539 B.C.). At the same time the sacerdotal tradition became strong; cf. Ezekiel's vision of the new temple (Ezek. 40-48) and the building of the second temple (520-515 B.C.). Now high priests were also anointed (Lev. 8:12), and in 520 B.C. the high priest Joshua was seen as a second Messiah beside the Davidic king Zerubbabel: "These are the two anointed who stand by the Lord of the whole earth" (Zech. 4:14; 6:12-13). High priests were now exalted at the expense of the royalty (Sirach 45:6-24). In the Testament of Levi (second half of second century B.C.) the priestly Messiah is given pre-eminence: "Then shall the Lord raise up a new priest. And to him all the words of the Lord shall be revealed.... The heavens shall be opened. And from the temple of glory shall come upon him sanctification, with the Father's voice.... In his priesthood shall sin come to an end ... and he shall open the gates of paradise" (Test. Lev. 18:1-14). The "Manual of Discipline" (first century B.C.) of the Qumran community speaks about "the Messiah of Aaron and Israel," referring probably to a priestly and a royal Messiah.

4. During the second and first centuries B.C. more and more Jews began to hope for the coming of a Messiah who would be the Saviour. Besides the above-mentioned messianic figures *other Old Testament texts and promises* were now seen in the light of the messianic expectations:

a. God had promised to Moses: "I will raise up for them a prophet like you from among their brethren; and I will put my words in his mouth, and he shall speak to them all that I command him" (Deut. 18:15-19). This hope became especially strong among the Samaritans. Also the prophet Malachi (*ca.* 450 B.C.) had linked the coming messianic age, the rising of "the sun of righteousness," with the return of a prophet, the prophet Elijah (Mal. 4:2-6).

b. The old oracle of the prophet Balaam about the star (Num. 24:15-17) was interpreted in an Aramaic paraphrase (Targum) as follows: "When the mighty king of the house of Jacob will reign and the Messiah, the mighty sceptre of Israel will be anointed ...."

c. Psalms such as Ps. 2 and 110, which had been sung at royal ceremonies, were now reread in the light of the messianic hope.

d. For a long time the "Servant of God" in the hymns of Isa. 42, 49, 50, and 53 played little or no role in the Jewish hope. Shortly before Christ this figure was probably related to the messianic expectations, but only the final triumph and not the vicarious suffering of this Servant was emphasized.

e. In the prophecies of Deutero-Zechariah (probably 330-300 B.C.), the coming Saviour is portrayed as the humble messianic king (Zech. 9:9-10), as the antitype of the wicked shepherd (Zech. 11:4-17; 13:7-9), and as the one who has been pierced (Zech. 12:10-14).

f. The figure of the Son of Man in the second century B.C. apocalyptic literature (Dan. 7:13; Enoch 37-71) was well known in the time of Jesus, but only after Christ was it related to the expected Messiah.

g. Although not identified with the Messiah the figure of the personified Wisdom (Prov. 8:22-31; Wisdom 7:21-8:1) played an important role in Jewish hope.

Task: Try to visualize the image of the Messiah and the changes of his "portrait" which occurred in Old Testament and intertestamental times.

Worksheet II/7b

The coming of the Christ

Mark: In his prologue Mark reveals to his readers the true identity of the main actor and the real nature of his struggle. Before the actual story begins, John the Baptist appears as the forerunner of the Mighty One (Mk 1:1-8). Then Jesus enters the scene. During his baptism the heavens are torn apart, and by God's Spirit and voice the main actor is acknowledged and empowered to be God's Son (Mk 1:9-11). Finally, Satan the antagonist enters, and the battle behind the whole of Jesus' life, death, and resurrection is joined (Mk 1:12-13).

John: The prologue is probably an ancient Christian hymn which the evangelist expands to show how in Christ all creation and redemption, both history and eternity, are united. The original hymn (possibly vv. 1-5, 9-14, 16) celebrates the creation and the redeeming knowledge through the word/wisdom, recalling many passages from the Old Testament and especially the late wisdom literature (cf. Gen. 1:1ff; Ps. 33:6, 9; Prov. 8:22-31; Wisdom 7: 21-30; 8:4; 9:9-10). The hymn affirms that this word/wisdom is not only personified but actually became incarnate in Jesus (1:14). He "tents" among us, just as the presence of God formerly dwelt among the people of Israel in the tabernacle (Exod. 25:8; 40:34-35). Through his editing of the hymn the evangelist firmly links this incarnation with history, that of John the Baptist (vv. 6-8, 15) and that of the history of salvation (vv. 17-18).

Both *Matthew* and *Luke* preface their gospels with two introductory chapters on the origin, birth, and early childhood of Jesus. They situate his birth in Bethlehem (Mt 2:1; Lk 2:4-6), in the time of Herod (Mt 2:1, Lk 1:5). Both insist on the intervention of the Holy Spirit (Mt 1:20; Lk 1:35), on the fact that Joseph belonged to the family of David (Mt 1:20; Lk 1:27), and that Jesus grew up in Nazareth (Mt 2:23; Lk 1:26). The virginity of Mary is affirmed by Luke (1:35) and alluded to by Matthew (1:18).

Despite these common affirmations Matthew and Luke clearly base their accounts on different traditions, probably ancient oral teachings of the church in the case of Matthew and perhaps already written sources in the case of Luke. Moreover, both evangelists edit their traditions in different styles, with different purposes and many particularities typical for each of them.

MATTHEW	LUKE
Mt, a Jew probably writing for a majority of Jewish Christians, answers in his introductory chapters the questions: Who is Jesus? From where does he come? How is he received?	Lk, a Gentile addressing essentially Gentile Christians, writes "an orderly account" (1:3) of the great deeds of God in Christ. He therefore begins with an almost biographical account of Jesus' conception, birth and early years.
Mt uses the style of a Jewish "midrash," that is, an interpretation of a biblical text often in the form of a story ("haggadah") which does not necessarily report historical facts. After the genealogy (1:1-17) follow five such interpretative stories with OT texts.	Lk writes in the style of a historian of salvation. He shows how the actors of the heavenly scene (God, the Spirit, angels) interact with the actors on the earthly scene (especially Zechariah, Elizabeth, Simeon, Mary, and Jesus) and how these human actors respond to God's great deeds with praise.
Mt starts with a genealogy (1:1-17) showing that through Joseph Jesus is "the son of David, son of Abraham" (descending genealogy).	Lk puts the genealogy (3:23-38) between Jesus' baptism and temptation (ascending genealogy up to "Adam, the son of God").
Mt remains rather vague in his localization of the various events, except the birth in Bethlehem, the flight to Egypt, and the settling of Jesus' family in Nazareth.	Lk specifies the localities: Mary comes from Nazareth, Elizabeth and Zechariah live in Judea. The temple in Jerusalem is the central place: annunciation to Zechariah, presentation of the child, Jesus among the teachers.
Mt remains vague with regard to time except the return from Egypt after the death of Herod (2:19) under the reign of Archelaus.	Lk wants to be precise: "In the days of the decree from Caesar Augustus" (2:1); "in the sixth month" (1:26); "at the end of eight days" (2:21), etc.
Mt assigns an important place to Joseph: he receives three decisive revelations in the dream: therefore he takes Mary into his house (1:18-25), later escapes with her and the child to Egypt (2:13-15), and finally comes back from Egypt to take residence in Nazareth (2:19-23). Yet in the	Lk assigns an important place to Mary: she hears from the angel about the child conceived (1:26-38); she visits Elizabeth (1:39-56); she guards the words of the shepherds in her heart (2:19); to her the words of Simeon are addressed (2:25-35).

Lk continually compares Jesus and John the Baptist: two announcements, two descriptions of their mission, two affirmations of their growth. This parallelism underlines the different roles of John and Jesus.

Lk makes many allusions to Old Testament texts especially in the "Magnificat" (1:46-55; cf. 1 Sam. 2:1-10), the "Benedictus" (1:68-79; cf. Mal. 4:5) and the "Nunc dimittis" (2:29-35; cf. Isa. 42:6). These texts are not explained but used for prayer.

Lk presents Jesus as "the Lord" whose people and way have been prepared by John the Baptist (1:17, 76). He is "the Son of the Most High" on the throne of David who will reign forever (1:32-33, 35). Therefore the mighty are put down and the poor exulted (1:51-55). The one called Jesus (1:31; 2:21) is "a horn of salvation" (1:69: "horn" in the OT is a metaphor for "strength"), that is the liberator (1:73). As such he is announced by the angels: "a Saviour, who is Christ the Lord" (2:11). His salvation and light are to reach all people and nations (2:30-32), but at the same time it will bring a crisis for the people of Israel (2:34-35). "Filled with wisdom" (2:40, 52), the twelve-year-old Jesus finds his rightful place in the temple of Jerusalem, his Father's house, thoughts, and presence (2:46-49). The priestly blessing which the dumbfounded Zechariah could not give at the beginning of the gospel (1:22) will be given by the ascending Jesus (24:50f) at the end of the gospel.

stories of the Magi (2:1-12) and the murder of children in Bethlehem (2:16-18), originally probably related, Joseph does not appear.

Mt builds his five scenes around five Old Testament quotations:

1:23 — Isaiah 7:14
2:6 — Micah 5:2 (2 Sam. 5:2)
2:15 — Hosea 11:1 (Exod. 4:22)
2:18 — Jeremiah 31:15
2:23 — "prophets" (Isa. 11:1?)

Mt presents Jesus ("he will save," 1:21) as the Emmanuel ("God with us," 1:23; cf. 28:20), the "king of the Jews" (2:2) and the Messiah ("the Christ," 2:4). The significance of the title "Nazarene" (2:23) is not clear: the one from Nazareth? A *nazir* = consecrated to God? The *netser* = "shoot" of Isa. 11:1? Going to Egypt and coming back from there Jesus sums up the story of the people of Israel, "God's son called out of Egypt" (2:15): cf. Mt 2:13-15 with Gen. 12:10; 46:2-5; Mt 2:16-18 with Exod. 1:1-22; Mt 2:19-23 with the whole Exodus story. Jesus appears as the new Moses.

Worksheet II/9

The shepherd and the sheep

MATTHEW

18:1-4 Who is the greatest in the kingdom?
18:5-9 Temptations and how to cope with sin
18:10-11 Warning not to despise the little ones

18:12-14 Parable of the lost sheep

12What do you think? If a man has a hundred sheep, and one of them has gone astray, does he not leave the ninety-nine on the hills and go in search of the one that went astray? 13And if he finds it, truly, I say to you, he rejoices over it more than over the ninety-nine that never went astray.

14So it is not the will of my Father who is in heaven that one of these little ones should perish.

LUKE

14:15-24 Invitation to the messianic feast
14:25-33 Conditions for discipleship
14:34-35 Useless salt
15:1-2 Pharisees shocked by Jesus' community with sinners

15:3-7 Parable of the lost sheep

3So he told them this parable:
4"What man of you, having a hundred sheep, if he has lost one of them, does not leave the ninety-nine in the wilderness, and go after the one which is lost, until he finds it? 5And when he has found it, he lays it on his shoulders, rejoicing.

6And when he comes home, he calls together his friends and his neighbors, saying to them, 'Rejoice with me, for I have found my sheep which was lost.' 7Just so, I tell you, there will be more joy in heaven over one sinner who repents than over ninety-nine righteous persons who need no repentance.

15:8-10 Parable of the lost coin

15:11-32 Parable of the prodigal son

18:15-17 If your brother sins
18:18-20 Binding and loosing
18:21-22 How often to forgive
18:23-35 Parable of the servant who does not forgive

Worksheet II/12

Who do you say that I am?

The earliest known written extra-biblical answers

Tacitus, a Roman historian living from about AD 55-120, mentions the persecutions of Christians under the Emperor Nero and then continues:

"Christus, from whom the name (sc. Christians) had its origin, suffered the extreme penalty during the reign of Tiberius at the hands of one of our procurators, Pontius Pilatus, and a most mischievous superstition, thus checked for the moment, again broke out not only in Judaea, the first source of the evil, but even in Rome, where all things hideous and shameful from every part of the world find their centre and become popular." (*Annals*, XV, 44, 5)

Flavius Josephus (*ca.* AD 37/38-110) wrote the following account around AD 90. The text is contested, and this version follows a hypothetical reconstruction of the original text:

"About this time (i.e. after two disturbances among the Jews) there lived Jesus, a wise man.... He was one who wrought surprising feats and was a teacher of such people as accept the truth gladly. He won over many Jews.... When Pilate, upon hearing him accused by men of the highest standing among us, had condemned him to be crucified, those who had in the first place come to love him did not give up their affection for him.... And the tribe of the Christians, so called after him, has still to this day not disappeared." (*Antiquities*, XVIII, 63-64).

Question: What strikes you in these two non-Christian texts on Jesus? and
What can we learn from them?

The answers of the first Christians

Even before the gospels were written and the earliest Christian creeds formulated, the church answered Jesus' question by assigning to him various titles: Jesus — the Messiah (= the Christ); — the Son of Man; — the Son of God; — the Son of David; — the Lord; — the Just One; — the Servant of God; — the Saviour; — the new Adam (= the new Man); — etc.

Question: Which of the above titles expresses most clearly your own and your church's faith as you attempt to witness to this faith in your own particular situation today?

The early Christians answered Jesus' question also by collecting the oral tradition about Jesus, first the stories of his sion and resurrection, but soon also the miracle stories, his words and accounts concerning his teaching. The conversation between Jesus and his disciples near Caesarea Philippi (Mark 8:27ff and parallels in Matthew 16:13ff and Luke 9:18ff; cf. also John 6:67ff) falls into this last category.

What did really happen?

During the period of oral and written transmission various words of Jesus have been grouped around the memory of a particular event or teaching in Jesus' life. This was the case also for the narrative on the conversation near Caesarea Philippi. When the evangelists wrote, the tradition concerning this conversation was not yet definitely fixed. See e.g. the important addition in Matt. 16:17-19, the omission of Mark 8:32-33 in Luke's version, and the variations of Peter's confession according to the following synopsis:

Matt. 16.15-16	Mark 8.29	Luke 9.20	John 6.67-69
15He said to them, "But who do you say that I am?" 16Simon Peter replied, "You are the Christ, the Son of the living God."	29And he asked them, "But who do you say that I am?" Peter answered him, "You are the Christ."	20And he said to them, "But who do you say that I am?" And Peter answered, "The Christ of God."	67Jesus said to the twelve, "Will you also go away?" 68Simon Peter answered him, "Lord, to whom shall we go? You have the words of eternal life; 69and we have believed, and have come to know, that you are the Holy One of God."

On the basis of a literary analysis of the narrative in Mark 8:27-35 several reconstructions of the original nucleus of this incident have been made. Yet even without such hypothetical reconstructions it is possible to guess what "Peter's confession" originally meant.

Question: If examined in the light of the Jewish messianic expectations and the political situation in Palestine of Jesus' time, what did "Peter's confession" originally mean?

Mark's witness to Jesus

Mark wrote his gospel some time within the period of AD. 65-72, probably for the church in Rome. In order to understand his particular witness to Jesus it is important to know something of the questions which Christians raised and of the situation in which the church then found itself in the world.

Mark's redaction (8:27-35, RSV):

(27) "Jesus went on with his disciples, to the villages of Caesarea Philippi; and on the way he asked his disciples, 'Who do men say that I am?'

(28) And they told him, 'John the Baptist; and others say, Elijah; and others one of the prophets.'

(29) And he asked them, 'But who do you say that I am?' Peter answered him, 'You are the Christ.'

(30) And he charged them to tell no one about him.

(31) And he began to teach them that the Son of man must suffer many things, and be rejected by the elders and the chief priests and the scribes, and be killed, and after three days rise again.

(32) And he said this plainly. And Peter took him, and began to rebuke him.

(33) But turning and seeing his disciples, he rebuked Peter, and said, 'Get behind me, Satan! For you are not on the side of God, but of men.'

(34) And he called to him the multitude with his disciples, and said to them, 'If any man would come after me, let him deny himself and take up his cross and follow me.

(35) For whoever would save his life will lose it; and whoever loses his life for my sake and the gospel's will save it.' "

Questions: (1) Where in this passage does the new teaching begin — and what is therefore the key-verse of the whole narrative according to Mark? (2) What does Jesus in this catechetical conversation teach about the true identity of Christians?

Worksheet II/15
The Lord's Supper

Matt. 26.26-29	Mark 14.22-25	Luke 22.15-20	1 Corinthians
		15 And he said to them, "I have earnestly desired to eat this passover with you before I suffer; 16 for I tell you I shall not eat it until it is fulfilled in the kingdom of God." 17 And he took a cup, and when he had given thanks he said, "Take this, and divide it among yourselves; 18 for I tell you that from now on I shall not drink of the fruit of the vine until the kingdom of God comes."	Chapter 10 16 The cup of blessing which we bless, is it not a participation in the blood of Christ? The bread which we break, is it not a participation in the body of Christ? 17 Because there is one loaf, we who are many are one body, for we all partake of the same loaf.
26 Now as they were eating, Jesus took bread, and blessed, and broke it, and gave it to the disciples and said, "Take, eat; this is my body."	22 And as they were eating, he took bread, and blessed, and broke it, and gave it to them, and said, "Take; this is my body."	19 And he took bread, and when he had given thanks he broke it and gave it to them, saying, "This is my body, [which is given for you. Do this in remembrance of me."	Chapter 11 23 For I received from the Lord what I also delivered to you, that the Lord Jesus on the night when he was betrayed took bread, 24 and when he had given thanks, he broke it, and said, "This is my body which is for you. Do this in remembrance of me." 25 In the same way also the cup, after supper, saying,
cp. v. 29	cp. v. 25		
27 And he took a cup, and when he had given thanks he gave it to them, saying,	23 And he took a cup, and when he had given thanks he gave it to them,	20 And the cup after supper likewise saying,	

"Drink of it, all of you;

my blood of the covenant,
which is poured out for
many for the forgiveness of sins.
²⁹ I tell you   I shall
not drink again of this
fruit of the vine until
that day when I drink it
new with you in my
Father's kingdom."

and they all drank of it. ²⁴And he said to them,   "This is

²⁸for this is

my blood of the covenant,
which is poured out for
many. ²⁵Truly, I say to you, I shall
not drink again of the
fruit of the vine until
that day when I drink it
new   in the
kingdom of God."

"This cup
which is poured out for
you is the new covenant in my
blood.]

"This
cup is the new covenant in my blood.
Do this, as often as you drink it, in
remembrance of me. ²⁶For as often
as you eat this bread and drink the
cup, you proclaim the Lord's death
until he comes."

JOHN 6

⁵¹ I am the
living bread which came down from
heaven; if any one eats of this bread,
he will live for ever; and the bread
which I shall give for the life of the
world is my flesh."

⁵² The Jews then disputed among
themselves, saying, "How can this
man give us his flesh to eat?" ⁵³ So
Jesus said to them, "Truly, truly, I
say to you, unless you eat the flesh of
the Son of man and drink his blood,
you have no life in you; ⁵⁴ he who eats
my flesh and drinks my blood has eternal life, and I will raise him up at the
last day. ⁵⁵ For my flesh is food indeed, and my blood is drink indeed.
⁵⁶ He who eats my flesh and drinks

LUKE 24

²⁵ And he said to
them, "O foolish men, and slow of
heart to believe all that the prophets
have spoken! ²⁶ Was it not necessary
that the Christ should suffer these
things and enter into his glory?"
²⁷ And beginning with Moses and all
the prophets, he interpreted to them
in all the scriptures the things concerning himself.

²⁸ So they drew near to the village
to which they were going. He appeared to be going further, ²⁹ but they
constrained him, saying, "Stay with
us, for it is toward evening and the
day is now far spent." So he went in
to stay with them. ³⁰ When he was
at table with them, he took the bread

JOHN 13

² And dur-
ing supper, when the devil had already put it into the heart of Judas
Iscariot, Simon's son, to betray him,
³ Jesus, knowing that the Father had
given all things into his hands, and
that he had come from God and was
going to God, ⁴ rose from supper, laid
aside his garments, and girded himself with a towel. ⁵ Then he poured
water into a basin, and began to wash
the disciples' feet, and to wipe them
with the towel with which he was
girded.

¹² When he had washed their feet,
and taken his garments, and resumed
his place, he said to them, "Do you
know what I have done to you? ¹³ You

(Luke 24 cont.)
and blessed, and broke it, and gave it to them. 31 And their eyes were opened and they recognized him; and he vanished out of their sight. 32 They said to each other, "Did not our hearts burn within us while he talked to us on the road, while he opened to us the scriptures?"

(John 13 cont.)
call me Teacher and Lord; and you are right, for so I am. 14 If I then, your Lord and Teacher, have washed your feet, you also ought to wash one another's feet. 15 For I have given you an example, that you also should do as I have done to you.

(John 6 cont.)
my blood abides in me, and I in him. 57 As the living Father sent me, and I live because of the Father, so he who eats me will live because of me. 58 This is the bread which came down from heaven, not such as the fathers ate and died; he who eats this bread will live for ever."

EVENT, LITURGICAL TRADITIONS AND INTERPRETATIONS

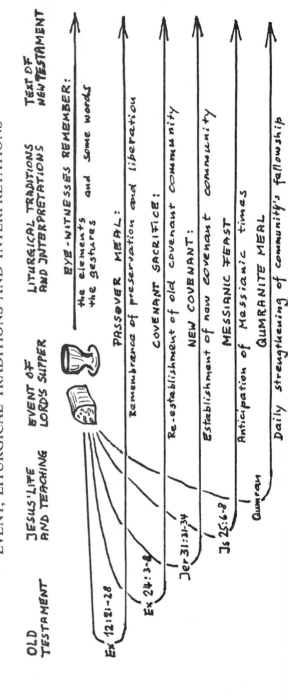

OLD TESTAMENT | JESUS' LIFE AND TEACHING | EVENT OF LORD'S SUPPER | LITURGICAL TRADITIONS AND INTERPRETATIONS | TEXT OF NEW TESTAMENT

EYE-WITNESSES REMEMBER: the elements the gestures and some words

PASSOVER MEAL: Remembrance of preservation and liberation

COVENANT SACRIFICE: Re-establishment of old covenant community

NEW COVENANT: Establishment of new covenant community

MESSIANIC FEAST: Anticipation of Messianic times

QUMRANITE MEAL: Daily strengthening of community's fellowship

Ex 12:21-28
Ex 24:3-8
Jer 31:31-34
Is 25:6-8
Qumran

Texts functioning as clues for understanding

Exodus 12:21-28: (21) Moses said: "Select lambs for yourselves according to your families, and kill the passover lamb. (22) Take a bunch of hyssop and dip it in the blood which is in the basin, and touch the lintel and the two doorposts with the blood.... (23) For the Lord will pass through to slay the Egyptians; and when he sees the blood on the lintel and on the two doorposts, the Lord will pass over the door, and will not allow the destroyer to enter your houses to slay you. (24) You shall observe this rite...."

Exodus 24:3-8: (3) Moses came and told the people all the words of the Lord and all the ordinances; and all the people answered with one voice, and said, "All the words which the Lord has spoken we will do...." (5) And he sent young men of the people of Israel, who offered burnt offerings and sacrificed peace offerings of oxen to the Lord.... (7) Then he took the book of the covenant and read it in the hearing of the people; and they said, "All that the Lord has spoken we will do, and we will be obedient." (8) And Moses took the blood and threw it upon the people, and said, "Behold the blood of the covenant which the Lord has made with you in accordance with all these words."

Jeremiah 31:31-34: (31) "Behold, the days are coming, says the Lord, when I will make a new covenant with the house of Israel and the house of Judah.... (33b) I will put my law within them, and I will write it upon their hearts; and I will be their God, and they shall be my people. (34) And no longer shall each man teach his neighbour and each his brother, saying, 'Know the Lord,' for they shall all know me, from the least of them to the greatest, says the Lord; for I will forgive their iniquity, and I will remember their sin no more."

Isaiah 25:6-8: (6) On this mountain the Lord of hosts will make for all peoples a feast of fat things, a feast of wine on the lees.... (7) And he will destroy on this mountain the covering that is cast over all peoples, the veil that is spread over all nations. (8) He will swallow up death for ever, and the Lord God will wipe away tears from all faces, and the reproach of his people he will take away from all the earth; for the Lord has spoken.

Qumran meal: "When the table is prepared for eating or wine for drinking, the priest shall first raise his hand so that the first portion of the bread and of the wine be blessed" (1QS VI, 4f).

Worksheet II/17
Come and see

Matt. 28.1-8	Mark 16.1-8	Luke 24.1-12
		56Then they returned, and prepared spices and ointments. On the sabbath they rested according to the commandment. (23.56)
1Now after the sabbath, toward the dawn of the first day of the week, Mary Magdalene and the other Mary went to see the sepulchre.	1And when the sabbath was past, Mary Magdalene, Mary the mother of James, and Salome bought spices; so that they might go and anoint him. 2And very early on the first day of the week they went to the tomb when the sun had risen.	1But on the first day of the week, at early dawn, they went to the tomb, taking the spices which they had prepared.
2And behold, there was a great earthquake; for an angel of the Lord descended from heaven and came and rolled back the stone, and sat upon it.	3And they were saying to one another, "Who will roll away the stone for us from the door of the tomb?" 4And looking up, they saw that the stone was rolled back; for it was very large. 5And entering the tomb, they saw a young man sitting on the right side,	2And they found the stone rolled away from the tomb, 3but when they went in they did not find the body. 4While they were perplexed about this, behold, two men stood by them

3His appearance was like lightning, and his raiment white as snow. 4And for fear of him the guards trembled and became like dead men.

5But the angel said to the women, "Do not be afraid; for I know that you seek Jesus who was crucified.

6He is not here; for he has risen, as he said. Come, see the place where he lay.

7Then go quickly and tell his disciples that he has risen from the dead, and behold, he is going before you to Galilee; there you will see him. Lo, I have told you." 8So they departed quickly from the tomb with fear and great joy, and ran to tell his disciples.

dressed in a white robe; and they were amazed.

6And he said to them, "Do not be amazed; you seek Jesus of Nazareth, who was crucified. He has risen, he is not here; see the place where they laid him.

7But go, tell his disciples and Peter that he is going before you to Galilee; there you will see him, as he told you." 8And they went out and fled from the tomb; for trembling and astonishment had come upon them; and they said nothing to any one, for they were afraid.

in dazzling apparel; 5and as they were frightened and bowed their faces to the ground, the men said to them, "Why do you seek the living among the dead? [He is not here, but has risen.] 6Remember how he told you, while he was still in Galilee, 7that the Son of man must be delivered into the hands of sinful men, and be crucified, and on the third day rise." 8And they remembered his words, 9and returning from the tomb they told all this to the eleven and to all the rest.

The Gospel of Peter

(Fragment of an apocryphal gospel from the middle of the second century)

(34) Early in the morning, when the Sabbath dawned, there came a crowd from Jerusalem and the country round about to see the sepulchre that had been sealed.

(35) Now in the night in which the Lord's day dawned, when the soldiers, two by two in every watch, were keeping guard, there rang out a loud voice in heaven, (36) and they saw the heavens opened and two men come down from there in a great brightness and draw nigh to the sepulchre. (37) That stone which had been laid against the entrance to the sepulchre started of itself to roll and gave way to the side, and the sepulchre was opened, and both the young men entered in. (38) When now those soldiers saw this, they awakened the centurion and the elders — for they also were there to assist at the watch. (39) And whilst they were relating what they had seen, they saw again three men come out from the sepulchre, and two of them sustaining the other, and a cross following them, (40) and the heads of the two reaching to heaven, but that of him who was led of them by the hand overpassing the heavens. (41) And they heard a voice out of the heavens crying, "Thou hast preached to them that sleep," (42) and from the cross there was heard the answer, "Yea." (43) Those men therefore took counsel with one another to go and report this to Pilate. (44) And whilst they were still deliberating, the heavens were again seen to open, and a man descended and entered into the sepulchre. (45) When those who were of the centurion's company saw this, they hastened by night to Pilate, abandoning the sepulchre which they were guarding, and reported everything that they had seen, being full of disquietude and saying, "In truth he was the Son of God." (46) Pilate answered and said, "I am clean from the blood of the Son of God, upon such a thing have you decided." (47) Then all came to him, beseeching him and urgently calling upon him to command the centurion and the soldiers to tell no one what they had seen. (48) "For it is better for us," they said, "to make ourselves guilty of the greatest sin before God than to fall into the hands of the people of the Jews and be stoned." (49) Pilate therefore commanded the centurion and the soldiers to say nothing.

(50) Early in the morning of the Lord's day Mary Magdalene, a woman disciple of the Lord — for fear of the Jews, since (they) were inflamed with wrath, she had not done at the sepulchre of the Lord what women are wont to do for those beloved of them who die — took (51) with her her women friends and came to the sepulchre where he was laid. (52) And they feared lest the Jews should see them, and said, "Although we could not weep and lament on that day when he was crucified, yet let us now do so at his sepulchre. (53) But who will roll away for us the stone also that is set on the

entrance to the sepulchre, that we may go in and sit beside him and do what is due? — (54) For the stone was great, — and we fear lest any one see us. And if we cannot do so, let us at least put down at the entrance what we bring for a memorial of him and let us weep and lament until we have again gone home." (55) So they went and found the sepulchre opened. And they came near, stooped down, and saw there a young man sitting in the midst of the sepulchre, comely and clothed with a brightly shining robe, who said to them, (56) "Wherefore are ye come? Whom seek ye? Not him that was crucified? He is risen and gone. But if ye believe not, stoop this way and see the place where he lay, for he is not here. For he is risen and is gone thither whence he was sent." (57) Then the women fled affrighted.

Worksheet II/18

Go quickly and tell

In all gospels the resurrection of Christ is intimately linked with the world-mission of the church. In order fully to appreciate how Matthew makes this link it is important to keep in mind two things: (1) throughout his gospel Matthew strongly emphasized the continuity between the Old Testament expectations and the ministry of Jesus; (2) Matthew's style is deeply influenced by the wisdom literature (e.g., the book of Proverbs) and therefore he often confronts the reader with alternatives.

Old Testament texts on "Mission"

Genesis 12:3: God spoke to Abraham: (3) "I will bless those who bless you, and him who curses you I will curse; and by you all the families of the earth will bless themselves" (other possible translation: "... in you all the families of the earth will be blessed").

Isaiah 2:2-3: (2) "It shall come to pass in the latter days that the mountain of the house of the Lord shall be established as the highest of the mountains, and shall be raised above the hills; and all the nations shall flow to it, (3) and many peoples shall come, and say: 'Come, let us go up to the mountain of the Lord, to the house of the God of Jacob; that he may teach us his ways and that we may walk in his paths.' For out of Zion shall go forth the law, and the word of the Lord from Jerusalem."

Isaiah 42:1-2, 4, 6b: (1) "Behold my servant, whom I uphold, my chosen, in whom my soul delights; I have put my Spirit upon him, he will bring forth justice to the nations. (2) He will not cry or lift up his voice, or make it heard in the street; ... (4) He will not fail or be discouraged till he has established justice in the earth; and the coastlands wait for his law.... (6b) I have given you as a covenant to the people, a light to the nations."

Isaiah 60:1-3: (1) "Arise, shine; for your light has come, and the glory of the Lord has risen upon you. (2) For behold, darkness shall cover the earth, and thick darkness the peoples; but the Lord will arise upon you, and his glory will be seen upon you. (3) And nations shall come to your light, and kings to the brightness of your rising."

The parable of the wedding feast
(italicized words and verses are typically Matthean terms and additions as compared to Luke's version in Luke 14:16-24)

Matthew 22:2-10: (2) "*The kingdom of heaven may be compared to a king who gave a marriage feast for his son,* (3) and sent his servants to call those who were invited to the marriage feast; but they would not come. (4) *Again he sent other servants, saying, 'Tell those who are invited, Behold, I have made ready my dinner, my oxen and my fat calves are killed, and everything is ready; come to the marriage feast.'* (5) But they made light of it and went off, one to his farm, another to his business, (6) *while the rest seized his servants, treated them shamefully, and killed them.* (7) *The king was angry, and he sent his troops and destroyed those murderers and burned their city.* (8) Then he said to his servants, '*The wedding is ready, but those invited were not worthy.* (9) Go therefore to the thoroughfares, and invite to the marriage feast as many as you find.' (10) And those servants went out into the streets and gathered all whom they found, *both bad and good; so the wedding hall was filled with guests.*"

The end of Matthew's gospel

Traditions and Composition

Material from a first special tradition of Matthew Mt 27:62-66	*Material from the synoptic tradition (underlined) and the first special tradition*	*Material from a second special tradition of Matthew*
62 Next day, that is, after the day of Preparation, the chief priests and the Pharisees gathered before Pilate 63 and said, "Sir, we remember how that impostor said, while he was still alive, 'After three days I will rise again.' 64 Therefore order the sepul-		

*Material from a first special tradi-
tion of Matthew*

Mt 27:62-66

chre to be made secure until the third
day, lest his disciples go and steal him
away, and tell the people, 'He has
risen from the dead', and the last
fraud will be worse than the first."
⁶⁵Pilate said to them, "You have a
guard of soldiers; go, make it as secure as you can." ⁶⁶So they went
and made the sepulchre secure by
sealing the stone and setting a guard.

*Material from the synoptic tradition
(underlined) and the first special tradition*

Mt 28:1-8

Now after the sabbath, toward the dawn of the first day
of the week, Mary Magdalene and
the other Mary went to see the sepulchre. ²And behold, there was a great
earthquake; for an angel of the Lord
descended from heaven and came and
rolled back the stone, and sat upon it.
³His appearance was like lightning,
and his raiment white as snow. ⁴And
for fear of him the guards trembled
and became like dead men. ⁵But the
angel said to the women, "Do not be
afraid; for I know that you seek Jesus
who was crucified. ⁶He is not here;
for he has risen, as he said. Come, see
the place where he lay. ⁷Then go
quickly and tell his disciples that he
has risen from the dead, and behold,
he is going before you to Galilee;
there you will see him. Lo, I have told
you." ⁸So they departed quickly from
the tomb with fear and great joy, and
ran to tell his disciples

*Material from a second special tra-
dition of Matthew*

Mt 28:9-10

⁹ And behold, Jesus met them and said, "Hail!" And they came up and took hold of his feet and worshiped him. ¹⁰ Then Jesus said to them, "Do not be afraid; go and tell my brethren to go to Galilee, and there they will see me."

Mt 28:16-20

16 Now the eleven disciples went to Galilee, to the mountain to which Jesus had directed them. ¹⁷ And when they saw him they worshiped him; but some doubted. ¹⁸ And Jesus came and said to them, "All authority in heaven and on earth has been given to me. ¹⁹ Go therefore and make disciples of all nations, baptizing them in the name of the Father and of the Son and of the Holy Spirit, ²⁰ teaching them to observe all that I have commanded you; and lo, I am with you, always, to the close of the age."

Mt. 28:11-15

11 While they were going, behold, some of the guard went into the city and told the chief priests all that had taken place. ¹² And when they had assembled with the elders and taken counsel, they gave a sum of money to the soldiers ¹³ and said, "Tell people, 'His disciples came by night and stole him away while we were asleep.' ¹⁴ And if this comes to the governor's ears, we will satisfy him and keep you out of trouble." ¹⁵ So they took the money and did as they were directed; and this story has been spread among the Jews to this day.

Worksheet II/22

The radical cure

(Gal 5:16-24, especially verse 24)

Paul's angry letter

Galatians is Paul's angry letter. Already in the address (Gal. 1:1) the passionate argument begins, and only in this letter has Paul omitted the usual initial thanksgiving/blessing (cf. e.g. Rom. 1:8ff with Gal. 1:6ff). What was it that "bewitched" the "foolish Galatians" (3:1), who were about to "fall from grace" (5:4)? Why were they "deserting" God and turning to "a different gospel" (1:6)?

The Galatians were almost certainly the converted Celts ("barbarians" to the Greeks and Romans) in "the region of Galatia" (Acts 16:6; 18:23) in the northern part of Asia Minor. After the powerful conversion-experience of salvation and liberation and after an initial period of spiritual enthusiasm the converts had difficulties with their *sarx*, their self-seeking human nature. The Galatians had received the Spirit and had been running well (3:2-5; 5:7). But then the great Christian liberty of living by grace alone and of walking by the Spirit and not by customs and the law had begun to frighten them. Misguided by false teachers they now doubted the authority of Paul's teaching. While still believing in the grace of the crucified Lord and the power of the Spirit they sought securities also in legal performances, especially circumcision (Gal. 2:3; 5:2ff; 6:12ff) and the observance of certain days and feasts (4:10).

In his passionate letter, written probably at his departure from Ephesus for Corinth in A.D. 56/57, Paul first re-established his apostolic authority (Gal. 1-2) and made his own confession of faith (2:19-21). Then he refuted the false teachers' interpretation of what it means to be "sons of Abraham" and gave his own, Christian-rabbinical exegesis with regard to this matter (3:6ff; 4:21ff). He showed that the seeking of salvation by way of the law, be it the Jewish law or former Celtic customs, inevitably leads to perdition. However, Christ has become a curse for us, opening the new way of salvation by grace. The curse was thus transformed into blessing (3:10-14) and the history of salvation was thereby led to its decisive turning point (4:4-7).

From this centre of Pauline faith — later more fully expounded in the letter to the Romans — the apostle then drew conclusions for the special problem of the Galatians: how can we live in the "flesh" (*sarx*) according to the Spirit (*pneuma*), if we are always tempted to live according to the *sarx*?

The problem with the sarx

Paul's answer is radical. The problem with the *sarx* cannot be solved by such legal safeguards as circumcision (5:1-12). Although the freedom in Christ is full of risks, we are called to freedom (5:13-15). There is no compromise possible between the *sarx* and its "works" and the Spirit and its "fruit" (5:16-23). Yet the problem with the *sarx* has already been solved: "those who belong to Christ Jesus have crucified the *sarx*" (5:24).

Usually in the New Testament the Greek word *sarx* (literally "flesh") is simply a translation of the Hebrew word *basar* which refers to earthly, mortal, bodily existence (e.g. John 1:14), sometimes in the combination "flesh and blood" (Gal. 1:16). *Sarx* designates then the creature before God, the corporeal person, the earthly condition, often with an emphasis on its fragility. It refers to the *whole* of the human psycho-somatic existence with its good and evil possibilities. There is in the Bible no anthropological dualism (e.g. the "flesh/body" versus the "soul").

A dualism in spiritualities exists, however. Especially in Galatians and Romans Paul used the term *sarx* also to designate the power opposing God's Spirit.* It then refers to sinful human beings abandoned to themselves and their self-seeking human nature ("flesh" RSV; "our lower nature" NEB; "our human nature" TEV; "self-indulgence" JB). The source and guidance of our life can either be God's Spirit or our self-indulgent ego. How do we make sure that it is the Spirit and not the *sarx* in this second, pejorative meaning which guides our life?

Paul's radical remedy

"Those who belong to Christ Jesus have crucified (*estaurōsan*, aorist active) the *sarx* with its passions and desires" (Gal. 5:24).

---

* Gnostic Christians have misunderstood this Pauline dualism of spiritualities as an anthropological dualism. This led in much of traditional Christian spirituality to a despising of the body, of sexuality, and of the female with which the evil *sarx* was equated, while the "soul" was thought to have a special relationship with the divine. Salvation then was thought of in terms of the "excarnation" of the soul out of the body, rather than the incarnation of God in the human Jesus.

Examine the meaning of this affirmation and its implications for Christian spirituality in the light of the following texts. (Note especially the tenses of the verbs. In Greek the *aorist* usually refers to a definite past event or telescopes a past action to a point. The *perfect* refers to a past event or action by insisting on its continuing effect until today). On the basis of this describe the main characteristics of the Christian spirituality as Paul taught it.

"Christ redeemed (*exēgorasen*, aorist active) us from the curse of the law, having become a curse for us — for it is written, 'Cursed be every one who hangs on a tree'" (Gal. 3:13).

"For I through the law died (*apethanon*, aorist active) to the law, that I might live to God. I have been crucified with Christ (*synestaurōmai*, perfect passive); it is no longer I who live, but Christ who lives in me, and the life I now live in the flesh (*en sarki*) I live by faith (*en pistei*) in the Son of God, who loved me and gave himself for me" (Gal. 2:19-20).

"Do you not know that all of us who have been baptized (*ebaptisthēmen*, aorist passive) into Christ Jesus were baptized into his death? ... We know that our old self (here not *sarx* but *ho palaios hēmōn anthrōpos* = "our old human being") was crucified with him (*synestaurōthē*, aorist passive) so that the sinful body (not *sarx* but *to sōma tēs hamartias* = "the body of the sin") might be destroyed, and we might no longer be enslaved to sin" (Rom. 6:3,6).

"Far be it from me to glory except in the cross of our Lord Jesus Christ, by which the world has been crucified (*estaurōtai*, perfect passive) to me, and I to the world" (Gal. 6:14).

"My self-seeking love (*eros*) has been crucified (*estaurōtai*, perfect passive)" (Letter of Ignatius to Romans, 7:2; early second century).

Worksheet II/23

Liturgy and life

Romans 6
vv. 3-11

(3) Do you not know that all of us who have been baptized[h] into Christ Jesus were baptized[h] into his death? (4) We were buried[h] therefore with him by baptism into death, so that as Christ was raised[h] from the dead by the glory of the Father, we too might walk[h] in newness of life. (5) For if we have been united[i] with him in a death like his, we shall certainly be united[k] with him in a resurrection like his. (6) We know that our old self was crucified[h] with him so that the sinful body might be destroyed[h], and we might no longer be enslaved to sin. (7) For he who has died[h] is freed[i] from sin. (8) But if we have died[h] with Christ, we believe that we shall also live[k] with him. (9) For we know that Christ being raised[h] from the dead will never die again; death no longer has dominion over him. (10) The death he died[h] he died[h] to sin, once for all, but the life he lives he lives to God. (11) So you also must consider yourselves dead to sin and alive to God in Christ Jesus.

EPHESIANS 2[a]
vv. 1-10

(1) And you[b] he made alive[e,h], when you were dead through the trespasses and sins (2) in which you once walked[h], following the course of this world, following the prince of the power of the air[c], the spirit that is now at work in the sons of disobedience. (3) Among these we all once lived[h] in the passions of our flesh[d], following the desires of body and mind, and so we were[l] by nature children of wrath, like the rest of mankind. (4) But God, who is rich in mercy, out of the great love with which he loved[h] us, (5) even when we were dead through our trespasses, made us alive[e,h] together with Christ (by grace you have been saved[i]), (6) and raised[h] us up with him, and made us sit[h] with him in the heavenly places in Christ Jesus, (7) that in the coming ages[f] he might show[h] the immeasurable riches of his grace in kindness towards us in Christ Jesus. (8) For by grace you have been saved[i] through faith; and this is not your own doing, it is the gift of God — (9) not because of works[g], lest any man should boast[i]. (10) For we are his workmanship, created[h] in Christ Jesus for good works, which God prepared[h] beforehand, that we should walk[h] in them.

Explanatory notes

a) *The structure of Eph. 2:1-10* consists of an introduction (vv. 1-3), followed by material from hymns (especially vv. 4-7, 10) which may have been part of an early Christian initiation hymn.

b) The *"you"* in vv. 1-2 refers to Christians from among Gentiles, while the *"we"* in v. 3 probably points to Christians from among the Jews. Both are included in the "us" and "we" from v. 4 onwards.

c) *"The power of the air"* and similar expressions like the "rule and authority and power and dominion" in Eph. 1:21 refer to the attack and impact of the "devil" mentioned in Eph. 4:27; 6:11. According to Ephesians the evil powers do not reside in hell or an underworld, but mainly in the "air," the "atmosphere," in this "age," and they work in a "spiritual" way.

d) In the New Testament *the term "flesh" (sarx)* usually designates the creature before God, the whole psycho-somatic existence with its good and evil possibilities. However, Paul especially used this term also to designate the power opposing God's Spirit. It then refers to sinful human beings abandoned to themselves and their self-seeking human nature.

e) *The verb "to make alive"* is often a synonym with "to rise from the dead." In the original Greek this verb does not appear in v. 1, which has neither subject nor verb. The "you he made alive" of Eph. 2:1 in the Revised Standard Version is taken out of v. 5 and put at the beginning of the exhortation.

f) *Another translation possible is*: "that he may prove to coming (attacking and hostile) aeons ...." The Greek term *aiōn* is not only a category of time and space ("age," "world"), but it designates also the (usually evil) ruler of that time and space. Thus in 200 B.C. the Alexandrinians worshipped a god called Aion. If the above second meaning is chosen, Eph. 2:7 must be read in the light 7 of Eph. 2:2; 1:21ff; 3:10; and 6:10ff.

g) Notice that the author uses in vv. 9-10 *the term "work"* in different ways: salvation does not come from self-righteous works which lead to boasting, but God enables us to do good works on the way on which he has set us. For we are his new creation, his work. The Greek for "workmanship" is *poiēma* which refers to "that which has been made," "the creator's work", or more specifically the "work of art," the "poem." The author probably did not intend the latter specific meaning, but it is revealing to think of a believer's life in Christ as God's poem and work of art.

h) These verbs are in *the aorist tense*, a verbal tense unknown in English which views the (usually past) action, irrespective of its duration, as telescoped to a point. It can then refer to the action as a whole or to the point of beginning or completion of a (past) action.

i) These verbs are in *the perfect tense* which in the Greek language is as much a present as a past tense. It denotes an action already accomplished but insists that the results of this action are still present at the time of speaking.

k) These verbs are in the *future tense*.

l) This verb is in *the imperfect tense* which in Greek points to a continued, repeated, or habitual action in the past.

N.B. All other verbs are in the present tense.

Task: Read and examine Eph. 2:1-10 with the help of the explanatory notes. Then compare the text from Ephesians with that from Paul's letter to the Romans. What are the striking particularities of the exhortation in Ephesians 2?

N.B. The conclusion of this study follows on the cassette.

An Early Christian baptismal hymn

"Awake, O sleeper,
arise from the dead,
and Christ shall give you light."
(Eph 5:14)